T-34

DEVELOPMENT & FIRST COMBAT

CONTENTS

Red Machines Vol.3 T-34 Development & First Combat

©Canfora Publishing 2021
ISBN 978-91-984776-4-1
Design: Toni Canfora
Print: Printbest, Tallinn, Estonia

Canfora Publishing
Industrivägen 19
171 48 Solna, Stockholm, Sweden
www.canfora.se, info@canfora.se

PUBLISHER'S INTRODUCTION

The T-34 is one of the best know tanks of World War Two, and indeed of all time. The tank is well known as a combat vehicle, and its service with the Red Army needs no reiteration here. The tank was the result of a long process of experimentation, both technical and tactical, the end result of many years of tank development that produced the ultimate balanced combination of firepower, armour and mobility, as it existed in 1941 when the T-34 entered combat.

The T-34 was not a tank designed in isolation however. The individual tank characteristics of the tank which made it so successful, namely the 76.2mm calibre main armament, the well sloped armour and the remarkable V-2 aluminium diesel engine were proven technical achievements beyond compare for a tank introduced into service in 1941. But the T-34 was also developed taking Soviet industrial specifics into consideration. The tank was designed for simplicity of operation, on the basis that typical farm employees with basic technical acumen could quickly learn to operate the tank. The T-34 was also the result of many years of development of the individual armament, armour, engine, transmission and suspension elements that were brought together in the final A-34 prototype design. These elements included improvement on imported foreign technology as appropriate, particularly with regard to the original designs of the US engineer Walter J. Christie, whose contribution towards what became the BT "fast tank" series has always been acknowledged by the Russians. The tank was also developed for ease of mass production, a factor that would be as critical as the technical details of the tank itself as the Soviet Union was plunged into a war for survival in June 1941. What the Soviet Union still lacked in any perceived qualitative difference was by 1942 already being made up for in quantity, and for this Nazi Germany had no ultimate solution.

Although the T-34 is well known as a combat vehicle, the design route by which it was ultimately developed, and the tactical parameters developed in the 1930s which favoured the use of Red Army tanks in breakthrough roles as opposed to infantry support operations, as favoured in much of the world with the notable other exception of Germany, is not well known in the West.

This book, by the foremost Russian historians and researchers on the T-34, Colonel (Retired) Igor Zheltov and Alexey Makarov, details the history of the development of both the tank types and mechanised warfare tank doctrine that ultimately resulted in the appearance of the T-34 tank as war loomed on the horizon in Europe. For the first time, the story of the designs, the designers, the prototype testing and the background of the rapidly industrialising Soviet Union are described in precise and accurate detail, and the T-34 put in into its proper Soviet context.

The material used in this book is taken entirely from Soviet original source documents, primarily Red Army and military manufacturing plant archives. As such this book relates the T-34 story from the perspective of the country that developed the tank. The book describes the struggles of the designers, the at times conflicting instructions, and the steps by which the T-34 was developed as the culmination of a decade of tank design developments. The book includes the story of the design development, prototype testing and the arguments as to what the Red Army should be equipped with in the way of tanks, leading to the famous final test run of the A-34 prototypes for demonstration to Stalin within the walls of the Kremlin in Moscow. The book also describes the first combat of the T-34, and the reaction of German Axis forces that encountered it in combat, and the test evaluations of Great Britain and the United States that were provided standard production samples by the Soviet Union.

In addition to working with formerly closed Soviet archives to describe as accurately as possible the birth of the T-34 from original documents, the authors also had the privilege of communicating with the direct descendants of three of the T-34's principal designers, Koshkin, Kucherenko and Morozov, such that the story of the T-34's development is brought alive within the context of the time. For the designers, and for the Soviet Union, the development of the T-34 was a personal as well as a State matter.

This book tells the story of the development of the T-34 from an entirely fresh perspective; that of those who designed and built it. In some cases the Russian word order and phraseology has been kept in the original format precisely so as to give perspective as to the differences in thought, mentality and process, then and now. The book is written by insiders with intimate technical and historic knowledge of Soviet tank design theory and practice, such that the development history of the T-34, and the technical, political and social environment in which it was created, might be better understood outside the country that designed and built one of the most famous tanks of all time.

Chapter 12 is collated from disparate material provided by the authors into one logical location. The UK and US foreign test report extracts were added by the Publisher to complete the story of the T-34 tanks shipped abroad to their wartime Allies by the Soviet Union, their evaluation and eventual fate. The book authors are not responsible for these additions. The colour artwork in this book provided by Andrey Aksenov are representations only for colour schematic purposes and not for technical study.

INTRODUCTION

The starting point in the creation of the legendary Soviet T-34 medium tank may be considered 15th August 1937, which was the date that Resolution №94ss of the Defence Committee of the SNK of the USSR (KO pri SNK SSSR) *"About the types of tanks for arming the tank forces of the Red Army and about tanks for production in 1938."* was issued. The document defined four new tank and two new armoured car types with which the armoured forces of the Red Army were to be equipped, with the respective assembly plants to be ready for series production of these new designs by January 1939. One of the tank types specified in Resolution №94ss was a new version of the BT wheel-track drive fast tank, with six driven wheels, a diesel engine and bulletproof armour pro-

tection. Work on this new tank, conducted at Plant №183 (the Komintern plant) in Kharkov under the leadership of Mikhail I. Koshkin would result in development of the first prototypes of the A-20 and A-32 tanks, and ultimately the series production T-34 medium tank. Resolution №94ss was a later development of Resolution №71ss of the Council of Labour and Defence dated 13th August 1933, which related to the operational use of armoured forces weapons* to be developed within the second Soviet Five Year Plan. This envisaged the development of mechanised combined-arms forces with independent and fast moving tank formations within which the BT fast tank, and later the T-34 medium tank, would be an integral part.

BT-7M, A-20 and T-34 tanks armed with the L-11 and F-34 gun.

---

* In Russian *"Bronetankovoye Vooruzhenie"* i.e including armoured cars, tanks and associated support vehicles.

Chapter 1

New Red Army Tank Requirements

The Soviet Union underwent rapid industrialisation in the early 20th Century, with the first Soviet Five Year Plan already transforming the formerly agrarian country into a leading industrial power. By the mid 1930s the industrial capacity of the country was exponentially greater than before the Russian Revolution of 1917. The expansion of heavy industry included the purchase of foreign military technology and machine tooling, allowing the country to developed its own indigenous tank industry in the pre-war years at a rate that would have been inconceivable only a few years before. Speaking to graduates of military academies of the Red Army in the Kremlin Palace on 4th May 1935, I. V. Stalin in his capacity as General Secretary of the Central Committee of the Communist Party (Bolshevik) (TsK VKP(b)) of the Soviet Union described the industrial transformation of the country:

"You know that we inherited from the past a backward and semi-poor, ruined country. Devastated by four years of imperialist war, repeated by three years of civil war, a country with a semi-literate population, with low technology, with separate oasis of industry, drowning in a sea of the smallest peasant farms - that is the country we inherited from the past. The task was to transfer this

country from the Middle Ages and darkness to the rails of modern industry and mechanised agriculture. The task, as you can see, was serious and difficult. The question was this: either we will quickly solve this problem and strengthen socialism in our country, or we will not solve it and then our country - weak technically and culturally dark - will lose its independence and become the object of the game of imperialist powers.

Our country then experienced a period of severe famine in the field of technology. There were not enough vehicles for industry. There were no vehicles for agriculture. There were no vehicles for transport. There was not the most elementary technical basis, without which the industrial transformation of the country was unthinkable. There were only some prerequisites for the creation of such a base. We had to create a first-class industry. It was necessary to direct this industry to reorganise technically not only industry but also agriculture, and our rail transport. And we had to make sacrifices and put in all of the most severe savings; it was necessary to economise on food, on schools, on textiles, in order to accumulate the necessary funds for industry. There was no other way to end the famine in the field of technology. <..> It is clear that in such a large and difficult situation it was impossible to wait for continuous and rapid success. In such a case, progress could be made only after a few years. It was therefore necessary to arm oneself with strong nerves, Bolshevik endurance and persistent patience in order to overcome the first failures and steadily move forward to the great goal, avoiding fluctuations and uncertainty in the ranks. You know, we handled things that way. But not all agreed. Some said: "what is your industrialisation and collectivisation, machines, ferrous metallurgy, tractors, combines, vehicles to us? It would be better to undertake manufacturing, buy raw materials for the production of consumer goods, and give to the population more of those little things that brighten people's lives. Creating an industry with our backwardness, and particularly a first-class industry, is a dangerous dream. "Of course, we could raise 3 billion roubles in foreign currency, which we have earned through the greatest austerity and spend it on creating our industry, and we could turn to importing raw materials and increasing the production of consumer goods. This would also be a kind of "plan". But with this "plan" we would have no metallurgy, no mechanical engineering, no tractors and vehicles, no aircraft and tanks. We would be unarmed before external enemies. We would undermine the foundations of socialism in our country. We would have been in the thrall of the bourgeoisie, internal and external. Obviously, it was necessary to choose between

Poster "Five-Year Plan in Four Years", 1932.

two plans: the plan of retreat, which would lead and could not (be allowed to) lead to the defeat of socialism, and the plan of offensive, which, as you know, has already led to the victory of socialism in our country. We chose a plan of attack, and went forward along the Leninist path, pulling back these comrades as people who saw something under their nose, but turned a blind eye to the immediate future of our country, the future of socialism in our country. Yes, comrades, we went confidently and rapidly on the way of industrialisation and collectivisation of our country. And now this path can be considered already traversed. Now everyone recognises that we have made great strides along the way. Now everyone recognises that we already have a powerful and first-class industry, powerful and mechanised agriculture, increased transport, and an organised and well-equipped Red Army"*   *"Pravda" №123, 6th May 1935.*

The beginning of industrialisation, as an integral part of the *"three-fold task of fundamental reorganisation of society"* (i.e. industrialisation, collectivisation of agriculture and cultural revolution), was laid out in the first Five Year Plan for the development of the Soviet national economy for the period from 1st October 1928 to 1st October 1933. The Main task of the first Five Year Plan was to rapidly increase the economic and military power of the Soviet State, with the original targets being achieved in late 1932, nine months ahead of schedule. The industrial base created during the first Five Year Plan was fundamental in providing the ability to undertake large-scale re-armament of the Red Army, including the provision of indigenously produced modern tanks and armoured cars. During the first Five Year Plan, Soviet defence spending increased to 10.8% of the State budget, but the armoured vehicles required by the Red Army remained to be defined.

At the time of the initial development of domestic tank forces in the 1920s, the technicalities of tank development and

The Soviet MS-1 Tank.

production, and the theory of tank deployment and application all required to be solved from scratch, as the Red Army had inherited from the Russian Imperial army neither tanks, nor experience of their application. However, despite the operational and technical challenges, there was in the early 1920s much interest in the Soviet Union in military-theoretical thought related to the operational use of tanks. In March 1921 the first specialised publication on the Soviet use of tanks, entitled "Bronevoye Delo" (the business of armour) began to be published, which reviewed the different tactics and techniques of armoured warfare as might be applied by the Red Army.

The first official guides on Red Army tank tactics were based on the results of accumulated Russian experience in the First World War and the Russian Civil War that followed the Russian Revolution of 1917. Instructions for the operational use of tanks were published in September 1920, followed in 1925 by a temporary field manual for the armoured forces of the Red Army. These armoured forces (which included tanks, armoured cars and armoured trains) were at the time considered as a secondary combat means, with the manuals stating that the main purpose of tank units was to support infantry and cavalry in attacks on the enemy - as was the case in other European nations at the time.

By the end of the 1920s the Soviet Union had also started production of its first indigenous armoured vehicles. Production of the MS-1 (T-18) tank began in November 1927, with series production of the BA-27 armoured car following in 1928. These two Soviet armoured vehicles, produced in relatively moderate numbers, equipped the first tank and mechanised units of the Red Army.

With the Red Army now being provided with indigenous tank and armoured car designs, consideration of the tactical application of these new armoured vehicles was correspondingly accelerated. In contrast with most European countries, with the notable later exception of Germany, Soviet armoured theory considered the dynamic operational use of these new weapons, confirmed in the Temporary Instructions on the Operational Use of Tanks (1928) and in the Field Charter of the RKKA (i.e. the Red Army) of 1929. These written State instructions envisaged that tanks would in an offensive battle operate in close cooperation with infantry, but in the form of an advanced, freely manoeuvring echelon, providing covering fire and suppressing and destroying artillery, command posts, communication centres and other important enemy assets. In most of contemporary Europe, tactics at the time envisaged tanks moving at slow pace in the direct support of infantry.

The developing Soviet form on the tactical use of tanks reflected the theory of deep combat, which was born at that

---

* *The spelling and punctuation in this and subsequent quoted texts is generally in accordance with the original sources, but the original word order has in some cases been changed to make it more readily readable in English.*

time, and would be refined in the first half of the 1930s. Performance of these new combat tasks naturally required equipment with new tactical and technical characteristics (TTKh's). Practical implementation of the new doctrine was entrusted to the first system of "tank-tractor-auto-armoured weapons of the Red Army", implemented in accordance with Resolution №29 approved at a meeting of the Revolutionary Military Council (RVS) of the USSR on 18th July 1929. According to this document, in the first Five Year Plan, Soviet industry was required to develop and master the series production of combat and transport vehicles with the following tactical and technical characteristics:

"a) **Tankette.** (wheel-track). Purpose-reconnaissance, surprise attack. Weight- not more than 3.3 tonnes. Preferably 2-2.5 tonnes. Speed- at least 60km/h on wheels and 40km/h on tracks. Armour must guarantee from penetration by armour-piercing rounds from a distance of 300m. Armament-1 machine gun with 360° horizontal arc of fire, or two, not simultaneously operating, with 360° horizontal arc of fire. Ammunition not less than 2,500 rounds. Crew-2. Radius of action 300km on tracks, 450km on wheels. Trench crossing-not less than 1.25m, vertical obstacle 0.5m, fording depth- 0.75m (preferably amphibious). Diameter of trees to be felled- 10cm. Transition from wheeled to tracked drive not more than 30 seconds without leaving the tankette. Height-no more than 1.5m. In addition, to manufacture a tankette with the same specifications, but armed with one 37mm gun for anti-tank use;

b) **Small tank.** Purpose-strike means of mechanised units, a breakthrough in terms of combat manoeuvre. Weight-7-7.5 tonnes.

Title page of the Field Charter of the RKKA (the Red Army) of 1929 (PU-29)

Speed-25-30km/h. Armour thickness must ensure against penetration of 37mm projectiles with an initial velocity of 700-1,000m/s. Armament-1x37mm gun and 2 machine guns, one being co-axial. Ammunition-minimum 75 shells and 3,500 cartridges. Crew-3. Range-200km, trench crossing at least 2m, vertical obstacle 0.6-0.8m, fording depth not less than 1.3m (preferably amphibious) and able to knock over trees with a diameter of 20cm. To also experimentally design a wheel-track small tank with the same data, but with a weight of not more than 8 tonnes, speed on wheels 45km/h and a range on wheels of 300km. Pending production of a new small tank, allow the MS-1 tank to be retained in use by Red Army units, and AU US RKKA to take all measures to increase its speed to 24-25km);

c) **Medium tank.** Purpose-breakthrough of fixed and mobile fortified zones. Weight-no more than 15-16 tonnes Speed-25-30km. Armour thickness must ensure against penetration of 37mm projectiles (with an initial speed of 700m/s) at a range of 750m. Armament-1x45mm gun and three machine guns. Ammunition not less than 100 rounds and 5,000 cartridges. Crew 4-5. Range-200km. Trench crossing not less than 2.5m. Vertical obstacle-1m, fording depth not less than 1.3m. Diameter of trees to fell 30cm;

d) Development work on a large tank to meantime be limited to theoretical consideration of the question by suggesting that VPU VSNKh by 1st October 1930 present a preliminary design, and then to solve the issue of inclusion in the system of armaments;

e) **Self-propelled gun for mechanised units.** Purpose-preparation and support of tank attack; combat against tanks (artillery supporting mechanised units). Chassis-small tank. Calibre-76mm. Weight-not more than 7-7.5 tonnes, travel speed-25-30km. Armour 7-10mm. Gun elevation not less than 30°. Horizontal traverse 12°. The barrel and breech must be standardised with divisional and regimental guns. Ammunition complement-not less than 24 rounds, with two crew in the gun compartment;

f) **Self-propelled anti-aircraft machine gun.** Purpose-protection of mechanised units on the march and in battle from attack aircraft. Chassis-small tank or medium tractor. Weight-7-7.5 tonnes. Travel speed-25-30km. Armour-7-10mm. Armament-universal 4-barrel 7.62mm machine gun (4M). The Installation should carry not less than two command crew and 4,000 rounds;

g) **Self-propelled anti-aircraft gun installation.** Purpose-defence of mechanised units on the march and in battle against attack by bomber aviation and also anti-tank weapons. Chassis-small or medium tractor. Weight-7-7.5 tonnes, travel speed-25-30km/h, side armour 7-10mm. Armament-twin 37mm anti-aircraft gun.

The unit must transport at least two gun-crew and 100 rounds;

h) *With regard to an infantry transporter on a small tank chassis, to be limited to theoretical development, inviting the VPU VSNKh to by 1st October 1930 submit a draft, and then solve the issue of its inclusion in the armaments system;*

i) **Radio tractor.** *Purpose-communication within large tank formations. Chassis-small or medium tractor. Weight-7-7.5 tonnes travel speed-25-30km/h. Thickness of side armour (shields) 7-10mm. Station with telegraph-telephone. Station range (Telegraph) 250km at halt; and 50km on the move.*

j) **Smoke tank.** *Purpose-production of dense smoke screens. Chassis-small or medium tractor. Weight-7-7.5 tonnes, travel speed-25-30 km/h. Armour thickness 7-10mm;*

k) *With regard to a bridging tank (MT) limit meantime to theoretical development, suggesting that VPU VSNKh by 1st October 1930 present a preliminary design, and then to solve the issue of his inclusion in the armaments system;*

l) **Light tractor.** *Purpose-transportation of the material of division artillery, transportation of staff and command structure and all parts of the motorised artillery. Weight-3-3.5 tonnes. Maximum speed with towed load-25-30km. Drive mechanism- track;*

M) **Medium tractor.** *Purpose-transportation of ARGK guns, weighing in transport order not more than 7 tonnes. Transport of corps artillery, mechanised unit loads (in trains of two trailers). The chassis should be standardised where possible with the light tank chassis. Full standardisation is desirable. Weight-about 7 tonnes. Trailer load capacity-7-7.5 tonnes. Maximum speed with trailer load 20km/h. (pending construction of a new small and medium tractors to replace the Red Army "Bolshevik" and "Kommunar" tractors. AU US RKKA to take measures to increase the speed of these tractors according to the modernisation plan);*

n) **Heavy tractor.** *Purpose-transportation of ARGK high power guns and all heavy loads. Weight, about 11 tonnes. Towed load-11-12 tonnes. Maximum speed with towed load-15km/h.*

3. *To recognise the need to design special new armoured vehicles and charge US RKKA together with the industry to study the issue of adaptation of machines (i.e. chassis) already in manufacture, namely:*
a) *Ford Model A*
b) *Ford Model AA "with "Jumbo*" rear axles (i.e. the GAZ-AAA) or other design*

c) *cargo truck.*

**"Jumbo"* refers to a US design truck axle used on the GAZ-AAA.*

4. **To adopt the following requirement for modified (wheeled) machines:**

(a) *Light armoured car (Ford Model A). Purpose-movable firing means in the composition of reconnaissance units. Armament-2 machine guns, 1 adapted for anti-aircraft use. Unarmoured, but with a front bullet shield. Preferably with a third axle. Maximum road speed 80-100km. Vehicle weight not more than 1.5 tonnes. Crew-3. The internal volume of the machine should allow a 2,000 round ammunition complement. Radius of action-250km. In addition, to recognise the need to construct the same machine, but for a 37mm gun with 360° horizontal fire instead of a machine gun;*

b) *Medium armoured car (Ford AA with "Jumbo" or similar rear axle). Purpose-combat reconnaissance in reconnaissance and mechanised units. Armament-2 machine guns, 1 with 360° traverse. Armour should guarantee against penetration by small arms fire from a distance of 150-200m. Maximum road speed-50km/h. Vehicle weight not over 3.8 tonnes. Crew-3. Range 200km. Minimum ammunition complement-3,000 machine-gun rounds.*

c) *Heavy armoured car (Autocar truck). Purpose-heavy reconnaissance vehicle and also for anti-tank combat. Weapons-1x37mm gun and a machine gun (not acting simultaneously) with 360° arc of fire, and one machine gun for firing in the direction of movement (angle of attack of 25-30°). Armoured vehicle should give a guarantee against penetration by armour-piercing bullets at distances up to 500m. Number of axles-3. The vehicle must have a (secondary) rear steering wheel. Road speed not less than 50km/h. Weight of machine-not exceeding 6 tonnes. Crew-4. Range 200km. The internal volume of the machine must allow an ammunition complement of at least 75 rounds, 3,000 machine-gun rounds and fuel for 5-6 hours duration. (Pending final development of specified machines, to allow for the continued service in the Red Army of the BA-27 armoured car)".*

RGVA F4. L18. C15. pp190-203

Implementation of this task-list was particularly difficult for the rapidly developing but still immature Soviet industry. Despite the difficulties, the armoured vehicle elements of the first Five Year Plan were nevertheless generally accomplished, and in some cases exceeded. Within the first Five Year Plan, the Red Army received modern tank types, designed both on the basis of the best foreign models from Great Britain and the

United States, and from rapid indigenous development. Soviet industry had mastered mass production of the T-27 tankette and the light twin-turreted T-26 tank (the T-26 M-1931); had replaced the obsolescent MS-1 (T-18) tank, and produced an experimental series of T-24 medium tanks. Directly relevant to the development of the later T-34 medium tank, series production of the BT-2 wheel-track fast tank had also commenced. The BT-2 was based on the design principles of the entrepreneurial American designer Walter J. Christie, whose efforts were rejected by the United States government as not in conformance with their own current tank development and operational philosophy. Christie's wheel-track design was however at that time one of the most modern and revolutionary tank designs in the world. And the country that was best positioned to take advantage of the available technology, having no significant pre-history of tank development or operational use, but now rapidly developing in industrial and military strength, was the Soviet Union.

The first series production T-26 and BT tanks had by the end of the first Five Year Plan been developed using the best of imported technology and design; and prototypes of the T-37 amphibious reconnaissance tank, the T-28 medium three-gun tank, and the first prototype of the T-35 heavy five-gun breakthrough tank had all been developed and manufactured to replace the first-generation and now obsolete T-27 tankette and the limited production T-24 medium tank. All of the new Soviet designs matched the philosophies behind armoured warfare being developed in the Soviet Union, and the country was meantime industrialising at an exponential rate to accommodate the demands for ever-heavier and more complex armoured vehicle production. Moreover, in 1932 the country had successfully carried out development work on uprating the

armament of both the T-26 and BT-2, which were now being armed as standard with a 45mm tank gun. Further, specialised armoured vehicles were also now being developed, with early T-26 variants including prototypes of MT bridge-laying tanks and KhT "chemical" tanks, the latter armed with flamethrower, smoke-laying and chemical area contamination equipment.

The results achieved in producing new tank types in the Soviet Union during the first Five Year Plan led to revision of the corresponding *"operational-tactical views on the use of tanks"*. The People's Commissar for Military and Maritime Affairs (NKVM) Klimenti E. Voroshilov gave the following assessment of the work carried out in the first Five Year Plan to equip the Red Army with modern weapons:

"The system of auto-armour-tank weapons, with which we entered the first Five Year Plan, was mainly based on the principle of introducing tanks into combined arms formations, as a means of strengthening them when acting in the tactical zone. However, during the first Five Year plan samples of the most advanced tanks have been put into mass production on the basis of the best foreign types and a range of sophisticated designs, and these technical achievements have created a solid background for fundamental changes in operational-tactical views on the use of tanks and requires a strong organisational change in mechanised troops toward the:

1) Creation of separate mechanical combined arms units;
2) Creation of a powerful tank reserve of the Main Command*;
3) Organisational equipping of cavalry divisions and brigades;
4) Organic vehicle tank units of infantry divisions.

The success of the Socialist construction has led to the creation of our own aircraft, automotive and tank base, and the first five years

BT-2 fast tanks (foreground) and twin-turreted T-26 light tanks (background)

* ГК (GK) in Russian

T-27 tankette.

T-24 medium tank.

have transformed the Red Army from being a backward army from a mechanised warfare perspective to being an advanced army, and in any event, the number and quality of (Soviet) combat vehicles is not (now) inferior to the most powerful capitalist army".

AP. Special Folder. F.3 L.46 C.381 pp134

The early 1930s in the Soviet Union was characterised by the rapid development of doctrinal theories of tank deployment based on the new opportunities associated with the industrialisation of the country and the overall and rapid technical reconstruction of the Red Army; in particular the provision in large numbers of new armoured vehicle types. Armoured (tank) forces within the Red Army moved rapidly at this time from being a specific weapon type into being a new type of tactical force, which had in its composition tank and mechanised units. At the beginning of the second Five Year Plan in 1933, mass tank production was based on the T-37 amphibious re-

Marshal K.E. Voroshilov.

connaissance tank, the 45mm armed T-26 light tank (the T-26 M-1933), the BT-5 fast tank and the T-28 medium tank. The Kharkov Steam Locomotive Plant (KhPZ) - later known as Plant №183 - had meantime also begun "series" production of the T-35 heavy breakthrough tank. Development work on new tank designs also continued unabated, with prototypes of the PT-1 wheel-tracked amphibious tank and the T-34 small tactical (war mobilisation) tank being undertaken that year.

As of 1st May 1933, the Red Army had 5,729 tanks and tankettes in inventory, made up of the following tank types: T-27 (2,430); T-37 (50); MS-1 (T-18) (950); T-26 (1,550); BT-2 and BT-5 (710); T-24 (25); T-28 (12) and T-35 (2). At the time 1,897 tanks and tankettes were assigned to mechanised formations and units of the two mechanised corps, six separate mechanised brigades, fourteen mechanised regiments and seven mechanised cavalry divisions; 849 tanks and tankettes were part of the Tank Reserve of the General Command (TRGK), with the remaining tanks and tankettes located within separate tank battalions and companies introduced into combined arms units, mainly located in infantry divisions.

Widespread deployment of tank and mechanised units within the Red Army naturally resulted in a sharp rise in the development of armoured warfare tactics. As a result of extensive development and experimental research in the first half of the 1930s a coherent system of tactics for the use of tanks in various types of fighting units in the Red Army was conceived. The theory of deep battle and operations became prevalent as described below:

"tanks in combined arms offensive combat associated with breaking the enemy's defence", it was envisaged to use such a way as to simultaneously affect the entire depth of an enemy tactical zone of defence, to be suppressed by coordinated air strikes and artillery fire, with the rapid breakthrough into the depth of the defence tank groups long-range (DD), determined by the advance of tanks for infantry support

(DPP), and non-stop attack infantry with tanks in direct support (NPO). Successful rapid breakthrough of the defence (at a rate of 2-3km/h) was considered possible only under the condition that the direction of the main attack tanks would involved massed formations, with a density of 75-100 tanks per km of front, i.e. up to one tank for every 100m of front. Specific attention of military-theoretical thought of the time was devoted to the operation of tanks in the encounter battle in which the fighting properties of armoured forces would be most extensively utilised. In the encounter battle, tanks were recommended to be used centrally, in cooperation with artillery and aircraft to defeat the main grouping of an enemy. In defensive operations, armoured forces combat units were to be used in the composition or as independent strike groups with the task of applying counterattacks to destroy or break into the depth of enemy defences. In favourable situations it was considered possible to combine the defending combined arms tank units for applying a powerful tank attack ahead of the front edge of the defensive zone of the enemy."

Questions of Tactics in Soviet Military Works
(1917 - 1940). M. Voenizdat, 1970, pp241-242

To develop the reality behind the theory of deep battle and operations required both appropriate equipment and a technical base. In the summer of 1933 the People's Commissariat for Military and Naval Affairs (NKVM) thereby developed and approved by the RVS of the USSR, the new system of "bronetankovaya" (armoured-tank) weapons of the Red Army, which for the most part reflected concurrent operational-tactical views on the use of tanks in various types of fighting formations. Under the new system the following types of machines were to be made available to the Red Army:

"1. Main tanks-5 types:
a) Reconnaissance - T-37;
b) Combined Arms - T-26;
c) Operational - BT, in future PT-1;
d) Tank of qualitative strengthening of TRGK - T-28;
e) Powerful special purpose tank - T-35.

2. Special tanks-7 types (on standard chassis, as above):
a) 3 Chemical types (on the chassis of combined arms, reconnaissance and operational tanks);
b) 2 Engineer types (chassis combined arms tanks and TRGK tank forces);
c) Self-Propelled artillery installation (on units of the combined arms tank);
d) Command tank (chassis combined arms tanks and TRGK forces);

3. Armoured cars - 2 types (on Ford-A and Ford-3A chassis):
a) Reconnaissance vehicle (on Ford-A chassis);
b) Combat vehicle (on Ford-3A chassis).

4. Train combat vehicles - 2 types:
a) Moto-armour-wagon; (MBV)
b) Reconnaissance armoured car (standardised with armoured car).

5. Tractors - 3 types (all general State use types):
a) Light high-speed tractor STZ-3;
b) Heavy high-speed tractor "Kommunar";
c) Heavy powerful tractor "Stalinets".

6. Transporters - 2 types:
a) Battlefield Ammunition Transporter (chassis standard reconnaissance tank);
b) Infantry Transporter (light tractor chassis).

7. Transport vehicles (existing mass production trucks with the installation of a 3-axle chassis and half-track drive for snow):
a) Ford-A;
b) Ford-AA;
c) AMO-5 (later known as ZiS-5)"

AP. Special folder. F.3 L.46 C.381 pp147-148

For approval of the armoured vehicles, Voroshilov as the People's Commissar for Military and Naval Affairs and Chair-

The original T-37 amphibious reconnaissance tank.

The T-26 M-1933 tank armed with a 45mm gun.

man of the RVS, prepared the report *"About the system of tank weapons for the second Five Year Plan"*, dated 15th July 1933, and sent it to the Chairman of the Commission of Defence at the Council of People's Commissars V. M. Molotov. In his report, Voroshilov stressed that *"the second Five Year Plan should make mechanisation one of the decisive elements of the future operations of the Red Army."* The report further stated:

"a) The best, most powerful and fast tanks should be grouped in a strong combined-arms operational and strategic value (mechanised brigade and the mechanised corps);

b) At the disposal of the General Command (GK) must be a strong tank reserve (quantity and quality), which would create absolute tank superiority over the enemy at impact areas;

c) Strategic cavalry retains its purpose, firmly fitted with a for-means and self-propelled artillery;

d) Combined arms (the majority of divisions, and later regiments) must have their organic mechanical units for reconnaissance and combat".

AP. Special folder. F.3 L.46 C. 381. pp144

Based on these requirements, Voroshilov suggested that in the nearest few years the main types of combat vehicles that should enter series production were:

"a) Reconnaissance tank (T-37 tank). Standard service tank-for military reconnaissance for combined arms and combat infantry units. Basic requirements: speed, all-terrain (including amphibious) maneuverability, small size, low cost and mass production.

b) Combined Arms tank (T-26 tank). Basic, organic tank of combined arms (units), and for TRGK reinforcement. Basic requirements: maneuverability on the battlefield, armour that protects against armour-piercing bullets, armed with a variety of weapons (guns, machine guns, flamethrower, chemical weapons), finally, low cost and mass production.

c) Operational tank (BT tank, in future PT-1 tank). Tank for independent combined arms units. Everything in this tank is subject to the requirements of speed, all-terrain (including amphibious) and powerful armament.

d) Support tank (TRGK) (T-28). Basic requirements: Powerful armament and strong armour, speed, allowing use in operation with combined arms units.

e) Powerful special purpose tank (the T-35 tank is meantime suitable). Tank quality, plus strengthening the breakout and advance against strongly fortified front lines. Main requirement-powerful weapons and armour that protects against small-calibre (i.e. artillery/anti-tank shells).

f) To provide the option for use and production during wartime of the existing prototype T-34* [small]tank (to be built in wartime) on the basis of the automotive industry".

AP. Special folder. F.3 L.46 C.381. pp145-146

The new system of armoured weapons as submitted by K. E. Voroshilov on 13th August 1933 was discussed at a meeting of the Council of Labour and Defence (STO), and approved almost without amendment by STO Resolution №71ss *"On the system of tank weapons of the Red Army"*. In the first section of this important resolution concerning for domestic tank production, of the decision it was stated:

"Approve for the second Five Year Plan the following system of armoured weapons of the Red Army:

1. Main tanks - 5 types:

a) Reconnaissance tank. Main service tank of all mechanised units.

The BT-5 fast tank.

Means of combat reconnaissance and infantry combat. Basic requirements: speed, all-terrain (including amphibious), maneuverability, small size, low cost and mass production.

b) *Combined Arms tank. The main tank quantitative strengthening tank (of the) TRGK, and combined arms units.*

c) *Operational tank. Tank mechanised units. Should be all-terrain, high-speed (including amphibious) and powerfully armed.*

d) *Tank (of) TRGK reinforcement. To overcome heavily fortified defensive lines. Basic requirements: powerful weapons and armour, speed, allowing use also in operation with combined arms units.*

e) *Powerful special purpose tank. Tank quality, plus enhancing TRGK (units in) the breakout through particularly strong and well fortified front lines. Main requirement-powerful weapons, armour that protects against small-calibre rounds. Capability to deal with concrete structures.*

2. Special tanks - 7 types (on standard chassis as above):

a) *3 chemical types (on the chassis of combined arms, reconnaissance and operational tanks);*

b) *2 engineer types (chassis combined arms tanks and tank power TRGK);*

c) *Self-propelled artillery installation (chassis of combined arms tank);*

d) *Command tank (chassis - combined arms tanks and TRGK tanks);*

3. Armoured car - two types:

a) *Reconnaissance (on Ford-A chassis);*

b) *Combat (on Ford-3A chassis).*

4. Train combat vehicles - two types:

a) *Moto-armour-wagon;*

b) *Reconnaissance section armoured car (standard with armoured car).*

5. Tractors - 3 types (all types state):

a) *Light high-speed tractor STZ-3;*

b) *Heavy high-speed tractor "Kommunar";*

c) *Heavy powerful tractor "Stalinets".*

6. Transporters - 2 types:

a) *Battlefield ammunition transporter (standard reconnaissance tank chassis);*

b) *Infantry Transporter (on light tractor chassis).*

7. Transport vehicles (for existing mass production with the installation of a 3-axle chassis and half-tracks for snow):

a) *Ford A;*

b) *FORD-AA;*

c) *AMO-5;*

d) *Ya-5".*

GARF. F. R-8418. L.28 C.2 pp74-76

To implement the approved system, it was decided to keep the following tanks in mass production for the first half of the Five Year Plan:

a) T-37 - reconnaissance tank;

b) T-26 - combined arms tank;

c) BT - operational tank;

d) T-28 - tank of TRGK qualitative strengthening;

e) T-35 - powerful special-purpose tank.

GARF. F. R-8418 L.28 C.2 pp76

In the future, these tanks were to be replaced by improved modifications. Two main directions of further tank improvement were set, namely that all tank types were to be powered by diesel engines; and all tank types (except the T-35) were to

The T-28 medium tank.

Prototype of the I-29-5 medium wheel-track tank.

---

* *The T-34 "small" tank was intended as a wartime emergency production tank, capable of being assembled at automotive rather than specialised tank plants with hull and turret amour sets provided by armour sub-contractors. The philosophy behind the T-34 "small" tank later gave birth to the wartime T-60 "small tank".*

Prototype of the PT-1 amphibious wheel-track tank.

be provided with wheel/track drive mechanisms. The gradual introduction of the PT-1 amphibious wheel-track tank design was envisaged from 1934, to by 1936 completely replace the BT-5 in mass production. The T-37, T-26 and T-28 tanks were from 1936 also to be modernised, in order to increase operational flexibility, by also being equipped with a wheel-track drive mechanism. For replacement of the T-35 tank, the tank industry was by 1937 obliged to develop and introduce a new, more powerful "special purpose" tank. In the event Soviet tank manufacturers were able to comply in full with the plans for the new system of armoured weapons, the following tanks were to be in series production by 1937:
- T-37 reconnaissance amphibious tank with wheel-track drive;
- T-26 light combined-arms tank with wheel-track drive;
- PT-1 light operational wheel-track amphibious tank;
- T-28 medium tank (TRGK) with wheel-track drive;
- A new "special purpose" heavy breakthrough tank - T-35 type.

All of these tanks were to be fitted with diesel engines. The following basic tactical and technical requirements (TTTs) for the above tank types were listed in the Annex to STO Resolution №71ss:

"1. Reconnaissance tank (T-37): combat weight 3.3 tonnes, speed-40km/h and armed with 1 machine gun; armour protection against armour-piercing rounds from a distance of 400m, design-amphibious.

2. Combined arms tank (T-26): combat weight 9.5 tonnes, speed-50km/h, armament-45mm gun (some with 76mm gun) and 1 machine gun, or 2 machine guns and 1 flamethrower, armour-protection from armour-piercing rounds, construction-preferably wheeled-tracked.

3. Operational tank (BT, in the future-PT-1): combat weight of 11-14.5 tonnes, speed-60km/h on tracks and 80km/h on whe-

els, armament-45mm gun (some with 76mm gun) and 3 machine guns, armour-protection from armour-piercing rounds, design-amphibious, wheeled-tracked.

4. TRGK reinforcement tank (T-28): Combat weigh 20-23 tonnes, speed-40km/h on tracks and 70km/h on wheels, armament -76mm gun and 3 rapid-firing machine guns, armour-protection from armour-piercing large-calibre rounds from any range; design-wheeled-tracked.

5. Powerful special purpose tank (T-35): combat weight-45 tonnes or more, speed-30km/h, armament-76mm or 152mm gun, two 45mm guns or one 45mm gun and 4-6 machine guns; armour-protection from armour-piercing large-calibre rounds from any distance and from small-calibre rounds (37-45mm) from a distance of 500-700m, construction-preferably wheeled-tracked"

GARF. F. R-8418 L.28 C.2 pp81

With regard to the T-34 "small tank" STO Resolution №71ss stated that production would not be considered in peacetime, but in the event of war the design was available for mass production by the automotive industry - a role that would later be undertaken by the T-60 "small tank" produced in 1941-42. The resolution separately defined measures for strengthening the firepower of existing tank designs. The industry was from 1934 obligated to produce the 76.2mm PS-3 tank gun and to in parallel start development of a new 45mm tank gun with improved ballistics. Less than two years after the adoption of Resolution STO №71ss, a meeting of the Labour and Defence Council was held on 19th June 1935, which summarised the preliminary results of work undertaken on the implementation of tanks and armoured vehicles within the second Five Year Plan. The efforts of Soviet tank designers and the industry to create new models of armoured vehicles was duly noted. In Leningrad, the Kirov Pilot Plant had designed and manufactured several T-46 light wheel-track tank prototypes, with two pairs of driving wheels, intended to replace the T-26 light tank, and two versions of a medium wheel-track tank with four pairs of driving wheels - the T-29-4 and T-29-5 tanks, intended to replace the tracked T-28 medium tank. Three models of amphibious reconnaissance tank were developed to potentially replace the T-37 amphibious tank. Two of these were wheel-track designs with two pairs of driving wheels, both developed under the T-43 index; one being designed at Plant №37 in Moscow, the other design at the Kirov pilot (experimental) plant in Leningrad. The other was the tracked T-38 amphibious tank which had also been designed at Plant №37. Meanwhile at KhPZ in Kharkov, further improvement of the BT tank series was undertaken. The BT-5 was in 1935 replaced in production by the BT-7 tank, fitted with a more powerful M-17 petrol engine. In parallel, a new BD-2 tank diesel engine had been developed at KhPZ (later given the better-known V-2 index), which was installed in the BT-5 tank and successfully tested at the plant for potential service.

The meeting of the Council of Labour and Defence adopted the Resolution №S-71ss *"On the implementation of the NKTP system of tank weapons based on the Resolution of the STO dated 13th August 1933"*, by which the following five types of tanks were determined for service with the Red Army:

"1. To adopt the T-38 - Plant №37; to improve the driver's accommodation and increase the ground clearance by 15mm, with the weight of the tank not increased by more than 150-200kg against a test sample.

2. To determine adoption of the T-46 tank from the Kirov pilot plant instead of the T-26; complete plant and field testing, in order to put the tank into production in 1936 at the Voroshilov plant.

3. To leave in service the BT tank. Decline replacement with the PT-1. In 1935 to produce BT tanks with the M-17 engine and in 1936 to move over to production of the same BT tank at the Kharkov Locomotive works (KhPZ) with a diesel engine installation.

Prototype T-34 small tank with gun armament.

Prototype T-46 wheel-track tank.

4. To determine adoption of the wheeled tracked T-29 tank instead of the T-28 tank; to finish its plant and military testing in order to put it into production at the Kirov plant in 1936.

5. To leave in service the T-35 produced at the Kharkov Locomotive Plant (KhPZ)".

GARF. F. R-8418. L.28 C.6 pp213-214

The PT-1 amphibious wheel-track tank was not accepted for service with the Red Army, as it offered no significant advantages compared with the BT-7 fast tank. The main armament, armour and mobility characteristics of the PT-1 and BT-7 tanks were almost identical, but due to the need for buoyancy, the combat weight of the PT-1 tank could not be increased. The PT-1 tank was also far more complex to manufacture. By the mid 1930s a defined plan was in place with regard to the tanks required by the Red Army in order to meet modern operational-tactical views on the use of tanks in different combat scenarios. Moreover, for almost all tank types, there was a preference for wheel-track drive systems over standard tracked types. The Soviet military preference for more complex wheel-track drive systems, and for several tank types, rather than conventional track-only drive systems, understanding the inevitable design, production and operational headaches involved, would appear somewhat illogical. But there was a very specific logic to the consideration of which drive system would be optimal for future Soviet tank designs.

T-38 amphibious reconnaissance tank.

T-35 heavy tank.

Chapter 2

In Search of the Optimal Tank Drive System

The invention of the internal combustion engine marked the most significant advance in military mobility for centuries; there now being a replacement for the horse for both cavalry and transport purposes. It also represented the beginning of the development and practical use of armoured fighting vehicles. The first examples of wheeled armoured combat vehicles appeared in the armies of different states at the beginning of the 20th Century. However, armoured cars were primarily used for reconnaissance and forward area communications roles rather than as combat vehicles. The mounting of armoured hulls and turrets on light wheeled chassis resulted in low power-to-weight ratios and poor all-terrain performance however, making them unsuitable for off-road combat use. To create a better fighting machine with high tactical mobility, a propulsion system was required which was capable of providing improved traction on soft ground. Ultimately for heavy armoured vehicles this required tracked propulsion. Wheeled and tracked armoured vehicles each provided advantages and disadvantages. Wheeled drive systems provided for a combat vehicle with high operational mobility - the ability to move on roads over long distances at relatively high speed, operating relatively quietly on roads, and being less negatively impacted by road travel. Wheeled drive systems were and remain inherently more reliable and durable than tracked systems, requiring significantly less maintenance and repair. Tracked drive systems by comparison provided signifi-

cantly higher all-terrain tractability and were less vulnerable in combat, but with significantly lower reliability and higher operational and maintenance requirements.

When creating the first armoured combat vehicles, capable of overcoming rugged terrain and various natural and artificial obstacles, preference was given to the tracked drive option. Thanks to the advantages of the tracked drive, a new type of combat vehicle - as first designated "tank" by the British based on the rail transport description used en-route to continental Europe during World War One - began to be used in combat, providing an acceptable level of tactical mobility on the battlefields of Europe. What tanks lacked by comparison with armoured cars was operational flexibility, overall reliability and durability between capital- rebuilds. To reduce the wear and tear on tracks when travelling over relatively long distances, for delivery to the front, or moving from one part of the front to another, tanks were transported either by rail or on special tractor-trailer combinations. To give the tank greater operational mobility new technical solutions were required, and after much experimentation, were ultimately found.

"Tracked drive, ensuring high tactical mobility, puts serious obstacles in the way of achieving tanks of adequate operational mobility, i.e., made them unsuitable for rapid and prolonged independent movement. Attempts to significantly increase speed when designing new types of tanks encountered serious obstacles, a consequence of the shortcomings of track drive. These disadvantages should be attributed primarily to the following:

- A sharp reduction in the gearbox (life) of the track drive with an increase in the speed of movement.
- Inability to drive on roads at high speeds without some significant damage to the roadway, especially on road bends.

Track service life is especially reduced by long transitions through sands and loose soil, due to contamination of the track link hinges. This prompted the designers with the first steps of tank development to look for other ways to resolve the problem of combining tank operational and tactical mobility. It was natural to go the way of using the existing constructive solutions to each of these tasks separately, i.e. to supply tanks with combined wheeled and tracked drive systems."

Tanki. Konstruktsiya i Raschet. Tank Department, VAMM
under the direction of Prof. N.I. Gruzdev, Tashkent, 1943 pp730

Transport of a KS tank by truck

In the latter half of the 1920s, some countries - notably Czechoslovakia, France, Great Britain, Sweden and the USA - created prototype tanks and tankettes provided with combined wheeled and tracked drive systems. These tanks were designated as wheel-track tanks. By design, the wheel-track tank designs were divided into two types:
- with two entirely separate and unconnected forms of propulsion - wheel and track;
- with combined wheel-track drive, with some elements involved when driving on tracks, and others when driving on wheels.

Most wheel-track tanks designed in the second half of the 1920s envisaged separate wheeled and tracked drive systems. The main disadvantages of this design compared to a design with a combined wheel-track drive were increased weight and dimensions (width or length) of the tank; a lower speed when driving on tracks; complexity of manufacture and vulnerability to damage. In this regard, tanks with separate wheeled and tracked drive systems were not widely adopted by those countries involved in such tank developments. The design of tanks with a combined wheeled-tracked system was by contrast widespread, especially in the Soviet Union. The most experienced Soviet tank plant involved in such work was the Kharkov Steam Locomotive Plant (KhPZ), which had since 1931 mastered production of the BT (Bystrokhodny - fast moving) series of wheel-track tanks. The development prototype for the original BT-2 tank series was an experimental wheeled tracked tank, developed on the basis of the "Model 1940" combat vehicle designed by the American engineer J. Walter Christie. The American prototype was simply designated "Christie" in the Soviet Union. On 28th April 1930 an agreement was signed between the American firm "U.S. Wheel and Track Layer Corporation" and the Soviet "Amtorg Trading Corporation", the latter representing the interests of the Soviet Union in the

Tanks - Design and Calculation - the Department of Tanks under the direction of Prof. A. Gruzdev. Tashkent, 1943

United States. By the signed agreement the Soviet side purchased "two military tanks" with a total cost of $60,000. The agreement also stipulated the rights to manufacture, sell and operationally use tanks within the borders of the USSR for a period of ten years.

Back in the USSR, preparation work was well advanced with regard to series production of the imported technology. Pursuant to the Order of the Supreme Council of National Economy of the USSR №73ss issued in May 1931, a new design bureau (KB) was established within the Kharkov Steam Locomotive Plant (KhPZ) under the supervision of chief engineer S. A. Ginsburg. The main task of the new KB was to rapidly develop production drawings to ensure the initiation of series assembly of the "Christie" tank design at KhPZ. Ginzburg headed this KB only from May to July 1931, being replaced in the role from July to December 1931 by military engineer 2nd rank N. M. Toskin. In the course of organising series produc-

Prototype British "Vickers" Medium Tank.

The American "M-1940" wheel-track design.

tion, the engineers and technologists over a period of seven months made some 1,293 changes in the original drawings of the experimental "Christie" tank design. Most changes were related to modifying the original Christie design documentation over from Imperial (U.S. Federal) measurements to the metric system used in the Soviet Union. The two tanks received from the United States were without turrets, and so KhPZ designers developed an indigenous turret and armament installation for the original Soviet tank development prototypes, designated BT-2. The designated main armament for the BT-2 tank was the 37mm B-3 tank gun, but as Soviet industry was unable to quickly provide the required volume of production, the BT-2 was as an interim measure initially fitted with a twin 7.62-mm Degtyarev (DT) machine gun installation.

BT-2 tanks were fitted with either a Soviet designed M-5 petrol engine or with an imported Liberty engine purchased in the USA with an operating power of 360hp, which provided the tank with the ability to move at speeds up to 52km/h on tracks and up to 72km/h on wheels. The main feature of the BT-2 tank that distinguished it from all other tanks then in Red Army service was the high operational flexibility provided by the combination wheel-track drive system. In wheeled mode, the tank moved on eight large diameter roadwheels with perforated rubber rims for shock absorption. The first pair of roadwheels served as steering wheels, and the last (fourth) as driving wheels. Torque transmission to the drive wheels was via final drives and gear reducers referred to as "guitars". The transition from one mode of movement to another took the

crew 30 minutes to complete. When preparing the tank for movement on wheels, each track was split into four sections that were placed on strengthened track guards and fastened with straps. Work on further improvement of the BT series tanks was conducted at KhPZ mainly within the experimental shop T2O ("T" - tank department, "2" - divisional ordinal number, "O" - pilot plant of Department T2). The prototype shop was established in March 1932 in the form of experimental research section T2K at the design office T2K, of which from 6th December 1931 the chief was A. O. Firsov.

The result of the work on further developing the BT-2 tank carried out by designer engineers at KhPZ at Kharkov in collaboration with the Directorate of Mechanisation and Motorization (UMiM) of the Red Army, was the creation of the BT-5 wheel-track tank, series production of which was organized at KhPZ in 1933. The BT-5 tank differed from the BT-2 primarily in the installation of a new, enlarged turret compatible with that used on the T-26 M-1933 light tank, and armed with a more powerful 45mm tank gun and co-axial DT machine gun, which increased the combat weight by 700kg to 11.7 metric tonnes.

In parallel with the production of BT-5 tanks at KhPZ, the T2K design bureau continued to improve the combat characteristics of the BT tank. The ultimate result of the experimental design work (OKR in Russian) was the modernised BT-7 wheel-track tank; created on the basis of the BT-5 tank, but with enhanced hull armour protection with the majority of the armour plates now welded rather than riveted. The turret and armament on the first-production tanks were the same as on

The "Christie" tank on trials at the Nakhabino polygon, west of Moscow.

the BT-5 tank, but the modified hull design also now allowed for the installation of a modified turret with a more powerful 76.2mm tank gun. Significant changes were made to the power plant. Instead of the Soviet M-5 or imported "Liberty" type engines installed in the BT-5, the more reliable M-17T engine was installed in the BT-7, with an operating power output of 400hp. A significant increase in the fuel tank capacity from 360 to 800 litres more than doubled the road range. Series production of the BT-7 began at KhPZ in 1935.

Thus, in the mid 1930s, the light BT-7 wheel-track or "fast" tank, despite some design weaknesses was in full compliance with the original tactical and technical characteristics (TTKhs) and fully consistent with best practices at the time and operational-tactical thought on the use of tanks. The combined wheel-track drive system of the BT tank series provided relatively high operational (wheeled) and tactical (tracked) mobility, which was an extremely important element in implementing the Soviet theory of mechanised deep battle and operations.

BT-2 Tank armed with twin DT machine guns.

Unsurprisingly, when choosing the type of propulsion for the new types of tanks for use in the development of a system of armoured weapons in the second Five Year Plan, preference was given to the wheel-track propulsion system that had been operationally tried and tested on the BT series. The design of wheel-track drive system used on BT tanks was not however entirely perfect; with movement on wheels on all but good roads leaving much to be desired. Military experts at the NIA-BT polygon of the Armoured Directorate (ABTU) of the Red Army described the shortcomings of the wheel-track drive system employed on the BT series drive system as follows:

"The existing BT-5 and BT-7 wheel-track tanks have the following main drawbacks:

a) Inability to convert to wheeled drive without the crew leaving the tank.

b) Inability of movement on tracks with the wheels engaged.

c) Limited scope of application of the wheel travel mode.

Due to these shortcomings, the BT-5 and BT-7 are not wheel-track tanks in every sense of the word, as using the driven wheeled mode of these tanks in combat with the destruction of one of the tracks, is not possible. The use of wheel travel for operational (i.e. sudden off-road) requirements is very limited due to the (only) two driven-wheeled mode. In the event of necessary detours from, or the in case of partial destruction of a road, or fast dispersal with the appearance of enemy planes - BT-5 and BT-7 tanks are in a relatively helpless position, as the weight on "soft ground" threatens the tank with bogging down, and the transition to tracked drive takes about 30 minutes and requires the crew to leave the tank".

RGVA. F.34014. L.2. C.806. pp3

A.O. Firsov.   N.F. Tsyganov.

In the development of new types of tanks as provided by Resolution STO №71ss dated 13th August 1933 and a later amendment S-71ss dated 19th June 1935, the disadvantages described above were tackled. Specifically, in order to increase tank tractability on wheels, the TTTs for the design of the T-46 and T-29 tanks increased the number of driving wheels to two pairs for the T-46 tank and four pairs for the T-29 tank, as well as specifying improvement of the (wheeled) steering mechanisms.

In parallel with the development of new tank models, the Soviet tank industry continued to work on the improvement of tanks then in mass production, including the BT tank series, with design work to improve the firepower, protection and mobility of the BT tank series in the mid 1930s being solely undertaken by the tank building industry. In April 1935 in the repair shops of the Ukrainian Military District (UVO), a talented inventor, a

BT-5 tank.

BT-7 M-1935 tank.

platoon commander of the 4th Tank Regiment, military technician 2nd rank N. F. Tsyganov developed together with a group of enthusiasts a new wheel-track variant, the BT-IS tank, on the basis of the BT tank series. The BT-IS design was undertaken to increase the protection of the BT series on the battlefield by improving the design of the wheel-track drive. Work on the design of the BT-IS tank was carried out on the direct instructions of the commander of the UVO, commander 1st rank I. Eh. Yakir.

The results achieved by the group of UVO enthusiasts were relayed, with colourful introductory wording, in a report written on 23rd April 1935 directly to the Secretary General of the Central Committee of the Communist Party - TsK VK-P(b) - Iosef V. Stalin and the People's Commissar of Defence (NKO) K.E. Voroshilov:

"Bolsheviks fighters and commanders of the Ukrainian Military District - enthusiasts of the great cause of mastering and further improvement of our powerful military equipment - report to You: Your instructions about the improvement of propulsion on BT tanks, have been carried out. We propose a new type of propulsion for BT tanks. The new wheeled propulsion consists of not one, but three driving pairs (II, III and IV) of wheels. The drawings of the new drive system are complete. Self-propelled models of the BT tank on a scale of 1/5 are also made. The model was tested. It fully confirmed your instructions and data provided in the summer of 1934. With a new propulsion the BT tank can be turned into even more powerful, highly manoeuvrable combat machine.

The BT tank with the new drive system has acquired the ability to move on its own, manoeuvre and fight, despite the most heavy damage in combat - loss of one or both tracks and four wheels from

eight. With a heavily damaged machine on four wheels (if the destroyed wheels have not unbalanced the machine) the crew has full ability to continue to fight and defeat the enemies of our glorious socialist Motherland, as we are taught by our great Bolshevik party of Lenin and Stalin - Bolshevik and every conscious worker and farmer are fighting to the last drop of blood and, if necessary, die but will not surrender to the enemy. The new type of propulsion increases the tractability of the BT tank on heavy (arable) ground by a factor of 4-5 times and makes it possible to overcome 25° ploughed inclines. The new design of the steering wheels halves the BT tank turning radius from 10 metres to 5-6 metres, thus increasing the maneuverability of the tank by a factor of two. The change from tracked to wheeled drive in the case of track damage, one or both, by enemy action is made automatically without stopping the tank and without the crew being required to leave the armoured hull. We gave the tank invention the name "BT-IS". Simultaneously with the draft of the new wheeled-drive, we started design and fabrication of a new track-roller drive for BT tanks, also now complete. All the drawings and experimental models in 1/5 full size scale are ready. Designed and manufactured is a new suspension of roller drive, and track. The BT tank in wheeled drive mode with a conventional M-5 engine according to our calculations develops on wheels and on tracks a speed of 105km/h, double the existing normal speed on standard tracks (norm 51.6 km/h)".

The tank mounted on its wheels and new track can rotate 360° in place. The rollers and tracks are rubber and give almost silent running. Tactical use of this machine follows from its high-speed all-terrain capability and quietness. In both types of machines we tried to minimise the changes from the existing BT-2 and BT-5 tanks, and achieved this. This allows to install new types of drive without major alterations to existing and experimental types of BT machines and makes the series production of new machines easy to master. The invention of both types of BT drives belongs to the young Bolshevik and young commander of the 4th Tank Regiment of the UVO, Tsyganov N. F., talented self-taught designer-inventor. In 1934, comrade Tsyganov was given an award by the People's Commissar of Defence comrade Voroshilov, the junior officer platoon commander given a gold watch for the invention of the automatic coupling of tanks BT, T-26 and T-27, adopted by the Red Army. We all were only conscientious assistants to him in the practical implementation of his inventions. Within 4 months the friendly team, directed by comrade Tsyganov directly under our Commander comrade Yakir, working 16-18 hours a day, have produced more than 500 drawings and about 3,000 components for the models of the designed machines. And today, in happy consciousness of the performed duty we report to you that the works on both types of drive are finished. We ask for your guidance and future tasks".

RGVA. F.33987. L.2. C.1362. pp1-2

On 23rd April 1935 - the same day this report was drawn up - the UVO commander, I. Eh. Yakir sent a letter to K. E. Voroshilov describing the inventions of N. F. Tsyganov with a request to *"approve a new type of BT drive mechanism and give instructions to industry about production of prototypes and series production of quoted machines."* After consultation with the People's Commissar of Heavy Industry (NKTP), G. K. Ordzhonikidze, Voroshilov at the end of April 1935 gave the director of "Spetsmashtrest" NKTP (in charge of prototype tank production) K. A. Neumann a private instruction in 1935 to produce six experimental tanks of the "latest design". Pursuant to this guidance, "Spetsmashtrest" was on 4th May 1935 issued an order №P-9ss that in particular, stated:

"The Director of KhPZ comrade Bondarenko is to immediately conclude an agreement with ABTU RKKA to manufacture three prototype tanks of the Tsyganov BT-IS design, with six driving and six controlled wheels, and director of the Kirov experimental plant comrade Barykov is to immediately conclude an agreement with ABTU RKKA to manufacture three prototypes of the BT-IS, tank designed by comrade Tsyganov, with new track and suspension".

Malyshev G. N. The Tank Factory named after S. M. Kirov.

Due to other heavy workload commitments, the leadership of both plants refused to sign agreements with ABTU, and therefore work on making a prototype of the tank BT-IS with six drive wheels was organised in the tank-automotive workshops of the Kharkov Military District (KhVO). Inspired by the support of the top leadership of the Red Army, the group of enthusiasts began to create the BT-IS prototype on the basis

Model of a BT tank with three pairs of driving wheels.

Model of a BT tank with experimental roller-track drive.

of the BT-2 tank. Taking into account the importance of N. F. Tsyganov's invention, the workshop chief, friend and combat comrade during the Civil War, hero of the famous novel "How the Steel was Tempered", N. A. Ostrovsky, Kombrig (brigade commander) N. N. Lisitsyn, and also the head of the Political Department of KhVO M. F. Berezkin has assumed overall leadership for the production of the BT-IS machines. Due to the combined efforts of the designers, military mechanics and civilian workers of the district workshop, a prototype BT-IS tank was quickly completed. Photographs of particularly distinguished workers were included in a photo album, which in late 1935 was sent to the People's Commissar of Defence K.E. Voroshilov in Moscow.

The prototype BT-IS, created in the second half of 1935 on the basis of the BT-2 tank, more or less corresponded to the Tsyganov's original project, in that in wheeled mode the second, third and fourth wheel pairs were driven. The exception was the number of controlled (i.e. adjustable) wheels - on the BT-IS tank, instead of three pairs of controlled wheels (1st, 2nd and 4th), provided for in the initial project, two pairs were controlled, namely the first and the second. This BT-IS design implemented the ability to move simultaneously by track on one side of the tank and on wheels on the other. The relative speed

The BT-IS design team.

adjustment between the wheels and the track was undertaken with the help of special synchronizer mechanisms. In addition, the tank could move on tracks with the drive torque gearing engaged with the second, third and fourth pairs of road wheels. Switching on and off of the drive mechanisms and speed synchronizers was undertaken from the driver-mechanic's position through system of levers and pulleys.

After completion on 15th December 1935, the BT-IS was delivered from the KhVO district workshop to Plant №48 where testing was undertaken from 17th December 1935 to 20th January 1936. The testing Commission concluded:

"1. Three pairs of driven wheels have an advantage over one and two pairs. 2. The advantages of two pairs of driven wheels are insignificant and have no practical effect (especially in winter conditions). 3. For the normal movement of the tank on one track it is necessary to change the gear ratio to the wheels at track speed in the range of 5-8 % less than the existing…"

RGVA. F. 31811. L. 3 C. 580 pp18

Further development of the BT-IS was approved by K. E. Voroshilov and G. K. Ordzhonikidze, with the joint decision

to in 1936 produce an experimental batch of ten BT-IS tanks at Plant №48 in Kharkov for the purpose of conducting further military trials. At the beginning of 1936, Plant №48 under the direction of N. F. Tsyganov and with the participation of ABTU engineers began work on developing for production an experimental series of BT-IS tanks based on the BT-5 fast tank, the new tank receiving the designation "BT-5-IS". The first three tanks from the experimental batch were completed in August 1936. The BT-5-IS tank was a wheel-track tank with six drive and two steering wheels; with speed synchronization when driving simultaneously on wheels and tracks.

By mid November 1936, the last of the BT-5-IS experimental series was completed at Plant №48. Immediately thereafter, by order of the head of ABTU, division commander G. G. Bokis, a non-stop run by three BT-5-IS tanks was organized for 18th - 19th November on a route Kharkov - Moscow. The run was deemed successful and the small (46 person) team behind the development and testing of the BT-5-IS were by ABTU Orders №229 & №230 dated 27th and 29th November 1936 respectively awarded significant cash prizes for their efforts.

As a result of the trial run, three BT-5-IS tanks (№05, №06 and №010) were modified in May-June 1937, and thereafter subjected to military trials in the area of Kharkov. From the report of ABTU military representative Pestov at Plant №48, dated 3rd July 1937 the BT-IS military trial results were as follows:

"I can report that the military Commission has completed testing of the BT-IS tanks at Plant №48. During the tests, the tanks have undertaken the following distances:
Note: the BT-5 tanks were taken after completed repairs for com-

BT-IS № 05	On Wheels	2,331 km	On tracks	109 km
BT-IS № 06	On Wheels	1,545 km	On tracks	328 km
BT-IS № 010	On Wheels	1,467 km	On tracks	191 km
BT-5	On Wheels	1,237 km	On tracks	150 km
		6,580 km		**778 km**

parison with the BT-IS and testing the quality of repair of the BTs at Plant №48. The Commission's assessment is positive for both BT-IS and for the repaired BT-5 tanks. The following main defects of the BT-IS are identified:

1. Weak (overloaded) synchroniser bevel gears of the synchronisers.
2. Overloaded rims on the rear wheels.
3. Seals of vertical shafts leaking grease lubrication.
4. Poor access to the additional transmission.

In addition to these flaws, there is a significant defect affecting the entire additional powertrain - split vertical suspension rod cushions, as well as stripped threads in these rods. Breakage of the rods, will assure failure of the spline connection and perhaps universal joints

and other parts. This defect was not detected because the tanks were repaired very often during the tests. [The last sentence was underlined in a pencil made notation: "not true"]. The BT-5 tank did not have serious defects for the distances travelled. All the BT-IS defects are repairable and solutions to eliminate them already available in the plant design Bureau".

RGVA. F.31811. L. 3 C.760. pp40

The report on military testing of the BT-5-IS and Annex dated 11th July 1937 were sent from Kharkov to Moscow to the chief of ABTU, G. G. Bokis on 15th July 1937, and on 21st July members of the Commission who took part in trials personally reported in Moscow to Bokis on their findings on the BT-IS tank. On the same day, the famous Soviet tank test driver, Captain E. A. Kulchitsky, then holding the post of head of the test Department of NIABT ABTU, reported in a letter addressed to G. G. Bokis, his conclusions on the BT-IS tank:

"In Leningrad you asked my opinion about the BT-IS tank. You were interested in the opinion of the "tankist". Then, I related based on experience of the distance travelled between Kharkov-Moscow and the first phase of military testing. Now I have an opportunity to confirm and supplement that opinion on the basis of a full study of the machine on test in Kharkov. As a test and as a "tankist" who hopes to wage a future war in a tank, I have the opportunity to know all the tanks of our army and have in mind the type of tank in which I would like to fight, if the choice is presented. After testing the BT-IS tank, I think that at the moment this machine can be better than all other machines taken into the army, which is especially important at

The BT-IS Fast Tank

BT-5-IS tank during trials.

the moment. The rectification of the faults on a proven new machine is achievable, and the result is a fundamentally new tank. Tests in Kharkov gave the necessary experience for the construction of reliable tanks. Plant №48 has greater experience than other plants on these machines, and under your leadership can deliver a batch of tanks this year. Staying with the №48 plant, considering the seriousness and responsibility of situation with building the proven BT-IS, and also your address in Leningrad, I address to you with a private letter. I appeal to you to give the most serious and immediate attention to the BT-IS tanks, because I am sure that not only sabotage, and accidental negligence in the selection of the plant for the production of tanks, or even deviation from accuracy in production, can once again deny the army good machines for a prolonged time, and the idea of synchronization can be taken into question, as difficult".

RGVA. F.31811. L. 3 C.760. pp45

Kulchitsky's concern about providing the Red Army with BT-IS tanks was caused not so much by the "structural and production defects" revealed during the standard tests, but was more focused on the difficult political and economic situation in the Soviet Union in 1937. The above-mentioned letter regarding domestic tank building was written at a time when there were problems with preparing the new T-46 light and T-29 medium wheel-track tanks for series production in Leningrad, with similar problems being experienced in Kharkov. In letter №12/252ss dated 17th July 1937, the acting head of the military group of the control commission for the TsK VKP(b), E. I. Vishnevsky, informed the senior Soviet leadership of the country regarding the unacceptable situation in the tank industry:

"As a result of the wrecking carried out in the tank industry and in the 8th Command of NKOP, the management of the command and tank plants are in a position of confusion and inability to quick-

ly liquidate the possible consequences of this wrecking. The lack of concrete and operational leadership in the field of tank construction led to the disruption of the tank program of the I-II quarter of this year and panic in the factories, the leaders of which say: "if the next few days do not give a significant shift in production and delivery, we will find ourselves in a deadlock." The absolutely unacceptable situation created in the tank industry can be characterised by the example of the Leningrad plants. An inspection found that in the Voroshilov plant only seventeen T-26 tanks were accepted (by Red Army military representatives) for 5 months of 1937 instead of 400-500 according to the plan; for development of the new T-46 tank the plant was unprepared; until now the most serious defects of the prototype reference sample T-46 have not been eliminated. As a result, the implementation of the 1937 program for the production of 600 T-26 tanks and 100 T-46 tanks is in danger of failure. The main reason of failure of T-26 tank production is engine damage. When putting the T-26 into production the engine was copied from the original Vickers tank. When copying the drawings of the engine and later in the production process, a number of deviations were made from the original design, deteriorating the quality of the engine. This led to a systematic breakage of the valves and damage to the seats in the cylinders, which disabled the engine. Despite this, the NKO made acceptance of these tanks and only at the end of 1936 showed the plant the requirement to guarantee the operation of the engine as 100 hours on the test bench and 200 hours installed in the tank. However, none of the engines subjected to long-term tests in January-February 1937 provided the required warranty running hours and acceptance of the machines by the military representative was terminated. Thus, instead of development of the new T-46 tank, the plant is instead working on "development" of the engine for the T-26, already in mass production for several years, and as a result neither the T-26 nor the T-46 program has in 1937 been fulfilled.

Serial production of the T-46 tank was delayed. The Red Army has been waiting for these tanks since 1934, but the factory management still to this day cannot give a clear answer on when production of the T-46 will start. One thing only is clear, that the plant does not guarantee the delivery of combat machines in 1937; the T-46 tanks will at best be released only for training purposes, i.e. the Red Army in 1937 will not receive this tank. It should be noted that the Voroshilov plant had also prepared for serial production of the T-46 based on the prototype drawings rather than awaiting the final production drawings, and as a result, the four T-46 tanks produced in 1936 are already out of commission, and the tools and fittings have also proven unfit for service. According to preliminary data, the loss from this was 20-25 million Roubles.

The main reason for the failure of the release for production of the T-46 was the failure of this machine in the prototype stage, as well as acts of "sabotage" carried out on this tank at the pilot plant. Experimental Plant №185 named after S. M. Kirov, was the only experimental tank plant in the Soviet Union that was in the hands of counter-revolutionaries, Trotskyists and saboteurs - agents of foreign intelligence services, building a nest under the patronage of the plant director Barykov, a former Trotskyist who was in 1924 excluded from the party but did not break communication with active Trotskyists until 1935. In 1931 Barykov invited Simonov, the former Secretary of Trotsky, to the factory as his deputy on return from exile. Knowing Simonov to be a sworn enemy of the party, Barykov, however, nevertheless recommends him in 1931 to the party. Having restored his party member rights, Simonov till the end of 1934 was actually the "owner" of the plant. During the secondary arrest and expulsion of Simonov in connection with the murder of Comrade Kirov, Barykov interceded to the Leningrad regional Committee of the VKP(b) about leaving Simonov in Leningrad. But after the expulsion of Simonov, Barykov still does not break off contact with him.

In addition to Simonov, there were at the factory a number of Trotskyists (Musatov, Stedenkan and others), to whom the NKVD have been sent, that Barykov knew to be enemies of the people, but were covered by his authority. Along with the Trotskyists from the factory the NKVD arrested 10 designer saboteurs. At the end of 1936, Siegel and Syachintov, who were delegated to guide the design of all prototypes, were arrested. The attitude of Barykov to the work saboteurs can be seen in the example with Siegel. Saboteur Siegel directs the development of the T-43-1 wheel-tracked amphibious tank project. However, the prototype of this tank neither floats nor moves on wheels. Despite this, Siegel is appointed responsible for the development of the T-29 standard tank, which is not completed, and he is then transferred to guide the design of the T-46-1. Siegel also doesn't finish work on the T-46-1 or provide it to the Red Army, but he is for "productive work" nevertheless awarded the Order of the Red Star. In response to the award, the plant management has made a commitment to create the high-speed Stalkanov (designed) T-44 wheel-track machine. The management of this tank is entru-

E. A. Kulchitsky

sted again to Siegel, who also fails in this work, with all T-44 projects being archived. Despite the "fruitfulness" of Siegel's work, he is entrusted with the management of the design of the T-46-5 tank. Feeling the support of Barykov, Siegel will become even more impudent and with the T-46-5 he leads the direct wrecking of the work. His career has now been stopped by the NKVD. In principle the work of saboteur Syachintov, who led the design of self-propelled guns and in 1936 was awarded the Order of Lenin was in the same manner. The result from the whole range of prototypes developed in the factory is that there are in serial production, only the T-28 and T-35 tanks and two self-propelled guns, the SU-5 and SU-14. The development of the T-46 and T-29 tanks launched in 1933 is still not completed, their serial production in 1936, and in 1937 is not established, although the prototypes were made in 1934. The situation is not better at other plants. The Kirovsky Zavod (LKZ) and similarly the Voroshilov factory are for a long time engaged in "development" for of the new T-29 tank to replace the T-28 tank in production. KhPZ is stalled with the production of the T-35 and BT-7, and Plant №37 still has not provided a combat-ready reconnaissance machine to replace the T-37".

RGVA. F.4. L.14. C.1897. pp286-290

Poster - "Don't Break the Five Year Plan or We Will Break Your Paws!"

Chapter 3

Cadres Are the Key to Everything!

The famous Russian slogan "Кадры решают все!" - the (choice of) cadres or personnel are the key to everything* - was proclaimed by Stalin on 4th May 1935 in the Kremlin Palace before the graduates of the military academies of the Red Army. In his speech, General Secretary of the Central Committee of the TsK VKP(b) Stalin explained:

"We used to say that: "technology decides everything". This slogan has helped us to eliminate the famine in the field of technology and has created the broadest technical basis in all fields of activity for the arming of our people with first-class equipment. That's very good. But that is far from enough. To set the equipment in motion and use it to the end, we need people who have mastered that equipment, we need personnel capable of mastering and artfully using this equipment. Such equipment without people who have mastered it, is dead. Equipment managed by people who have mastered that equipment can and should perform miracles. If our world-class mills and factories, our state and collective farms and our Red Army had a sufficient number of personnel able to use this equipment, our country would obtain an effect three or four times more than it has now. That is why the emphasis must now be placed on people, on personnel, on workers who have mastered the use of equipment. That is why the old slogan "technology solves everything", which is a reflection of the past period, when we had a hunger in the field of technology, should now be replaced by a new slogan, the slogan that "cadres are the key to everything". This is now important.

Cadres are the Key to Everything, Stalin's 1935 speech as reported in the press.

Can we say that our people have understood and fully understood the great importance of this new slogan? I wouldn't say that. Otherwise, we would not have had that ugly attitude to people, to personnel, to employees, which we often observe in our practice. The slogan "cadres are the key to everything" requires our managers to show the most caring attitude to our employees in whatever field they work, grow them carefully, help them when they need support, encourage them when they show their first successes, put them forward, etc. Meanwhile, in reality we have cases of a heartlessly bureaucratic and ugly attitude to employees. This, indeed, explains that instead of having to study people and only afterwards looking to put them into posts, (we are) often throwing people about like pawns".

In the final part of his speech, Stalin stressed that:

"of all the valuable capital available in the world, the most valuable and the most decisive capital is cadres, people. It is necessary to understand that under our current conditions that cadres decide everything. There will be good and numerous options in industry, in agriculture, in transport, in our army, - our country will be invincible. But if we will not have such cadres - we will limp on both legs".

"Pravda" newspaper №123 dated 6th May, 1935.

One striking example of the real-life implementation of the proclaimed slogan was the appointment at the end of December 1936 of Mikhail Koshkin to the post of head of the T2K tank design department (KB T2K) at the Kharkov Locomotive Plant (KhPZ). Koshkin had previously held the post of Deputy Head of the design department at the experimental S. M. Kirov mechanical engineering plant in Leningrad. Given that Koshkin received his qualification as a mechanical engineer only in May 1934, when he graduated from the Leningrad Institute of Mechanical Engineering, defending his diploma project with an assessment of "excellent", such rapid progress was remarkable. One of the creators of the legendary T-34 tank, Ya.I. Baran, would later write of Koshkin:

"Son of a poor peasant from Yaroslavl province, Koshkin had begun work at enterprises in Moscow, and had participated in the First World War. After the Russian Revolution, he had volunteered for the Red Army, and fought against White Guards and interventionist forces. A member of the Bolshevik Party from 1919, he graduated

---

* The Russian statement literally translates as cadres decide, or resolve, everything; however the actual Russian meaning is that the choice of cadres or personnel are the key to everything, which is what Stalin was relaying in his speech.

Mikhail Ilyich Koshkin.

from the Communist University named after Ya. M. Sverdlov, specialised on economic and party work. After attending the Leningrad Institute of Mechanical Engineering, he successfully graduated and was assigned to the KB of the prototype tank plant (the Kirov plant). There he revealed his talent as a designer. In January 1937 Mikhail Ilyich Koshkin appeared in our design bureau. I found time to talk to each designer and remember my first conversation with Mikhail Ilyich. He was deeply interested in the work that I did, tactfully finding out how I had became a designer, my attitude to this work, and the study undertaken at evening Institute. Subsequently, while working on assembly on the night shift, he in a free moment talked about his life, work, and plans for the future. He was a man with a capital letter. For three and a half years working at the Kharkov plant, he taught us a lot. His ability to talk to people, his modesty, and determination in critical moments of work were a good example."

T-34: Path to Victory: The Memoirs of Tank Builders and Tank Crews. K. M. Slobodin, V. D. Listrovoy, Publishing House of Political Literature of Ukraine, 1989, pp26-27.

The appointment of M. I. Koshkin to the new position was not incidental. By the autumn of 1936 the situation at KhPZ in Kharkov had become extremely tense. This was primarily due to investigations by the Main Directorate of State Security (GUGB) of the NKVD (the People's Commissariat for Internal Affairs) of the USSR into the causes of failure in Red Army operational service of the BT-7 fast tank series, production of which had commenced at KhPZ in 1935. In one of the numerous documents relating to this issue - a special message *"on the situation with the new BT-7 tanks"* dated 14th July 1936, compiled by the head of the special Department of GUGB NKVD, M.I Gaem, was noted:

"In the auto-armour-tank forces of the Red Army from August 1935 to March 1936 were received more than 700 new BT-7 tanks, representing the former tank BT-5, with modernised construction, equipped with a more powerful engine (M-17 developing 500-650hp instead of the previous M-5 developing 400hp). In service there are some major failures of BT-7 components, with serious damage, leading to tanks being removed from service. The most typical failures are:

1) *Failure in the gearshift mechanism (with most serious failure being of the cone gears);*
2) *Failure of wheel mounting bolts*
3) *Parting of the tracks.*

Special tests undertaken within the last three months in connection with this by the Armoured Forces Directorate of the RKKA and the Kharkov Locomotive Plant (KhPZ) confirmed the unsuitability of the BT-7 gearbox and, therefore, the unreliability of all prior manufactured BT-7 tanks so fitted with this gearbox, as the gearbox is one of the most important and vital components of the tank, and damage puts the tank out of commission for a long period. The situation is so serious that the production of BT-7 tanks is suspended at the plant, and newly manufactured tanks (about 300) have not been given military acceptance. The whole assembly shop is crammed with tanks from which the gearboxes have been removed for use as spare parts for BT-5 tanks, because they are unfit for the BT-7. The situation is exacerbated by the fact that the production of BT-7 tanks has been stopped for three months, and according to all reports, will not soon be re-established, and, therefore, the restoration of the "BT" tank fleet (the BT-5 has been removed from production) will stretch indefinitely. The materials available to us indicate that the situation is not accidental, but is the result of criminal negligence committed in the design of the BT-7 tank, with no less criminal negligence related to its testing before commissioning into mass production."

D.31-P/O-6/6-3 pp6-10

Urgent measures to strengthen the transmissions were undertaken, allowing KhPZ to re-start BT-7 production in the mid-summer of 1936. However, investigation into *"results of criminal negligence committed in the design of the BT-7 tank"* had only begun. During the investigation, the chief of the T2K KB, A. O. Firsov, was demoted senior designer, before on 14th March 1937 being arrested and charged with sabotage. The transmission problem with the BT-7 was not the only one encountered, and during 1936, NKVD investigations: *"revealed and eliminated a number of counter-revolutionary fascist and terrorist groups"* among the staff at the plant, totalling 67 people. In early 1937 the Commission of Soviet Control (KSK) pri SNK SSSR also began an investigation into delays in construction of the diesel engine workshop at KhPZ and thereby the start of serial production of the urgently required BD-2 diesel engine. The results of the audit were outlined in Memorandum №282ss, dated 20th April 1937 from group leader of the Military Control of KSK, KomKor V. N. Sokolov to the KSK Chairman N. K. Antipov within which the report the activities of the plant management and primarily its director I. P. Bondarenko were characterised in extremely negative terms:

"Recruitment and the state of affairs at the plant makes us think that we are dealing, at best, with a degenerate person who has lost all his party form, or with the direct organiser and head of a saboteur group at the defence plant."

RGVA. L.4. C.1897. pp69

The Firsov Design Bureau team.

The report by Sokolov and its conclusions about the plant management was of course confirmed by the Party Secretary of KP (b) U - the Kharkov Regional Committee of the Communist Party, N. F. Gikalo in a letter dated 20th March 1937 addressed to the Secretary of the TsK VKP (b), A.A. Andreev, describing the situation at the plant and the specific activities of Bondarenko:

"Comrade Bondarenko now, working at the plant, has actually broken away from the party organisation, with opinions that are not adequate and on a number of questions opposes the party organisation".

RGAEh. F.7515. L.1. C.4. pp12

Meanwhile, the former head of the operations department of the tank department at KhPZ, N. A. Sobol, described the prevailing atmosphere in the plant:

"The arrests of a number of experienced managers, who had the authority and respect of the workers, caused increased nervousness in people, bordering on passivity: "What is it?" "What more can you expect?" It looked like in such cases people say: "I lived through the day, thank God, and what will happen tomorrow, if we live until then, we will see." The tension at the plant, and the complexity of the production processes for a long time led to a situation whereby, although at KhPZ it was possible to earn more money than at other enterprises, there were few people wishing to work there. In view of this fact the city authorities repeatedly had to give other enterprises in the city orders about directing workers to permanent work at the locomotive plant".

Sobol. N.A. Recollections of the Plant Director. Ed: A.S. Epshtein. Kh. Prapor. pp43

It was within this tense environment that the approximately 45 staff of the T2K design bureau within the tank department of the plant worked, only six of whom were members of the VKP(b) - the Communist Party. Nine were Communist Youth Union members, and the rest were non-party members, including the Deputy Chief of the design bureau N. Kucherenko, and the heads of all sections - P. N. Gorun, A. A. Morozov, V. M. Doroshenko, M. I. Tarshinov, V. Ya. Kurasov, A. S. Bondarenko, G. M. Fomin, V. A. Fesino and A. Ya. Mitnik. Their collective apparent "lack of conformity" was always in the background if things did not go well. At the time, over half of the T2K KB staff were also under 30 years of age.

It was within the above background situation that the People's Commissariat of the Defence Industry (NKOP) - formed on 8th December 1936 by separating from the NKTP structure

I.P. Bondarenko.

N.A. Kucherenko.

- made the decision to strengthen the KB of one of the leading Soviet tank production plants. This was achieved by sending there the 38 year old design engineer - and Bolshevik Party member since 1919 - Mikhail I. Koshkin, who was appointed as head of the T2K KB on 25th December 1936 by the order of the Main Artillery-Tank Command of the NKOP. Before moving to KhPZ and his subsequent career, Koshkin already had extensive practical experience in the design of wheel-track tanks. For his active participation in the creation of the T-29 medium wheel-track tank at the S. M. Kirov plant in Leningrad, Koshkin had in April 1936 been awarded the Soviet Order of the Red Star.

Almost simultaneously with the appointment of Koshkin into his new office, the People's Commissariat of Defence Industry (NKOP) on 30th December 1936 issued Resulotion №06ss, according to which KhPZ - in full known as the Kharkov Locomotive Plant in the name of Komintern NKOP SSSR - was given a numerical designation, becoming known thereafter as "Plant №183". In January 1937, three-digit numbers were also introduced for the plant departments and workshops. The T2 tank department was designated as Department "100", the T2K design Bureau headed by Koshkin became KB "190" and workshop T2O became Workshop "191". KB-190 was located on the third floor of department building "100". On the floor below were the offices of the military representatives of the ABTU and AU (the auto-armour and artillery directorates) and the office of the chief of tank department "100". Koshkin originally had a relatively small design team tasked with ensuring the technical currency of design documentation for the serial production BT-7 tank. It also worked on improving the design of BT-7 components and assemblies, and designing potential BT-7 modernisations and derivatives. The volume of experimental work carried out at the T2O workshop being undertaken in December 1936 can be judged by the report of the assistant military ABTU representative at KhPZ, military engineer 3rd rank K.V. Olkhovsky:

"I. installation of remote control (control of tank movement from workplace of tank commander) on BT-7 tanks.

One BT-7 machine with remote control was factory tested. The tank made two trips with the target to travel 200km on each run. The first run of the tank was not completed due to the loss of air pressure as a result of a burst pipe between the compressor and an air cylinder, and a holed gasket in a side friction clutch air cylinder. The tank also did not finish the second run because of differential gear failure. <...> Imperfection of the remote control system creates conditions of difficulty control, and the machine has a reduced speed. At this time, the installation continues on installing remote control on another two BT-7 machines.

II. Testing progress of BT-8 machines [BT-7 with BD-2 diesel].

Collected two tanks. One machine after travelling 100km required repair due to a broken fan. The second twice had fan failures and therefore did not complete the test.

III. Test of new gearbox designs.

Continued test of four BT-7 service machines with a 3-speed transmission design by engineers Morozov and Doroshenko. The M-17T engine was fitted on all tanks. <...> Of the four tanks, two went on plant transmission tests. Of these, one tank, with a gearbox by design engineer Morozov completed 5,015km. The other tank with the same transmission completed 3,505km. The machine did not run regularly, as the shop T2O cannot cope with the volume of (repair) work.

IV. Tested new track designs.

1. Track with reduced links and with pin diameter 22mm. One set of tracks lasted 646km, the second set 834km.

2. Serial production track with special profiled links lasted 372km before to track links broke, damaging a drive sprocket.

3. Track of serial production 8-hinge type with guide horn, with extended and enlarged track shoes, with 6mm retaining studs set in the track edges. One set of such tracks after two repairs lasted 1,048km. The second set of tracks after one repair lasted 656km before being removed due to parting.

4. Began testing of track developed by design engineer Tarshinov. Track has passed 156km. The tests continue."

RGVA. F.31811. L.3. C.1017. pp8-10

At the beginning of 1937, the ABTU work plan for 1937 added the following to the above experimental works:
- project development and working drawings for a command tank for the commander of mechanised units and reconnaissance on the basis of the BT-7 tank;
- project development and working drawings for improved BT-2 and BT-5 tanks fitted with BD-2 diesel engines;
- project development and working drawings of a BT-7 tank with "gas generator set";
- manufacture and testing of "tanks BT-5 and BT-7 insulated for winter conditions";
- development, production and tests of the prototype *"of the artillery self-propelled wheel and tracked installation on the basis of the BT tank"* (an artillery tank with 76.2mm gun installation).

Even by modern standards, with the use of AutoCad design systems rather than manually prepared drawings, the workload for a team of only 45 staff was significant. The new KB chief had to simultaneously get acquainted with the *"cadres who resolved everything"*, organise the timely and qualitative implementation of contracts and explain to subordinates the policy of the Bolshevik party. By the first half of February 1937, Mikhail I. Koshkin had already participated in the design improvement of components and assemblies for the BT-7. A list of these activities was developed at a meeting held on 9th February in Moscow with the assistant to the chief of the ABTU, V.D. Sviridov, and recorded in a Protocol signed by the Deputy Director of Plant №183, F. I. Lyash and others.

The planned terms of modifications and the production of prototypes were reflected in NKOP Order №0035ss dated 15th February 1937, according to which on the basis of operation combat experience the design of the BT-7 tank was to be improved on 19 separate points. The stipulated project delivery terms were extremely short. For installation of a machine gun alomgside the driver-mechanic, installation of a radio station in the hull, increased ammunition complement and other modifications the plant was given only two months. Less than two weeks later, on 28th February 1937, Plant №183 was provided the tactical and technical requirements (TTTs) for the design and manufacture of the BT-9 wheel-tracked tank, which was designed for the following tasks:

a) *Destruction of tanks, anti-tank weapons, and enemy manpower.*

b) *Independent operation in isolation from other types of troops behind enemy lines and in joint action with infantry, cavalry, etc. in various types of combat.*

c) Conduct reconnaissance, as single machines or as part of units.
d) Support and combat support of the tanks of the RGK.
e) Penetration into enemy territory by transport in aircraft.

RGVA. F.31811. L.3. C.975. pp5

The estimated combat weight of the BT-9 tank was set in the range of 12-13 metric tonnes, while in the design TTTs it was intriguingly stated that:

"The weight of the tank must be at a minimum in order to have the possibility of carrying it by aircraft. For this purpose, it is necessary to introduce the machining and stamping of parts, as well as the use of light alloys and alloy metals. The final weight shall be determined when the sketch design is submitted."

RGVA. F.31811. L.3. C.975. pp13

The armament of the BT-9 tank was to consist of a 45mm tank gun, co-axial DT machine gun, secondary DT machine gun (in the turret rear), a removable flamethrower, anti-aircraft machine gun, and a "sub-machine gun" for the driver mechanic. In addition, the tank was to be fitted with the "Orion" gun stabiliser acting as *"the stabiliser of the turret in a horizontal position when the tank is manoeuvring in a snaking manner with frequent twists and turns"*. The tank hull was to be designed with inclined welded armour plates, with a conical turret. The minimum angles of the hull and turret armour plates were to be at least 15°. The BT-9 was to be fitted with the BD-2 diesel engine rated at 400hp, with a planned maximum speed of 80km/h on wheels or tracks. Cruising range on tracks was to be 500km, increasing to 700km when driving on wheels on made roads. The number of driven wheels in wheeled mode was to be at least six, while the speed of movement on wheels and on tracks (or a single track) was to be synchronized by selection of appropriate gear ratios in the transmission, i.e. without the use of synchronisers. According to the TTTs the KB-190 designers were required to design the BT-9 tank with:

"a) Maximising the use of existing equipment so transition to a new tank does not require conversion of the plant.
b) Maximum use of standards and standard parts.
c) Reduction of total number of components on the tank as a whole.
d) when using parts and assemblies of the existing production to provide their improvement based on operational data".

RGVA. F.31811. L.3. C.975. pp13-14

A few days after receiving the task for designing the BT-9 tank in KB-190, the TTTs for design and manufacture of another new BT-7 tank variant, the BT-7-B-IS had also been studied. These requirements were approved by the deputy

A.A Morozov   V.D. Sviridov.

chief of ABTU, Sviridov on 2nd March 1937 and the first copy of this document sent that day from Moscow to Plant №183 in Kharkov. According to the TTTs, the BT-7B-IS tank was supposed to be a BT-7-B tank with six driving wheels and synchronized speeds on the wheels and tracks, allowing *"to increase the manoeuvrability of the tank when moving on wheels and maintain the possibility of movement in case of breakage of one of the tracks."* The technical requirements for the transmission required:

"a) movement on tracks with the wheeled drive disconnected;
b) movement on tracks with the wheeled drive connected;
c) simultaneous movement on tracks and wheels (one side on tracks, the other on wheels)"

RGVA. F.31811. L.3. C.760. pp22-23

In addition, the BT-7-B-IS was to incorporate all the design improvements made to the BT-7-B, with a factory warranty of 2,500km. The combat weight of the tank was not to exceed 13.5 tonnes. In the 1930s, the addition of the letter "B" to the tank nomenclature indicated that the tank was produced in accordance with "B" revision drawings, i.e. after the elimination of all previously identified deficiencies found in trials and initial Red Army service. Looking ahead, in the spring of 1937 the TTTs for the design and manufacture of the BT-7-B-IS tank would be significantly changed, and three months later, on 4th June 1937, new TTTs for the BT-7-B-IS tank would be approved by the People's Commissar of Defence, K. E. Voroshilov. The revision of the TTTs for a new BT-7-B-IS tank variant was as a result of the study and incorporation of experience in the use of Soviet-built tanks in combat in Spain. In mid 1936, with the support of both Nazi Germany and Fascist Italy, General Franco had organized a military rebellion in Spain. The resulting civil war involved not only the Spanish Republicans and those opposing them, but also involved direct German and Italian intervention.

The Soviet Union duly provided considerable military assistance to the Republicans. In the period between 4th October 1936 and 27ᵗʰ February 1937 alone, the Soviet Union sent more than 200 T-26 tanks by sea to Republican Spain. Republican forces and Soviet volunteers on Spanish territory began to act as an operational military intelligence gathering source for the Red Army. Detailed information about the situation in Spain, the use of various types of troops and modern military equipment came to the Intelligence Directorate of the Red Army, with individual and collated reports promptly sent to the leadership of the country and the military command of the Red Army. Among the many documents stored in the funds of the Russian State military archive, is a compendium of reports about the civil war in Spain, composed in the second decade of February 1937 by the Deputy of the Chief Intelligence Directorate of the Red Army, Divisional Commander A. M. Nikonov. In the section *"the most Important lessons of operations in Spain"*, it was in particular noted that:

"The experience sorely tested modern tanks in action. Their strength in the suppression of enemy firing points and infantry is revealed; the ability of tanks to fight against enemy tanks is proven. Especially clearly manifested is the power of tanks in sudden attacks of tanks on cavalry, wagons, and unprepared concentrations of enemy infantry. In battles near the village of Sesenya (south of Madrid) in late October 1936, the battle northwest of Madrid in early January 1937, the last battle on the river Jarama, Republican tanks created havoc in rebel ranks, destroying at one stroke a whole enemy company.

At the same time, it is clearly established that tanks produce the greatest effect in close cooperation with infantry, when the latter moves directly behind them, occupying the space seized by them. With this method the Republicans have managed to achieve success on 11ᵗʰ-12ᵗʰ January in the area of Majadahonda, where tanks, step by step suppressed the order of battle of the rebels from their front edge, and the infantry brigades were very attentive to the moving tanks. The only drawback with the advancing infantry was the passivity of the other nearby parts of the Spanish Republicans, which did not allow in this battle a more decisive success.

By contrast, the action of tanks separated from infantry, even with great valour shown by the tank crews, led only to a partial suppression of the enemy and was accompanied by heavy losses of tanks and personnel.

Tanks with skilful use proved a powerful tool, not only in the attack but also in defence. In the critical days of the onslaught of the Fascists on Madrid (3ʳᵈ - 7ᵗʰ November 1936) almost the entire Madrid area was defended by a company of tanks, which threw itself against each of the attacking enemy columns and threw them back. The infantry of the Republicans at this time were quite unfit for action. Under the cover of the actions of this company of tanks the Republicans organised the more or less steady defence of Madrid, and established some system of machine-gun and artille-

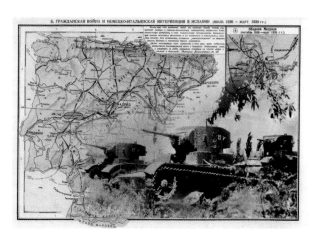

Map of the T-26 and the Civil War in Spain 1936-1939.

ry fire. Along with this, there was effective use of modern anti-tank guns (in particular, German). Rapid-fire anti-tank guns quickly learned to hit the tanks even when because of the terrain they show only the turret; with direct hits they struck a tank, and although not destroying it completely, disabling the tank and caused loss of personnel, and (thereby) tanks. True, the tanks in turn destroyed and captured a significant number of anti-tank guns".

RGVA. F.37967. L.8. C.1181. pp105-106

Thus, at the initial stage of the war in Spain, the T-26 tank, despite its relatively weak armour protection was given a generally positive assessment. However, operational combat revealed some weaknesses; in particular it was found that the T-26 was not well adapted for fighting in built up areas. To resolve this issue, the People's Commissar of Defence, Voroshilov, on 21ˢᵗ March 1937 sent Letter №4250ss to the head of ABTU, G. G. Bokis stating:

"Comrade Bokis. You need to call comrade Barikov and the designers of KhPZ and Plant №37. Work through the detail, and then I invite you to see me."

RGVA. F.31811. L.3. C.975. pp75

In order to discuss the new requirements for the tank designed for combat in urban environments formulated by Voroshilov, a meeting was held on 8ᵗʰ and 9ᵗʰ April 1937 in Moscow with the assistant chief of ABTU brigade engineer V. D. Sviridov. In this meeting also participated the head of the 11ᵗʰ Department of ABTU, military engineer 2ⁿᵈ rank Ya. L. Skvirsky, the KB heads of Plants №174 and №183 - S. A. Ginsburg, and M. I. Koshkin; and also - just returned from Spain; Colonel S. M. Krivoshein and Hero of the Soviet Union, Major P. M. Arman (Tiltinsh).

As a result of a comprehensive study of the creation of a new type of tank designed for street combat, the meeting came to the following conclusions, recorded in the Protocol:

"1. It is necessary to create a tank designed to conduct street combat, and this tank must simultaneously solve combat problems in the field.

2. The development of such a tank should be carried out in two parallel ways: creation of a special tank design, and adaptation of existing tanks.

3. The design of the special tank should meet the requirements set out in the letter of the People's Commissar and have a powerful armament and strong armour protection. The calibre of the main armament of the tank should be not less than 76mm. Armour needs to protect from a 45mm anti-tank gun shell fired from a distance of 1,000m. Such a tank will be able to fully perform the tasks normally assigned to medium and heavy tanks.

4. The existing types of tanks (T-26, BT, T-28 and T-35) can be adapted by strengthening the battering-ram capability; giving the weapon large elevation angles (60-70°); and improving surveillance. Otherwise the adapted tanks retain the existing properties.

5. To obtain from tank guns angles of elevation of 60-70°, it is necessary to rework the recoil mechanism, elevation mechanism, gun mask, sighting devices, and to check the reliability of the gun breech.

6. The requirements set out in the letter of the People's Commissioner, do not meet special technical difficulties, except for the protection of tracks from attack with bundles of hand grenades. To resolve this issue, a lot of experimental work is needed not only by ABTU, but also by the Engineering Command of the RKKA."

RGVA. F.31811. L.3. C.974. pp57-58

Following the ABTU meeting, TTTs were developed for the design and manufacture of a new tank designed for combat in the built up areas, together with TTTs providing modification of the BT-7, T-46, T-29 and T-35 tanks for the same purpose. The head of ABTU, G. G. Bokis reported on 22nd April 1937 by Letter №179443s to the People's Commissar of Defence, Marshal of the Soviet Union Voroshilov on the results of the work done. In the final part of the letter, Bokis asked Voroshilov to set a date for a joint report with the designers of the plants on the newly developed TTTs. However, in lieu of a report a meeting was organised by Voroshilov set for 7th May 1937, chaired by the assistant chief of ABTU Brigade Engineer V. D. Sviridov. The composition of the meeting was essentially the same as that held on 8th and 9th April. Sviridov was joined by the head of the 11th Division of the Red Army, military engineer 2nd rank Ya. L. Skvirsky, chief of the KB of Plant №174, S. A., Ginsburg, heads of the tank KB of Plant №183 M. I. Koshkin, and I. S. Ber, and the head of KBs №1 at Plant №185, Rosse. The purpose of the meeting was to clarify the tactical and technical requirements, on "both design and production side."

"As a result of the discussion" it was noted in the minutes "the me-

eting reached the following conclusions:

1. Adopt the developed tactical and technical requirements as indicative for the development of only draft projects, followed by clarification of these requirements.

2. Development of adaptations of the existing tanks for conducting street fight is expedient to make in the following order:

a) Develop a draft design for the installation of a 45mm gun with an elevation angle of up to 70° in existing BT-7 and T-46 tanks. This development does not require large alterations in the tank and requires the development of a special turret design. Installing the same 76mm gun with an elevation angle of up to 70° in existing BT-7 tanks and the T-46-1 will require large alterations in the hull, transmission and chassis.

b) Develop the sketch project of a 76mm gun installation with elevation angles to 70° on the basis of the developed projects BT-7-B-IS (Plant №183) and T-46-3 (Plant №174).

c) Develop the preliminary design for installation of a 76mm gun in the large turret of the T-35 with elevation angles to 70°. This development will require small alterations in the tank and can be performed by replacing the existing large turret with a special design. The solution to the problem of creating a tank adapted for street combat, on the basis of existing tanks is best resolved on the BT-7-B-IS and T-46-3, but will require more time, since factually a new tank is being developed.

3. Development of a special tank, adapted for street combat, must be performed in two versions:

a) Development of a draft design for a three-turret tank with a 76mm gun with gun elevation of up to 70° in a large turret, with DK machine guns with co-axial DT machine guns in the two small two turrets. Korpus* (hull and turret) with oblique armour plate increased to 30mm. The layout of the turrets according to the T-29 tank type. The tank should be wheeled-tracked. Weight will be about 35 tonnes.

b) Develop the sketch design of the single-turret tank in two versions, with installation of 76mm and 45mm guns with elevation up to 70°. Hull and turret with 40-50mm thick inclined armour.

G.G Bokis.   I.A Khalepsky

---

* In Russian the term Korpus (a building, structure) in tank terms refers to a complete hull and turret set rather than just the hull.

Tank - tracked. Weight about 25-30 tonnes.
The development of a draft project of a special three-turret tank designed to conduct street combat, it is advisable to perform at the Kirov plant, and a single-turret tank at Plant №185.
4. For normal firing at elevation angles up to 70°, it is necessary to make changes to the design of the recoil mechanism, to ensure the operation of the semi-automatic (gun breech) and accordingly change the sighting device. Modification of the 45mm and 76mm guns, sighting devices and adjust them for firing at angles of elevation up to 70° to be made by order of the Chief Artillery Directorate RKKA".

RGVA. F.4. L.14. C.1897. pp93-94

P.M Arman.

The minutes of the meeting, TTTs and a draft letter addressed to the People's Commissar of the Defence Industry, M. L. Rukhimovich, with a request to give instructions to the plants to urgently begin the development of tanks suitable for fighting in populated areas, G.G. Bokis as the head of the ABTU on 28th May 1937 sent to the People's Commissar of Defence Voroshilov. In the covering Letter, №180304ss Bokis asked the People's Commissar of Defence to approve the agreed TTTs: *"to develop conceptual designs: a) tank BT-7-B-IS and b) special medium tank, specifically designed for the conduct of street fighting"* and explained that *"now you can start to design only these two tanks, as the KB of Plant №174 and the Kirovsky Plant are loaded with current production work."*

On 4th June 1937, Voroshilov approved the presented TTTs *"on the design and fabrication of a prototype of the tank BT-7-B-IS adapted for combat in the mountains and cities."* And TTTs *"for design and construction of a medium tank developed for action in mountainous terrain and in combat conditions in settlements".* On the same day, the approved TTTs and Letter №27222ss signed by Voroshilov were sent to the People's Commissariat of the Defence Industry of the USSR. After consideration of the submitted documents by NKOP, on 21st June 1937 the deputy head of the 8th Main Directorate of the NKOP, K. P. Farmanyants sent orders to the Directors of Plants №183 and №185 to begin works on designing of the new tanks, the TTTs of which were approved by Voroshilov. In Letter №6-396/2147 dated 21st June 1937, addressed to the Director of the Plant №183, it was stated in particular:

"On the basis of personal instruction of the People's Commissar of Defence, Marshal of the Soviet Union, comrade Voroshilov K. E. and the People's Commissar of Defence Industry, comrade Rukhimovich M. is transmitted to you the tactical and technical requirements for a prototype BT-7-B-IS tank adapted for combat in the mountains and cities. You must immediately begin the development of draft designs:
(a) Installation of a 45mm gun with an elevation angle of up to 70° in an existing BT-7 tank.
b) Installation of a 76mm gun with an elevation angle up to 70°

in the BT-7-B-IS tank.
c) Installation of a 76mm gun with an elevation angle up to 70° in the large turret of the T-35 tank.
From the very beginning of the design it is necessary to establish a close working relationship with the AU RKKA with regard to the artillery part of the system and with the ABTU RKKA on the technical characteristics of the machine.
It is necessary to bear in mind that the specified works shall be performed in the shortest possible time, even at the expense of delay of other works. All your considerations, the proposed plan of work, dates of availability, and the responsible persons are to report to the Division within five days. In case of need of revision, in connection with this work, the plan of developmental works approved to you immediately send to Glavk via your responsible worker for approval.
In the future, starting from 1st July, you need to send the Glavk every ten days, reports on the progress of the work."

RGVA. F.31811. L.3. C.975. pp110

Concurrently, K. P. Farmanyants reported to the head of the Secretariat of the People's Commissariat of the Defence Industry V.V. Kryukov about the specifics provided to the factory directors:

"Forwarding herewith your material №1042ss from 8th June and copies of our orders to the Directors of Plants №185 and №183 to inform you of the respective instructions to the Directors of the factories".

RGAEh. F.7515. L.1. C.11. pp99

The amount of work being assigned to the KB-190 design bureau was constantly increasing in the first half of 1937, while the composition of the design team remained virtually unchanged. According to the personnel list made by the assistant to the Director of Plant №183, all of 48 designers worked in KB-190 as of 1st July 1937. By the time TTTs for the design and manufacture of a prototype BT-7-B-IS tank adapted for combat in the mountains and in cities arrived at Plant №183, KB-190 had already completed the development of a draft design for a new wheel-tracked BT tank type with a wider hull and six driving wheels. The new tank developed in the draft design was factually neither a BT-9 tank nor a BT-7-B-IS tank, since it did not meet the TTTs for either machine. The factory workers themselves called this tank "BT-IS", but in further correspondence with ABTU the tank was also referred to as "BT-IS of design Bureau 190". Thus, instead of developing two draft projects of new tanks (the BT-9 and BT-7-B-IS) as required by ABTU, KB-190 actually developed and presented a draft design of only one wheel-tracked tank. At the time, KB-190 designers were already overloaded with making improving the design of individual components of the series production BT-7 tank, and the design of modernisations of this tank and machines developed on its basis.

In the period January-April 1937, with the direct participation of KB-190 at Plant №183, the following experimental design works were carried out: installation on the BT-7 of remote control of tank movement from the workplace of the tank commander; installation of "tele-apparatus" equipment on the BT-7 for remote control of the tank; installation on the BT-5 of a three-stage, instead of four-stage, gearbox; development and testing of a new track with a pitch of 167mm and drive sprocket wheel with six roller bearings; development and testing of a BT-7 tank with a 76.2mm gun mounted in the T-26-4 turret. In addition, during this period, KB-190 carried out work on the fine-tuning of the BT-8 (A-8) tank; development of a prototype BT-7 tank armed with a flame thrower, as well as more than 100 activities related to the improvement of the design of individual BT-7 tank components, including those directed under the NKOP Order №0035ss. All the above work was done by a team of less than 50 engineers, including the Chief of the Design Bureau, M. I. Koshkin and his Deputy N. Kucherenko.

The preliminary design of the BT-IS tank developed at KB-190 was considered on 21st June at Plant №183 by a Commission under the leadership of the deputy of ABTU, brigade engineer V. D. Sviridov, who had been specially sent for this purpose to Kharkov Plant №183. The Commission was charged with:

"Preliminary calculation of the strength of the transmission parts of the BT-IS tank and the following drawings:
a) General view of the machine (side view).
b) Cross-section of the machine.
c) General view of the transmission drive wheels.
d) Final drive (Option №2).
e) A driving wheel with side box.
f) Spring suspension and rubber dampers.
g) Scheme of the cardan shaft balancer and spring suspension.
h) General view of the drive to the wheels of the 2nd, 3rd and 4th pairs".

RGVA. F.31811. L.3. C.760. pp85

From the "client's"* side in the work of the Commission for the review of the draft design took part: the district engineer ABTU Plant №183 military engineer 2nd rank Saprygin D. S., senior engineer of the 11th Division ABTU military technician 1st rank L. Bron and adjunct of the Military Academy of Mechanisation and Motorisation (VAMM) of the Red Army military engineer 3rd rank A.Ya. Dik. The participation of Dik in the Commission was not accidental.

While still a student at the design faculty of VAMM, military technician 1st rank A. Ya. Dik at the Department of "Tanks and Tractors" engaged in the problems of improving the tank mobility. In the journal "Mechanisation and Motorisation of the Red Army" №12, 1935, and №4, 1936 were published his articles *"On the dynamic equilibrium of tracked vehicles".* In November 1936, the drawings and explanatory note on the gearbox of his diploma project, were sent as deserving attention, the leadership of ABTU for review in the T2K KB at KhPZ. In January 1937 military engineer 3rd rank A. Ya. Dik was enrolled into the permanent composition of VAMM with the position of adjunct at the Department of "Tanks and Tractors". In March-April, 1937, Dik was on a business trip to Kharkov, where he became acquainted with the design of the BT-IS tank at KB-190 within Plant №183 as developed at Plant No48 by N.F. Tsyganov. In May and June 1937, Dik, together with Captain E. A. Kulchitsky, and military technician 2nd rank N. F. Tsyganov took part in the military trials of three BT-5-IS tanks in the Kharkov region. Dik was thereby well versed in the design of the chassis and drive-train of the wheel-track tank.

The conceptual design of the BT-IS tank presented to the Commission identified the following main tactical and technical characteristics: combat weight of 14 metric tonnes, crew-3, length-5.42m, width-2.46m, height-2.374m, track width-2.15m, ground clearance on wheels-390mm, ground clearance on tracks-410mm, transmission-4 speed, minimum speed on wheels and tracks-10.9km/h, maximum speed 64.6km/h, fuel capacity-600 litres. When driving on wheels, the transmission of torque from the side gearboxes to the three pairs of road wheels was carried out through two longitudinal side shafts and six telescopic gimbals. The results of BT-IS concept design review was reported on 22nd June 1937 in letter №397 by the acting Director of Plant №183, Lyash to the assistant chief of ABTU, Sviridov, which, in particular, noted:

"1. The presented for approval transmission scheme for the tank BT-IS has the following main drawbacks, which are unacceptable:
a) cardans (cardan shafts) are not protected;
b) Access to transmission - requires removal of engine;
c) the presence of a gear in the wheel.
2. In addition, the presented scheme has a defect in the sense of the

---

* In Russian "Zakazchik" - client, or customer; the term including the State as the provision of work to manufacturing plants.

location of the balancers. 2 and 4 balancers are located against the direction of travel of the machine, which causes some "braking of the wheel" with the moving of the balancer. The balancers must be positioned in the direction of travel of the machine.

3. In connection with proposals for a guitar gear arrangement on the wheel, I consider it necessary before the start of production of the sample, on the proposed plant scheme, develop a project guitar and calculation of transmission and suspension.

4. The development of the option available to the plant should be continued, taking into account all the defects noted in the discussion of the project in the design bureau.

5. Notes on constructive assemblies and calculations, running gear and box will be given the plant Design Bureaus by 26 June. (signed) comrades Saprygin, Dik and Bron.

<...>

7. Development of the korpus (hull and turret) for the tank "BT-IS" must be done in such a way that the side sheets are combined with vertical inclined - (vertical armour at the bottom of the wheel). It is desirable that the lower vertical armour near the wheel is shielded (i.e. by additional armour sheet).

8. For the detailed development of the project should be taken into account all the data indicate the order of People's Commissar of Defence Industry comrade. Rukhimovich № 0035ss.

9. Please following the project guitar transmission, and suspension of your deadline 15 July, report me to share with You finally choose the transmission scheme on wheels and suspension for the tank "BT-IS"".

RGVA. F.31811. L.3. C.760. pp37

The list of comments to the preliminary design of the BT-IS designed by KB-190 was on 27th June 1937 sent by S. D. Saprygin by Letter №408s to the deputy chief of ABTU in Moscow, Sviridov, with a second copy of the letter sent to the head of tank department "100" of Plant №183, S. N. Makhonin.

In the list of remarks to the draft prepared by Saprygin, Bron, and Dik, it was stated:

"1. Designed machine "BT-IS" is not an upgrade of the tank BT-7-B, as provided for by the contract and the tactical and technical requirements of ABTU RKKA, and is a new wheel-tracked tank type BT with 6 driven wheels. From series production BT-7 tanks, the project involves the use of only the main friction [clutch], the side clutches, the fan and the steering mechanism.

2. The project also does not meet the tactical and technical requirements for the BT-9 tank.

3. The transmission scheme implemented on the example BT-5-IS, proved better than other schemes of our tanks, because the drive wheel and the actuator on the track for the side clutch enables easy and convenient control, eliminates track drive wheel spin on turns,

Article by A. Ya. Dik in "Mechanisation and Motorisation, April 1936.

reduces the number of brakes by two and increases agility when driving on a single track. Wheeled tank with this scheme, transmission and control was worse due to the lack of a differential, but when using the on-board friction clutches and brakes turning on solid ground is no different from the turning with tracked drive.

4. Synchronisation of wheel and track speeds are calculated so that the nominal perimeter of the wheel (2,607.5 mm) larger than the nominal length of track corresponding to one revolution of the wheel 24.4mm, i.e. of 0.965%, according to the testing tank BT-5-IS lies resolution of the wheeled drive arrangement.

5. The equation of wheeled and tracked speeds produced by the deterioration of the dynamic characteristics of the tank: the maximum wheel speed is reduced to 64.4km/h, and the 1st gear speed (10.9km/h) is too great for a tracked drive (overcoming obstacles, towing, etc.). When designing a new high-speed wheel-tracked tank with speed synchronisation, it is necessary to make at least five steps in the gearbox with a transmission ratio of about 8.

6. The project does not provide for the possibility of disengaging the individual driving wheels.

7. The advantages of the adopted design of the drive from the longitudinal shafts on the wheels is a simple mounting of the wheel and the balancer and reducing the effort in the longitudinal and Cardan shafts. But this drive has the following main disadvantages, which cannot be eliminated with this design:

a) Access to the central and rear side gearboxes - requires removal of the engine and other units.

b) Cardans are not protected from dust, dirt, water, etc., that will lead to their increased wear.

c) The cardans are poorly protected from bullet hits.

d) Cut outs in the side armour plates for the cardans and suspension weaken the hull.

e) The presence of open cardan shafts will not allow the tank to overcome MZP (small unseen) obstacles.

8. Another major drawback of the designed drive system is that the

second and fourth cranks of the balancers are directed forward against the movement. This reduces the permeability of the tank through stumps, bursts, etc., as well as causes tremors and shocks in the suspension and transmission when passing irregularities. This is getting worse by the device, the wheel gear of one pair of cylindrical gears external gearing. Cranks needed to guide the knee back. Preferably, the external engagement is to replace the internal gear of the cylindrical gear wheel reducers.

9. *Shock absorbers must be installed on the tank to dampen longitudinal vibrations of the tank.*

10. *It is necessary to provide possibility of transition from tracks on wheels and back without over-regulation of a candle [springs of suspension units].*

11. *At the same time with further work on the design of the tank as a whole, it is necessary to design a new small-link track for the BT-IS tank since the existing production track will not fit due to the increase in the width of the road wheels.*

12. *The width of the bandages (rims) should be chosen so that the period of their service is not less than 2,500km.*

13. *The transmission of the tank will need to calculate the full torque of the engine, i.e. 320kg/m². Especially check the strength of the assemblies taken from the BT-7 and, if necessary, revise them.*

14. *It is necessary to achieve a significant improvement in the cooling conditions of the engine compared to BT-7.*

15. *Benzine (petrol) for the BT-IS tank must be at least 600-650 litres (without additional tanks). The machine must not be fitted with a rear fuel tank.*

16. *It is necessary to revise the design of the seals, providing adaptations for their adjustment and lifting."*

RGVA. F.31811. L.3. C.760. pp85-87

When considering the draft design of the BT-IS tank, the ABTU representatives on 21st June 1937 also put forward proposals for developing a new design of the drive for the torque supply to the second, third and fourth pairs of road wheels using "guitar transmission". The suggested drive design option was to be developed in parallel with the drive variant offered by KB-190 (with use of Cardan shafts), and on reconsideration of the sketch project by the Commission it was necessary to choose for use in the prototype the best of the designed variants of transmission. To implement this proposal it was agreed between the deputy chief of ABTU, V. D. Sviridov and the acting Director of Plant №183, F. I. Lyash to develop the project drive with the "guitar gear" to be be undertaken by A. Ya. Dik, with Plant №183 required to by 25th June 1937 identify three highly qualified designers to assist him. Due to the excessive workload at KB-190, only two designers were actually assigned, on 1st and 17th July 1937. The arrival of Dik at the plant, and the requirement to allocate to his disposal three highly qu-

S.N. Makhonin.

alified designers in an already overworked environment, naturally did not cause great delight in the leadership of KB-190.

District engineer D. S. Saprygin on 26th July 1937 notified the chief of ABTU, Bokis, regarding the failure of Plant №183 in its commitments and the "distress" situation within the group headed by A. Ya. Dik in a telegram:

"The plant does not provide the development of the project of the guitar drive. Dik still had only one (additional) designer and was recently given the second. The group, which developed the gimbal drive for four months, has six people. It is necessary to increase Dik's team with three additional designers".

RGVA. F.31811. L.3. C.760. pp46

To normalise the situation around the work of A. Ya. Dik, the deputy chief of the ABTU, V. D. Sviridov, on 13th August 1937 sent the acting Director of Plant №183, F. I. Lyash Letter №182275 stating:

"By personal arrangement with you for the detailed development of several variants of the conceptual design of the BT-IS tank was sent to your plant VAMM military engineer 3rd rank A. Ya. Dik. It would seem that the plant should be interested in careful study of all possible variants of projects of the new tank and would therefore create all conditions for the fruitful work of A. Ya. Dik, having given him necessary help and support. In reality, however, Bureau "190" in the face of its chief M. Koshkin has become an obstacle to the work of the office of comrade Dik. As a result, instead of a case of healthy competition benefit, it turned out the situation doomed the work of Dik to failure. This resulted in not recruiting a brigade of designers for comrade Dik, and the creation of an unhealthy environment around all of his work. I do not want to think that Bureau "190" finally went in this direction to prevent the plant accommodating fresh thoughts, as has been the case before."

RGVA. F.31811. L.3. C.760. pp53

In August 1937 a third designer joined the A. Ya. Dik design group, and eventually by the end of the month, this small team managed to develop a rough draft of the "guitar drive" and suspension arrangements for the BT-IS tank. Currently, at the end of August 1937, the staff of KB-190 under Koshkin's leadership completed the draft design of the BT-IS tank. The circumstances surrounding the development of this machine were described in detail by the ABTU district engineer at Plant №183, military engineer 2nd rank D. S. Saprygin in the report *"About the new design of the combat vehicle"* completed on 20th August 1937. In this document, addressed to Bokis, the chief of ABTU, Saprygin, reported:

"The course of the new design at Plant №183 does not provide the creation of the required Army machine. The design direction is on the basis of to "get away with" a new project in pursuance of the plant contract with ABTU RKKA. The plant management is obliged to produce in the current year 1937 two tanks: BT-9 of a new design according to the set tactical and technical requirements, and BT-IS representing modernisation of the BT-7 with a new drive on three sets of wheels, with other assemblies unchanged. But since the Plant management missed all the deadlines, so it decided to design only one machine. This machine was made in a hurry, within two months, and was presented to Brigade Engineer ABTU RKKA, comrade. Sviridov on 21/V-1937 [misprint in the document, should have been VI]. The presented project had significant errors, as a result of which it was rejected. The project gives a new tank with a new widened hull, new chassis, etc. Essentially it is not the BT-9; nor does it correspond to the ABTU tactical and technical requirements for the BT-9 and BT-7-IS. And the design is deliberately subordinated only to the convenience of production and commercial considerations, and is made without (adherence to) the tactical-technical requirements. Particularly striking is that the design does not take into account the requirements of the army and does not use all the experience of tank building. The Design Bureau of comrade Koshkin states: "I solve only one problem, of the wheel drive, basically I keep everything that is possible from the old components." This line (of thinking) results in the failure in improvement of the entire machine as a whole and is essentially a continuation of the old wrecking work based on the show of an "improvement" of a single node due to the weakening and deterioration of the working conditions of other nodes and, therefore, the designed machine BT-7-IS already at this time, during the process of design, marked by the following significant defects:

1. *Wheel drive with a transverse propeller shaft dramatically reduces the fighting qualities of the tank (much weakened side armour and large cut-outs for the cardans, MZP [low-observable obstacles] become an insurmountable obstacle).*
2. *The final reduction gear is outside the armour inside the wheel*

rim, so it is poorly protected.
3. *There is no mechanism to disconnect individual wheels (inside or outside the machine), so if one wheel is damaged, it will lock-up and disable the entire side from service.*
4. *The wheel drive is not accessible for operation and repair, as it cuts deep inside the hull - in the engine and combat compartment (more than 300mm on each side).*
5. *The engine cooling is worsened due to the fact that the wheel drive reduces the radiators by 170mm in height.*
6. *The small vertical wheel travel (160mm up and 90mm down) and thus large (17°- 20°) angles in the cardan connection turn out.*
7. *The planned 4-speed transmission gives poor dynamic performance (torque), when installing the BD-2 diesel, the dynamic factor on the lower gear will be about three times lower than on the BT-7 with the M-17T engine and twice lower than the BT-5 with The M-5 engine, which will entail the engine stalling on heavy obstacles, since the weight of the tank increases by 2 tonnes. In addition, it not produced by dynamic calculation, which should be the basis of all calculations. Moreover, the designed gearbox is laid within the old dimensions of the BT-7 gearboxes, although the new extended housing significant free space.*
8. *Despite the fact that the tank's weight was increased by two tonnes, the old springs [spring suspension units] were used, which were feeble, even for the BT-7.*

A number of gross errors were made in the wheel drive system:
   a) *The second and fourth beams are directed forward against the motion (against the "grain").*
   b) *The wheel reducer has an external gearing, which further increases the so-called "trickle", when the wheels on the hill, especially under braking.*

The following long-term problems have not been solved: the armour inclination, the shielding of the hull, the longitudinal hull vibrations and its reduction, the working position of the driver, gunner and commander, ramming capability, the cardan and telescopic shafts, etc.

Under pressure as a result of errors and omissions in the Design Bureau headed by Koshkin, designer A. Morozov and others were forced to agree to alter the project, though they still did not radically change the project, although their drive design with transverse shafts resulted in irreparable shortcomings. And since they announced and insisted that the guitar drive is out-dated, heavy, fragile, very difficult to manufacture and unreliable in operation hence Brigade Engineer Sviridov instructed adjunct VAMM military engineer 3rd rank comrade Dik to try provide a good guitar design, because the guitar has a number of good qualities if used in combat vehicles (small cut of armour, not afraid of MZPs, durable, an absence of universal joints and telescopic shafts, etc.). The work of the Dik showed:

1. *Guitar can be made solid, reliable and easy to manufacture and exploit, if this guitar is directed back, halving, make the case wi-*

Telegram on the "guitar situation" at Kharkov.

der and solid, wheel to put the hub directly on the slots, etc.

2. The drive with the prop-shaft in the longitudinal plane revealed an undeniable advantage over the transverse propeller shaft, if the longitudinal shaft is passed in the middle or at the bottom of the hull (the entire mechanism is easily accessible, fits in the space between the between armour openings and, most importantly, requires only small cuts in the side armour.

But the course of work on the design showed that it is necessary to sharply raise the question of the reconstruction of the whole machine on the basis of the experience of military units, polygon, repair plants and serial production of the Plant №183 in the first place. But the representatives of the KB Department "100" headed by comrade Koshkin did not undertake a thorough reworking and finishing touches for their project, and after some resistance were compelled to correct only certain mistakes that they have been specifically identified in the letter by comrade Sviridov, to the plant director, engineer Lyash.

Among the remedial measures required are:
1. The balancers facing backwards.
2. Outdoor gear relocated internally.
3. Cardans (to be) enclosed.

Along with this, the following developments by comrade Dik were used:
1. Springs reconsidered and strengthened.
2. Somewhat improved suspension characteristic by tilting the springs.
3. Reinforced side transmissions, but the design was left unchanged.

Completely refused to introduce the following improvements:
1. A five-speed gearbox, which when synchronising wheel and track speeds should be employed to ensure that the lowest gear downgrades speed to 7km/h, and the highest increases to 75-80km/h.
2. Installation of a 5th pair of wheels, which gives significant advantages for the tank (there is no need to widen the wheels and the track, increased tractability, reduces the risk of track pin and track wear, especially MZP etc.).
3. Switch off the individual wheels from the outside or from the inside (i.e. the "control" referred to earlier).

4. Change the on-board gear (leave the old stub-axle, strings, riveted neck, etc.).
5. Replace universal joints cross-longitudinal.
6. Set the camber to prevent overloading and melting of the rubber on the inner rim.
7. Set the slope of at least only the upper side armour.
8. Make a hatch in the fighting compartment floor to eject the casings and for (emergency) crew egress.
9. Install a hook for towing.
10. Increase the rigidity of the hull floor.
11. Improve the working places of driver, commander and gunner.
12. To make sloping roofs, etc.

All these and a number of other issues that are strongly required in the combat working conditions of tanks, are completely discarded, in order to quickly finish the rework and this time is used to decorate the drawings. Thus the hope that comrade Dik with all changes will not manage to finish the project in time and therefore will not be able to protect it. The head of the Design Bureau of Department "100" comrade Koshkin is a line on the failure of the work carried out by comrade Dik.

By agreement of Brigade Engineer comrade Sviridov with the plant Director comrade Lyash, comrade Dik had to be by 25/6-37 given three good designers. The implementation of this agreement was as follows: one designer to be given by 1/7-37, the second by 17/7-37, while the group of comrade Morozov was strengthened to six people with a much smaller volume of work carried out by the group of comrade Morozov.

Despite my categorical demand, to date comrade Dik works with three designers, which comrade Koshkin is trying to demoralise with talk that comrade Dik is engaged in fruitless design and will not succeed. Therefore, these already not strong designers put their hands in the air. Recently, when you can see that the design of comrade Dik has positive results, work went faster and better.

Summary.
1. The design of the new tank has on the part of the Plant management the wrong focus and is in danger of failure.
2. The design, conducted by comrade Dik is undertaken taking into account the modern requirements for tanks, but this design not only does not receive support and assistance from the plant management, but they even deliberately break the project.

In order to create normal conditions for the construction of a modern tank, the following is necessary:
1. To urgently clarify in detail the tactical and technical characteristics of the projected new tank (TTTs attached).
2. The group of comrade Dik is to be given 20-30 student designers from VAMM RKKA (list attached).
3. Fully provide designers with reference material for all combat

vehicles in service with the Red Army and the Western Armies (drawings, test reports, data exploitation, etc.).
4. To provide expert advice from professors and experienced designers.

No matter what grades the separate projects will receive, it is necessary to develop, manufacture and test in parallel two versions in order to avoid risk and to ensure the speedy production of a high quality tank. If one project does not pass into series production, the other will take into account all the advantages of the first. The planned events for the new design with your full provided support will provide the chance to give the Red Army a new fighting machine, completely meeting modern requirements".

RGVA. F.31811. L.3. C.760. pp57-64

Having reviewed this report, Bokis on 26th August 1937 gave his assistant Sviridov the following guidelines:

"1. To be guided by the plan approved by the government.
2. When developing the design to take into account these proposals.
3. When considering projects to attract comrades Saprygin and Dik.
4. Design the order on ABTU about the orderly consideration of design projects".

RGVA. F.31811. L.3. C.760. pp75

On the instruction of Bokis, Sviridov on 29th August 1937 by "Lightning" (Series "G") telegram notified the management of Plant №183 to urgently send ABTU the materials on the design of the BT-IS tank design project, which included 13 drawings and 46 pages of notes, which were duly dispatched from Kharkov to Moscow on 31st August with transmittal Letter №SO2568. The following day, 1st September, together with transmittal Letter №SO2569, 33 drawings and a folder with the calculations of conceptual design of the "guitar drive" and BT-IS suspension developed by the design group under the leadership of A. Ya. Dik were also sent to ABTU.

In early September 1937, at a special meeting held in ABTU with the participation of representatives of Plant №183, the revised draft design of the BT-IS tank was reviewed for the second time, over a three day period, and the developments of the A. Ya. Dik group also considered. The results of the reconsideration of the conceptual BT-IS design and about the decisions, the chief of ABTU, G. G. Bokis notified the deputy chief of the 8th GU NKOP, K. P. Farmanyants and acting Director of Plant №183 F. I. Lyash by Letter №182987 dated 11th September 1937:

"The proceedings of the meeting were reviewed by myself along with my assistant, Brigade Engineer T. Sviridov, and the chief of the VAMM Red Army comrade Lebedev, resulting as follows:
1. The project still contains a number of design shortcomings, which

we pointed out to the plant during the design process (unprotected shaft for the wheel drive, poor access to the side gearboxes, deterioration of cooling, etc.).
2. In fact, the project provides for a radical alteration of the entire tank as a whole. All its units are designed anew. At the same time, the tank basically retains a number of fundamental disadvantages inherent in BT tanks (weak armour, no inclination of the side armour plate, short service life, maintenance complexity, etc.). This is especially unacceptable, given that it is a question of designing a new technically more advanced tank.
3. The drive scheme on wheels with transverse shafts does not meet our requirements for reliability and ease of operation.

On this basis, I consider it necessary to stop further development of the presented project. The design of the new tank, according to the tactical and technical requirements adopted by the government on 14 August, is necessary to organise in Department 100 of Plant №183 in the following direction:
1. To develop three projects of the new tank differing, mainly, in the wheel drive, namely:
First option - with a mid-mounted drive shaft.
Second option - with guitar drive.
Third option - with a lower mounted drive shaft according to the Straussler scheme.

All variants should be designed in such a way that only the best two are put into pilot production. When designing a new tank, it is necessary to take into account all the comments made on the projects when considering them in ABTU, as well as using the experience of polygon trials and existing tank construction.
Given that the current organisation of the new design at Plant №183 did not provide the required quality and pace of work, I consider it necessary for the design of the new sample tank to create a new project design group within Department №100, reporting directly to the plant manager. The new group should consist of the best designers of Plant №183 in number not less than 20 people. I agree to guide this group to be assigned to military engineer 3rd rank comrade Dik. In addition, since October the plant can be sent up to 20 student 5-year graduates of VAMM RKKA. I can second Comrade Dik for the time required for the design and manufacture of a prototype of a new tank, and can go to the plant at any time. In view of the importance and urgency of this issue, please inform me of your decision."

RGVA. F.31811. L.3. C.760. pp56

The leadership of ABTU had thereby concluded that work on the BT-IS tank should cease at KB-190, with Plant №183 organising for a new wheel-track tank design for which the performance characteristics were approved at the meeting of the Defence Committee of the SNK SSSR on 14th Aug 1937.

Chapter 4

A New Government Task

As noted earlier, the starting point in the creation of the legendary T-34 medium tank is 15th August 1937 - the day when Decree №94ss of the Defence Committee of the USSR *"on types of tanks for arming the tank troops of the Red Army and tanks for production in 1938"* was adopted. The Resolution was a further development of the system of armoured weapons of the Red Army approved for the second Five Year Plan in 1933, by the Council of Labour and Defence.

Revision of the system of armoured weapons within the existing second Five Year Plan was in the summer of 1937 urgent due to many factors. Firstly, combat experience gained with Soviet tanks in Spain showed the requirement to strengthen all the basic combat and technical characteristics of tanks (i.e. armament, armour, and mobility). Secondly, by the summer of 1937, it had become clear to the leadership of the country that Soviet industry would not be able to introduce the new armoured weapon types approved for the second Five Year Plan in full, or on time. To recall, according to Resolution STO №71ss dated 13th August 1933, serial production in 1937 (the final year of the second Five Year Plan) was expected to be of five basic types of tanks, all to be fitted with diesel engines:

1. Amphibious reconnaissance tank T-37 with wheel-track drive;
2. Light tank T-26 with wheel-track drive;
3. Light operational wheel-tracked amphibious tank PT-1;
4. Medium tank, TRGK reinforcement, of T-28 type with wheel-track drive;
5. New "special purpose" heavy tank - of the T-35 breakthrough tank type.

In fact, by July 1937, industry had actually implemented:

1. The T-38 amphibious light tank was adopted for service and put into production for the Red Army to replace the "amphibious reconnaissance wheel-tracked tank like the T-37";
2. The T-46 wheel-track light tank was accepted for service with the Red Army, but there were delays with the prototype and the industry continued to produce the T-26 tank;
3. Instead of the PT-1 "light operational" wheel-track amphibious tank entering series production, the BT-7 remained in series production, powered by the M-17 petrol engine;
4. The T-29 medium wheel-track tank was accepted for service,

but had also not entered production, the T-28 remaining in series production;
5. Production of the T-35 continued at a leisurely pace.

Despite great intentions, none of these tanks were provided with diesel engines. Further, the planned introduction of new tank designs during the second Five Year Plan was incomplete; with the T-46 and T-29 having both been accepted for Red Army service, but with both having failed to subsequently enter series production, being a particular setback.

In addition, feedback from operational Red Army units at Military District (VO) level added to the fray. On 20th April 1937 the commander of the Leningrad Military District (LVO) Komandarm 1st rank B. M. Shaposhnikov sent the People's Commissar of Defence, Marshal K. E. Voroshilov Letter №25965 a detailed report listing design and manufacturing deficiencies identified during Red Army operational use of the T-37, T-38, T-26, BT-7 and T-28 tanks, and the FAI armoured car. The defect list for the BT-7 ran to 46 items; however, the report stated that the tank nevertheless fully met the requirements of the mechanised forces. The defect list on the T-28 was no shorter, with 47 defects listed.

Together with listing the individual defects, Shaposhnikov's report detailed logistics issues, not least that: *"Currently, mechanised brigades are armed with machines running on four different fuel types"*. Some vehicles ran on two grades of benzene (petrol), some on a single (higher octane) grade. Some ran on "Baku" and "Grozny" grades of aviation benzene, referring

B.M. Shaposhnikov.   I. F. Fedko

BT-7 Tanks during driver training.

to the Soviet oilfields from where the crude oil was extracted. Shaposhnikov concluded somewhat matter-of-factly that: *"The presence of such a diversity of fuel creates great inconvenience and requires special care and accurate calculation. Incorrect refuelling of combat vehicles with the wrong fuel would stop them. It is necessary to transfer all vehicles to fuel of one grade".*

The above somewhat seemingly obvious and disarming statement illustrates the interface between engineer-designers and operational users, a problem that was not peculiar to the armed forces of the Soviet Union.

RGVA. F. 4. L. 14. C. 1826. pp. 21

In the final part of the LVO commander's report were made the following suggestions to improve the combat and operational qualities of BT and T-26 tanks:

"1. Increasing the viewing devices; in these machines visibility is very limited.

2. Install periscopic sights.

3. Create the possibility of lateral exit from the turret rear, which in a combat situation will allow the crew to egress in any direction, regardless of the position of the machine.

4. All military vehicles need to set the machine guns to fire to the rear of machine movements.

5. Improve crew convenience, especially the driver-mechanic.

6. Improve the turret, as regards crew ergonomics, and ease of firing (stabilising system).

7. Reduce the noise (slamming) of BT tracks and improve the engine (noise) output - i.e. fit silencers.

8. Increase the hermetic sealing of the korpus. (hull and turret).

9. Put the question of the transfer of combat vehicles to the use of engine heavy fuel (diesel), which has great advantages over benzene (petrol).

10. Oblige manufacturers to consider and resolve all the structural and operational deficiencies noted on the above combat vehicles".

RGVA. F. 4. L. 14. C. 1826. pp. 21 - 22

After reading the report, Voroshilov in early May 1937, sent a report to B. M. Shaposhnikov, the chief of ABTU G. G. Bokis requesting consideration and resolution. In pursuance of this order, Bokis by Letter №1798 of 13th May 1937 addressed to K. E. Voroshilov the following conclusion on this report was sent:

"1. Our tanks in the course of development by industry had a number of production and constructive shortcomings which from year to year were eliminated. The tanks manufactured in 1937 were dramatically different to the best of the tanks released in 1932, but military operational use revealed a number of additional requirements on elimination of defects. The latter are taken into account annually and when revising drawings for next year's orders, and specific changes made on the basis of a preliminary inspection of the new design on prototypes. Early version tanks, in service with the army, are modernised during overhaul at the industrial plants. If not for this there would be a problem with the provision of spare parts. Turning to the individual types of machines, it is necessary to state the following:

1. BT.

I personally believe, that this tank is the best tank existing in the armoured forces of modern armies. The BT tank in its tactical and technical characteristics is not only not inferior, as writes comrade Shaposhnikov, to tanks of the American army, but, in my opinion, is superior, especially in having twice the travel range. This tank is better armed than the American one, as it has a gun-armed turret and in 1937 was also established a flamethrower to protect the tank from the rear. The weak spot remains track fragility. In 1937 we worked hard on strengthening the tracks, but finally failed to resolve this issue as we would like. Currently, 4 variants of new tracks are being manufactured, including one variant according to the type of American tank track (with rubber pads i.e rubber-metal hinge). In the BT-7 tank in the past year, as you know, was found a major defect in the failure of the pair of conical gears in the gearbox, due to the increased torque of the M-17 engine. Last year, these unsuitable gearboxes were replaced with reinforced ones and this year we switched to a new one, tested for 5,000km.

2. T-26.

Tank T-26, in the opinion of all participants of special exercises, is a good tank, able to perform all the essential tactical tasks asked of it. You also know the order of comrade Rukhimovich on the elimination of specific defects. Currently, series production of the tank has revealed new not previously known defects as a mass phenomenon. Now bench testing is damaged valves. To eliminate this defect (we have) mobilised a number of engineers, in connection with which we do not have the release (i.e. production delivery) of these tanks to supply the army.

3. T-28.

T-28 tank in its tactical and technical characteristics meets all our basic requirements. Existing defects in this tank, according to the decision made with your participation, are eliminated. These defects are mainly described by army commander 1st rank comrade Shaposhnikov.

4. T-35.

This tank in its armament is quite a modern tank. The only weak point is the low power output of the M-17 engine, developing 500hp, which limits the speed of the tank in operation. It would

be desirable to install an 800hp engine. On the development of a (diesel) engine for this tank type, some work has been undertaken by the designers at KhPZ.

5. T-37.

In its tactical and technical characteristics the tank cannot serve as a reconnaissance tool in mechanised formations, because of its inferior speed to the BT tank. For the same reason it is not good for mechanised regiments, but it can perfectly perform reconnaissance for tank battalions of infantry divisions. <...> Summarising, it must be said that all the tanks in Red Army are quite modern. The only exception is the weakness of the front suspension on the T-37 tank. For this tank, whatever upgrades needed during 1938 should be undertaken. Currently, we are already finishing the development of appropriate designs".

RGVA. F.4. L.14. C.1826. pp23-24

As can be seen from the written opinion, Bokis believed the tanks that were in Red Army service were relatively modern and, despite known flaws, highly appreciated their combat performance. However, the Red Army continued to provide alternative feedback. On 11th June 1937, the commander of Kiev Military District (KVO) army commander 2nd rank I. F. Fedko sent a report together with cover Letter №Eh-8/00650 to K. E. Voroshilov, similar in content to the report of B. M. Shaposhnikov. The introduction noted that:

"Experience has shown very significant and troubling shortcomings in the design of existing combat vehicles. All these design and technical shortcomings can be stated with full responsibility, as these shortcomings continue to remain unresolved for several years. The materiel remains intact and not modernised. The last releases of

BT-7 tank maintenance.

combat vehicles would naturally have to improve, but in fact a number of shortcomings remained, and in some cases even increased. Designers did not go in the direction of releasing improvement, but followed the direction of seeking new types of machines. It is more necessary to improve first of all the existing machines and, on the basis of experience, to produce new types, taking into account all the identified shortcomings and modern requirements".

RGVA F.4. L.14. C.1826. pp25

The KVO commander subsequently listed the design flaws of the T-37, T-26, BT-2, BT-5, BT-7, T-28 and the FAI armoured car, almost completely replicating Shaposhnikov's list. The issue of modernisation was in the summer of 1937 highly relevant, taking into account Red Army feedback from significant operational experience of tanks in the Military Districts, and recent experience of the combat use of Soviet built tanks in Spain. Another factor was the inability of the tank industry to master production of the wheel-track tank T-46 and T-29 tanks that had been adopted into Red Army service but had not entered series production. The issue of *"establishing types of tanks, their weapons and on the implementation of the programme of 1937"* was considered at the meeting of the Defence Committee of the SNK (KO pri SNK SSSR) held on 1st August 1937, with the following outcome:

"1. On the basis of the exchange of views that took place at the meeting and given by the Committee of Defence installations, commissioning comrades Voroshilov, Rukhimovich and Mezhlauk (are) in five days to give the agreed proposals, bearing in mind; abandonment of production of the T-46 tank and the production of the T-38, replacing them with all-terrain armoured vehicles; to leave production of the wheeled-tracked tank T-29, increasing the frontal armour; to make a tracked tank T-35 (type), increasing the frontal armour up to 70mm.

2. The same Commission to develop systems of artillery and tank small arms.

3. Director of STZ (Stalingrad Tractor Plant) comrade Fokine to continue work on the STZ tank design, keeping in mind: 120hp engine installation; armour reinforcement in the most important places from 20-25mm; wheel-track drive with removable track; travel speed with enhanced armour not less than 30km/h. In parallel, not at the expense of the main task, STZ to work out the question of the transition from petrol to diesel engines.

4. Take note of the statement of comrades Rukhimovich and Mezhlauk that the installed tank program in 1937 is NKOP and NKTP is undertaken".

RGAEh. F.7515. L.1. C.176. pp85

On 3rd August 1937, the day following the Defence Committee session, the chief of ABTU, Divisional Commander G. G.

Bokis, sent K.E. Voroshilov with letter №174179ss the eight-page draft of the Defence Committee resolution *"On the types of tanks"*. The review of the Defence Committee Resolution between NKO, NKOP and the NKTP took a week, with, G. G. Bokis as a result on 9th August 1937 sending Voroshilov with Letter №174200ss the second version of the draft Resolution of the Defence Committee *"On the types of tanks"* now on 11 pages, mostly in agreement with the People's Commissar of the Defence Industry (M. L. Rukhimovich) and of Heavy Industry (V. I. Mezhlauk).

In this version of the draft decree the ABTU command offered as a *"set for arming the tank forces of the Red Army"*, four new tank types and two new armoured reconnaissance half-tracks. At the same time, it was proposed to abandon the production of (as yet un-established) T-46 and series T-38 tank production. The following day, on 10th August 1937, at the request of K. E. Voroshilov, the draft resolution was sent to the Secretary of the Committee of Defence in SNK Komkor G. D. Bazilevich, with the historically significant for the future T-34 meeting of the Committee of Defence in SNK being held in the Kremlin by 14th August 1937. According to Protocol №14 of the meeting the fifth item on the agenda addressed the issue *"About the types of tanks for tank weapons for the Red Army and tanks for production in 1938"*. After discussion of this issue the original ABTU draft decree was amended, including previously proposals by the people's Commissars of defence and heavy industry, and taking into account the amendments submitted by the NKO and NKOP, the draft resolution was approved. The full text of the Resolution 94ss of the Defence Committee of the SNK USSR *"About the types of tank weapons for armoured forces of the Red Army and tanks for production in 1938"*, was received on 15th August 1937, as will be reviewed in the "Documents" section of this book which will review its main provisions. As suggested by ABTU, four new types of tanks and two new types of armoured vehicles were established:

- for arming tank battalions of infantry divisions - a new light wheel-track tank developed in the Stalingrad Tractor Plant (STZ) on the basis of the experimental STZ-24 tank (later further developed as the STZ-34);
- for arming mechanised units and mechanised cavalry regiments - a new light wheel-tracked BT series tank with enhanced armour, BD-2 diesel engine and six driving wheels;
- for arming RGK mechanised brigades - upgraded T-29 wheel-track tank with enhanced armour and diesel engine;
- for arming RGK heavy tank brigades - T-35 tank with enhanced armour protection and remote control, and in the future (from 1940) a diesel engine;

The development of half-track armoured vehicles was abandoned at the request of V. I. Mezhlauk, with armoured and mechanised cavalry units having as reconnaissance machines two armoured types - light (2-axle) and medium (3-axle). The transition to the production of six new tank and armoured vehicle types was planned from the beginning of 1939, with production of the T-38 and the planned T-46 cancelled. Before beginning production of the new tank and armoured vehicle types, industry had in 1938 however to provide:

"1. Plant №174

(a) A T-26 Tank with a conical turret. Require transfer (to manufacture) of turret box with sloped sheets from 1 July, 1938. Experienced a series of tanks in equipment for underwater movement.
b) Artillery support tank (AT-1).

2. Plant №183

a) First half of 1938 - produce BT-7 tank with a conical turret, with M-17 engine, and 45mm gun and an experimental series of tanks with equipment for underwater movement.
b) Second half of 1938 - produce BT-8 with a conical turret, with diesel engine, and 45mm gun.
c) Tank BT-7 and BT-8 armed with a 76mm gun.
d) Prototypes of BT-IS tanks with 6 driving wheels, diesel engine, with a conical turret, with 45mm and 76mm guns, with inclined sheets of armour of the turret substructure in order to ensure the transition to the production of BT-IS tanks with 6 driving wheels in 1939.
d) Existing T-35 tank type to from 1 July 1938, produce with heavier armour, conical turrets, with M-17 engine.
e) Self-propelled 203mm howitzer B-4 to be removed from production.

3. Kirov plant

a) T-28 tank with conical turrets with heavy-duty suspension;
b) In the fourth quarter of 1938, produce a series of T-29 tanks, upgraded at the Kirov Plant in order to complete the transition of production to the T-29 from 1 January 1939.

4. Stalingrad Tractor Plant

a) Establishment Lot of tanks of the Stalingrad Tractor Plant (STZ) design in the amount of 25pcs.

5. Izhora plant

a) Medium armoured car on the GAZ-3A chassis (three-axle) with a conical turret and 45mm gun. A quantity of the armoured vehicles must be fitted with heavy machine guns;
b) Prototypes of armoured cars with 100-110hp engines (ZiS-101).

6. The Vyksa plant DRO

a) Light armoured car on the (GAZ) M-1 chassis with a conical turret and a DT machine gun;

M.L.Rukhimovich.   V.I. Mezhlauk.

b) Prototype of an armoured car with a conical turret, with a 70hp engine."

GARF. F. 8418. C. 28. L. 27. pp. 85 - 86

In accordance with the Resolution, Plant № 183 was, in addition to serial production of BT-7 tanks with M-17 and BD-2 engines, and production of T-35 tanks, to in 1938 produce a prototype of a light wheel-tracked tank with a diesel engine and six driven wheels with the following tactical and technical characteristics:

"Weight-13-14 tonnes.
Speed-52 km/h on tracks and 72km/h on wheels.
Engine-diesel, 400hp
Chassis type-track-wheel.
Armour: frontal-25mm;
Conical turret-20mm;
Side and rear-13mm,
Roof and floor-10mm.
Armament: 1-45mm gun with stabilisers or 1-76mm gun; 2-DT machine guns; A flamethrower for self-defence;
Every fifth tank should have anti-aircraft (machine gun) fitted.
Ammunition: 130-150 45mm or 50 76mm rounds. 2,500 DT cartridges.
Communication devices: every fifth tank should have a duplex radio station with an ariel antenna mounted along the side of the tank. The rest of the tanks should have a VHF radio.
Observation: periscopic sight, telescopic sight, commander's panoramic view.
Stowage: tools, accessories, set of spare parts, chemical equipment (masks, costumes), crew personal belongings and a one-day food ration.
Range-300km.
Crew-3.
The tank should have the integrity to protect against OV*, and to overcome water obstacles".

GARF. F.R-8418. L.28. C.27. pp81-82

---

* OV - Otravlyayushchiye Veschestva - Poisonous material

It should be recalled that in the first decade of September 1937, ABTU had again considered and "rejected" a proposed design of the BT-IS tank developed by KB-190 at Plant №183, as described earlier. After review of the sketch project the ABTU command sent the 8th GU NKOP and the Plant №183 Letter №182987 dated 11th September 1937 on the proposal to discontinue work at KB-190 on the BT-IS tank and create within Department №100 a new design of wheel-tracked tank with performance characteristics as approved per Resolution KO №94ss. Additionally, in the opinion of the chief of ABTU, G. G. Bokis, the "new" design should be developed under the management of VAMM military engineer 3rd rank A. Ya. Dik.

After receiving this letter, the 8th GU NKOP organised the creation at Plant №183 of a separate (independent) design bureau (OKB) for developing new fighting vehicles. A list of planned activity was on 28th September 1937 sent to the Director of Plant №183, I. P. Bondarenko by Letter №4-233-3411s, signed by the acting head of the 8th GU NKOP, K. P. Farmanyants:

"The Government's decision №94ss 15-8-1937, (is that) 8th Main Directorate (is) to design and fabricate prototypes, and prepare for serial production of a high-speed wheel-track tank with a synchronised drive in 1939.

This work should be carried out at your plant. In view of the extreme seriousness of this work and the very tight deadlines set by the Government, the 8th Main Directorate considers the following activities necessary:

1. To create at Plant №183 a separate design bureau (OKB) to design the machine, subordinate directly to the chief engineer of the plant.

2. By agreement with the Head of VAMM and ABTU, VAMM military engineer 3rd grade Dik, Adolf Yakovlevich (is) appointed head of the office of associate, and shall allocate work in the office from 5th October to 30 VAMM graduates and from 1st December, an additional 20 people. You are required to provide housing and all conditions for normal operation for the arriving graduate engineers.

3. In agreement with the Chief of ABTU RKKA, to appoint as chief consultant on this tank, Captain Evgeny A. Kulchitsky.

4. Not later than 30th September to allocate work in the OKB to the top 8 tank plant designers for the purpose of leading separate groups, one standardisor, a secretary and archivist.

5. Approve allocation of 50 people at the state special design bureau of VAMM (including arriving academics) for the period of the development of the technical project with a further increase to 100 people for the development of the working drawings.

6. Create at the OKB a model mock-up workshop and provide extraordinary performance of the works connected with new design in all shops of plant.

7. Considering the necessity of the machine being for mass production, to design 3 variants at the technical project stage and make 2 versions of prototypes approved by the Commission for the review of projects.

8. To conduct this work to conclude an agreement with ABTU RKKA not later than 15 October 1937 with the simultaneous approval of the tactical and technical requirements (TTTs) of the machine for NKO and 8th Glavka (main directorate).

9. Provide performance of works on stages in the following terms:

a) Submission of technical project with preliminary calculations and layout by 1 February 1938 (the wheeled drive to be developed in 3 versions).

b) Develop a working draft of the machine for the two options approved by the Commission by 1 May 1938.

c) Produce machine prototypes on two options by 1 September 1938.

d) Test prototypes and eliminate defects revealed during test by 1 December 1938.

e) Prepare serial (production) drawings and carry out production preparation for delivery of a finally approved sample by 1 May 1939 so that series production commences from 1/5-39.

10. In the course of design and production of the prototype the chief of the bureau to engage and pay professionals for consultation and development of individual issues, as well as to send employees of the bureau to other plants.

11. To participate in the development of tactical and technical requirements, instruct diploma students and selection of necessary materials for the design no later than 2 October to send to Moscow Chief of OKB comrade Dik with heads of the groups allocated by plant.

12. The working room for OKB is necessary for convenience of use of archive of Department 190 to allocate in Department 100 and completely to equip it by the time of the beginning of work, i.e. by 10 October.

To provide all work necessary to install in all the listed events your personal observation and leadership."

RGVA. F. 31811. L. 3. C. 974. pp. 97 - 98

A copy of the letter was on 29th September 1937 received by the chief of ABTU, divisional commander G. G. Bokis; he immediately ordering the chief of the Military Academy of Mechanization and Motorization (VAMM) of the Red Army, brigade engineer I. A. Lebedev to send on secondment to Plant №183 the adjunct of the faculty of tanks and tractors, military engineer 3rd rank, A. Y. Dik. The forthcoming trip by Dik to Plant №183 would as it turned out last only from 1st to 18th October 1937.

In early October 1937, the chief of the 11th Department of ABTU, military engineer 1st rank Ya. L. Skvirsky with the participation of Major V. P. Puganov, developed *"Tactical and technical requirements for the design and manufacture of the light wheel-track-*

ed high-speed tank BT-20", - the designation BT-20 was now given to the tank created at Plant №183 on the basis of the tactical and technical requirements (TTTs) previously developed by Ya. L. Skvirsky for the aborted BT-9 tank, with amendments and additions developed taking into account new requirements specified in Resolution №94ss. In addition, preparation of the TTTs for the BT-20 tank used additional requirements: *"TTTs for the design and manufacture of a new light tank BT"*, compiled by the ABTU district engineer at Plant №183, engineer 2nd rank D. S. Saprygin in August 1937. The latter additional specifications again took into account the experience of long-term operation use of tanks in the Red Army, the experience of combat use of Soviet tanks in Spain and the latest scientific and technical developments in the defence industry. The TTTs for the design and manufacture of the tank BT-20 were on 11th October 1937 approved by the chief of ABTU, Bokis, and the next day, 13th October immediately sent to the Director of Plant №183, I. P. Bondarenko by the military Commissar of ABTU, brigade engineer P.S. Alliluev. In the covering Letter, №183715, a copy of which was sent to the ABTU district engineer at Plant №183 D. S. Saprygin noted:

"We forward you the approved TTTs for the design and manufacture of a new wheel-tracked BT-20 tank.

As you know, this type of tank has been approved by the governing bodies for mass production at your plant from 1939. Please provide, in ABTU RKKA's estimate at the conclusion of the contract as well as the estimated timing of the draft to view his special Commission."

RGVA. F. 31811. L. 3. C. 974. pp. 1

The management of Plant №183 was not however in a hurry to implement either the ABTU request as set out in the letter, or to implement the proposals of the 8th GU NKOP on establishing at the plant an independent design bureau under the leadership of A. Ya. Dik, as directed by K. P. Farmanyants on 28th September 1937 to the plant Director I. P. Bondarenko. The "delay" in response can be explained by many factors, and primarily by the internal situation in the People's Commissariat of the Defence Industry. On 15th October 1937, the People's Commissar, M. L. Rukhimovich was himself removed from his position, and the following day he was arrested by the NKVD. Meanwhile, and adding to the lack of operational action, the Director of Plant №183, I. P. Bondarenko had from March to September 1937 been on a foreign business trip, and on his return it took him some time to familiarise himself with all the current issues at such a complex and diversified enterprise as Plant №183. To force some movement in the delay of new tank development, the chief of ABTU, G. G. Bokis on 20th October 1937 sent the newly appointed People's Commissar of the Defence industry, M. Kaganovich, Letter №174266ss stating:

"On 15th August 1937 <...> the government took a special decision about preparing at Plant №183 a prototype BT tank with a development timetable such that the new tank type would by no later than 1 January 1939 be in series production. From the moment of that decision two months have passed. Mikhail Moiseevich, I urge you to personally intervene in this matter and order, as the 8th Main Directorate and Plant №183 to engage in the present implementation the most important resolution of the Government of arming the Workers and Peasants Red Army (i.e. RKKA - the Red Army) with modern types of tanks.

My suggestions basically boil down to the following:

1. No later than 1 November of this year to create at Plant №183 a special design team for the new type of BT tank, for which purpose to allocate at least 30 highly qualified, experienced designers to the Design Bureau, not counting less qualified and auxiliary drawing power.

2. To oblige the Chief of the 8th Main Directorate and Director of the Plant №183 comrade Bondarenko to create a special experimental base for testing of individual units of the designed machine. To create such a base no later than 1st November of this year.

3. To instruct the 8th Main Directorate to submit for approval a special schedule for the production of drawings, separate components, models, etc.

4. Provide development of designs and production of the prototype with necessary appropriations on the line of the National Commissariat of the Defence Industry".

This letter took effect on 29th October 1937 at a special meeting regarding the organization of the new OKB for design of the BT-20 tank at Plant №183, which was personally attended by the chief of ABTU Bokis, together with the Director of Plant №183, I. P. Bondarenko and the chief of the 8th GU NKOP V.D. Sviridov (by NKOP Order №365 dated 27th October 1937, Sviridov was appointed chief of the 8th GU (Main Directorate) of NKOP.

Ya. L. Skvirsky.   M.M Kaganovich.

By the same order K. P. Farmanyants who to that point had performed the duties of chief 8th GU NKOP was returned to his former duties as deputy chief of the 8th GU NKOP).

Three days before this meeting, on 25th October 1937, ABTU had printed the documents directly related to the creation of the new OKB at Plant №183 for design of the BT-20 tank and included: *"proposals for the establishment of an OKB"; "List of designers of the Plant №183, which are allocated for the new design OKB."; "List of persons whom ABTU RKKA sends Plant №183 to draft a new tank"; "the List of experimental works of the first stage; "Schedule of pilot works of the first stage" and "Organization of a separate Design Bureau (OKB) of Plant №183. Communist international."*

The author of these documents, VAMM military engineer 3rd rank A. Ya. Dik, had meantime already returned from Kharkov to Moscow. The proposals of Dik on the OKB organisation were:

"1. Create at Plant №183 a separate Design Bureau (OKB) which is not connected with mass production and subordinated directly to the plant director.

2. To ensure that the best factory tank designers are allocated to work in the critical design areas. (see Annex).

3. For design work to allocate 10 more factory engineers and to allow 40 graduate students of VAMM to work in the OKB planned for real design.

4. To expand the work of OKB on 9.11.37, for which prepare and equip the premises by 5.11.37.

5. Make comprehensive use of the experience of other tank-building plants (domestic and foreign), and also scientific-test establishments:

a) To assign test-tanker Captain Kulchitsky as main permanent consultant on the new design;

b) Send to the address of Plant №183 by 7.11.37 fully equipped latest samples of T-26, T-28, T-46 and T-29 tanks, as well as drawings and calculations for them;

c) The chief of the OKB to give the right to engage and pay for advice and work as individual specialists and institutions (VAMM, TsAGI, NATI, etc.);

d) ABTU to constantly inform the OKB of intelligence data on foreign tanks;

e) The KB chief to give the right to send designers to other plants to examine their manufacturing, testing and new design, and for collecting material for the bureau, which should be sent to OKB on an urgent basis.

6. Immediately have experienced contractors test the individual components and assemblies even before the approval of technical designs and rough prototypes to resolve the issues outlined in the list of experimental work in the 1st stage.

7. To ensure the timely pilot works of the 1st stage, proceed by 9.11.37 with experimental works, namely:

Ya.I. Baran.

D.G. Pavlov

a) Transfer the prototype shop of Department 100 to the Chief of separate design bureau (OKB) by 1.11.37.

b) To increase and upgrade the pilot plant machine tooling, and to replenish the staff of highly skilled turners, fitters, welders, and carpenters, for prototype work. Term 5.11.37.

c) To give the order for extraordinary performance of work quickly complete work design bureau and pilot plant in all divisions and departments of the plant;

d) Finish as scheduled started basic tests: of the tracks and the engine, for BT-IS the type of the plant, flamethrower, and air cleaner;

e) Other small works (clips, seals, etc.) and works of 1938 to transfer to delivery workshop of Department 100 where to organise the skilled site;

f) Transfer to the OKB prototype workshop the 2 first samples of future diesel engines for installation in the tank (term on 15 December 1937)".

RGVA. F.31811. L.3. C.974. pp110-111

The documents developed by A. Ya. Dik had a number of provisions, the implementation of which would significantly complicate the work of Plant №183 as regards the further improvement of series production BT-7 tanks. First of all, it related to the proposal to transfer of division 100 to the experimental workshop №191 in a chief to the newly formed OKB.

The role of A.Ya. Dik in the meeting held on 29th October 1937 is is not known. But what is known is that during the exchange of views it became clear that the leadership of Plant №183 was not fully in accordance with the requirements and recommendations of the ABTU RKKA and the 8th GU NKOP on the organisation of the Bureau, especially in its personnel policy and of the significant power of the future head of the new OKB. It is also known that at the meeting, despite pressure from the ABTU RKKA and the 8th GU NKOP, I. P. Bondarenko defended their point of view, contesting the transfer of pilot plant "191" and also the appointment of A. Ya. Dik as OKB chief. According to the Director of Plant №183, I. P. Bondarenko the design team for the new BT-20 should not be seconded for a time "enemies" from VAMM RKKA, and his factory "checked in" design engineer, subordinated directly to the management of the plant. In the first half of November 1937, such a design team, designated "Bureau 24" (KB-24), was established, with M. I. Koshkin appointed the chief of KB-24 and the vacant position of the chief of KB "190" tank division "100" assigned to N. Kucherenko. This was detailed in the memoirs of one of the creators of the T-34 tank, designer Ya. I. Baran:

"The task of the zakazchik (customer)* was received in October 1937. In view of the particular seriousness of the work of Mikhail I. Koshkin did not consider it possible to design the tank within an existing KB, as people would in this case consider the work just "routine". It was decided to assign a group of the most qualified employees to the special design bureau, relieving them of all other duties. The chief designer of this KB was himself, M. I. Koshkin. As his Deputy he appointed A. Morozov, depending on the outstanding design talent of this man. The selection of staff in the newly created Bureau of M. I. Koshkin and A. Morozov was paid particular attention, and soon there was a solid team, which was dominated by the spirit of creativity and camaraderie. Development of the project began immediately."

T-34: Path to Victory: the memoirs of tank builders and tank crews. Ed. : K. M. Slobodin, V. D. Listrovoy, Publishing House of Political Literature of Ukraine, 1989, p. 27

The head of the 8th GU NKOP, V. D. Sviridov informed the People's Commissar of Defence Industry M. M. Kaganovich on the establishment of Bureau "24" at Plant №183 and the beginning of work on the design of a new BT-20 tank by letter №4249s dated 29th November 1937:

"1. The design group for the new type of BT tank was established at Plant №183 with 18 qualified designers from 15th November 1937. As the design work unfolds, this team will be strengthened.

2. Plant №183 has no special experimental base to test individual components of the projected machine. The experimental inspection of the units of the designed machine will be carried out in the existing small pilot shop of the tank Department of Plant №183. The extension of the experimental workshop of Plant №183 provided in the cover appropriations for capital construction at Plant №183 in 1938 is a cost of 3-4 million Roubles.

3. The schedule of production of drawings and production of the prototype can be submitted for your approval on 1st January 1938 after the design team has made the first sketches for the developed machine.

4. I believe that the design development and production of the prototype should be carried out at the expense of NKO, not at the expense of NKOP.

All of the above I reported to comrade Bokis."

RGAEh. F.7515. L.1. C.143. pp353

Only a week before the sending of this letter, the chief of ABTU, G.G. Bokis was on 23rd November 1937, ABTU head of the Red Army was accused of participating in a "fascist conspiracy", removed from office and arrested. By order of NKO №3889 dated 28th November 1937 the new chief of ABTU became D. G. Pavlov, who was until July 1937 the Deputy to Bokis. A month before these events, in late October 1937, several departments were reorganised within ABTU. So, the 11th (Scientific and Technical) division, the chief of which was military engineer 1st rank Ya. L. Skvirsky, merged into the 8th division, keeping the same features. As for military engineer 3rd rank A. Ya. Dik who had failed to become the OKB chief; he in early November 1937 continued to work in the Department of Tanks and Tractors at VAMM. In accordance with NKO personal Letter №1974 dated 7th August 1938, Dik, together with the head of maintenance at the Department of Technical Supplies and Ammunition at VAMM, military engineer 2nd rank R. F. Miller were transferred to the army reserve under paragraph "a" of Article 43, i.e. made redundant.

Returning back from Moscow to Kharkov, a team of 19 designers at Bureau "24" at Plant №183 from November 1937 to March 1938 developed a draft design of the BT-20 high-speed wheel-track tank, with the tank at the plant having immediately been assigned the plant index A-20. In future official correspondence the factory designation A-20 began to prevail over the designation BT-20, with the tank from this point being more commonly referred to known as the A-20.

"The structure is small - about twenty people - and a very friendly team". So wrote Plant №183 veteran K. M. Slobodin in his book *"the KB takes up the challenge"* published in 1987:

"entered Mikhail Tarshinov, Alexey Moloshtanov, Narkis Korotchenko, Vasiliy Matyukhin, Yakob Baran, Piotr Vasilyev, Grigory Fomenko, Vasiliy Kalendin, Mikhail Kotov, Fyodor Kozlov, Semyon Braginsky, Aaron Mitnik and others. All of them were released from their current work so as to fully focus on their new special tasks. Koshkin appointed Alexander Alexandrovich Morozov as his Deputy and project leader. Direct management of the BT-7 and BT-7M was assigned to Nikolai Alekseevich Kucherenko, who for the time being remained as though "in the reserve of the main command". When the hour will come, he will also be put forward on the front line of the fight for a new tank and will prove himself to be the best.

The Bureau is located in a large room on the second floor of the main office building, with admittance through the guarded entrance only with special permits. Even the "seriishiki" (series production tank designers) can't come in here. These measures were not unnecessary. No matter how casually one looked at the office desks and drawing boards, the success of those who took their places, and how they would be able to keep it secret was - without exaggeration -

---

* *The Russian term "Zakazchik", in manufacturing refers to a client or customer that orders something to be made, whether State or commercial.*

the course and outcome of battles on the fields of future war, and the lives of many people. And although there is no war yet, and the country, speaking in newspaper language, is on labour watch, they, the Soviet designers, already today have to enter into an invisible fight with a skilled, well-trained opponent - experts of technically advanced Germany who, as it is easy to guess, also do not sit idly by.

The secrecy simultaneously rendered another good service: no one distracts the designers from their work. At first, there were such attempts, and there were a lot of people willing to go to one or another of them to clarify something, something, to consult, just to chat. But the strict and adamant shifts quite soon managed to inculcate into respect to established order, time, putting an end to similar liberties. Behind the mysterious door the work was at full swing.

The lights were on late in the windows of the second floor. I do not count how many times Mikhail Ilyich (Koshkin) and other employees of the Bureau had to go on foot across the city (i.e. after the public transport had stopped working), or stayed in the design bureau until morning. They worked with the special passion that only exists when people are not chained to rigid regulations and requirements, have freedom of initiative, the ability to express them-selves and show what they can do. Incredibly exciting is a competition of abilities, healthy self-esteem, technical erudition, and performance - all the best that is in each of the participants. And this is the best that manifested it-self in all areas of machine design. The "korpusniki" (hull designers) Tarshinov and Fomenko worked excellently. The "zakazchik" (client) had stipulated that the armour of the hull should have a thickness of up to 20mm, a clear task that does not allow any discrepancies. But so many paths lead to its embodiment in metal, and it is necessary to find the most rational and the only correct one. It is here that, in addition to my own experience, will fit the experience of the self-taught inventor Nikolai Tsyganov.

Koshkin thoroughly studied this issue, discussed it at the technical meeting of the team, where former associates of Nikolai Tsyganov, and now the leading designers of the design Bureau Vasily Matyukhin and Peter Vasiliev told about all the vicissitudes of work on the Tsyganov BT-IS project. The feasibility of using sloped armour plates was not in doubt. But what angles of inclination are optimal? And is there no other, even more effective solution? Only a painstaking se-arch could answer these questions. Sketches, calculations, layouts... ".

Slobodin. K.M. The KB Takes the Challenge. Verkh. Volzh. Publishing House, Yaroslavl, pp59-61.

Despite the relatively small team, the designers of Bureau "24" as of 1st March 1938, developed 42 of the drawings and to complete calculations on: dynamic, 5-speed transmission, two actuator options for transferring input torque to the road wheels, of steering clutches, final drives and calculation of cooling components and assemblies located in the tank engine and transmission compartments.

The senior ABTU military representative of Plant №183, military engineer 2nd rank I. P. Petrov, sent a progress report on the design of the new A-20 wheel-track tank to the head of the 8th Directorate ABTU, military engineer 1st rank Ya. l Skvirsky on 5th March 1938 in transmittal Letter №0132s. The report gave a detailed description done by Bureau "24" work on the design of the A-20 tank and observed the following organisational deficiencies:

"1. There are still few workers. In the annual report we pointed out that by order of the Director of the plant was scheduled to have 33 engineers, but as of 1.1-38 worked only 6 engineers and 10 technicians, a total of (only) 16 people. Currently, 19 people work, including 10 engineers, 9 technicians, 1 copier and 1 Secretary.

2. There is not yet any experimental work. Already now it would be necessary to make a number of models, to determine the centre of gravity of one BT-7 chassis to start tests of tracks and tracked wheels, check the cooling system (fans, radiators, air ducts), to test lever controlled wheel, to check the exploitation of the BT-7-IS (braking, turning, wheel slip, efficiency, dynamics, engine), etc. But the skilled work is not conducted, because there are no means and no people. It is imperative that the Command of ABTU RKKA provide the necessary funds to assist in the staffing of the OKB."

RGVA. F.31811. L.2. c.773. pp90

In early March 1938, ABTU considered the draft design of the A-20, as the acting chief of ABTU, Colonel V. P. Puganov notified the Director of Plant №183 I. P. Bondarenko in Letter №283316, dated 7th March 1938:

"For consideration and approval of the draft design of the BT-20 tank, I request your order to send to ABTU all the materials you have on this issue. Concurrently, please send your representatives by 15.3.38. Materials must arrive in ABTU RKKA not later than 13th March this year. The beginning of consideration of the project is scheduled for 15 March 15 at 10.00 and will last until 20 March this year."

RGVA. F.31811. L.2. C.773. pp71

Interestingly, while this letter was still in transit, on 9th March 1938 I. P. Bondarenko sent to ABTU in the name of D. G. Pavlov and Ya. L. Skvirskiy telegram series G, with a request to send to the Plant №183 the Commission for consideration and approval of the draft design of the A-20 tank. Thus, due to the lack of an initial agreement, each of the parties - Plant №183 and ABTU - wanted to review the draft project on its own territory. However, the more insistent was the client, and on Sunday 13th March 1938, the acting head of ABTU Colonel V. P. Puganov sent I. P. Bondarenko the following telegram:

"KHARKOV KOMINTERN PLANT BONDARENKO SE-RIES Year. CONFIRM AGAIN THE SENDING OF THE KOSHKIN PROJECTS FOR ABTU CONSIDERATION. PU-GANOV."

Preparation of all necessary documents took the plant three days, and on 17th March 1938, the Deputy Director of Plant №183, F. I. Lyash and the head of KB-24, M. I. Koshkin sent to the chief of ABTU, corps commander D. G. Pavlov together with transmittal Letter №SO1103 the following: *"Explanatory note to the conceptual design of high-speed wheel-track tank A-20"* in 32 pages; and *"Technical calculations for the mechanisms of the A-20 tank"* in 299 sheets, together with 74 sheet of drawings of the A-20 tank.

In the end, a technical review meeting of the preliminary design of the A-20 tank was held at ABTU in Moscow on 25th March 1938 - ten days behind schedule. From the explanatory notes submitted for consideration to the draft project it followed that:

"The A-20 wheel-tracked tank displays a further improvement of the A-7 [BT-7] tank series. Taking into account the preliminary design of the tank, all the demands on the machine, its tactical properties, and on the other hand, the conditions of production of Plant №183, the design of the A-20 tank has taken into account the following:

1. *Implementation of tactical and technical requirements for the designed tank.*
2. *Taking into account the production capabilities of the manufacturing plant.*
3. *Taking into account the direction in the tank technology and in the technology of anti-tank protection.*
4. *The experience of operating combat vehicles in the army.*
5. *Ensuring the minimum possible weight of the tank.*
6. *Providing the best conditions for the combat operation of the tank crew.*
7. *The maximum possible increase of firepower for the tank.*
8. *Providing convenient maintenance of the tank mechanisms, etc.*

In its dimensions, the designed A-20 tank corresponds to the A-7 tank, except for its width, which is equal to 2,500mm for the A-20, i.e. increased by 242mm. The hull expansion of the A-20 tank was 152mm, the rest of the expansion of the machine is caused exclusively by an increase in the size of the arrangement of the wheels and the distance between the axes of the idler wheels, and the track wheels are old. All balancers are directed in the course of movement, i.e. back, and are interchangeable for each side of the tank. The placement of the main mechanisms in the tank remain similar to the A-7 tank, except for the placement of fuel tanks, which are now located on the sides in the fighting compartment of the tank. <...> The ammunition complement is located on the sides of the hull and under the floor in the fighting compartment of the tank. The total ammunition complement in the tank is designed in accordance with the requirements of the Tactical and Technical Conditions (TTKhs). The fighting compartment interior was increased in length in comparison with the A-7 tank, by 188mm".

RGAEh. F.7719. L.70. C.70. pp5-6

In the presented draft design, the hull of the A-20 tank was made in two versions: with a narrow and wide glacis, with a DT machine gun mounted in the glacis next to the driver-mechanic in both versions. The enlarged glacis and fighting compartment allowed for the placement of a bow machine gun and a fourth crewmember.

In both versions the glacis, stern and upper side plates of the hull were inclined. The only hull armour plates located vertically were the lower side armour plates. The hull was of entirely welded construction without any additional reinforcement as on the BT-7. There were pockets cut in the hull for the rocker-arms, and for the convenience of installation of the road wheel mountings the armour plates of the hull were removable. The upper glacis was made of a single 16mm armour plate with a rectangular cut-out for the driver-mechanic's hatch. In the version with a wide glacis, the front tube was excluded from the number of elements of the body, and the extension of the bow was achieved by installing longitudinal rigidity sheets and niche assemblies to accommodate the swinging levers of the controlled wheels (support rollers). In neither version did the hull glacis protrude beyond the front idler wheels, i.e. neither tank provided a "ram capable" hull to destroy obstacles - a deviation from the TTTs. All small hull fitments, such as hinges and spring hatches were located inside the hull, thereby ensuring their protection against damage. The tank hull was also: *"designed with the expectation of underwater transit"* and accordingly *"all hatches, manholes and other openings in the body had the appropriate seals"*. The A-20 turret draft design was also made in two versions - both using 20mm side armour plate but sloped at differing inclinations of 18° and 23°. The turret variants otherwise differed mainly in the number of crew hatches, and the location of the anti-aircraft machine gun installation. Two round hatches were designed in the turret roof of the turret with the 18° side plate slope, and one large trapezoidal-shaped hatch in the roof of the turret with the 23° side plate slope. A new turret race was designed for both turrets; with a special seal to prevent water ingress while the tank was traversing entirely submerged across rivers. The internal equipment arrangement of the A-20 turret did not differ in principle from that of the BT-7 turret in either variant.

The 45mm armament was provided in the preliminary design with a new elevation mechanism and gun mantlet allowing an elevation/depression range of +65° to -7°, with a co-axial 7.62mm DT machine gun. Another DT machine gun was installed in the rear of the turret. In the turret bustle was to be located additional shells in line tanks or a radio in command tanks. The 45mm gun and co-axial DT machine gun were provided with telescopic and periscopic sights. The gun was stabilised in the vertical plane by means of the new "Orion" gun stabiliser to ensure that the aim was fired from the course on the A-20 tank.

The A-20 tank was to be powered by the BD-2 diesel. Engine starting was in the draft design by means of two electric starters with a capacity of 3hp each, plus a back-up compressed air start, for which the tank was provided with two air cylinders with a volume of 10 litres each. All fuel tanks, with a total capacity of 500 litres, were located inside the tank hull within the combat and transmission compartments. The engine cooling system was a closed loop type and its main part was two tubular type radiators, located either side of the engine. The cooling surface area of each radiator was 49.61m², some 60% greater than the radiator of the BT-7 tank. The cooling system was designed for an engine with a power output of 500hp running at an ambient temperature of +35° C.

Two alternative gearboxes were considered for the preliminary A-20 design. The first version had five forward and one reverse gears, a forward speed range from 8.17km/h to 56.6km/h and a reverse speed of 9.9km/h. The gear synchronizers operated by the movement of the gears on the shaft slots. The second version had four forward and one reverse gears, a forward speed range from 8.98km/h to 65.13km/h and a reverse speed of 8.40km/h. The design of the main and side frictions, brakes and on-board gearboxes of the A-20 tank generally matched the design of similar mechanisms on the BT-7 tank, but modified to transmit higher torques. To reduce the effort when exposed to the control drives of the main and on-board frictions, instead of bronze ratchet ball mechanisms were introduced shutdown. And in the final drives were added nodes to transmit torque from the spur gear side gear side to the longitudinal drive shaft to the road wheels (when driving a tank on wheels).

First and last pages of the explanatory notes for the conceptual design of the A-20.

The torque transmission drive to the second, third and fourth pairs of road wheels in the design of the A-20 tank was designed in four versions: with transverse Cardan shaft and wheel reducer; with longitudinal Cardan shaft and wheel reducer; "guitar" (with three gears in the gearbox) and balanced Cardan with bevel gear in the wheel reducer. The developers of the project gave preference to the first and third options as most satisfying all imposed conditions. However, given the fact that the design of the actuator with a cross propeller shaft and wheel reducer, had already proven reliable on the PT-1 and T-29 tanks (with M. I. Koshkin having partaken in the development of the latter), Bureau "24" thereby recommended this actuator variant for the A-20 tank.

Many chassis elements of the A-20 design such as the drive sprocket/wheel and idler wheels were left the same as in the BT-7 production tank. The design of the road wheels and suspension units of the A-20 tank were however strengthened relative to the BT-7 tank. In connection with the increase in weight of the A-20 tank to 16 metric tonnes, and with driving the tank on wheels, the width of the rubber wheel rims was increased from 110 mm on the BT-7 to 145mm, while for the same purpose in the A-20 tank the camber was in the range of 1-1.5. It should be noted that on the BT-7 tank it was known that the rubber rimmed road wheels already worked at the limit of their capabilities an that a further increase in tank combat weight without modifying the roadwheel construction would preclude prolonged movement without tracks. For example, on the BT-7 tank powered by a BD-2 diesel engine (combat weight 14.5 tonnes) destruction of the rubber rims occurred after travelling 50-100km by road on wheels; however when moving on the tracks the wheel rims endured up to 2,000km.

The track for the A-20 tank was designed in two versions: with comb and with hitch gearing. Moreover, the track pitch and the number of rewound tracks leading wheel in one of its

Telegram on Project A-7 dated 9th March 1938.

turnover (in both cases) were selected in such a way that the speed of the machine on track synchronized with the rotation speed of the road wheels receiving the torque from the actuators to the wheel gearboxes. The track with crest gearing had a pitch of 167mm and a width of 320mm, the track with hitch gearing being respectively 111mm and 354mm.

In order to obtain a more steep characteristics of the load on the road wheels, the spring of the 2nd and 4th suspension units were located at an angle in the hull of the tank.

Questions of internal and external communication, *"warming"* of the tank, laying outside and inside the tank and *"all kinds of carried property and equipment"*, and also electric equipment were not considered in the draft project.

The conceptual design of the A-20 tank was attended by the Chief of ABTU, D. G. Pavlov together with P. S. Alliluyev and a large number of ABTU professionals. As a result of discussions, the draft design was with a number of comments approved for the development of a full technical design and the production of a prototype. The A-20 tank design with a wide hull bow, 4-speed transmission, and a drive torque transmission to the road wheels for use when driving a tank on wheels and using the cross-Cardan shafts and wheel gearbox option was chosen for further development. In the minutes of the technical meeting that considered the draft design of the A-20 tank approved by D. G. Pavlov on 26th March 1938 it was noted:

"The draft design is approved for further development of the technical design and production of the prototype with the following remarks:
1. The combat weight of the tank should be no more than 15.5 tonnes.
2. Armour must protect against (12.7mm) "DK" machine gun rounds. The shape of the hull should be with a wide nose with the removal of the leading edge of the latter. The front edge of the hull is not advocating idler.
Armour: turret 20mm at 25° minimum angle; 16mm-swing box-tilt at 35° minimum angle. Vertical lower hull sheets in two versions - a) ekranami (screen) 15mm+5m or 13mm+7mm, or homogeneous improved 20mm. Roof is sloping, smooth-10mm homogeneous. Hull and rear 20mm armour set at angles above 45°.
Lower side sheet from 16mm of homogeneous armour at an angle of 30°. Floor is 10mm smooth armour.
The driver's hatch cover-inclined, thickness 25mm, should withstand "DK" rounds. The driver's seat shall provide side vision and protection against lead spatter.
The service - Approved project.
45mm gun paired with a "DT", elevation angle of 45°.
Machine gun "DT" in the turret rear, tourelle (AAMG) installation, frontal "DT" machine gun beside the driver.
To provide installation in the same turret type L-10 gun.
Turret with one hatch and installation of a P-40 (tourelle anti-
aircraft mount) over the commander's seat (left).
The radio is located at the front of the tank.
Crew: 4. In the front next to the driver to develop a design to fit 4 persons, providing them the opportunity of observation and firing from the forward gun.
Scheme of the transmission and the drive wheel stroke is fundamentally approved. To provide shutdown of each wheel separately. Gearbox-4 speed. Final drive without the tube. Drive wheel to turn the wheel with the cross-shaft and a curved rocker. Between the engine and the gearbox it is desirable to provide a flexible coupling. Suspension: the scheme is approved. Loads on the roadwheels should be levelled whenever possible. The rear wheel it is desirable to push back. It is desirable to have a front driven wheel on the General balancer and with removal of a spring from the fighting compartment. The angle of rotation of the wheels is not less than 15°. The rubber bandage (rim) should be perforated for cooling.
Wheel travel 160mm-desirable an increase to 180 to 200mm.
Track-for the prototype is allowed BT-7 type track. At the same time, a rubber-metal track is to be developed.
The engine installation. An engine start system to be developed in two variants:
a) four batteries and one starter 10hp, with secondary air start;
b) two batteries and run an additional motor.
Speed of movement. When installing 4-speed boxes, to have the following: minimum-9km/h; maximum-65km/h with an engine speed of 1,700rpm.
Equipment. The tank should be equipped for PKh and protected from OV, and it is desirable to provide defrosting for work in winter conditions.

When developing the technical project to take all necessary measures to ensure free access to the components of the tank. New units of the tank shall be designed with the possibility of fitting them on the A-7 (BT-7) machine in the case of its modernisation. Simultaneously with the development of the technical project, the plant is obliged to produce a full-scale model of the tank. The plant is further obliged in parallel with the development of technical design and working drawings to test the main tank components, both on the stand and on the A-7 machine. Primarily to make experimentation with the tyres on the A-7 machine".

RGVA. F.31811. L.2. C.733. pp157-159

Copies of this Protocol were sent to the Director of Plant №183, I. P. Bondarenko and chief of the 8th GU NKOP D. V. Sviridov on 29th March 1938 as an Annex to the signed D. G. Pavlov and S. P. Alliluyev by Letter №283765 follows:

"The presented draft design of the BT-20 tank as a whole meets the tactical and technical requirements of the ABTU and was approved by me with separate comments for further development

Longitudinal section drawing of the A-20 tank.

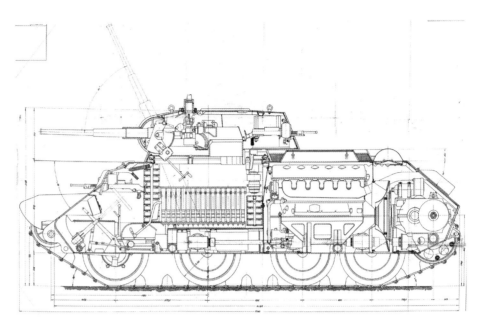

and production of the prototype. Sending you the project approval Protocol, at the same time I draw your attention to the following:

1. All work on the production of a prototype tank must be deployed to complete the course in order for this tank, as specified in the decision of the government was prepared to have it in production 1939. Therefore, the production of the prototype should be forced as much as possible. Keep in mind that up to now you have been working very slowly and have lost about 7 months only on design, while you have had every opportunity to do this work in a shorter time. For our part, we will take all measures not to delay this work and will provide timely and appropriate advice on all issues. It is now necessary to expand the design bureau and to deploy experimental work on those components that are for the first time used in tank construction or cause some fears in their performance. Only in this way is it possible to obtain quality and timely needs of the army tank. In this regard, I ask you to take all necessary measures for the timely production of a prototype tank within the deadlines set for you by the Government decision of 15 August 1937. About your events, please keep me informed".

RGVA. F.31811. L.2 C.773. pp156

After considering the draft design of the A-20 tank, all drawings and technical calculations were sent to Plant №183 on 27th March 1938 with Letter №283691s. Upon receipt of this project documentation, the KB-24 design team began to formally develop the technical design of the A-20 wheel-tracked tank. In order to force further work on the design of the A-20 tank, the head of the 8th GU NKOP, V. D. Sviridov on 20th April 1938 sent to the Director of Plant №183, I. P. Bondarenko letter №52-1404s as follows:

"Further development of the project of the A-20 machine in the Bureau of comrade Koshkin is at an unacceptable slow pace, which jeopardizes the timely implementation of Government Resolution №95ss [typo, should read №94ss] of 15/VIII-37. One of the reasons hindering the work on the A-20 machine is lack of staff in the Bureau of comrade Koshkin. It is quite clear to you that the Bureau's available staff will not be able to cope with the amount of work that is entrusted to it. According to my talks with you, immediately take action to requisition for the Bureau of comrade Koshkin, engineers from other departments and divisions of the plant:

1. 4 series production developers from Department "100".

2. 3 persons from production Department "500".

3. 4 persons from the design offices of Department "400".

The relocation of the personnel takes a 3-day period. From my side, measures are taken to second to Plant №183 at the disposal of the Bureau of comrade Koshkin:

1. 3 persons from Plant №185

2. 2 persons from Plant №37

For a period of 3 months. The plant should take into your account travel costs for these comrades, and provide them with hotel accommodation."

RGVA. F.31811. L.2. C.773. pp215

A copy of this letter was sent to the chief of ABTU, D. G. Pavlov, under whose leadership at this time there was intensive preparation for a special "tank" meeting, devoted entirely to the creation of new tank designs.

Chapter 5

New Management - New Requirements

As previously noted, D. G. Pavlov, having since July 1937 held the post of deputy head of ABTU, was on 28th November 1937 promoted to head of ABTU in accordance with NKO Order №3889. Before his appointment to the Armoured Directorate, Pavlov had from October 1936 to June 1937 served in Spain, where he commanded the joint group of armoured brigades in the army of the Republicans. For the successful implementation of special tasks he was by Decree of the Presidium of the Supreme Soviet of the USSR dated 21st June 1937 awarded the title Hero of the Soviet Union. The Spanish Civil War had given the new head of ABTU experience of both the direct command of armoured forces in modern combat, and the operation of armoured vehicles in combat conditions.

It took the new chief of ABTU only two months to fully grasp the main tasks required for future development. By mid February 1938, Pavlov, having assessed the state of the Red Army tank park, had concluded what changes in the existing system of armoured forces were required. One of his first initiatives in his new position was revising the GKO Resolution №94ss dated 15th August 1937, *"On types of tanks for the tank forces of the Red Army and tanks for production in 1938"*. On 21st February 1938, Pavlov, along with the Military Commissioner of ABTU, brigade engineer P.S. Alliluyev sent the People's Commissar of Defence of the USSR, Marshal of the Soviet Union K. E. Voroshilov a detailed report, in the introduction of which was noted:

"Currently, the Red Army has 9 types of tanks (T-27, T-37, T-26, T-38, BT-2, BT-5, BT-7, T-28, T-35). According to the Defence Committee (KO) Resolution №94ss, 7 new types of tanks (amphibious, STZ tank, wheel-track reconnaissance tank, BT with diesel, BT with six driving wheels, T-29, and T-35 with reinforced armour and engine power output of 1,000hp are to be additionally introduced from 1939. In fact, the number of tank types is much higher, as the above list does not include artillery, chemical, engineer and tele-tanks. The same situation we have with armoured cars. In the Red Army there are 10 types (D-8, D-12, D-13, BA-27, FAI, BAI, BA-3, BA-6, BA-10 and BA-20). In addition, according to KO Resolution №94, in 1939 will be introduced two additional new types".

RGVA. F.4. L.55. pp1

According to Pavlov as the new Chief of ABTU, the operation of numerous different tank and armoured vehicle types

D. G. Pavlov.

had proven detrimental for mechanised forces, complicating maintenance and repair, provision spare parts and training. The different tactical and technical characteristics (in speed, mobility, armour and armament) of these vehicles operating together had also led to their incorrect combat use. *"If you consider this many types of vehicles, tractors and special machine parks"* stated the authors of the report *"the necessity of radical revision of the whole system of auto-armour-tank weapons becomes clear"*. Specific proposals for such a "radical revision" and for the existing Red Army tank park were contained in the main body of the report:

"1. Available (are) 862 T-18 (tanks) to be used in fortified areas as anti-tank defence vehicles based on satisfactory modernisation. Modernisation of the T-18 is underway, the negative outcome of which will result in their withdrawal from Red Army and their being melted down in the smelter. Spare parts for the T-18 are incomplete, and are no longer manufactured.

2. Available in the Red Army (discontinued) T-27 tankettes-2,690 pcs. To be used in infantry divisions as a means of communication and the fortified areas of individual companies of battalions.

3. Available in the Red Army (discontinued) T-37 and T-38 amphibious tanks-3,851 pcs. For use as tanks of the Reserve Command, organising those units for the capture of bridgeheads [river embankments] during assault crossings. In peacetime, these tanks (T-37 and T-38) are not produced, only parts. Industry

BT-2 and T-26 tanks on tactical exercises.

should be prepared for production of T-38 tanks in time of war, and to continue adopting new and better types, such as amphibians with armour impervious to small arms at all distances.

4. Tanks T-26-6,748pcs. As a mass-production tank for infantry support (main tracked tank type), used for combined action with infantry. Production of the T-26 and spare parts is to continue, improving the T-26 with regard to full interchangeability of components and parts throughout the existing tank park. A more powerful engine and running gear is to be installed on the T-26 (work underway).

The type of tank provided by Resolution KO №94ss for production at the STZ plant, and intended to replace the T-26 per NKO requirements resulting in the creation for the Red Army of a new type of tank is for its fighting qualities, little different from T-26. It should not be included in the system of tank forces and work on the tank at STZ is to stop. Maintain the (existing) T-26 at STZ as a mobilisation option.

5. BT tanks, BT-2-618 pcs., BT-5-1,841 pcs., BT-7-2,346 pcs. (basic type of wheeled-tracked tank). For use by mobile combined und independent forces. Production of BT tanks and spare parts to continue, modernised by means of installation of a diesel engine and improved suspension according with the principle of unit

interchangeability, pending the adopting of a modernised whe-eled-tracked tank with 6 driven wheels and diesel engine.

6. Available in the Red Army tanks T-28 - 262pcs. and T-35 - 41 pcs. To use as tanks of the Reserve Command. T-28 and T-35 tanks do not protect their crews and vital parts of the tanks from 37mm armour-piercing shells firing from a distance of approximately 1,000m, i.e. these tanks can be disabled before they can open fire. The increase in the armour thickness from 20mm to 30mm (conical turrets and sides), as provided for by Resolution KO №94ss for the T-35 tank, does not ressolve protection of the tank from PTO (anti-tank guns), since a tank with such armour fired on by a 45mm armour-piercing projectile from a distance of 2,000m remains vulnerable. Increasing the armour basis on the T-35 to 30mm will require the development of a completely new tank design and does not resolve the question of armour penetration. We need a PTO (anti-tank gun engagement) tank with armour that protects from damage by armour-piercing shells up to 47mm calibre at all ranges. T-28 and T-35 tanks do not correspond to their combat role of destroying fortified areas and, especially, for combatting PTOs (anti-tank guns) and (in the case of) the T-28, to fight other tanks. There is a need to replace both tank types with a single tracked breakthrough tank type capable of

engaging tanks and PTOs, with armour thickness of 50-55mm. This tank must easily destroy anti-tank guns and carry out the task of UR (reinforced region) breakthrough. Production of the T-28 and T-35 is to continue, but in accordance with the principle of component interchangeability. Development of the T-35 variant with 30mm armour and an engine developing 1,000hp under KO Resolution №94ss is to be cancelled.

Resolution №94 provides for a wheeled-tracked T-29 tank designed to replace the T-28 tank in 1939. The T-29 tank as with the T-28 and T-35 has armour that does not protect against damage by (45mm calibre) anti-tank guns. In addition, wheeled travel of such a heavy type of tank is impractical. Currently, the technical design of the T-29 is coming to an end. I consider it necessary to stop work on T-29".

RGVA. F.4. L.19. C.55. pp2-4

Regarding the development of new tank designs, D. G. Pavlov and P. S. Alliluyev suggested:

"Along with the production and supply to the army of existing tank types, it is necessary to work on the creation of more advanced tank types intended to replace the existing models, according to the following system:

1. Amphibious tracked tank: to replace the T-37 and T-38. *This type of tank for its fighting qualities (armour, weapons, speed on land and afloat, suspension, etc.) should exceed the T-38. Armour should be impervious to armour-piercing rounds at all ranges. Engine power output to be increased.*

2. Tracked tank for combined action with infantry (T-26 type). *Is a further improvement of the existing T-26 tank, including: increased engine power output, enhanced armour, strengthened chassis, etc. by the principle of inter-changeability of components.*

The T-18 tank.

3. Wheeled-tracked tank for combined arms and cavalry (BT type). *Is a further development of the BT tank to have enhanced combat performance in terms of: strengthened armour, installation of a diesel engine, movement on wheels, etc.*

4. Tracked Tank-Istribitel PTO* - also a breakthrough tank. *Represents a new tank type intended to replace the T-28, T-29 and T-35 tanks. The main feature of this tank is 50-55mm armour thickness, defeating armour-piercing shells up to 47mm calibre. For this tank can be used the existing M-100 aircraft engine developing 860hp, followed by transition to a diesel engine."*

RGVA. F.4. L.19. C.55. pp5

In addition, Pavlov and Alliluyev requested the adoption of the new reconnaissance wheel-tracked tank prescribed by KO Resolution №94ss be cancelled on the basis of it being inexpedient to further increase the number of different tank types, together with the possibility of other existing Red Army tanks being used to conduct reconnaissance. However, ongoing work on the design of this tank was nevertheless proposed to continue because:

"It is considered necessary to continue this work, with the aim being not the creation of a special reconnaissance-type tank, but the development of a tank prototype that is likely to give a new, best solution for tanks working with infantry, and tank combined arms units, and cavalry, changing the tactical and technical requirements respectively.

With the existing T-26 and BT tanks the "tight place" (i.e. bottleneck) is the suspension and especially the tracks. In the new development, these existing problems should be eliminated. Prototypes need to be produced in two versions: wheel-tracked and tracked for the final decision on the choice of type (tracked or wheel-tracked). Upon availability of running gear (including the track) of a purely tracked tank with a duration of at least 3,000km, it will be possible to abandon the wheel-tracked type of tank."

RGVA. F.4. L.19. C.55. pp6

It should be noted that D. G. Pavlov himself was a supporter of tanks with tracked (only) drive. On 1st February 1938 at a meeting of ABTU within the VAMM offices, on being questioned about his views on the use of wheel-tracked and tracked alternative drive systems for tanks, Pavlov stated:

"Tanks such as the Vickers (T-26) after given the "stop" command can fire the first round after two seconds. We have other data - tanks such as the Christie (BT) gives the first round at eight seconds after the "stop" command. Frankly speaking, when he is put on the dead brake (i.e. put on the spot when entering combat), the tank shouts: "Hello and goodbye!".

---

* PTO - Anti-Tank Armaments (i.e. anti-tank guns)

Early production T-38 tanks during amphibious manoeuvres.

Pavlov continued:

"Here, in the argument between the wheel-track tank and tracked tank, I am not making blame, I am a patriot of tracked tanks. I love the T-26 "lyagushka" (frog) and would not change it for any other existing tank. If you ask me which one is best to go into battle with, it is the T-26. The T-28 is also a wonderful machine, but I am talking about my personal opinion. If you need a point of view from the army as to which tank is better, wheeled and tracked, or tracked, the answer is that all of Europe declined from the use of wheel-tracked machines for two reasons - (they are) difficult to manufacture, difficult to repair - and the design also does not give special advantages. As for our point of view, I think during future tank production you will yourselves understand this point of view from within our military forces. In the process of (working with) existing weapons you feel how the whole structure is built, what tanks are for independent action, what tanks for combined action with infantry. This is simple. The type of tank shall be determined by the appropriate structure and arrangement of the units."

RGVA. F.31811 L.2. C.799. pp148-149

Also in the report presented by Pavlov and Alliluyev to Voroshilov was noted the requirement to develop and have accepted for service a new 76.2mm tank gun, and a large-calibre machine gun:

"The (current) 76mm gun, mounted on the T-28 and T-35 and artillery tanks, does not meet the needs of mechanised forces due to the trajectory and low initial velocity (381m/sec). A 76mm gun

with a flat trajectory is needed, for which an initial muzzle velocity not less than 560m/s is required. These guns need to re-equip the (existing) park of T-28, T-35 tanks. In mechanised forces is also missing a small-sized heavy machine gun, crucial for tanks, especially amphibious, and armoured cars. The existing (12.7mm) DK heavy machine gun requires a turret little different in size from the turret for the 45mm gun installation. A dimensionally smaller heavy machine gun is needed."

RGVA. F.4. L.19. C.55. pp7

In the final part of the report, the ABTU leaders requested the NKO, in event of its approval, to raise the question of revising Resolution №94ss at a meeting of the Defence Committee (KO pri SNK SSSR). After reviewing the presented report, Voroshilov on 28th February 1938 gave the order to Pavlov about the preparation of necessary documents for submission to the Government. Pursuant to this order, ABTU on 14th March 1938 sent the NKO the draft KO resolution: *"About the types of tanks for arming the armoured forces of the Red Army"* and the draft of a letter on behalf of the People's Commissar of Defence of the USSR addressed to the Chairman of the SNK of the USSR, V. M. Molotov. The text of the draft letter addressed to Molotov almost completely replicated the text of Pavlov's report of 21st February 1938, with the - significant to the future - exception of paragraphs 2 and 3 of the second section of the original report. The amended paragraphs concerned further development of the T-26 (tracked) and BT (wheel-tracked) types, that the letter addressed to Molotov now recommended to be combined into a single new tank type:

"2. The tank intended for actions with infantry (cavalry) and as a part of independent tank units shall be one and the same tank type. To achieve this goal, it is necessary to develop two types of tank, one purely tracked and the other - wheeled-tracked,

T-26 tank of the 11th Interbrigade. Spain, September 1937

comprehensively test them during 1939, and after that to adopt (for service), replacing the T-26 and BT tanks, that tank option which will meet all requirements".

RGVA. F.4. L.19. C.55. pp14

The letter addressed to Molotov also added a paragraph on the need to develop a new 7.62mm tank machine gun. The KO draft resolution: *"types of tanks for arming the armoured forces of the Red Army"* and the draft letter addressed to Molotov were received in a quantity of ten copies by the NKO command on 17th March 1938. The text of the letter remained unchanged, with minor corrections made only to the draft resolution regarding the date of manufacture of the prototype amphibious tracked tank. The final version of the draft resolution dated 17th March 1938 was however another document:

"The Committee of Defence (KO pri SNK SSSR) Has Decided:

I. Use of Tanks in the Red Army:

1. *The production of T-26 tanks (standard tracked tank) and spare parts is to continue, with improvement in terms of increased engine power, increased hull and turret bullet resistance, improved suspension and better weapons - all these works are to be carried out according to the principle of complete interchangeability of components and mechanisms with the existing tank park. To compel NKOP to by 1.1.1939 present for State tests an upgraded prototype sample T-26 type tank.*

2. *The production of BT-7 tanks and spare parts to continue with improvements, including: the installation of a diesel engine, increased hull and turret bullet resistance, strengthened chassis and improved weapons - all these works to be carried out according to the principle of complete interchangeability of components and mechanisms on the existing park (tank fleet).*

3. *The production of T-28 tanks and spare parts to continue, improving them by installing a gun with high initial velocity (L-10), increased armour resistance and strengthened suspension - all these works to be carried out according to the principle of complete interchangeability of units and mechanisms on the existing park.*

4. *The production of T-35 tanks and spare parts to continue, improving them by installing the (76.2mm) L-10 gun, increased armour resistance, strengthened transmission and running gear - all these works to be carried out according to the principle of complete interchangeability of components and mechanisms on the existing Park. To compel NKOP to by 1.1-1939 present on State tests an upgraded sample T-35 prototype tank.*

5. *Production of spare parts for amphibious T-37, T-38 and T-27 tanks to continue.*

6. *Tanks T-26, BT-7, T-28, T-35 and T-38 to maintain as mobilisation (i.e. wartime) tanks, pending the adoption and preparation for serial production of more advanced types of tanks, replacing those discontinued.*

T-35 tank with 76.2mm M-1927/32 (KT-28) gun installed in the main turret.

II. Development of New Tank Designs:

Along with production and supply of the RKKA (Red Army) with the tanks specified in section I of this Resolution to perform works on the creation of improved tank models intended for replacement of the existing types:

1. To create amphibious tank intended to replace the T-27, T-37 and T-38. Purpose: The capture of major river obstacles, participation in landing operations, coastal defence.
   Type of tank-tracked. Armament-12.7mm heavy machine gun, paired with a standard 7.62mm calibre machine gun. Armour that protects against 7.62mm armour-piercing rounds from all distances. Maximum road speed 45-50km/h; water-7-8km/h. Weight without crew no more than 4 tonnes.
   To compel NKOP to by 1.12-1938 present on State trials the developed prototype of the tank.

2. Create two prototypes of a light tank.
   The first, pure tracked, armed with a 45mm gun, coaxial machine gun and 2 extra machine guns, with armour that can withstand armour-piercing 12.7mm rounds from all distances. Speed 50-60km/h, weight not over 13 tonnes. The second, wheel-track with 6 driving wheels, with the same armament and armour and a speed of 50-60km/h on tracks and wheels, not weighing more than 15 tonnes. A diesel engine to be common to both options.
   Both version of the tank are to be tested, and based on test results to take one of the tank options (tracked or wheel-tracked) into service to replace the existing T-26 and BT tanks.
   To compel NKOP to by 1.I-1939 to present on state tests both versions of these tanks.

3. To create a tank fighter, PTO, breakthrough tank.
   Type of tank-tracked. Armament-1x76mm gun, 2x45mm guns, co-axial machine gun and 3 machine guns.
   Armour to protect against 47mm calibre armour-piercing rounds at all distances. Speed not less than 35km/h. Weight not more than 55 tonnes. Tank to be taken into service to replace the T-28, T-29 and T-35 as having weak armour not protecting from damage by 37mm armour-piercing projectiles fired from a range of 1,000m. To oblige NKOP and NKMash to by 1.I-1939 present this tank on State trials. For the prototype, it is allowed to install the M-100 aircraft engine, followed by a transition to a 1,000hp diesel engine.

4. To oblige NKOP:
   a) Before 1.I-1939 to establish series production of 76mm tank guns with an initial velocity of [armour-piercing projectile] not lower than 560m/s;
   b) Develop and produce samples of a smaller-size large calibre machine gun for tanks and armoured cars and a standard calibre machine gun for replacement of the existing DT machine gun.

5. To oblige NKOP to in 1938 force work on making available armour impenetrable by a 47mm armour-piercing round from all distances.

6. In view of the fact that in existing tank types track service life is inadequate, to compel NKOP and NKMash to in 1938 provide sample tracks for all existing and planned tank types with a track life of at least 3,000km.

III. About the Types of Armoured Vehicles:

1. Production of BA-10 medium armoured cars on the GAZ-AAA chassis with M-1 engine and BA-20 light armoured cars on the M-1 chassis (is) to continue, upgrading them to strengthen the chassis and increase the bullet resistance of the armour, pending adoption of more sophisticated types.

2. To replace the existing armoured vehicles with more advanced ones, order NKMash and NKOP to create two types of armoured vehicle and present them for state trial no later than 1.12-38:
   a) A medium armoured vehicle with a 45mm gun with coaxial and additional machine gun, with armour protecting it from 7.62mm armour-piercing rounds from all distances, with a maximum speed of not less than 60km/hour; not weighing more than 7 tonnes, (mounted on a) three-axle chassis of the Stalin Plant (i.e. ZiS);
   b) Light armoured car with machine gun armament, with armour providing protection from 7.62mm calibre standard rounds from all distances, with maximum speed not below 70km/h, weighing 3-3.5 tonnes, on a Molotov plant based chassis (i.e. GAZ).

In accordance with the tank weapons system adopted by this Resolution to discontinue work on the following:
1) T-35 tank with 30mm armour;
2) T-29 tank;
3) STZ wheel-track tank;
4) Special reconnaissance tank, per Resolution KO №94ss".

RGVA F. 4. L. 14. C. 1974. pp. 9 - 13

Before submitting the above for discussion in the Defence Committee and reviewing the issue of changing the existing system of tank and other armoured weapons, it was resolved to convene a meeting of the newly created Supreme or Main Military Council of the Red Army (GVS), to which was assigned the consideration of major questions of organisation and infrastructure, military and mobilisation training, armaments and technical equipment of the Red Army. Copies of the draft letters to Molotov and the draft decision: *"About types of tanks for arming the armoured forces of the Red Army"* were by order of Voroshilov sent to members of the GVS for review and discussion. The meeting to consider the issue of changing the system of armored weapons was scheduled for 20th April 1938.

The Main Military Council (GVS) of the Red Army was

created on 13th March 1938 by a joint Resolution №322 of the Central Committee of the CPSU (b) and the SNK SSSR as an advisory body for the NKO. The same resolution appointed the People's Commissar of Defence of the Soviet Union, Marshal of the Soviet Union K. E. Voroshilov and the GVS members: Secretary of the Central Committee of the CPSU(b) Iosef Stalin; Deputy People's Commissar of Defence, Army Commander 1st rank I. F. Fedko; Deputy People's Commissar of Defence, Chief of the Political Directorate of the Red Army, Commissar 2nd rank L. Z. Mekhlis; Deputy People's Commissar of Defence, chief, command and personnel of the Red Army, Commissar 2nd rank E.A. Shchadenko; Deputy People's Commissar of Defence, chief of the General Staff of the Red Army, Commander 1st rank B. M. Shaposhnikov; the commander of OKDA, Marshal V. K. Blucher; the commander of the Moscow Military District (MVO), Marshal of the Soviet Union S. M. Budyonny and the chief of the Artillery Directorate of the Red Army, commander 2nd rank G.I. Kulik. By Resolution of the Central Committee of the TsK VKP(b) and SNK USSR №375 dated 22nd March 1938 the chief of GVS, Komkor A. D. Loktionov and the chief of ABTU, Komkor, D. G. Pavlov were also taken into the GVS structure.

In preparation for the planned 20th April 1938 meeting of the GVS, the report abstracts were drawn up, which set out Pavlov's views as chief of ABTU on the operational and tactical use of tanks in a future war, on the requirements for modern tanks, and on armoured weapons generally. In preparation for the meeting, Pavlov also collated materials on the main characteristics of tanks and armoured vehicles in service with the armies of "probable enemies" (specifically Germany, Poland and Japan), as well as on the anti-tank weapons of the armies of these countries. The envisioned use of tanks in a future war, was described by the chief of ABTU, as follows:

a) *The location of tank formations in the most important operational areas in peacetime will allow them to be used as invasion groups during the initial period of the war. The purpose of these groups:*

1) *Disruption of mobilisation, concentration and deployment of enemy forces in the main operational areas;*

2) *Capture and retention of the most important boundaries of operational and strategic importance;*

3) *Most importantly, postponing the outbreak of hostilities in enemy territory.*

4) *Ensuring that the situation is turned.*

b) *During wartime, tank units are one of the crucial means of defeating the main forces of the enemy, the action on the flanks and to the rear. In interaction with aircraft, cavalry and motorised infantry, tank units ensure defeat of the enemy attacked from the front.*

c) *Tactical use of tanks on the battlefield has become crucial. No army in the world, even the most backward, could conceive of fighting without the use of tanks. Tanks are the main weapon capable to fight successfully against the "scourge" of infantry machine guns".*

RGVA. F. 31811. L. 2. C. 804. pp. 1

Based on the tasks assigned to tank forces in any future war, Pavlov's report outlined the following basic requirements for modern tanks:

"a) Greater operational and tactical mobility, so that tanks can independently make large transitions and can quickly manoeuvre on the modern battlefield. This latter is necessary to hit more targets in a given time, but also for successful combat against the main enemy of tanks - small calibre (anti-tank) guns.

b) *Powerful armament - every tank must be able not only to attack but also to directly combat enemy armoured forces, i.e. to have a tank gun and only in extreme cases when it is impossible to break any of the basic requirements of tanks (weight, buoyancy etc.) is a heavy machine gun permissible. Machine gun armament is obligatory in all cases to combat infantry targets. The machine gun must have a higher rate of fire than in the infantry, so that in a very short moment (due to the pitching of the tank) it can aim, and fire the number of rounds needed to defeat the target.*

It is highly desirable to equip the tank with a powerful gun to obtain a strong explosive projectile effect, but since this is almost impossible, it is necessary to go have some tanks with powerful (76mm) guns. Hence the need to have "art-tanki" (artillery tanks) organisationally included in the tank units, that accompany tanks throughout the battle.

c) *Armour - to have shellproof armour on all machines is impossible. However, it is necessary in the weapon system of the army to have at least part of these machines with armour that will resist shells of up to 47mm at all distances. Such tanks would have special tasks - combatting enemy anti-tank guns - and thus allowing other tanks not to be distracted from their main task - the fight against anti-personnel means.*

d) *It is Necessary to have some tanks which could be applied for capture and holding of large river barriers, to work as a part of landings and to fight on water with landings of the opponent, i.e. amphibious machines are necessary".*

In addition, the thesis emphasized that "only the mass use of tanks, whether in cooperation with infantry or independently, can bring success. Massed use of tanks is absolutely necessary, if we consider the saturation of modern guns for the defence of our probable opponents, when only special anti-tank guns have up to 10pcs per battalion (on a front of 2-3km), not counting the heavy machine guns in the battalions and the divisional and regimental guns of 75mm cali-

bre. Given the probability of defeat of tanks at a ratio of up to 3 times more than the guns of the tanks (i.e. each tank destroys three tanks in a battle), we can assume that less than two battalions of tanks against the front of defence is impractical. Of course, artillery bombardment can significantly reduce that figure, but the fact remains, you need a larger number of tanks to achieve a solution."

RGVA. F. 31811. L. 2. C. 804. pp. 3

Domestic tanks and armoured vehicles in service with the Red Army were, in general, considered highly. According to Pavlov, in overall combat properties, Soviet tanks were not only not inferior, but were in fact superior to most tanks produced in capitalist countries. *"However, as was rightly noted in the thesis of the report, technology is moving forward, all kinds of forces are developing further towards improvement, and we can not lag behind if we want to fulfil the tasks set before us. The socialist industry can supply us with all the necessary machines and we have to give it our order."* But to issue the order to industry, (we as) command of the Red Army first of all have to find out what types of armoured weapons were necessary for the army at the time". Setting himself the question: *"What do we need?",* Pavlov responded to his own question:

"a) **Breakthrough tank-PTO** *(anti-tank gun) fighter that will perform its tasks without fear of anti-tank guns - the main enemy of tanks. Type of tank-tracked. Armament 1x76mm and 2x45mm gun; co-axial machine gun and 3 machine guns. Armour that protects from armour-piercing 37mm shells from all distances. Speed not below 35km/h. Weight not more than 55 tonnes. This tank should replace the T-28 and T-35 tanks, as they are vulnerable to defeat from 37mm rounds fired from 1,000m range.*

b) **Light tank** *to replace the BT and T-26, for which to create two tank types:*

1) **Wheel-track tank** *with 6 wheels, armed with a 45mm gun, co-axial machine gun and 2 extra machine guns, with armour impenetrable to 12.7mm calibre armour-piercing bullets from all distances; with a speed 50-60km/h on wheels and tracks; weight not exceeding 15 tonnes. Engine-diesel.*

2) **A purely tracked tank** *with the same characteristics as a whe-el-tracked tank, but weighing not more than 14 tonnes. After extensive testing to adopt one of these two tanks.*

c) **An amphibious tank** *is needed to replace the T-37 and T-38 tanks. Purpose-capture of large river barriers, participation in landing operations, coastal defence. Tracked tank. Armament-12.7mm large-calibre machine gun, paired with a standard 7.62mm calibre machine gun. Armour must protect against 7.62mm armour-piercing rounds from all distances; maximum speed on roads 45-50km/h; on water 7-8km/h. Weight without crew not more than 4 tonnes.*

d) **Armoured reconnaissance vehicles of 2 types:**

The first type is a light armoured vehicle, armed with a 12.7mm heavy machine gun paired with a standard calibre machine-gun with armour impervious to a standard calibre bullet. The second type is a medium armoured vehicle armed with a 45mm gun paired with a machine gun to support the light armoured vehicle.

3. **Today we have a huge tank Park of fighting vehicles that will remain for the next years in our system of arms.** *This Park must be actively improved and upgraded, preserving however, the main requirement that the components of upgraded machines must be interchangeable.*

4. **On what design and modernisation directions should new machines develop?**

a) **Armour** *- the creation of two-layer and multi-layer armour. A (sealing) device on the tank's hull and turret should allow crossing of water obstacles to a depth of not less than 5 metres along the bottom.*

b) **Weight** *should decrease due to an improvement in armour quality and reducing the weight of non-critical parts.*

c) **Dimensions** *of new machines must meet the following conditions: heavy tanks-must allow to their transportation by rail. Light and amphibious tanks-must allow for transportation by vehicles, without reducing battlefield potency.*

d) **Engine power** *for heavy (tank) 860-1,000hp, for BT-500hp, for T-26-125hp, for amphibians 70-80hp, armoured cars-standard engines of the automotive industry.*

d) **Speed of movement** *should increase.*

e) **Suspension** *- to achieve from tracks a service life of at least 3,000km travel on gravel ground.*

f) **Transmission** *- must have enough strength to withstand dynamic forces on the battlefield. To increase the margin of safety against current standards*

g) **Turret** *- increase the volume to improve the conditions of loading weapons, laying ammunition and placement of communication and control mechanisms. Simplify the traverse mechanisms and make them more durable. To seal the connection between the turret and the hull.*

h) **Armament** *- to improve the position of aiming mechanisms. To solve the problem of ejecting the shell casings from the tank, using the hatch in the hull floor for crew exit. Maximise tank the ammunition complement.*

i) **Observation and aiming devices.** *Together with optical devices have mechanical sights in case of failure of the former. Improve and expanding the field of view from the tank. Consider small observation devices for the hatches.*

j) **Location of mechanisms.** *All mechanisms must have easy access for adjustment and replacement.*

k) **The range of the tank of any type.** *To be not less than 200km.*

l) **Finally, install the communication system inside the machine and between tanks.** *To reduce the dimensions of VHF ra-*

dio to a minimum, to provide to line tanks without reducing the ammunition of the latter.

m) To provide a simple device to overcome swamps. *Not all amphibious tanks are able to do go under water"*

RGVA. F.31811. L.2. C.804. pp11-14

Along with the abstracts of Pavlov's report, ABTU leadership in preparation for the upcoming meeting of the GVS of the Red Army on 8th April 1938 drafted the GVS decision *"on types of tanks for arming tank forces of the Red Army"*. The content of this document is almost fully consistent with the draft decision of the KO of 17th March 1938 with the exception of absence of instruction to the Commissariats of the Defence Industry (NKO) and Machine Building (NKMash) on the date of manufacture of tank and armoured vehicle prototypes. Looking ahead, the GVS draft resolution dated 8th April 1938 was rejected. However, almost all of the listed events to change the system of armoured weapons of the Red Army was reflected in Protocol №4 of the GVS meeting held in the Kremlin on 20th April 1938, attended by all GVS members, except the commander of OKDA, Marshal V. K. Blucher. Among those invited to the meeting, was the Military Commissar of ABTU, brigade-engineer Alliluyev. The second point on the agenda of the meeting was the issue: *"on the system of tank weapons and the plan of NKO orders (purchases) for 1938"*. As a result of the discussion, the following decision was made:

"Given the experience of combat training and operation requirements for tanks in modern warfare the following system of tank weapons is to be adopted:

1. In the army have four main types of tanks:

1) Breakthrough tank (PTO fighter.) (i.e. to overcome anti-tank guns) with the following tactical and technical data

a) Tracked type;

b) Armour-60mm, impenetrable at all distances by anti-tank guns up to 47mm in calibre;

c) Engine-M-34, taking into account in the design the tank transition to diesel engine;

d) Armament-1x76mm, with an initial muzzle velocity of not less than 560m/s; 2x45mm guns, coaxial machine gun; one machine gun with anti-aircraft guns;

e) Speed - 25-35km/h;

f) Range - 200-250km/h;

g) Weight-no more than 55 tonnes, with dimensions allowing railway transportation.

To ask the Defence Committee to oblige the People's Commissariat of Machine Building (NKMash) to manufacture a prototype breakthrough tank and to begin trials in February 1939.

2) Leave the army with T-26 and BT tanks, improving them with part shell-proof armour, improved suspension and better weapons. In addition, for the T-26 tank, install the 120hp engine, and for BT tanks, install a diesel engine.

The listed improvements are to be made on the principle of full interchangeability of units and mechanisms on the existing tank park.

3) To be armed with an amphibious tank with the following basic tactical and technical data:

a) Tracked type;

b) Armour-protecting from 7.62mm calibre armour-piercing rounds from all distances;

c) Engine - "Dodge" (75hp);

d) Armament - heavy machine gun, standard calibre coaxial machine gun;

d) Speed on road - 45-50km/h, on water - 7-8 km/h;

e) Road range - 200-250km;

f) Total weight - no more than 4 tonnes.

The amphibious tank is intended to replace the existing T-37 and T-38.

Pending the production of a new amphibious tank, to maintain the mobilisation assignment in 1938 to T-38 tanks.

To ask the Defence Committee to oblige the People's Commissariat of the Defence Industry (NKOP)to put an amphibious tank on test no later than January 1939.

4) To continue production of T-28 and T-35 tanks and spare parts for them, improving the armament by installing the (76.2mm)"L-10" gun, to increase the armour resistance and strengthen the drivetrain and chassis. Improve the design on the principle of full interchangeability of components and mechanisms with the existing Park of machines.

With the (attainment of) mass production of breakthrough tanks referred to in paragraph 1, to remove the T-28 and T-35 tanks from production. < ... >

2. In order to further improve the tanks, to create two prototypes - one tracked and the second wheel-tracked with six drive wheels. Both tanks must meet the following basic tactical and technical requirements:

a) Armour on vulnerable places-30mm;

b) Engine-diesel engine common for both tanks;

c) Armament-1x45mm gun with co-axial standard calibre machine gun and 2 additional machine guns, 1 adapted for anti-aircraft fire;

g) Speed - 50-60km/h;

e) Range - 250-300km;

f) Weight - on tracks 13-14 tonnes, and on wheels 15-16 tonnes.

To request the Defence Committee to oblige the NKOP to hand over both types of tanks for testing no later than February 1939.

3. *Reducing the armour thickness requires a sharp improvement in its quality and resilience, and to reduce the weight of the tank. To ask the Defence Committee to take the necessary steps for the production of two-layer and ekrani (shielded) armour.*

4. *To ask the Defence Committee to oblige the People's Commissariat of the Defence Industry (NKOP) and the People's Commissariat of Machine Building (NKMash) to improve the quality of tracks by manufacturing in 1938 samples of tracks a track life of not less than 3,000km. (currently track duration is 1,000-1,500km.).*

< ... >

7. *To ask the Defence Committee to stop development of the T-29 tank, the STZ wheel-tracked tank and the reconnaissance tank, as not meeting performance requirements.*

8. *In order to fully identify the combat and operational data in armoured tanks and to discuss the tactical and technical conditions proposed by this Protocol for new models, a tank meeting is to be convened on 28 April.*

Invite to the meeting:

1) Management of the tank units and crews with training and combat experience;

2) Designers and engineers of the tank industry.

The People's Commissar of Defence to determine the number of participants.

9. *The attached proposal of the Head of the Armoured Directorate (ABTU) on the withdrawal from service and utilisation of existing obsolete types of tanks, to approve and submit for (further) approval to the Committee of Defence."*

RVGA. F. 4. L. 19. C. 28. pp. 36-46

Only a few days were left to determine the composition of the tank meetings, as demanded by Paragraph 8 of the Protocol №4 of the meeting of the GVS. The document entitled *"draft composition of the meeting"* was signed on 22nd April 1938 by Pavlov and Alliluyev. The meeting was to include representatives of the Red Army ABTU, VAMM, the tank industry, and about 40 "tankisti" from Red Army tank crews with combat experience, to the mechanised corps commanders. The Tank meeting was held as planned in the Kremlin on 28th April 1938, but due to the large volume of issues to be discussed, was continued the following day in the buildings of ABTU RKKA. The Tank meeting was attended by over 70 people, including management of the auto-armoured-tank, artillery, engineering and chemical commands of the army; the command of communications of the Red Army; representatives of the NKOP and NKMash, the heads of the 7th and 8th GU NKOP, the KB (design bureau) heads of Plants №37, 174, 183, 185 and the Kirovsky plant, and representatives from military units - the aforementioned tankers with combat experience.

Before the Tank meeting started, the bulk of its partici-

pants were on 27th April 1938 required to sign a non-disclosure agreement - putting their signatures opposite their names in the list printed after the words: *"I UNDERTAKE NOT to DISCLOSE and KEEP in COMPLETE SECRECY ALL HEARD at the SPECIAL MEETING, 27 APRIL in 1938 in ABTU, of DESIGNERS AND REPRESENTATIVES of MILITARY units"*. As a result of comprehensive discussions, the participants of the Tank meeting were of the unanimous opinion that the decision about the new system of armoured forces adopted at the original meeting of GVS on 20th April 1938 fully met the needs of the Red Army. The meeting discussed in detail the characteristics of the new tanks and developed TTTs for the design and manufacture of prototypes of the new breakthrough tank, the T-40 tracked amphibious tank, as well as significantly adjusted TTTs for the A-20 tank, the design of which was returned to Plant №183 for further development. In addition, the meeting identified actions to improve the combat characteristics of tanks and armoured vehicles already in Red Army service and in mass production.

The main differences between the TTTs for the design and manufacture of the A-20 tank from the TTTs for the same tank originally approved in October 1937, were:

- Increase in tank weight up to 16.5 tonnes;
- Increased thickness of the main armour parts of the hull and turret;
- Crew increased to 4;
- Increased 76.2mm ammunition complement to 75 rounds;
- Deletion of the flamethrower for self-defence.

Following the Protocol of the Tank Meeting, discussion of the design of light wheel-track and tracked tanks was undertaken by 17 people, including the head of Bureau "24" (KB-24) at Plant №183, M. I. Koshkin, the chief of ABTU, D. G. Pavlov, recently returned from Spain where he had served as Commander of the International tank regiment, S. I. Kondratyev; his technical Deputy A. A. Vetrov, and other tankers involved in the fighting.

The requirements and proposals to improve the design of the designed A-20 tank put forward by Pavlov during the discussion were: *"to recognise the design proposed by Plant №183 as acceptable, with the reinforcement of the frontal armour. Electrical wiring to be simplified. Turret to be adapted for mounting 76mm armament. 4 crew, the antenna mounted on the hull. Radio operator alongside the driver. Move the radio from the turret. Communication between the commander and the radio operator by means of talk-tubes (TPU system). Gun elevation 45°"*. The meeting participants adopted the improvements unanimously.

RGVA. F.31811. L.2. C.745. pp38

Also at the Tank meeting, an agreement was reached between the heads of the tank and chemical departments of the Red Army on the development of TTTs for the design and manufacture of removable smoke dischargers for the A-20, T-38 and the new "breakthrough tank", as well as TTTs for a stationary flamethrower for the A-20 tank. Already on 11th May 1938 the specified TTTs were together with Letter № 437138ss, signed by the head of chemical control of the Red Army Corps, Commander M. O. Stepanov and acting military Commissioner of the Department, Regimental Commissar, G. N. Dmitriev, and sent to ABTU.

It took the staff of the 8th Department of ABTU two weeks to process the tank design for the plan submission meeting with the People's Commissar of Defence of the USSR. On 13th May 1938, Pavlov and Alliluyev sent to the chief of the NKO administration Kombrig (brigade commander) M. G. Snegov with Letter №284797ss a packet of documents, including the report in the name of K. E. Voroshilov, the TTTs for the design and manufacture of prototypes of the breakthrough tank, wheel-tracked A-20 tank, amphibious T-40 tank, and the STZ-25 and STZ-35 tanks, all in triplicate, together with one copy of the lists of works to improve the combat and technical characteristics of serial production tanks and armoured vehicles, as well as their weapons and communications.

Referring in a letter to Snegov, ABTU leadership requested not only to: *"report to the People's Commissar of Defence Marshal of the Soviet Union comrade Voroshilov all materials with the project of the decision of the Supreme Military Council of the Red Army №4 dated 20 April"*, but considered it *"required that all the mate-*

rials to combine in one or two draft resolution on the whole system of armaments, and the removal of unfit and obsolete tanks."

RGVA. F. 31811. L. 2. C. 842. pp. 7

In addition, by Letter №284797ss dated 14th May 1938 the chief of the 4th Department of ABTU, military engineer 1st rank N. T. Minaev sent to Snegov the second and third copies of lists of works on improvement of combat and technical characteristics of the series of tanks and armoured vehicles, signed by Pavlov and Alliluyev. At the end of May 1938, ABTU prepared draft resolutions of the Defence Committee (KO) *"On the system of tank weapons and on the use of existing in the Red Army of non-series production old tank types"*. On 31st May 1938 this draft resolution together with Letter №285293 was sent to the NKO for subsequent approval by the Defence Committee. The TTTs for the breakthrough tank and T-40 amphibious tank, and the modified TTTs for the A-20 tank were approved by K. E. Voroshilov on 2nd June 1938. Minor changes were made to the draft resolution of the KO *"on the system of tank weapons"*, after which a set of documents was formed within the management of NKO, sent to the KO Chairman V. M. Molotov by Letter №9608ss signed by K. E. Voroshilov on 14th June 1938. The final version of the draft resolution *"on the system of tank weapons"* had significant differences from the first version, which was called *"on the types of tanks for arming the tank troops of the Red Army"* and developed in March 1938 in ABTU under the leadership of D. G. Pavlov.

In the last version of the draft resolution, the procedure for the development and manufacture of prototype breakthrough tanks was spelled out more specifically. Design work on STZ light tanks with enhanced armour - the wheel-tracked STZ-25 and tracked STZ-35, was also, contrary to the initial opinion of Pavlov, proposed to continue. Having reviewed the above set of documents, the KO proceeded to adopt the draft Resolution *"On the system of tank armaments"* between all concerned in its implementation, namely the NKO, NKOP and NKMash commissariats. The first comments and suggestions to the text of the draft resolution were received from the People's Commissar of the Defence Industry M. Kaganovich in Letter №1159ss dated 23rd June 1938, addressed to the People's Commissar of Defence of the USSR, K. E. Voroshilov, in which he in particular, noted:

"1. The presented tactical and technical requirements for new tank types are endorsed by me. However, given that they contain a number of new challenges for the Design Bureau, I would consider it necessary to amend the draft resolution with an additional paragraph as follows: "After the development of the draft design tactical and technical requirements for tanks specified in the resolution (paragraphs 1 - 4 section 1) are subject to clarification of the NKO together with NKOP." The need for this paragraph is

List of individuals undertaking to keep secret everything heard at the "tank meeting". A rare document, dated 27th April 1938, with the signatures of the tank plant KB chiefs.

dictated by the considerations that the resolution of new design problems existing in tactical and technical requirements can create a greater delay in the design and creation of new models and disrupt the time specified in the draft resolution."

RGVA. F.4. L.19. C.55. pp127

A similar letter was sent by the KO M. M. Kaganovich. Comments and suggestions from the People's Commissariat of Machine Building (NKmash), mainly related to the production timing of new tank prototypes, were later provided to the KO. The delay in the submission of comments to the draft decree was caused by a change of leadership at the People's Commissariat following the arrest of A. D. Bruskin on charges of participating in a *"counter-revolutionary terrorist organisation"*. He was replaced by V. K. Lvov, who had previously held the position of Director of the Kirov plant in Leningrad; he being appointed as the People's Commissar of Machine Building (NKMash) on 16th July 1938. The draft Decree №198ss/s *"On the system tank weapons"* was after all approvals ultimately adopted at a meeting of the Defence Committee on 7th August 1938. The previous week, on 1st August 1938, Resolution №180ss *"On the use of existing Red Army custom-made old tank types"* had been passed at a meeting of the Defence Committee.

Thus, with the adoption of KO Resolution №198ss/ov dated 7th August 1938 and Resolution №180ss from 1st August 1938, the question of a fundamental revision of the system of the armoured weapons of the Red Army raised by the ABTU chief Pavlov in February 1938, had been resolved positively in less than six months. KO Resolution №198ss/s adopted a new system of armoured forces armaments, including the following types of tanks:

"1. Breakthrough tank (PTO fighter) tracked type is made according to ABTU tactical and technical data, developed on the basis of the Tank Meeting and approved by the People's Commissar of Defence (Annex №1).

a) To Oblige NKMmash to produce and transfer to NKO for testing a prototype breakthrough tank by May 1, 1939.

b) To Compel NKOP to produce and transfer to NKO for test a prototype breakthrough tank by July 1, 1939. A wooden model of the breakthrough tank to be presented to the Commission by September 1, 1938.

c) To Oblige NKO to demonstrate prototypes of breakthrough tanks with comprehensive testing, and choose one sample meeting the requirements for a breakthrough tank to present to the Red Army.

d) A statement on the mass production of T-28 and T-35 breakthrough tanks, and their removal from production.

2. In order to further improve the tanks create using the ABTU

tactical and technical data developed in a tank meeting and approved by the People's Commissar of Defence, produce three prototype tanks, two tracked and one wheeled-tracked with 6 wheels (Appendix №2). One of the tracked tanks is manufactured as a chemical tank type.

a) To Compel NKOP to produce and transfer to NKO for test, prototypes of tanks by June 1, 1939. A wooden mock-up model of the tank to present to the Commission by 1 October, 1938.

b) To Oblige NKO to expose tank prototypes to comprehensive comparative tests and choose one sample to present to the army, completely meeting designated tank requirements.

3. To oblige NKMash to create at the Stalingrad tractor plant (STZ) based on the tactical and technical characteristics approved by the People's Commissar of Defence (Appendix 3), three samples of light tanks with reinforced armour-two tracked and one wheel-tracked. One tracked tank to be manufactured as a chemical tank.

a) Two samples of light tanks-tracked and wheel-tracked to be transferred to NKO for test by 1 January, 1939, the third sample of the light tank-tracked chemical tank-to transfer to NKO for testing by July 1, 1939. The wooden mock-up model of the tank to transfer to the Commission by 1 September, 1938.

b) To Oblige NKO to subject the tank prototypes, prepared by NKMash to comprehensive comparative tests with the T-26 tank to address the question of presenting the best of the samples for the armed forces, replacing the T-26.

4. Create based on the tactical and technical data approved by the People's Commissar of Defence, an amphibious tracked tank with a more powerful engine, weapons and armour, intended to replace the existing T-37 and T-38 tanks (Annex №4).

(a) Require NKOP to manufacture and submit to NKO for testing a prototype amphibious tank by 1 January 1939. A wooden mock-up model of an amphibious tank to present to the Commission to September 1, 1938".

GARF. F.8418. L.28. C.35. pp215-216

The People's Commissariats of the Defence Industry (NKOP) and Machine-Building (NKMash) were also instructed *"in the development of prototypes of combat vehicles to provide the maximum possible inclination of plates on hulls and turrets."* The same Resolution listed for NKOP and NKMash controlled plants the tank types subject to serial production in 1938 and in 1939, NKOP undertook *"in order to improve armour resistance"* to *"sharply improve armour quality and to boost production of thicker armour for breakthrough tanks by means of double-layer and ekranirovanni (shielded) armour"*. The results of the work on improving armour durability was required to be reported to the KO by 1st October 1938.

In addition, pursuant to Resolution №198ss/s, all work on

the wheel-tracked T-29 and T-46 tanks, the unnamed reconnaissance tank, AT-1 artillery tank and self-propelled 203mm howitzer B-4 installation was discontinued, and in accordance with KO Resolution №94ss dated 15th August 1937, was cancelled in its entirety.

Pursuant to Defence Committee Resolution №198ss/s *"on the system of tank weapons of the Red Army"* People's Commissar of NKOP, M. Kaganovich on 21st August 1938 signed Order № 335ss, according to which the head of the 8th GU NKOP, demanded that:

"By June 1, 1939 Plant №183 is to produce and transmit to NKO for testing three tank prototypes, two tracked and one wheel-tracked with 6 driven wheels. One tracked tank is to be produced as a chemical tank type. Tanks shall be made according to the ABTU tactical and technical data approved by the People's Commissar of Defence (Appendix №2). A wooden model of the tank is to be presented to the prototype Commission to October 1, 1938".

RGAEh. F.7515. L.1. C.231. pp46

While in the spring and summer of 1938 the upper echelons of power in Moscow reviewed changes to the system of armoured weapons of the Red Army, work continued at KB-24 at Plant №183 in Kharkov on the A-20 wheel-tracked tank design. After the previously noted A-20 draft design technical meeting held in ABTU on 25th March 1938, a still understaffed team at KB-24 began to develop a technical project of the new machine. In order to accelerate work on the A-20 tank design at the urgent request of the chief of the 8th GU NKOP, V.D. Sviridov, the staff of KB-24 was at the end of April 1938 increased from 19 to 29 employees by transferring engineers from other departments at Plant №183, albeit the staff complement at KB-24 should have already been 37 people by that date. Nevertheless, despite the shortage of specialists, the staff of KB-24, headed by M.I. Koshkin, worked to complete the government task in a timely manner. Recalling that period, one of the creators of the T-34 tank, A. A. Moloshtanov described the atmosphere that reigned in KB-24:

"I can not say that M. I. Koshkin was a born organiser. But (his) energy really was boiling, he was obsessed with the new tank and managed to convey that obsession to all of us. Despite the extreme complexity of the task, we did not doubt its reality for a moment and did not spare ourselves for the sake of achieving the goal. I was instructed to develop a blueprint for the conical turret with the largest possible angle of inclination of the side armour. Like everyone else in the KB, I worked with great enthusiasm and was proud of this honour".

T-34: Path to Victory: The Memoirs of Tank Builders and Tank Crews. Ed. : K. M. Slobodin, V. D. Listrov, Publishing House of Political Literature of Ukraine, 1989, pp. 16

Until 15th May 1938 the primary initial materials for the development of the technical design of the A-20 tank were the TTTs dated 11th October 1937 and the comments set out in the minutes of the meeting on the consideration of the draft design of this tank, approved on 26th March 1938 by D. G. Pavlov. In the second half of May, 1938 at a meeting in the 8th GU NKOP, representatives of ABTU at Plant №183 were presented with the changes to the TTTs reviewed at the Tank Meeting (but not yet approved by Voroshilov) for the design and manufacture of the A-20 tank. In accordance with these new requirements, M. I. Koshkin was as the head of KB-24 asked by the leadership of the 8th Department of ABTU to rework the previously approved draft design of the A-20 wheel-tracked tank, as well as to begin work on the design of an A-20 variant with tracked (only) drive.

A difficult situation again existed at Plant №183 at the end of May 1938. On 25th May 1938 the Director of Plant №183, I. P. Bondarenko was arrested on charges of leading an *"anti-Soviet right-wing organisation"* and *"cooperation with German intelligence"*. Prior to the appointment of a new director, his responsibilities were until the end of October 1938 undertaken by the head of the Production Department of Plant №183, P. Parfenov. On 7th and 8th July 1938, Parfenov hosted ABTU management who had arrived at the plant for a review of future tank developments, organised by ABTU chief Pavlov and division engineer Alliluyev.

During these two days, ABTU leadership now on the ground at Kharkov learned the situation regarding series BT-7 tank production, preparation of the V-2 diesel engine for serial production and for the A-8 (planned BT-8) tank fitted with this new diesel engine. Being in Kharkov, Pavlov and Alliluyev also inspected two tanks developed by F. Tsyganov - the BT-5-IS tank with six driven wheels, and the BT-SV-2 "Cherepakha" tank based on the BT-7 tank but with heavily sloped hull and turret armour. It was due to the peculiar shape of the hull that the BT-SV-2 tank was called "Cherepakha" * even in official correspondence.

M. I. Koshkin (KB-24) and N. Kucherenko (KB-190) were present during the ABTU senior management inspection of the BT-SV-2 tank at Plant №183. The extent to which Koshkin's acquaintance with the "Cherepakha" influenced the subsequent design of the hull and turret of the A-20, and subsequently the T-34, is to date not confirmed from available documents. However, in several memoirs written by direct participants of those meetings, it is noted that the shape of the armoured hull of the BT-SV-2 tank as proposed by N. F. Tsyganov was adopted for the base hull design of the T-34 tank. E. A. Kulchitsky, who led the testing of both the BT-SV-2 and A-20 tanks, recollected in his memoirs that:

"In 1935 senior military engineer N. F. Tsyganov arrived in Moscow with proposals to improve the BT tank. With the aim of

---

* *"Cherepakha" in Russian can be translated both as turtle, and as tortoise.*

68

increasing the armour protection of the hull it was suggested to place the armour plates not vertically per tradition, but at a large angle of inclination. Apart from the ideas and pencil drawings of the machine, and its shape resembling a "Cherepakha", there was nothing (new) from Tsyganov. But, thanks to his energy and dedication, he was able to interest the highest authorities, and as a result of the work done on their behalf, it was found that the ideas deserved attention. Plant №183 was recommended in the future when designing new machines to take into account these proposals."*

T-34: Path to Victory: The memoirs of tank builders and tank crews. Ed. : K. M. Slobodin, V. D. Listrov, Publishing House of Political Literature of Ukraine, 1989, pp. 16

P. Vasiliev, one of the designers of the "thirty four", and winner of the Stalin Prize in the Preface to the documentary novel by Ya. L. Resnik, "The Creation of Armour" issued by the (Soviet) military publishing house in 1987, wrote the following:

"In "the creation of the armour" characters were under their real names, except M. I. Koshkin, appearing within several other characters. These are, in particular, the successor to Mikhail Ilyich Koshkin for KB the talented designer Alexander Morozov, a veteran of the plant Vasily Fomich Zakharov and deputy tank company inventor Nikolai Fedorovich Tsyganov. I worked there in the years of his military service; the shape of the hull of the BT-IS (Tsyganov's machine) was adopted in the hull of the T-34".

From a draft of the response by Kucherenko on the letter by P. N. Goryun on the preparation of the V. D. Listrov books about the creation of the T-34 (written notes dated March 1976):

"What is it you, Pasha, worried about Tsyganov? It will not scratch it out. He was a natural, though, and adventurer. Were we not

adventurers? And moreover there there is in the machine from Tsyganov (something of value) not to remove from a tank (design)…"*

*Nikolia Kucherenko: Fifty years in the battle for tanks of the USSR. L. N. Vasilyeva, I. G. Zheltov RKPOO "Atlantis - XXI century", 2009, p. 273

Back in July 1938, with Pavlov and Alliluyev having returned to Moscow, KB-24 increased the development temp on the technical project for the A-20 wheel-tracked tank. The project had already studied two versions of the tank - one with a wheel-tracked chassis, the other tracked, with the latter tank having received the designation "A-20 Gus."**

Despite the fact that the modified TTTs for the A-20 tank were approved by K. E. Voroshilov on 2nd June 1938, the text of these new requirements was not received at Plant №183 until the development of the technical project was almost complete, and design of the tank required a number of clarifying documents and instructions. As Koshkin rightly noted, *"all this in the process of developing the project of the A-20 tank required several times to process the same components of the tank and subject the latter to strength test calculations"*. The development of the technical project failed to be completed by the end of the summer, and only on 27th August 1938, the head of KB-24 M. I. Koshkin and the Project Director A. Morozov signed an "Explanatory Memorandum to the technical project of the A-20 and A-20 tank."

The explanatory note, 110 drawings, 10 technical calculations on the strength of individual components and mechanisms of the A-20 and A-20 "Gus." tanks together with the model of the A-20 tank were on 6th September 1938 provided to the prototype Committee chaired by the chief of the 8th Department of ABTU RKKA, military engineer 1st rank Y. L. Skvirskiy at Plant № 183.

The BT-SV-2 "Cherepakha" tank developed by N.F. Tsyganov.

** *Gus. - Gusenichny (tracked).*

Chapter 6

From Design to Prototypes

The technical design of the A-20 wheel-track tank as developed within Bureau "24" had a number of significant changes in comparison with the draft design, mainly related to improving the armour protection. Based on the modified TTTs the hull and turret armour plate thickness was increased from 20mm to 25mm, with the angle of inclination also increased (see diagram). The horizontal armour plates were unchanged.

In addition to the armour changes, the hull of the A-20 was also modified in the technical project. In order to provide better working conditions for the driver-mechanic and machine-gunner-radio operator, the frontal part of the hull was widened, with the vertical side armour moved forward as far as possible. To ensure correct operation of the front pair of steering wheels the hull nose was 122mm narrower than the rest of the hull, which had a width of 1,784mm. The narrowing of the hull began at the level of the second suspension unit balancer.

To simplify production, the lower vertical section hull sides consisted of two side plates. The join between these plates was angled at 20°, with the plates connected by a docking bar, located within the hull. In the forward part of the front side plate, where it connected with the hull floor there was a cutout, designed for passage of the suspension mounting of the first road wheel closed internally by two armour parts forming a niche "pocket" for the suspension rocker arm. The height of the upper part of the hull sides (i.e. above the track guards) was increased from 400 to 430mm compared with the draft design.

The hull glacis, according to the technical project, consisted of upper and lower armour plates, the thickness of which

relative to the conceptual design was increased from 16mm to 20mm. In order to strengthen the glacis for use as a form of battering ram for destroyimg obstacles, the lower glacis plate was made of armour plate located at an angle of 64° with a radius of curvature of 110mm. The lower plate was angled at 57° to the vertical, and the upper plate set at an angle of 53°. To enhance the ballistic strength of the lower glacis at the point of bending an additional 10mm thick armour plate was welded internally across the entire width of the hull.

The design of the A-20 hull rear was simplified compared with the draft design. Instead of three armoured sections, it now consisted of 16mm thick upper and lower armour plates, both set at an angle of 45° to the vertical. The hull floor escape hatch, located in the fighting compartment near the engine bulkhead in the conceptual design, was moved directly in front of the driver-mechanic's seat. The calculated weight of the A-20 "korpus" (hull and turret) was 5,800kg of which 4,650kg was armour.

The thickness of the A-20 turret side armour plates was in the technical project now 25mm, angled at 25° from the vertical. The turret race was increased in diameter by 70mm, providing for an enlarged turret with better internal space. The turret rear DT machine gun was deleted; and on the turret roof a P-40 mount was provided for a DT anti-aircraft machine gun. The maximum elevation of the 45mm tank gun and co-axial 7.62mm DT machine gun was reduced from 65° to a still significant 45°. Sighting and observation devices, and the placement of the ammunition complement remained generally as in the draft project. The additional armour basis increased the design weight of the A-20 to 17 tonnes, which in accordance

A-20 tank armour layout.

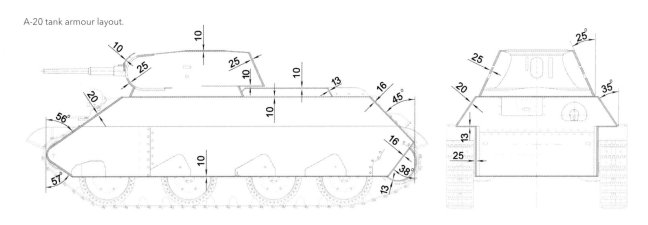

Title and last pages of the A-20 and A-20 Gus.
tank technical project summary.

with contemporary Soviet tank weight classification moved the A-20 tank from being designated as a light tank to being a classified as a medium tank.

The chassis, engine and transmission of the A-20 tank did not undergo significant changes compared with the draft design. The A-20 gearbox was according to revised ABTU data now a four-speed type. Of the four options originally considered for transmission of torque to the 2nd, 3rd and 4th road wheel pairs, as considered in the original technical project, the first option was chosen - with a transverse drive shaft and gear reducers. Moreover, the drive to the road wheels was selected in such a way that the wheel and track speed was identical. This feature of synchronous operation allowed the tank to move even when *"one side is working on tracks and one on wheels"*, and in addition, the tank could still move on tracks using the driven road wheels even if the main drive wheel was damaged. The design provided for the shutdown of drive to one side of the tank, and to each wheel separately. Due to the enlargement of the driver-mechanic's compartment, the angle of rotation of the steering wheel was reduced to 15°, and the track tension mechanisms were relocated within the hull glacis.

Pursuant to decision of the Defence Committee (KO) №198ss/s dated 7th August 1938, the designers of "Bureau-24" (KB-24) simultaneously with the A-20 wheel-track tank designed a tracked only version designated A-20 Gus. (Gus - "gusenichny" - tracked), developed as a separate technical project, with the explanatory memorandum to the technical project for the A-20 Gus. stating:

"With the cancellation of the (need for) wheeled travel, the design of the A-20 tank is greatly simplified, and the resulting reduction in

the total weight of the tank allows for placement in the turret of a more powerful weapon in the form of an L-10 gun, without increasing the weight of the tank, over the estimated 1,700kg. The simplification of the tank design entails the cancellation of a number of parts that were inherent to the wheeled vehicle, namely:

1) Gears - 30pcs. 2) Spline couplings and bushings - 42pcs.
3) Ball bearings - 46pcs. 4) Universal joints - 12pcs.
5) Steel castings - 14pcs.

Besides, when this is achieved, together with complete inter-changeability of all wheels and balancers on the machine, with eliminates the necessity of manufacturing right and left handed balancers. The design of the tank hull with cancellation of the front steering wheels straightens the hull, increasing the width of the hull in this (driver's) location by 122mm, which provides greater freedom in placing the crew in the front of the hull. Ammunition stowage in the floor of the tank becomes a simpler construction design and ensures the placement of more ammunition. Roughly we can expect an (unspecified) increase in 45mm shells and 630 machine-gun rounds (10 clips). <...> All other components and mechanisms of the tank remain universal between the wheel-tracked and purely tracked vehicles."

RGVA. F.31811. L.2. C.842. pp312-314

The tactical and technical characteristics (TTKhs) of the A-20 and A-20 Gus. tanks in comparison with the BT-7 tank were presented in the form of Annex №1 to the Explanatory Memorandum to the technical project.

The technical design and layout of the A-20 tank was reviewed in the beginning of September 1938 by a development Commission under the chairmanship of the chief of the 8th Department of ABTU, Military Engineer 1st rank Ya. L. Skvirsky, who had arrived at Plant №183 to review progress. According to the results of the "maketny" (prototype) Commission, a working Protocol (agreement on works) was drawn up on 6th September 1938, which indicated:

"The project is approved with the following main amendments and additions:
1. To produce one wheel-tracked tank with a 45mm gun, two tracked tanks with 76.2mm gun and one (hull and turret set) for firing trials (i.e. armour integrity tests).
2. The combat weight of the tank must not exceed 16.5 tonnes.
3. The specific pressure on the track shall not exceed 0.65kg/cm² without immersion (i.e. sinking into ground).
4. To design and install an observation cupola without optical devices.
5. Reduce the required pressure on the side friction clutch brake band.
6. Develop a hydraulic shock absorber for the suspension.
7. The front sheet of the hull floor to make 13mm instead of 10mm.

8. Driver's hatch to make 30mm.

9. There should be several "triplex" (viewing) devices in the turret.

10. Hull floor hatch should be easily opened and have a lock.

11. To provide 2-3 DT magazines for ground use should the crew need to leave the tank.

12. Develop and submit for approval the installation of a smoke generating device and flamethrower.

13. To develop a servo-control system.

14. Ammunition for the 76.2mm gun shall be 85-100 rounds."

TsAMO. F.38. L.11355. C.931. pp3

I. F. Tevosyan.

A.A. Goreglyad.

Almost all of the Protocol amendments and additions the designers of "Bureau-24" had to develop independently, the only exception being item 13 - equipping the tank with a servo-control system. It should be noted that in the second half of the 1930s one of the known problems associated with decreased tank mobility was excessive driver fatigue, which appeared due to the great effort (to 60kg/cm²) that the driver was forced to apply to the pedals and levers to control tank movement. One solution was the introduction of a servo mechanism for the driver controls, the development of servo controls for tanks being an ABTU instruction undertaken at the Moscow Scientific Research Institute №20 (NII-20) Special Technical Department of NKOP. At the end of 1937, the Institute developed a closed-type pneumatic servo control system, with testing on the BT-7 and T-28 tanks yielding positive results. In order to equip the tanks with pneumatic servo control system, the head of ABTU Komkor (Corps Commander) D. G. Pavlov and divisional engineer P. S. Alliluyev sent Letter №288201 to the Deputy People's Commissar of the Defence Industry I. F. Tevosyan on 4th September 1938, stating:

"ABTU carries out a number of experimental works on the installation of servo equipment on tanks, which significantly improves machine control. We believe that it is timely to raise the question of Plant №183, making preparations for the production of tanks provided with servos. Plant №183 together with NII-20 have provided working drawings of servo mechanisms and in the first quarter of 1939 will produce a prototype BT-7 tank with servo controls. Production of the prototype will be preceded by all the necessary tests of these mechanisms, and it should take into account all corrections made by tests at the site and in the army. We ask your instructions to Plant №183 regarding the raised questions".

RVGA F.31811 L.2 C.842 pp172

Following the correspondence between the leadership of Plant №183 and Tevosyan about the joint development of pneumatic servo drive control systems with NII-20, the Bureau "24" designers, together with those at NII-20 prepared the technical designs for such a system for the A-20 tank in the first half of October 1938. The technical design of the servo control system for the A-20 tank was reviewed and adopted at a meeting held on 14th October 1938 at KB-24 within Plant №183. The minutes of the technical meeting, inter alia, noted:

"The presented project of pneumatic servo control is accepted. When developing working drawings, it is necessary to take into account decreasing the total weight of the servo control mechanisms. Ensure the tightness of all connections in the closed loop of the air lines."

RVGA F.31811 L.2. C.842 pp323-324

The technical project review for the A-20 tank servo control system was sent with transmittal Letter №SO6702 to the chief of the 8th Department of ABTU, military engineer 1st rank Ya. L. Skvirsky and the Director of NII-20, V. F. Zakharov. The technical meeting held in Bureau "24" also announced the appointment of A. A. Goreglyad as the new head of 8th GU (Main Directorate) of NKOP; appointed to this position at the end of September 1938 in replacement of his predecessor, V.D. Sviridov, who was on 7th September 1938 convicted by the Military Collegium of the Supreme Court of the USSR on charges of *"participation in a military-fascist conspiracy"*. Prior to his appointment as chief of GlavK (central command) in NKOP, A. A. Goreglyad had served as controller of the party control Commission of the Central Committee of the TsK VKP(b) - the Communist Party (Bolshevik). In his new position, Goreglyad addressed streamlining of the design processes, manufacture and serial production of tank prototypes, modernisation of serial production machines, changes in the drawing and design documentation, and re-organisation of interactions with the Red Army. In order to remedy serious shortcomings in scientific-research and experimental design work in NKOP plants, improve the training of designers, the technical equipment of pilot plants; that of the laboratories and test stations of NKOP plants, and to strengthen links with military units, Goreglyad on 1st Dec 1938 issued Order №P-38 from the 8th GU NKOP stating:

"1. *Despite a number of directives on the procedure of designing and serial production of prototypes, there is still lack of clarity with regard to making changes in drawings and specifications, as well as the procedure of modernisation of serial machines, and there are extremely adverse comments on the quality of machines, the normal course of production, and the date of manufacture of the new machines.*

2. *The lack of improvement in machines, and personnel, at factories and the (lack of) modernisation of machines brings completely unsatisfactory results to the operational tank park (tank fleet). Also unsatisfactory is the modernisation of tanks undergoing major overhaul at repair bases. Due to this, the fighting qualities of previously produced machines are far behind the fighting qualities of later machines of the same type.*

3. *The experience of previous years shows that the timing of bringing a design into service can stretch for 3-5 years.*

The main reasons for these serious shortcomings as follows:

1. *Lack of proper organisation of design, experimental and research works at the plants.*

2. *The scientific research and experimental base at Plant №185, which has to generalise and use the experience of the operation of existing machines and lead the guidance of promising work on designing tanks, cannot cope with the tasks assigned to it.*

3. *Lack of attention to the issues of standardisation, normalisation and (component) substitutes in production, and to the resolution of these matters by contact with related industries (aircraft, auto-tractor).*

4. *Weak, quantitatively and qualitatively, design capability in tank plants. Lack of attention to the professional development of tank designers.*

5. *Poor technical equipment of pilot (prototype) plants, laboratories and test stations in the plants.*

6. *Unsatisfactory communication between plants and military units, repair bases with regard to operational experience of tanks in various conditions.*

To eliminate these shortcomings:

1. *The Appendix attached to the order is approved for steady execution: a) about the order and terms of design and production of prototypes; b) about the serial production of new samples; c) about the order of agreements on serial production; d) about the order of modification of machines in serial production; e) about repair and modernisation of fighting vehicles at repair bases.*

2. *To Directors of Plant №s 183, 174, 37, 234, 48, 104 and 105*

- *strengthen the design departments and pilot plants. To by 1/5 1939 staff these departments and workshops with all necessary equipment so that workshops are able to produce parts and prototype test samples within established deadlines.*

3. *Personnel Department GlavK - comrade Kovalev:*

a) *Arrange the return to work of special tank cadres, VAMM (technical university) graduates of previous years;*

b) *By 1/1-1939 to make the plan for utilising the young specialists designers prepared for the Tank Industry by the Bauman Institute NKOP (the Bauman Institute MHTS military department, Moscow - formed in 1938).*

4. *Directors of plants by no later than 1/1-1939 to strengthen bureaus of standardisation and normalisation through which to carry out all designs developed by plants. Standardisation, normalisation and substitution for the tank industry in general to by 1/1-1939 focus within the Research Institute of the Tank Industry (Plant №185).*

5. *Directors of plants to by 1/1-1939 strengthen operational departments with appropriate staff to which to assign responsibilities:*

a) *Instruction in military units on the exploitation and proper care of machines;*

b) *Regular informing of plant departments about all operational malfunctions for the purpose of prevention their repetition, both on produced machines, and on the existing tank park;*

c) *Testing of machines under different operational conditions;*

d) *Familiarisation with combat vehicle repair bases and the use of that experience for making necessary improvements to machines;*

e) *Provide regular information to military units and rembaza (repair bases), by issuing bulletins on the modernisation of machines for implementation in the current park of all improvements made to the machine design at the plant.*

6. *At the time of development of working drawings of prototypes intended for mass production to carry out consultation with technical personnel of the plant where serial production of the machine is to be undertaken.*

7. *Directors of plants to provide the order (structure) within which the prototypes shall be produced before serial production orders.*

8. *For the consideration of design and technical projects, and to develop testing of prototypes, to create at the 8th Main Directorate (GU) of the NKOP a permanent inter-Ministerial technical (expert) Commission of the 8th GU, ABTU, with the main designers of the plants included in its composition.*

The head of the 3rd Department to submit to me no later than 1/12-38 for approval by the expert Commission.

9. *I forbid all plants designing and manufacturing prototypes of military equipment, to independently accept and execute orders for the development of prototype designs".*

RGVA F.31811 L.3 C.1634 pp59-64

Copies of №P-38 and its attachments were sent to ABTU KA and all plant directors in the 8th GU NKOP, including the new director of Plant №183, Yu. E. Maksarev, who had been appointed to this position in early November 1938. Maksarev had previously worked as the head of the special armoured division at the Kirov plant in Leningrad.

But back from Moscow to Kharkov. Throughout the autumn of 1938, the staff of the Bureau "24" continued work on the implementation of the amendments proposed by the members of the Prototype Committee on 6th September 1938 when considering technical design and a model of the A-20 tank. In early December, Bureau "24" chief M. I. Koshkin and lead project engineer A. A. Morozov arrived in Moscow to participate in the meeting of the Supreme Military Council (GVS) of the Red Army, which took place in the Kremlin on 9-10th December 1938 under the chairmanship of the People's Commissar of Defence, Marshal K. E. Voroshilov. The Council was attended by its permanent members: I. V. Stalin, L. Z. Mekhlis, E. A. Schadenko, S. M. Budyonny, and G. I. Kulik, A. D. Loktionov and D. G. Pavlov. The first question at the GVS meeting was devoted to the adoption of the T-100 and SMK heavy, A-20 medium and T-40 amphibious light tanks, developed in accordance with the Resolution of Committee of Defence in SNK №198ss/s dated 7th August 1938. In addition to the permanent members of the Council, discussion of the tank models was also attended by the following invited representatives from ABTU and from industry: M. V. Zakharov, I. V. Smorodinov, G. K. Savchenko, M.M. Kaganovich, A. A. Goreglyad, P. G. Sukov V. I. Makarov, B. M. Korobkov, A. F. Kravtsev, P. K. Voroshilov, I. G. Panov, V. V. Kulikov, I. M., Saltzman, Zh. Ya. Kotin, A. S. Ermolaev, N. V. Barykov, Eh. M. Paley, G. V. Gudkov, M. I. Koshkin, A. A. Morozov, M. I. Shor, G. S. Surenyan and N. A. Astrov. The main report was made by the head of ABTU, Corps Commander D. G. Pavlov. The A-20 and A-20 Gus. (A-32) tank projects were introduced by Koshkin and Morozov. Being himself a direct participant in the tank review, Morozov later recalled how the A-20 tank model was considered:

"I well remember how anxiously M. I. Koshkin quite unconfidently reported to the Supreme Military Council about the assignment on the new tank A-20 and quite shyly substantiated the feasibility of further development of our "initiative" variant (the A-32 tank). I.V. Stalin, who was present at the Council, sitting to the side with his usual pipe and a pack of "Herzegovina Flor" cigarettes, did not interfere with the conduct of the meeting and our reports either by his appearance or his participation. After our reports there had been critical, sharp, heated performances. Then all those present gathered around the wooden models of tanks and in the form of open and business-like noisy conversation continued the discussion of our proposals. The-

Yu. E. Maksarev.

re were a lot of arguments "for" and "against". Special activity was shown by opponents of the new samples, and, relying on examples of the successful fighting application of BT and T-26 tanks (in Spain) tried to prove the absence of need for risky, in their opinion, deviations from the generally accepted direction in tank building. It seemed that the failure of our proposals is pre-determined, and if we approve something, then most likely it will be the A-20 project. But suddenly, interrupting this heated discussion, Stalin calmly, slowly, without gestures, staring off into space, quietly said in the silence: "let's not disturb the designers. Let them make the tank they themselves offer, and we'll see if it's really as good as they say it is." Suddenly all stood in its place. The A-20 and A-32 projects were approved and allowed us to produce one prototype of (each of) these tanks."

In his memoirs, A. A. Morozov described the appearance of the A-32 "Initiative tank" - which at that time still had the plant designation A-20 Gus. - coming to the fore after a short speech by Stalin, in which he proposed *"not to restrict the initiative of the plant, to give the team the opportunity to work."* This quote is taken from an article *"Chief Designer"*, published on 27th September 1940 in the factory newspaper "Kominternovets" Issue №229. The article was written by Plant №183 Director, Yu. E. Maksarev and the plant Chief Engineer S. N. Makhonin; the duties of chief designer of Plant №183 having just been taken over by A. A. Morozov due to the death of M. I. Koshkin the previous day. Due to the secret nature of the work conducted under the leadership of M. I. Koshkin, information relating to the design of new tanks in the newspaper - available to a wide range of readers - was by necessity limited. Further, in this article, Stalin's phrase *"not to hamper the initiative of the plant, to give the staff the opportunity to work"* was gradually transformed into the assertion that Mikhail Koshkin developed the A-20 Gus. tracked version of the A-20 tank as an initiative design, which later received the index A-32. This is however incorrect; the development of the tracked A-32 tank was carried out by Plant №183 not as a plant initiative, but according to NKOP Order № 335ss dated 21st August 1938, issued pursuant to Resolution №198ss/s. Declassified archival documents show that a proposal to create a tracked version of the A-20 tank was first introduced by the Defence Committee in the names of the head of ABTU, D. G. Pavlov and the People's Commissar of Defence of the USSR, K. E. Voroshilov, in the spring of 1938. When considering the technical design of both variants of the A-20 tank at the meeting of the GVS at a time when most of the participants were in favour of further development of only a wheel-track version of the tank, it was however Koshkin that took the initiative to continue to develop a tracked-only version of the tank, in order to make prototypes of both tanks for comparative tests. It was this initiative that was supported by Stalin at the aforementioned meeting of the GVS. In Protocol №28 resulting from the GVS meeting held on 9-10th December 1938 regarding the A-20 and A-20 Gus. tanks the following was noted:

"Pursuant to the decision of the Supreme Military Council as of 20 April, 1938 (minute №4 p.2) to approve the proposed models of tanks to create prototypes with the following key tactical and technical requirements:

<...> 3. Tank A-20 of Plant №183 (lead engineer comrade Morozov):

a) Type - one sample wheel-tracked machine, driven by 6 (six) wheels, the other - tracked;

b) Armour - protection against large-calibre 12.7mm armour-piercing rounds from all distances (both samples);

c) Engine - diesel, Plant №183 - 500hp (both examples);

d) Armament: for wheel-tracked model - 45mm gun, with co-axial machine gun, an anti-aircraft machine gun with 360° traverse, and a machine gun in the glacis next to the driver-mechanic. Consider the possibility of installing a 76mm gun in the turret. On the tracked prototype - to install a 76mm gun in the turret, of the same design as the wheel-tracked tank prototype. Angles of depression and elevation -7 to +25-30°;

e) Total weight of 16.5 tonnes with 45mm gun for the wheel-track sample, and should not exceed 17.0 tonnes for the tracked sample with 76mm gun;

f) Specific pressure 0,57kg/cm² without immersion, when the track width is 400mm for the wheel-track sample and 0.5kg/cm² for the tracked sample. Calculation of specific pressure at the track-bearing surface on 22 track shoes;

g) Ammunition - 45mm shells - 150pcs, cartridges - 3,024 pieces, 76mm shells - 85pcs. ;

h) Speed - the same on tracks, and on wheels. Maximum of 65km/h, minimum 9km/h;

i) Range - 300km (on tracks).

<...>

5. In the manufacture of prototypes to provide maximum use of sloped armour.

6. Terms of production of prototypes remain according to the order of the State №198ss".

RGVA F.4 L.18 C.46 pp259-261

Questions of Defence Technology - Book Cover, Series 6. Armoured vehicles. - Central Research Institute of Information, 1985. - Vol. 2 (120) pp15.

As can be seen from the text of the Protocol adopted for the GVS of the Red Army, the refined TTTs for the A-20 and A-20 Gus. tanks were not significantly modified from the previously set requirements. The refinements primarily concerned the reduction of the maximum angle of elevation of the gun from 45° to 30° and the reduction of the average ground pressure from 0.65 kg/cm² to 0.57 kg/cm² for the A-20 tank and to 0.50kg/cm² on the tracked A-20 Gus. tank. In addition, according to the personal order of D. G. Pavlov regarding prototype manufacture, the thickness of the side vertical armour of the A-20 Gus. tank hull was increased from 25mm to 30mm.

After returning from Moscow to Kharkov, Koshkin and Morozov congratulated the staff of Bureau "24" with their achievement. With the approval of the GVS, the designers of Plant №183 had developed the draft and layout of the A-20 tank and worked on the production of the A-20 and A-20 Gus. prototypes. In the second half of December 1938, the staff of Bureau "24" produced the working drawings for the production of prototypes of the A-20 and A-20 Gus. tanks. Taking into account the specified requirements adopted at the GVS meeting. The acting senior military representative of ABTU at Plant №183, military engineer 2nd rank K. V. Olhovsky in the report of the head of the 4th Department of ABTU, military engineer 1st rank N. N. Alimov described the work of Bureau of "24" in 1938:

"Over the past year, the KB at the plant completed a project and model of the wheel-tracked tank A-20 that was presented to the Commission on 6/9-38. The result was the outlining of a number of observations, which are mostly now implemented by the KB. The situation on the execution of work on the drawings as of January 1, 1939, is expressed in the following:

1. Complete the hull and turret layout drawings such that by the end of January armour can be ordered:

2. Provide in tracing paper (engineering drawings):

a) Drive wheel for track with guide horn links.

b) Steering wheel suspension. c) Cooling fan.

d) Armour detail for a turret armed with a 45mm gun.

e) Side friction clutches. f) Cardan shafts.

g) Side gearboxes for drive on wheels (90%).

3. Made in pencil:

a) Vertical suspension of the wheels.

b) Vertical transmission.

c) Idler wheel and track tension mechanism.

d) Main gearbox (90%).

e) Steering column and control rods.

f) Water radiators. g) Driver's seat. h) Steerable wheel.

i) Oil tanks.

j) Separate armature units for oil, water and fuel.

4. The bottlenecks in the KB are as follows:

a) There are no designers working on the hull of the machine, which forces the KB to transfer the chassis designers to work on the development and layout of the hull drawings.

b) Delay of accomplishment of drawings on the wheel-tracked tank for 25 days in connection with change of the task on specific track ground pressure (i.e. the initial projected 0.65- 0.58kg/cm²).

c) There is not at present a scheduled workshop in which to produce parts and mechanisms.

d) There is no room in the KB for copying of drawings.

e) The KB is not fully staffed, instead of 37 people, according to the order of the plant, there are only 29 people, including 25 designers and drawing copiers.

f) There are no tactical and technical requirements for a tracked prototype."

RGVA. F. 31811. L. 2. C. 938. pp. 41 - 42

After receiving similar information from other plants, the chief of ABTU, D. G. Pavlov and the Commissar P. N. Kulikov (appointed ABTU Commisar at the end of December 1938 in place of P. S. Alliluyev who died of a heart attack on 2ⁿᵈ November 1938), on 17ᵗʰ January 1939 by Letter №202393ss reported progress to the People's Commissar of Defence Voroshilov on the designing and production of prototypes of tanks and armoured vehicles performed according to Resolution KO №198ss/s. Regarding the work on the creation of the A-20 and A-20 Gus tanks the letter noted the following:

"I report on the condition of works on the prototype fighting machines carried out by the decision of the Government on 15.1.39. < ... >

3. Plant №183 - tank A-20.

On the wheel-tracked version of the tank, working drawings are

P.N. Kulikov.

I.A. Likhachev.

made except for the hull and turret. Work has started on development of a tracked version. Government deadline for production of tanks - 1.6.39".

RGVA. F.4. L.14. C. 2222. pp2-3

It should be noted here that in early 1939, while the staff of Plant №183 worked intensively on the creation of the A-20 tank, a number of Soviet ministries began large-scale reorganizations. By a Decree of the Presidium of the Supreme Soviet of the USSR dated 11ᵗʰ January 1939 the People's Commissariat of Defence Industry (Defence Production) of the USSR (NKOP) was divided into four People's Commissariats - the People's Commissariat of Aviation Industry (NKAP); the People's Commissariat of Shipbuilding Industry of the USSR (NKSP); the People's Commissariat of Ammunition (NKB) and the People's Commissariat of Armaments (NKV). The cumbersome structure of the NKOP, which consisted of more than twenty main departments responsible for the development and production of aircraft, ships, artillery, tanks, small arms, armour, sights, ammunition, all types of artillery shells, propellants, and other defence equipment, was thereby radically transformed.

As a result of the reorganization, the 8ᵗʰ GU of NKOP, which dealt with tank construction and all organizations and enterprises subordinated to it (including Plant №183), temporarily became a part of the People's Commissariat of the Aviation Industry. This somewhat non-standard situation was corrected after the formation of the People's Commissariat of Medium Machine Building of the USSR. This ministry was formed in accordance with the Decree of the Presidium of the Supreme Soviet on 5ᵗʰ February 1939. The People's Commissariat of Machine Building of the USSR (NKmash) was meantime divided into three Commissariats: heavy (NKTM), general (NKOM) and medium (NKSM) machine building. On the basis of the Resolution SNK USSR №240-32s dated 28ᵗʰ February 1939, the 8ᵗʰ Main Directorate of the NKAP structure was transferred to NKSM and existed as such until 2ⁿᵈ July 1939, when it was reorganised into the Main Directorate of Special Machine Building (Glavspetsmash) NKSM. Doubtless in no small part due to the large-scale reorganization of the Commissariat, the draft resolution *"On approval of the layout of tanks"* sent to Voroshilov at the Defence Committee (KO) was adopted as Resolution №45ss only on 27th February 1939, in absentia rather than at a formal meeting, on the basis of the Secretary of the KO, I. A. Safonov's survey of the permanent members of the Defence Committee, which voted unanimously "Za" (for). The text of Resolution №45 almost completely repeated the text set out in Protocol №28 of the meeting of the GVS on 9-10th December 1938, with the exception of the preamble and the date of manufacture of the prototype of the amphibious T-40 tank.

In pursuance of this Resolution and previously adopted Resolution KO №198ss/s from 7th August 1938 *"On the system tank weapons of the Red Army"* the People's Commissar of Medium Machine Building, I. A. Likhachev on 17th March 1939, signed Order №21ss, according to which the Director of Plant №183 Yu. E. Maksarev was ordered:

"1. To deliver for testing by ABTU RKKA machine "T-20" by 1st June 1939 in two versions: wheel-tracked and tracked type with factory pre-testing in the following tactical and technical requirements:

a) Type - one sample wheel-tracked, six-wheel drive, the other tracked.

b) Armour protection against 12.7mm large-calibre armour-piercing bullets from all distances (for both samples).

c) Engine - from the DMZ diesel plant - 500hp (on both samples).

d) Armament for the wheel-track prototype - 45mm gun, coaxial machine gun; anti-aircraft machine gun in the turret with 360° traverse, and a machine gun in the front glacis, near the driver-mechanic. To provide for the possibility of installation of a 76mm gun in the same turret design. On the tracked sample install a 76mm gun in the turret of a single sample of the wheeled-tracked tank. Angles of gun depression and elevation -7 +25 +30°.

e) Total weight of 16.5 tonnes with 45mm gun for the wheel-tracked sample; for tracked sample with 76mm gun combat weight should not exceed 17 tonnes.

f) Specific ground pressure 0,57kg/cm², without immersion with track width 400mm for the wheel-track sample and 0.50kg/cm² for the tracked model. Calculation of the specific (ground) pressure based on 22 track links in contact with the ground.

g) Ammunition - 45mm-150pcs., 76mm-85pcs., 7.62mm cartridges - 3,024pcs.

h) Speed is the same both on tracks and wheels. Maximum speed - 65km/h. Minimum speed - 9km/h.

i) Range - 300km (on tracks).

2. To allocate responsible persons for the production of the A-20 machine across all sites, divisions and departments; also the na-

mes of the responsible persons should be submitted to the Central Committee by 20 March 1939.

3. To submit the schedule of release of A-20 machines for GlavK approval taking into account factory run-in. Deadline is 25 March 1939.

Every ten days to submit a report on manufacturing of the A-20 machines to GlavK from 20 March, 1939".

RGAEh F.8115. L.8. C.16 pp18-19

The same order also given to the chief of the 8th GU NKSM, A. A. Goreglyad, assigned a requirement to report monthly to the NKSM on the status of work on the A-20 tank. One copy of this most secret order of 19th March 1939 was sent to Plant №183 in Kharkov, where KB-24 made working drawings of the parts, assemblies and units of the wheeled-tracked A-20 tank and the tracked A-20 Gus. variant. Work on the production of drawing and design documentation for the A-20 Gus. tank had nevertheless actually started on 10th February 1939. With the forthcoming ABTU trials on the new A-20 and A-20 Gus. tanks only two months away, and the volume of drawings and documents required to produce test prototypes being significant, the leadership of Plant №183 made the decision to significantly expand the staff of Bureau "24" at the expense of design engineers and draftsmen of Tank Department "100", Tractor Department "200", Locomotive Department "300" and Diesel Department "500". In addition, it was decided to introduce a new position, that of Plant Chief Designer, for which position the head of Bureau "24", M. I. Koshkin was nominated on 1st April 1939. The required documents and materials for approval of the chief designer of Plant №183 were sent to the 8th GU NKSM. In the supporting letter signed by the director of plant, Yu. E. Maksarev on 16th April 1939, in particular, noted:

"Working as the Head of the Design Bureau, Koshkin has done a great job as part of the improvement of the modernisation of machine construction. Qualified design engineer, fully prepared for the post of Chief Designer of the plant. With initiative, energetic and persistent. Good organiser and leader, has authority among the management of the plant. Work still in progress in terms of improvement of their technical knowledge. Actively participates in party and public work. The post of Chief Designer of the plant corresponds".

RGAEh. F. 7719. L. 2. C. 235. pp. 7.

By mid May 1939, M. I. Koshkin was approved in his new position. Concurrently, the reorganisation of the tank design bureau was completed, now with the new index "520" (hereafter in later text KB-520). A.A. Morozov was appointed as the chief of KB-520, with N.A. Kucherenko and A. V. Kolesnikov as deputies, heading up the design departments "100" and

"500" respectively. The design bureau would continue under the index "520" until 13th November 1971 when it was merged with prototype workshop "540" as the Ural KB for Transport Machine Building (UKBTM). KB-520 was evacuated together with Plant №183 from Kharkov to Nizhny Tagil in the Urals in the autumn of 1941, but more of that later. The first combat vehicles created within this famous design Bureau were the A-20 and A-20 Gus. With the beginning of assembly and of prototype the designation of the latter tank was changed from A-20 Gus. to the better known A-32.

So, who was directly involved in the design of the A-20 and A-32 tanks? Besides the above-mentioned team of KB-520, development of the new tank types was undertaken by a total of twelve separate design groups. Under the guidance of the head of design section M. I. Tarshinov, designers B. A. Chernyak and N. Ivanov developed the drawings of the main armour sections of the A-20 and A-32 hulls. Development of other parts of the tank hull was carried out within design groups led by G. S. Mironov and G. P. Fomenko. In these two groups worked designers: V. D. Gaplevsky, A. N. Lozov, E. M. Medvedev, A. Ya. Mitnik, I. P. Radoychin and four other constructors, whose names are yet not established.

The head of the design section, M. I. Tarshinov, in addition to the above group, in parallel headed two more design groups that developed the turrets, weapons installation and ammunition stowage. The composition of these groups included the designers A. A. Moloshtanov, M. A. Nabutovsky, U. E. Khlopenko, V. S. Kaledin, Ya. L., Guntman and B. M. Shevchenko. The viewing-device arrangements were developed by designer N. G. Izosimov.

Development of drawings of the engines used in the A-20 and A-32 tanks was carried out in the design team led by N. S. Korotchenko. The liquid-cooling system of the V-2 diesel engine was developed by the designers F. N. Kozlov, V. Kotov, and B. M. Shevchenko. The circulating lubrication system was designed by P.S. Sentyurin and E. I. Rosenberg. The combined type air cleaner was designed by design engineer A. F. Savenko. The fuel system was designed by designer M. I. Kotov, the drive to the fuel pump of the engine and the exhaust gas system was developed by F. N. Koslov. The names of another two designers within N.S. Korotchenko's group have not to date been established.

The gearbox for the A-20 and A-32 tanks was designed by Ya. I. Baran, and the main clutch and associated cooling fan by A.I. Shpaikhler and E. I. Rosenberg. In addition, Shpaikhler developed the side friction clutches and brakes for both.

Designers S.M. Braginsky and S. S. Libman, in one of two groups headed by V.G. Matyukhin, designed the final drives and the transfer gearboxes to the driven wheels of the tank A-20. Within the second group, led by G. V. Matyukhin, the designer A. S. Bondarenko developed the drive wheel and supporting rollers (road wheels), G. S. Mironov developed part of the suspension units of the tanks and A. I. Shpaikhler worked on the track engagement system.

The development of the pneumatic servo-control systems was undertaken by two groups, under the leadership of P. P. Vasilyev and I. Baran. The composition of these groups included the designers K. Oleinik, Konilets and B.M. Pokorny. The tank drive control systems were developed within a group under the leadership of P. P. Vasilyev with the designers engaged in the group including Konilets, S. S. Libman, K. Oleinik, and M. Ya. Shtitelman.

The group headed by V. Ya. Kurasov, with designers G. P. Volov, K. I. Zelenov, M. Ya. Katsznelson and V. E. Moisenko designed the electrical equipment of the A-20 and A-32 tanks. In the same group, designer A. A. Gorbachev developed the radio station and TPU-2 intercom installation.

Placement of spare parts, tools and devices was under the leadership of A.S. Bondarenko, with a group of designers including I. Gashinsky, V. O. Drobotenko, F. P. Peterson and another designer whose name has not yet been established.

The calculations group, which carried out control and generalisation of calculations of the main assemblies of the A-20 and A-32 tanks was directed by E. A. Berkovsky.

In addition to the numerous design engineer collectives (working groups), it is necessary to add also the collective of drafters and copywriters who were also a part of KB-520 and took direct part in the creation of drawing and design documentation for the A-20 and A-32 tanks. This team consisted of over twenty people, among which were: Anisimov, A. Butovskay, G. Gavrikov, Katz, Kondrikov, Kryazhkov, E. Martinov, Pilipnets, Pletnev, Popov, Nesterenko, Ryutin, Tkachenko, L. Umanets, Ushakov, I. Firsov, Chubarov, T. Shevchenko, Shalyapin, L. Shcherbakov and others.

During development of the A-20 and A-32 tank prototype working drawings, a new procedure for registration of technical documentation was introduced at Plant №183. A new system of part designations was introduced, and the drawing "corner stamp" noting revisions and approvals was changed, which with minor modifications has survived to the present day. In the new parts and assembly designations, the first group of digits indicated the factory index of the article (encrypted tank type), the second - the number of the group of tank parts, the third - the serial number of the part in the group. Assembly drawings were also indicated by three groups of figures, but with the addition of "sb" Examples are: 12.44.001 (12 - A-20 tank factory index, 44 - tracked, 001 - track links with guide horn) and 12.02.2 sb. (12 - A-20 tank factory index, 02 - cooling system, 2sb. - radiator left).

As they became available, working drawings were immediately sent to the plant or to other plants for the manufacturing of relevant parts, components or mechanisms of the A-20 and A-32 tanks. This parallel method of working between engineers and producers was selected in order to very quickly produce prototypes of new combat vehicles.

From a tank production perspective, the most time-consuming process was that of making the hull and turret, hence the working drawings for manufacture of the relevant armour parts were among the first to be sent to the "Ilyich" plant in Mariupol*. In the first half of April 1939, the A-20 hull and turret sets were produced in Workshop №5 at the Mariupol plant and shipped to Plant №183. The process of manufacturing two sets of hull and turret armour parts for the A-32 tank was somewhat delayed, the reasons for which were detailed by ABTU military representative at the "Ilyich" plant in Mariupol, military engineer 2nd rank V. A. Dmitrusenko in the operational summary №49ss dated 16th April 1939:

"In connection with the scrapping of the 8 hull nose parts, 30mm thick (in the original document there is a typo, it should read 20mm), the fault of wrong drawing size, and scrapping of 3 hull side parts with a thickness of 30mm, due to 1 side sheet being scrapped and 2 side sheets being cracked when straightened during rolling, production time of two hull (and turret) sets are held back."

RGVA. F. 31811. L. 2. C. 958. pp. 138

Ultimately, two hull and turret armour sets for the A-32 tank, with the exception of two side sections, were shipped to Plant №183 on 30th April 1939, with the two missing sections shipped on 3rd May. After this the Mariupol "Lenin" plant, as can be seen from situation report №53ss, began manufacturing armour parts for one A-20 turret and two A-32 turrets. No less stressful than the workload at the Mariupol plant was the work in early May 1939 on the production of the A-20 and A-32 tank prototypes at Plant №183 in Kharkov. The Operational Summary №0322/s dated 6th May 1939, compiled by the acting military representative of ABTU Plant №183 military engineer 2nd rank K. V. Olkhovskiy, noted:

"I report the condition of works on the A-20 tank on 4 / 5-39.:
1. *To date, drawings and detailed descriptions for 8 groups (of parts) have not been prepared.*
2. *So far no part with the exception of the brake band has been received.*
3. *The hull for the variant will appear in Department 500 for machining and assembly not earlier than 8 May.*
4. *Armour for the turret has not yet been received at Plant №183,*

with anticipated arrival of 20 May, that will not give the opportunity to produce turrets by the time the machines are complete.
5. *Hull armour for the 2nd (i.e. A-32) tank (has) arrived at the plant. Preparatory work for assembly of this hull is not yet conducted (no drawings).*
6. *To ensure the release of the A-20 machine at the scheduled time by the Director, it is necessary to produce in the machine shops about 500 parts by 10-11 May, 1939.*
7. *The Assembly of the gearbox is currently under way. The final drive needs to be produced by 10 May, 1939, the main friction (clutch) also by 10 May. The production specification side clutch has two designations: 12-09-008 and 12-09-009 that are both late due to the fault of the shop fixtures (i.e. with factory machine tooling).*
8. *Press-forms and bandages (wheel rims) sent to the Leningrad "Krasny Treugolnik" plant on 1 May. Need help from the ABTU on the early production of the load bearing i.e. (road) wheels, which should be at Plant №183 no later than 14-15 May.*
9. *All necessary bearings are obtained by the plant. On the machines will be installed bearings of domestic production, with the exception of two bearings №29-20 and №23-17, which are absent from the plant. In place of them on the first KPP (gearbox) will be supplied SKF (i.e. imported) bearings.*
10. *To ensure the above deadlines, the following activities are undertaken:*
a) *The Mechanical shop of Department 500 almost entirely moves on to a 3rd shift work pattern.*
b) *On 5 May, the department administration monitors the load of each (workshop) bay separately.*
c) *Release of A-20 parts will go out of sequence, to the detriment of spare parts for the "B" machine (T-35 tank) and some parts of the A-7 machine (the BT-7 tank), and parts for the machine "100" (the T-100 prototype tank)."*

RGVA. F. 31811. L. 2. C. 888. pp. 50-51

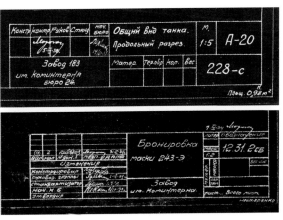

Samples of design drawing signature boxes

---

* *"Ilyich" - named after the patronym of Vladimir Ilyich Lenin.*

As can be seen from situation Report №57ss, composed by the military representative of ABTU on the Mariupol "Ilyich" plant, A.V. Dmitrusenko, production of three sets of armoured parts for A-20 and A-32 tank turrets was completed by the plant on 11th May 1939, and sent by rail to Plant №183 in Kharkov.

In mid-May of 1939, Department "500" of Plant №183 under the leadership of I. F. Rumyantsev worked intensively on assembling a prototype A-20 tank and parts and mechanisms for the A-32 tank. Thanks to the hard work of the staff of the Department "500" the prototype A-20 tank minus the main armament was assembled on 26th May 1939, and on the same day a trial run of the new machine took place on the territory of the plant. About this important event, the acting military representative of ABTU Plant №183 military engineer 2nd rank K. V. Olkhovsky and his assistant military engineer 3rd rank P. P. Baikov on 28th May 1939 notified their immediate superiors in operational summary №0375/s:

*"**Report on state of the machine A-20 on 26/5-39.***

1. The first version of the A-20 machine is assembled, moved on wheels inside the plant in 1st and 2nd gear about 1km. The final installations should be completed on 29 May, 1939.

2. Welding of the hull of the second variant (A-32 tank) was delayed; there were some design defects, namely inconsistency in the heat treatment of the hull parts, which led to a delay in welding work. The hull for the second variant will be ready before 30 May 1939.

3. There are still no finished parts for assembling the 2nd option. Most parts of the main units are ready.

4. Machining of parts according to the 2nd variant in the machine shop goes out of sequence, leading to failure of production of parts for the machine "100".

5. On the 1st variant of the A-20 machine is installed a 45mm gun with a push button control".

RGVA. F. 31811. L.3. C.1633 pp9

For plant testing purposes a prototype of the A-20 tank was completed on 31st May 1939, and the next day the machine was driven 174km on wheels. The supervisor at Plant №183 on A-20 and A-32 tank manufacturing, leading engineer of the 1st Department of the 8th department of ABTU, Major I. G. Panov in a summary entitled *"On the course of experimental work at Plant №183 as of 4.6.39."* reported to his direct chief, military engineer 1st rank Ya. L. Skvirsky the following:

"The A-20 machine on 1.6.39. ran on wheels 174km, and the mechanisms worked perfectly. The temperature regime of water and oil was within 60-70°C. The main disadvantages found during the run:
a) Leak of the left rear fuel tank. [written in pencil:] "replaced"
b) Slight leakage of the left radiator. [written in pencil:] "corrected".

c) Drips of oil from the gearbox.

d) An oil seal nut for the additional transmission gearbox has been lost, due to the unreliable cotter pin design, which caused damage to the coupling connecting the shaft of the additional transmission. [written in pencil:] "removed".

From the conversation with the driver, the machine is well controlled, is smooth running, but has significantly increased noise due to the gear connection of the additional transmission.

From conversations with those present during testing the behaviour of the machine is good and movement is steady.

Machine weight: without tracks, machine guns, command, observation devices and without full combat loading - 15,840kg.
Combat weight to be expected:
15,840kg; 1,300kg track; 350kg crew; 80kg radio;
200kg vision devices, ammunition, guns, tools
*= **17,600kg - 18,000kg.***

Proving run on 4.6.39 on tracks 155 [corrected at 175] km on a good dirt road. Movement was steady. The mechanisms worked smoothly. The water temperature was 70°C; the oil 85-90°C.
The speed was brought to 65km/h at 1,400-1,800rpm. Noted somewhat increased heating of the gearbox and side frictions.

The machine was loaded to full combat order, and then driven 200km on heavy ground and cross-country.

About the A-32.
The hull situation became boring. It was expected to start assembly on 6th but availability of parts is poor. Not avilable are parts for the side gearboxes, side frictions (clutches, stub-axles, balancers and not fully prepared traction. Especially delayed is the production of side gears. Gathered all the materials, and on the 4th will discuss with the Director of the plant, how to put things right. I believe on 10 -13 June the machine shall be driven to the first run-in."

RGVA. F. 31811. L. 3. C. 1633. pp. 5-6

At the request of the head of Administration of NKO, Kombrig M. G. Snegov, the chief of ABTU, D. G. Pavlov and the Military Commissioner P. N. Kulikov on 13th June 1939 in Letter №207024ss reported the People's Commissar of Defence Voroshilov on the progress on design and production of prototypes of tanks and armoured vehicles, as performed in response to KO Resolution №198ss/s. Regarding the A-20 and A-32 tanks it was noted within the letter:

"Built the 1st wheel-track sample (A-20), which is factory tested. On wheels the tank travelled 174km and on tracks 175km, and in total 349km. During the factory tests the transmission coupling and two rear wheel bearings failed and were replaced. The causes of breakdowns are identified and eliminated. Currently, the machine

is delivered in fully outfitted state. From 13 June to start running tests in more severe conditions. The second example of the tank (the A-32) is in the assembly stage and should be complete 15-16 June".

RGVA. F. 4. L. 14. C. 2222. pp. 12

On the same day, 13th June 1939, D. G. Pavlov and P. N. Kulikov appointed the Commission to conduct field tests of the A-20 and A-32 prototypes. The Chairman of the Commission was appointed head of the test department of the Scientific testing polygon (NIABT) of ABTU RKKA, Major E. A. Kulchitsky, and his deputy, Major I. G. Panov. On 13th June 1939 in ABTU the program of field tests of the A-20 and A-32 tank prototypes in summer conditions was made. The approved testing program and Order on appointment of the Commission, dated 16th June 1939 was together with transmittal Letter №207091s sent from ABTU to 8th GU NKSM in Moscow, as well as to the Directors of Plants №183 and №75 in Kharkov. It was decided to carry out polygon tests in Kharkov at Plant №183, with the Commission ordered to start work on 27th June 1939. However, due to the unavailability of the A-20 and A-32 prototypes, it was not possible to start the polygon tests within the specified period. The Operational Summary №0495/ s dated 2nd July 1939 made by the military representative of ABTU at Plant №183 P. P. Baykov explained the situation:

"I report the status of prototypes and units in Department of "500": (following numbering sequence is as per original document)

1. Machine A-20 is equipped, with the exception of the device "70" and the radio (no specified wiring diagram). Machine has moved on tracks and on wheels about 700km. During this time there were found the following defects:

1. The main clutch bearing "flew" (failed) due to poor lubrication and poor quality of manufacture of the bearing itself.

2. The bearings of the right rear wheel "flew" (failed) twice. The alleged cause of the breakdowns is weak retainers, which are now replaced by reinforced ones. In addition, there was a jamming in the splined joints; to eliminate this phenomenon the spline surface of one shaft was chromed.

3. Oil leak from the neck of KPP*. (design flaw). Currently, the machine A-20 is ready for testing.

2. Machine 32 (A-32) is assembled, but not fully equipped. Passed two proving runs (total distance of about 110km). During the run, there was found a strong "knocking-out" (leaking) from the oil tank (from the grid communicating with the atmosphere). The second machine "32" will not be ready before 6 July, 1939".

The summary *"on the course of experimental work at Plant №183 as of 6.7.39."* signed by Major I. G. Panov advised his superiors in ABTU that:

"Tank A-20.

Total distance travelled 800km. In addition to the previously described, failures were as follows:

a) The stud threads for the additional transmission for the right rear wheel sheared (not an emergency - trial continued).

b) After replenishment [refuelling and oil checks] a clogged oil filter caused the oil from the reservoir to be pumped into the other, and then the pressure dropped.

c) The coupling nut connecting the idler wheel with the hull glacis broke because of slipping tracks.

d) Slipping right side friction (clutch) - strong contamination.The machine performs quite well in sand - it handles a 26° slope and the same on a reverse slope. The "Vosmyorka" (the "8", meaning the A-8 tank) in this situation suffered from track slip. Movement on marschland, depth of immersion of 300-450mm - is good. The "8" bogged down after twenty metres.

Side slope of 32° on grassy black earth the machine overcomes easily. The A-7 and A-8 gave track slippage; the reason: track was underworked (on the edge of throwing both tracks). Develops a maximum speed of 85km/h.

Overcoming a deep ford at high speed, the machine was submerged and stuck in the water for 2.5-3 hours. After retrieval, cleaning was carried out by the crew, and the machine returned under its own power to the plant.

At this time, the machine is delivered for inspection, cleaning and retrofitting.

A-32.

The installation has been completed - ammunition stowage is not worked out yet. <...> Managed well, the movement is steady. Maximum speed up to 70km/h. On sand it performed well, as did the A-20. The maximum slope overcome was 40.5°, which is not the tank's limit. <...> Temperature conditions - more than 90°C, which for both machines are not fixed. Testing of mirror devices is conducted, but not yet finally developed. <...> Field testing can only begin 10.7.39".

RGVA. F.31811 L.3 C.1633 pp111-112

The forecast given by Major I. G. Panov for the start date of A-20 and A-32 field tests proved inaccurate. After factory tests and rework, the first A-32 tank prototype was transferred to military representatives to conduct field tests only on 17th July 1939. The same procedure was performed with a prototype of the A-20 tank two days earlier, on 15th July 1939. During the factory tests the tank A-20 covered 872km, of which 217km was on tracks - and 655km on wheels, while the A-32 covered 235km during plant testing. Polygon tests of one A-20 and one A-32 prototype began in the area of Kharkov on 18th July 1939.

---

* KPP - Gearbox

Chapter 7

General Arrangement of the A-20 Tank

The A-20 was an experimental wheel-track tank, which, according to the tactical and technical requirements (TTTs), was intended *"for independent actions as part of tank formations and for actions in tactical interaction with other branches of the armed forces."* The tank had a combat weight of 18 metric tonnes, which was within the medium tank classification (16-35 tonnes) in force in 1939.

The main armament of the A-20 tank was a turret-mounted 45mm tank gun, with two 7.62mm machine guns, one co-axially mounted with the main armament; the other ball-mounted in the glacis. The armour protected against armour-piercing rounds of up to 12.7mm in calibre from all ranges, and from shrapnel grenades, mines and shells exploding near the tank.

The A-20 was powered by a V-2 diesel engine coupled via the transmission to a combined wheel-tracked drive system. Moving on tracks, the tank could travel on roads and terrain, and surmount natural and artificial obstacles. With the tracks removed, the tank could perform long distance road marches on wheels. The combined wheel-track propulsion also allowed the tank

to enter combat with one or both tracks lost and with up to two drive wheels on either side of the tank damaged. The road wheel and track speed of the A-20 tank was synchronized, so allowing conventional movement on track, synchronised movement with track fitted on one side of the tank and the tank travelling on its road wheels on the other, or movement on tracks with the engaged drives supplying torque directly to the road wheels. Engagement of the individual drives to the road wheels was undertaken from the workplace of the driver-mechanic. To operate the main on-board friction clutches during turns and braking, and increase the overall efficiency of the driver mechanic, a pneumatic servo control system was installed on the A-20 tank.

Ensuring high combat and technical performance of the A-20 tank within a given combat weight was achieved due to a well considered layout arrangement that placed all crew members in the hull and turret of the tank directly in accordance with their functions in combat, with the placement of the main armament in a rotating turret, and with the engine and transmission compartments at the rear of the tank. Most tanks pro-

The A-20 tank prototype.

duced in the second half of the 20th Century have had exactly this arrangement of main components, units, mechanisms and crew roles, which would in the post war years be referred to as the "classic tank layout."

In the late 1930s however more than half of both foreign and Soviet domestic light tanks (such as the T-26) had a layout with the transmission located at the front of the hull with the combined transmission and control (i.e. driver-mechanic's) compartments greatly simplifying the design of the control linkages and easing transmission maintenance. However, the layout also had significant drawbacks, the main one being that the drive shaft connecting the engine to the transmission passed through the entire combat compartment at some height from the hull floor, which both complicated the layout and led to a

significant increase in the height of the tank. Placement of the steering mechanisms in the hull front also prevented positioning of the frontal hull armour at steep angles of inclination, reducing its projectile resistance. Locating the transmission in the front section of the hull also complicated the cooling of the drivetrain and especially the brakes, increasing the air temperature in the fighting compartment with removal and installation of transmission units for repair also being time-consuming. Locating the transmission at the hull rear, as done in the A-20 tank, alleviated such shortcomings, however the design of the linkages controlling tank movement, the workload on the linkages, and the driver-mechanic operating them, was now of greater concern.

The control compartment, where the driver-mechanic and machine-gunner-radio operator were seated, was in the

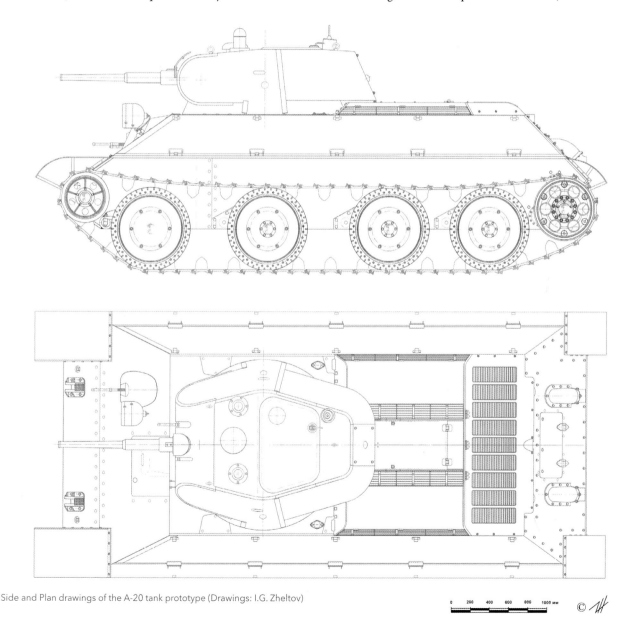

Side and Plan drawings of the A-20 tank prototype (Drawings: I.G. Zheltov)

0   200   400   600   800   1000 мм

hull front, with the seats for the driver (left) and radio operator (right) mounted to the hull floor. The seat cushion was located on supports tilted backwards, the angle of the semi-soft seats being adjustable for the height of the driver or radio operator. The further back the seat cushions were moved, the greater the distance to the hull roof. For ease of crew movement inside the tank, the seat backs were hinged. Under the driver's seat in the hull floor was located an oval emergency exit hatch.

In the hull glacis armour, there was a hinged rectangular hatch for the driver-mechanic with a viewing slot through which the driver in combat carried out terrain observation. For protection against bullets and shrapnel, the slot was from the inside closed by an observation device fitted with bulletproof glass, similar in design to that installed on the BT-7 tank. When not in combat, the hatch cover was fixed open by a stopper, and

the driver observed through the open hatch. The working place of the driver-mechanic was equipped with the driving controls, the actuator for the transverse louvres for the engine cooling system fan and two panels mounting the engine and electrical equipment controls. Alongside the driver-mechanic sat the machine gunner-radio operator, who operated the ball-mounted 7.62mm DT machine gun but able to monitor terrain only through an aperture in the ball unit, which was also used for aiming the machine gun. At the front of the control compartment were mounted two compressed air cylinders used for backup engine starting.

The fighting compartment was located in the centre of the tank hull and in the turret. The turret housed the 45mm tank gun and coaxial 7.62mm machine gun, the work places of the tank commander and loader, and the sighting and observations

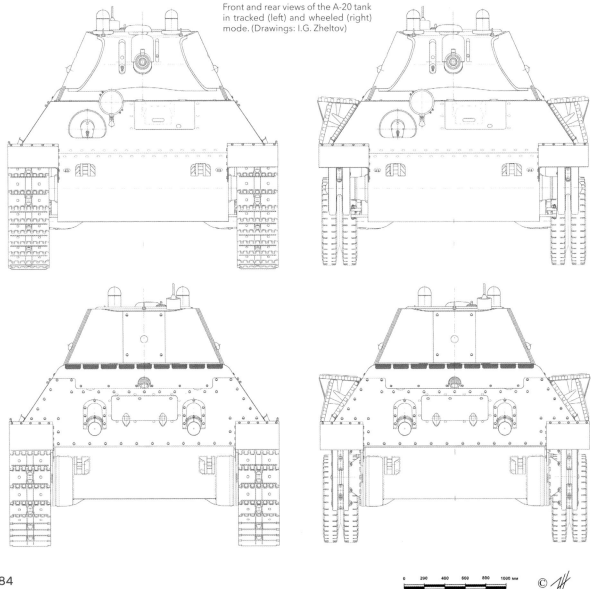

Front and rear views of the A-20 tank in tracked (left) and wheeled (right) mode. (Drawings: I.G. Zheltov)

devices. In the hull were the front fuel tanks, enclosed by re-movable steel sheets forming bulkheads, ammunition, the ex-haust fan and a 71-TK-3 radio station.

The commander (left) and loader (right) were provided with semi-soft seats, fastened to the upper section of the turret race. There was an armoured hatch in the turret roof for both turret crew members. The tank commander also performed the role of tank gunner, which allowed him to quickly strike the de-tected target, without wasting time on transfering information about its location to the gunner as in the case where these ro-les were separated. However, acting in both roles complicated the role of being commander, especially when he was also the commander of a platoon, company or battalion. The comman-der carried out battlefield observation through the TOP-1 and PT-1 optical sights, as well as an observation slot located in the left side of the turret, also protected by an observation devi-

ce with bulletproof glass. The loader observed the battlefield through a PTK panorama tank sight installed in the turret roof, and through the observation slot located in the right side of the turret, identical to the one on the left side.

The rear engine compartment was separated from the figh-ting compartment by a vertical bulkhead with hatches closed with removable covers. The V-2 diesel engine was mounted longitudinally together with the air cleaner. Either side of the engine were located the engine cooling radiators, engine lubri-cation oil tanks and four storage batteries mounted two on each side between the lower engine crankcase and the radiators.

The transmission compartment at the rear hull housed the main clutch and the centrifugal cooling system fan for the en-gine and transmission, side friction clutches with band brakes, the two side gear-reducers, two rear fuel tanks, electric starting system and air servo systems.

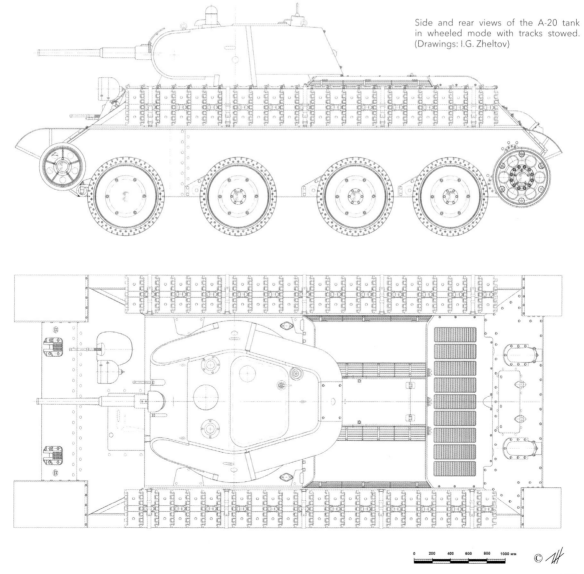

Side and rear views of the A-20 tank in wheeled mode with tracks stowed. (Drawings: I.G. Zheltov)

0 200 400 600 800 1000 мм

Tank Hull

The armoured hull was assembled from welded, and some riveted, armour plates with two transverse partitions for the engine and transmission compartments. The removable engine and transmission compartment roof sections were bolted to the hull. For ease of transmission access, the upper hull rear plate was also removable. To maximise the projectile resistance of the hull, the glacis, rear and upper side plates (in Russian "wing plates") were obliquely angled. The only hull armour located vertically was the lower side plates. The thicknesses and angle of inclination of the A-20 tank hull and turret armour components are shown in the following table.

Part Description	Thickness (mm)	Inclination angle to vertical (°)
Upper glacis plate	20	56
Lower glacis plate (top)	20	56
Lower nose plate (middle part)	20+6	Curved surface
Lower nose plate (lower part)	20	57
Driver's hatch cover	25	25
Side plate	25	0
Side plate of rocker arm niche	20	0
Front plate of rocker arm niche	10	0
Cover for rocker-arm (balancer) niches	25	0
Final drive casing	13	Cylindrical surface
Wing plate (armour above track guard)	20	35
Plate under wing plate	13	90
Top rear plate	16	45
Lower rear plate	16	38
Exhaust pipe covers	10	Cylindrical surface
Turret sub-plate	10	90
Roof plates - engine compartment	10	90
Side plates - engine cover	13	30 & 45
Caps above the longitudinal air louvres	10	90
Roof plates - transmission compartment	10	0 & 90
Hull floor	10	90
Turret front	25	Cylindrical surface
Turret side plate	25	25
Turret roof plate	10	0
Turret bustle lower section	10	90

The A-20 hull weighed 6,128kg, with hull rigidity ensured by the thickness of the armour plates and the hull partitions. Increasing the rigidity of the hull floor was achieved by connecting it with the suspension arrangements, engine mounting, partitions and the plate under the gearbox.

According to TTTs on which basis the A-20 tank was cre-

ated, the hull should be *"hermetic and suitable for deep wading without additional equipment."* This requirement was on the A-20 tank partially implemented by the installation of rubber seals on all the removable armour plates of the hull and turret; the plates adjacent to the radiators and transmission compartment louvres and the engine and transmission compartment covers; a special turret race design, and the ability to install "PKh" deep wading exhaust valves, preventing water penetration into a stalled engine when deep wading.

The hull glacis consisted of 20mm thick upper and lower armour plates, connected by riveteted butt connections. The upper hull glacis plate was located at an angle 56° to the vertical. In order to give greater strength to the hull front, for use as a "battering ram", the lower hull was made of armour plate angled at 67° and then with a curvature radius of 110mm. The bottom section of the plate was angled at 57° to the vertical and the upper section at 56° and mated with the top plate in the same plane. To enhance the strength and projectile resistance of the plate at the point of bending, over the entire width of the hull was welded an additional 6mm thick armour plate. On the left side of the tank on the upper glacis was a rectangular (470×558mm) driver's hatch, with an armoured cover with external hinges attached to the turret sub-structure. The driver's 25mm thick armoured cover had a 120mm× 30mm viewing slot, closed internally by a viewing device with bulletproof glass. Over the observation slot there was a swage line, which partially housed a viewing device. The flange for the driver-mechanic's hatch also provided protection against penetration of flammable liquid and shrapnel. On the right upper section of the glacis was welded an armoured sponson, housing a ball-mounted machine-gun. A single headlight was centrally mounted on a bracket located between the driver-mechanic's hatch and the machine gun sponson. On the lower section of the glacis were located two towing eyes, attached with rivets and welding incorporating a step for climbing on the tank, and an aperture providing access to the worm-drive of the track tension mechanism.

The angled upper side armour had was 13mm thick with a sloped plate thickness of 20mm. The height of the upper armour above the track guards, welded to the lower side armour plates, was 430mm angled at 35° to the vertical. Along each side were welded 120mm wide metal track guards.

To the inclined upper side armour on each side was attached a special platform and clamps for stowing the removed tracks when driving on wheels. To increase the turning angle of the steered front wheel pair, the front section of the A-20 hull was 122mm narrower than the rest of the hull. The narrowing of the hull began at the level of the second wheel balancers. To simplify production, the lower part of the hull side armour consisted of 25mm thick front and rear side plates, with the front plate at its junction with the rear side plate being bent at an angle of 20°. The front and rear side plates were joined by means of a docking bar welded and riveted to the side plates on the within the hull. In the front side plate, where it connected to the hull floor was a 520mm×220mm cut-out, to accommodate the rocker-arm of the first road wheel, closed internally with two armour parts, which formed a niche or "pocket" for the rocker-arm - consisting of a 10mm thick front plate, and a curved side sheet 20mm thick, welded together, and then welded to the front side sheet and the hull floor. Over the rocker-arm the niche was closed with a removable cover, attached with 14 bolts. A bracket was welded to each front side plate for mounting the idler wheel. In the rear side plates there were three cuts for the rocker-arm stub-axles and balancers of the second, third and fourth suspension units, closed by removable 25mm thick armoured caps, fastened by five bolts. To the rear side plate on the inside were welded three suspension box-shafts, in which were installed the second, third and fourth suspension units. At the rear of the rear side plate there was a cut-out for mounting the final drive.

The rest of the A-20 tank hull consisted of 16mm thick upper and lower sloped armour plates, the upper plates inclined at 45° to the vertical, and the lower at 38°. For transmission compartment maintenance, the top plate was removable, fastened by 42 bolts. In the centre of the upper rear plate was a rectangular hatch for transmission compartment access, closed with a hinged armoured cover fitted with a lock. Either side of

the hatch, there were oval cut outs for the exhaust pipes, protected by 10mm thick armoured caps, fastened to the upper rear plate by seven bolts. Welded flanges were attached to the ends of the armour caps, directly attached to the exhaust pipes. When preparing to overcome rivers, the exhaust pipes were dismantled and "PKh" (deep wading) valves installed in their place. A flat lower rear hull plate joined the sloped upper plate to the hull floor plate. At the edges of the lower rear plate were located rectangular cut-outs, to the edges of which were welded the armoured housings of the gear reducers. Two towing points were welded on the lower rear plate.

The hull roof of the A-20 tank consisted of a 10mm thick frontal welded turret sub-structure armour plate and the roof decking over the engine and transmission compartments. The turret ring diameter was 1,480mm. 20mm from the edge of the turret ring there were 36 equidistant holes for the bolts securing the lower turret race bearings. In the front of the turret sub-plate on either side above the shafts for the second units of the spring suspension were located cut outs for suspension access, closed externally by removable armoured covers. Also on the edges of the plate on both sides, closer to the engine compartment, were housed the 65mm diameter hatches covering the front fuel tank refuelling necks, covered externally by removable 10mm thick diamond shaped armour covers, each fastened by two bolts.

The engine and transmission compartment roof was a

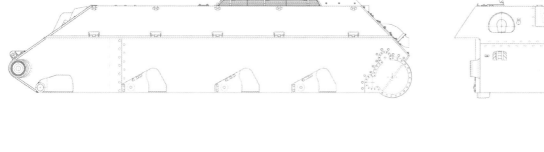

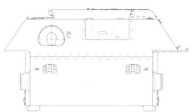

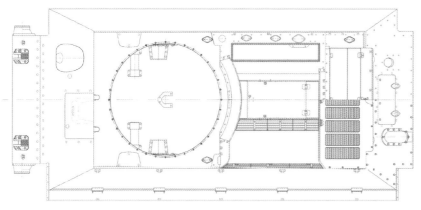

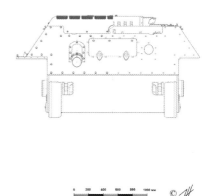

The A-20 hull layout. (Drawings: I. G. Zheltov)

welded construction of 10mm armour plates. In the middle part of the roof was a raised platform in the shape of a truncated pyramid made from 13mm armour plate, under which was located the air cleaner, which was directly mounted on the engine. Located on the cover was a 10mm thick 500×800mm hinged rectangular hatch access to the air cleaner and the engine. The side plates had rectangular cut-outs for the supply of air to the radiators with armoured strips welded to the edges to prevent liquid (whether rain or burning fuel) from entering the tank. The longitudinal shutters in their armoured housings were opened and closed using worm screw mechanisms installed either side of the fighting compartment near the engine bulkhead. At the longitudinal edges of each roof plate along the sides were located four round hatches, two 90mm diameter hatches intended for access to the 3rd and 4th suspension units and two 65mm diameter hatches used for access to the fuel filler neck and the valve for the oil tank-radiators. Over the longitudinal roof plates, flush with the engine deck plate, were installed removable U-shaped 10mm thick armour covers protecting the engine compartment against ingress of dirt or shrapnel when operating with open shutters.

The roof over the transmission compartment was a complex welded structure constructed of 10mm armour plates. Its main elements were left and right side longitudinal sheets, located above the rear fuel tanks, and front and rear transverse sheets with attached hinged double-blade louvre blinds for exhaust heat. The double shutters and the rear transverse roof plate were located 110mm below the level of the rest of the roof, forming a space for the louvre slats, which could be moved from horizontal (louvres closed) to vertical (louvres fully open), with their position being controlled by the driver operating the hand wheel worm-drive, located by the housing of the second left suspension unit. The louvres could be fixed at any angle from 0° to 90°. The longitudinal roof sheets had 65mm diameter apertures for filling the rear fuel tanks, closed externally with removable diamond-shaped 10mm thick armoured covers, closed with two bolts each.

The top of the roof compartment above the transverse louvres was closed by an (unarmoured) hinged cover, which had nine rectangular openings for exhaust heat and an aperture for mounting the tail convoy light. Each rectangular cut-out was closed from the inside by longitudinal grilles, again preventing the ingress of foreign objects with the shutters open. The folding cover was fastened to the engine deck plates by three hinges and fixed down with twelve bolts.

The A-20 hull floor consisted of front and rear 10mm thick armour plates, joined by a seam weld, reinforced by steel T-shaped cross section beam, forming the lower part of the frame of the engine bulkhead. In front of the driver's seat was located an oval-shaped escape hatch measuring 380×480mm, used for tank crew egress in combat when exit through the upper hatches was dangerous. At the rear of the hull floor plate there were two hatches. One (rectangular) hatch was located under the engine for access to the water and oil pumps. The second (round) hatch also served to drain the oil from the transmission. To ensure the hermetic sealing of the hull, all hatches were fitted with rubber gaskets. For draining fuel and oil, six 105mm diameter holes were located in the hull floor - two in the front hull floor plate for the front fuel tanks, and four in the rear hull plate for the oil tank-radiators and rear fuel tanks. The drain holes were closed externally with rubber plugs. In addition, there were eight rectangular cut outs in the hull floor, located under the shafts of the 2nd and 4th suspension units and niches of the rocker-arm of the 1st support rollers, as well as six 50mm diameter holes for accessing the lubrication points of the universal joints of the road wheel final drives. In the front section of the hull were located the driver's main controls, the driver's and machine-gunner-radio operator's seats, ammunition, and a bracket for the rotating ВКУ (VKU) contact device. Within the hull were located the steering rods and the tubing of the wheel balancers, bracketed to the hull floor. To reduce dirt, dust and snow on the hull, turret and the observation devices while driving, front and rear mud flaps and track guards were fitted.

Turret

The A-20 tank turret was designed to accommodate the main and co-axial weapons with the weight of a fully equipped turret with weapons and radio station installed being 1,750kg. The welded turret had an oval streamlined shape consisting of frontal, left and right side, turret base, roof, lower turret bustle plates and removable rear plates. The turret bustle was provided for balance. The 25mm thick frontal turret plate was a geometrically complex shape, bent along a radius of 225mm at an angle of 174° 39' with three cut-outs: central (45mm gun), right (co-axial DT machine gun) and left (TOP-1 telescopic sight). In addition, in the upper part of the frontal plate there were two holes for the installation of lifting eyes for maintenance purposes.

Each side of the turret consisted of 25mm thick front and rear side plates, with the joining weld reinforced by additional welded armour strips. The side plates were angled at 25° to the vertical. In each of the frontal turret side sheets was located a 120×30mm observation slot, protected from the inside by an observation device with bulletproof glass. Under the observation slots were pistol-firing ports fitted with an armoured plug. If necessary, the tank commander or loader pushed the plug forward; releasing it, but retained by a chain attached to the turret inner wall. A removable 25mm thick rear turret plate, angled at 25° to the vertical, and attached by four bolts, allowed mounting and dismounting of the armament. In the centre of the rear plate was a hole with a firing port.

The 10mm thick turret roof consisted of a frontal section armour plate, tilted towards the frontal sheet of the turret at an angle of 5º 21' and a rear section. There was a hatch for ventilation, protected by an armoured cap, and two holes for installing the armour protected optics of the PT-1 periscopic sight (over the commander's workplace) and the PTK panorama (over the loader's workplace).

In the middle of the roof there was a 10mm thick trapezoidal hatch for turret crew entry and egress, attached to the turret roof internally by a single large hinge with a spring-balance to assist opening and closing. In the open position, the hatch cover was fixed by a stopper and in the closed position it could be locked. The right side of the hatch had a 172mm diameter port for flag signalling, closed by an armoured cap. The A-20 tank design provided for the placement of a P-40 anti-aircraft machine gun mount, but this was not implemented on the prototype. At the rear of the turret roof, tilted at 3º 30' towards the turret rear, there were two embrasures for the installation of a lifting ring, and for the radio station antenna input, which was protected by an armoured "cup" welded to the roof.

All turret hatches and openings had hermetic seals that protected the internal turret equipment and crew from liquid, dust and dirt ingress. The base of the turret was in the form of a truncated cone structure consisting of two semi-circular shells (front and rear) welded to the frontal, side and turret bustle lower plates. The lower part of the front side plates also formed part of the turret base. The turret base armour was 25mm thick, angled at 25° to the vertical. Around the entire circumference of the turret base there were internally located welded lock plates, bolted to the upper turret ring.

The roller bearing turret race consisted of upper and lower turret sections with grooves for the hardened steel ball bearings. On the inside of the lower shoulder around the turret ring were the machined teeth that engaged with the turret rotation gear mechanism. To the upper ring seven locking bars were bolted that protruded beyond the lower edge of the ring and held the turret in place. Six sheet steel safety covers were attached to the upper shoulder, designed to protect the lower turret race from dirt and debris, and the crew from injury.

To ensure water tightness of the turret race when the tank was deep wading with the turret static, a rubber inner tube with nipple was installed in a groove in the lower outer section of the turret ring. When preparing the tank for deep wading, the tube was filled with air via a charging nipple in the fighting compartment, so sealing the turret ring and preventing water ingress via the turret ring. There was also a secondary large diameter groove with rubber seal around the turret shoulder where it met the turret sub-plate. In order to seal and protect the turret race from rain, dust and dirt, rubber washers were fitted in the holes around the turret race.

The 1,400mm diameter turret race provided 360° turret rotation. The turret and had both a manual drive and an electric motor. The planetary gearbox turret rotation mechanism in the turret provided for independent or combined use of manual or electrical drives. In transit, the turret was locked in position by a stopper, locking the upper shoulder of the turret race.

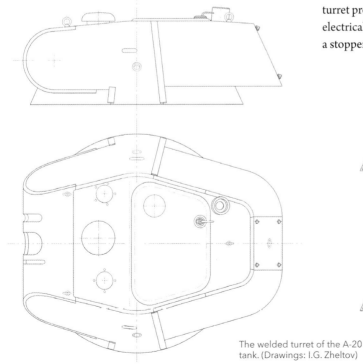

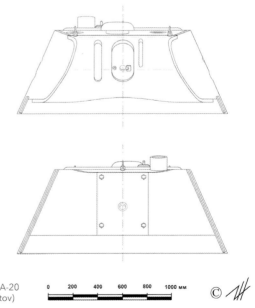

The welded turret of the A-20 tank. (Drawings: I.G. Zheltov)

The seats of the commander and loader, located respectively on the left and right side of the gun, were fastened to the upper turret by brackets such that they moved with the turret. The seats were height adjustable and had semi-soft cushions and backrests.

Armament

The armament of the A-20 tank consisted of a 45mm M-1934 semi-automatic tank gun with an electrically operated breech (Plant №183 index 243Э), two 7.62mm DT machine guns (co-axial and hull glacis), a TOP-1 optical telescopic sight with a stabilised aiming, and a PT-1 optical periscopic panoramic sight.

45mm Tank Gun M-1934 with Electric Breech Device

The 45mm M-1934 tank gun represented an improved 45mm M-1932 gun and was intended for firing on tanks, armoured cars, artillery located in the open, machine-gun firing points and enemy manpower. The gun consisted of the following main parts: barrel, semi-automatic breech, cradles, recoil and recuperator devices, masks, lifting mechanism, firing mechanisms, a shield with a shell casing catcher and drive to the periscope sight. The basic data of the gun are shown in the following table.

Basic data - 45mm M-1934 Tank Gun.

Calibre (mm)	45
Number of rifling grooves	16
Steepness of rifling (constant) (klb)	25
Length of barrel (klb)	Approx. 46 (L/46)
Typical recoil (armour-piercing projectile) (mm)	230 - 270
Typical recoil (HE-Frag projectile) (mm)	180-220
Maximum recoil length (mm)	275
Oil in recoil system (litres)	10.6
Time to recoil and recover at 15°C (seconds)	2
Limited rate of fire (rounds/minute)	Approx. 25
Working rate of fire (rounds/minute)	Approx.12
Weight of assembled gun (kg)	Approx. 313
Initial muzzle velocity (armour-piercing round) (m/s)	760
Initial muzzle velocity (HE-Frag projectile) (m/s)	335

Gun Barrel

The gun barrel consisted of thermally bonded gun tube, the main part of the barrel, and a casing with breech mechanism. When assembling the barrel, the casing was heated to about 400°C and slid on the tube. On cooling, the casing compressed the tube, redistributing the stresses in the metal of both parts, resulting in a more uniform load of the barrel walls during firing. By design, the barrel belonged to the "bonded barrel" type of construction, consisting of the barrel, chamber, breech and loading tray. The barrel had 16 clockwise rifling grooves

for generating projectile spin. On the barrel muzzle there were vertical and horizontal location points for attaching devices for calibrating the sighting on a remote target. At the trunk of the barrel was located the wedge type breech. Above the breech was located an area for the gun control mechanisms, and below was the "beard", by which the barrel connected with the recoil cylinder mechanism. In the lower part of the barrel assembly was the slide mechanism on which the barrel moved during firing, and the recoil and recuperation mechanisms.

Gun Breech

The vertical wedge gate was designed for secure and durable sealing of the barrel bore, firing the round and ejection of the spent shell cartridge. The breech locking mechanism, which contained the explosive forces induced on firing, consisted of a wedge gate, which locked the barrel for firing, and the mechanisms for the breech block and the gate or shutter, located in the left shoulder of the breech and intended to hold the breech in the closed position until the hammer was cocked. The opening mechanism was operated by a handle designed to open the shutter manually and to connect the semi-automatic with the shutter. The opening mechanism transformed the action the shutter handle, activated the breech shutter and when closed lifted the firing mechanism, intended to strike the percussion cap of the shell casings to fire the round. A shutter safety mechanism consisted of a "fuse of premature descent" and an inertial fuse. The fuse of premature descent was a lock-release latch intended to prevent accidental firing during tank movement with a loaded gun in the stowed position. For firing, the stopper of the trigger latch had to be put in the "Fire" position. The inertial fuse prevented normal opening of the shutter in the case of a prolonged shot or misfire. When fired, the recoil was automatic by inertial force action. The ejection mechanism was intended to discharge the shell casing then hold the breech in the open position for loading a new shell in the gun chamber.

The 45mm M-1934 tank gun was of the Soviet termed "semi-automatic" type, which provided automatic closing of the breech after shell loading, and automatically opening the breech after firing the shot, and the ejection of the spent cartridge case. The mechanism worked in full "semi-automatic" mode only when firing armour-piercing rounds. When firing fragmentation rounds, the "semi-automatic" automatically closed the breech after loading of the shell, but opening the breech and ejection of spent casings after firing was done manually.

Gun Cradle

The gun cradle included the slide mechanism for retaining and guiding the barrel movement during recoil and recuperation, and mounted the fixed elements of the recoil devices. The crad-

The 45mm M-1934 tank gun and co-axial 7.62mm DT machine gun as mounted in the A-20 turret.

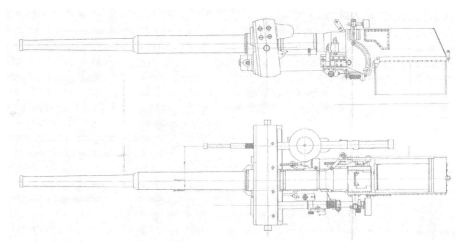

le was connected to the gun mask and was a bent steel trough. To the cradle was attached the bracket for the gun elevation mechanism, telescopic sight bracket, the bracket for the loading tray, parts of the "semi-automatic" (breech) and trigger. In addition, to the rear of the cradle was attached support for the recoil system. After the barrel moved back under recoil, sliding on the gun cradle skid rails, the recuperator returned the barrel to its original position.

Recoil System

The recoil devices were placed inside the cradle and consisted of a hydraulic recoil brake and spring recuperator. The recoil and recuperator devices were designed to provide elastic connection of the barrel with the cradle, to dampen the recoil and recuperation, to return the recoiled barrel to its original position after firing and hold it in this position for the next shot. The recuperator system returned the sliding part of the gun barrel into position by means of the mechanical energy of two compressed springs mounted in the cylinder brake recuperator assembly.

Firing Mechanism

The gun was equipped with two mechanical firing mechanisms, hand and foot pedal. The foot pedal was placed on a sliding rod attached to the bracket of the gun elevation mechanism, on the lower end of which was located a height-adjustable foot device with two trigger pedals. The left pedal was connected by a steel cable to the gun elevation mechanism, the right to the co-axial machine gun elevation mechanism.

It should be noted that when firing, the speed of firing a round is critical, since the slightest delay, with resultant vertical plane movement of the tank gun, moves the target trajectory relative to the axis of gun bore. With the aim of increasing the rate of fire of the 45mm M-1934 tank gun, it was from 1937 equipped with an electric assisted breech. The electric circuit elements on the lifting mechanism and electric breech were supplied with power via the main electrical power supply to the gun firing mechanism, which activated the firing cap of artillery rounds. On pressing the electric trigger, voltage was applied to the electro-percussion cap, heating and thereby igniting the percussion cap of the shell casing, firing the round. When firing electrically versus by foot pedal, the rate of fire was

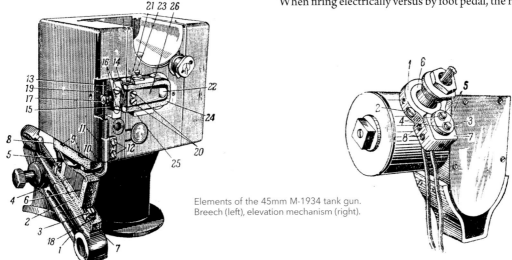

Elements of the 45mm M-1934 tank gun. Breech (left), elevation mechanism (right).

significantly increased (by reducing to a minimum the time before voltage was applied to the casing), with increasing firing accuracy, especially on the move.

Shield with Casing Catcher

A shield and casing catcher was located behind the breech, intended to protect the tank commander (gunner) and loader from the sliding parts of the gun during firing, and for catching spent cartridges ejected after the shot, but also to balance the gun. The shield with the casing catcher was attached to the gun cradle with bolts and consisted of two stamped side sheets and a rear inclined wall to deflect casings ejected from the breech assembly after firing. The folding shield had two positions - travel (lowered) and combat (horizontal along the barrel axis). On the left side of the shield was a riveted cushion for the right cheek of the gunner when using the TOP-1 sight, and there was also a socket for the bracket of the head of the TOP-1 telescopic sight. Under the shield was hung a canvas bag for spent shell casings.

Ammunition Complement, Stowage and Usage

The A-20 ammunition complement consisted of 152 shells and 43 machine gun magazines. The 45mm tank gun M-1934 employed the following unitary rounds:

1. Unitary artillery shrapnel (HE-Frag) УО-243 (UO-243) round with KT-1 and KTM-1 fuses - for defeat of infantry and against anti-tank guns. Weight of shell with KT-1 fuse - 2.135kg; with KTM-1 fuse - 2.117kg. Weight of СП (SP) propellant charge - 0.135kg. Unitary artillery rounds did not exceed 3.3 kg in weight;

2. Unitary artillery УБР-243 (UBR-243) round with an armour piercing-tracing (AP-T) projectile and МД-5 (MD-5) fuse, and armour-piercing (AP) projectile with МД-2 (MD-2) fuse.

These rounds were intended for use against tanks, armoured cars and fortified weapon emplacements. Weight of an AP-T projectile with MD-5 fuse - 1.433kg; AP projectile with MD-2 fuse - 1.425kg. Weight of SP propellant was 0.383kg. Total weight of unitary AP rounds did not exceed 2.5kg;

3. Blank artillery shots (with short sleeve), intended to simulate live firing on military exercises and for salutes.

Training (mock-up) artillery rounds were provided for training purposes.

For electric firing the same artillery rounds were used as for firing by the normal (shock) method, but they were fitted with an electric ignition sleeve, that ignited either via a Ni-Chromium filament (heated by applied electrical voltage), or by conventional breaking of the percussion cap by the firing pin of the firing mechanism. If the electric lock circuit failed, the shot could be fired using the foot or hand firing mechanisms.

All ammunition stowage was located in the fighting compartment. Ammunition use was divided into first and second stage access with the former placed vertically in a row in clips mounted on the bulkheads that covered the fuel tanks, with 20 unitary artillery rounds located on each side of the tank. The second stage ammunition was located on the hull floor, with 112 unitary artillery rounds located in 28 metal containers with "suitcase" type covers. These formed the floor of the fighting compartment. Machine-gun magazines for first-stage use were located in racks in the niche of the right hull inner wing, with the second stage use magazines located under the fightning compartment floor. There were 63 rounds in each drum magazine.

Installation of Gun and Co-axial Machine Gun

The 45mm gun and coaxial machine gun were mounted in a gun-mantlet assembly including the welded-box design gun mantlet, gun cradle and recoil system, with the ball machine gun mount and gun mounted to the gun mask. The gun was located and moved vertically on pressed and welded trunnions

The ammunition types used with the 45mm M-1934 tank gun.

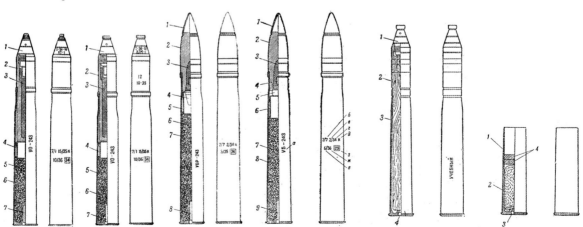

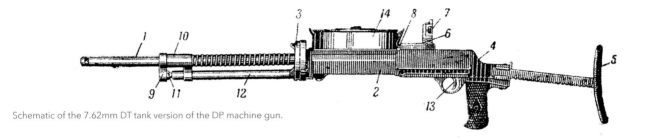

Schematic of the 7.62mm DT tank version of the DP machine gun.

mounted in bronze bushings, in the "cheeks" of the frontal turret armour. The worm-gear type manual gun elevation mechanism used in the A-20 tank provided the gun and coaxial machine gun elevation and depression in the range of +42° 30' to -6°, with one revolution of the hand-wheel elevation gear changing the angle of the armament by 2° 5'. During prolonged tank marches a détente (stop) with a fixing rod with screw thread tightening mechanism locked the gun at 0° elevation. In the front wall of the gun mantlet mask were four embrasures, for the gun barrel (central), telescopic sight (left side), coaxial machine gun (lower right) and the embrasure for machine-gun aiming. The telescopic sight and co-axial machine gun embrasures were provided with armour plugs. The outer gun mask was closed by a complex welded construction, consisting of the 20mm thick armoured gun mask and an 8mm thick armour casing protecting part of the gun barrel. A 10mm thick armoured shield protected the upper part of the gun embrasure in the frontal turret plate, fitted with a bracket for a searchlight-projector for illuminating targets at night. To provide a hermetic seal during deep wading, the co-axial machine gun embrasure in the gun mask had an armoured cap fitted with a rubber seal. When removing the machine gun from the ball-socket mount, an armoured cover was closed and held in this position by a hinged spring.

7.62mm DT Machine Gun

For engaging manpower and enemy positions the A-20 tank had two 7.62mm DT tank machine guns, located frontally in the control compartment, and co-axially with the main armament mounted in the turret. The DT was fed by a disc magazine mounted on top of the receiver, with cartridge feed carried out by a coil spring assembly within the magazine. The air-cooled machine gun barrel had four clockwise rifling grooves for imparting stability in flight. The trigger-operated weapon was designed only for automatic fire. The minimum dimensions of the receiver, achieved through the use of a sliding shutter and direct supply of cartridges from the magazine cartridge holder to the receiver also contributed to the small dimensions and weight of the machine gun. Specially designed small diameter (190mm) disk magazines and a retractable metal stock reduced the overall dimensions of the weapon for tank use, with the DT weighing 8.35kg. The weapon was simple and well tried, with almost no failures during firing. The weapon could fire short and long bursts, primarily at distances of up to 600m. Firing at distances of 600-800m was only effective when firing at large and un-armoured targets. The weapon target range was 1,000m and the maximum bullet range about 3,500m, thus the lethal force of a bullet remained to the maximum target range. Scales with divisions on the pad sight were applied after 200m, with range scales starting at 400m and thereafter at 600m, 800m and 1,000m. Combat rate of fire

The 7.62mm DT machine guns as fitted in the turret and hull glacis of the A-20 could be fitted with a bipod for ground use.

The DT tank magazine was designed for compactness within an armoured vehicle.

The DT machine gun casing catcher.

(ROF) was 100 rounds/min, and technical ROF - 600 rounds/min. Weight of a disc magazine with 63 cartridges was 3.1kg. The weapon fired Moisin-Nagant M-1891/30 rifle ammunition, namely the M-1908 light bullet (9.7g), M-1930 heavy bullet (11.9g), M-1930 steel-core armour-piercing bullet (11.9g) and M-1930 tracer bullet (9.6g). The initial muzzle velocity of the light bullet was 840m/s. The co-axial machine gun had the same angles of elevation and depression as the main gun. If necessary, the loader could operate the gun regardless of gun position. The sector of fire from the DT machine gun ball mounted in the hull glacis was in a vertical plane from -5° to +12°, and the horizontal plane 22° right and 3° left. The DT was provided with a bipod for ground use outside the tank.

Tank Sights

For surveillance in a combat situation and aiming the 45mm gun and coaxial machine gun at targets intended for direct fire, the A-20 tank commander used PT-1 and TOP-1 optical monocular sights. The TOP-1 with stabiliser was considered the main sight, and the PT-1 the firing and also surveillance sight.

TOP-1 Sight

The TOP-1 telescopic tank sight with line of sight stabilisation (to avoid confusion it was in 1940 belatedly renamed TOS M-1938) was located on the left side of the gun and rigidly bracketed to the mask of the co-axial machine gun. The sight had the following optical characteristics: magnification - 2.5x; field of view - 15°; aperture - 13mm. The diameter of the exit pupil of the sight was 23mm. The line of sight stabilisation independent of the vertical movement of the gun barrel was achieved by using a gyroscope, forming the main part of the stabiliser of the sight.

The optical system of the TOP-1 sight did not differ from the optical system of the TOP-1 M-1930, with the exception of the lower prism of the sight head, now movable and connected with the stabiliser. The sight scales were divided into internal and external. The commander viewed the internal scales in the sight concurrently with the target image. To work with the external scales located on the outside of the sight body, the com-

mander had to break away from the eyepiece. In the sight field were the sighting crosshairs, and a grid for lateral corrections and for firing from the co-axial DT machine gun. The horizontal grid lines were a scale for firing from the co-axial machine gun, and the vertical scale for lateral corrections (pre-empting direction, target direction, wind factor and derivation). In a window placed within a box in the aiming angle mechanism, to the left of the eyepiece, were two scales: the left, designated by the letter "Б" (B) - the remote scale for firing armour-piercing rounds, and the right, designated by the letter "О" (O) - the remote scale for firing fragmental rounds. The resolution of these scales relative to the horizontal thread observed in the same window, was performed using a hand-wheel.

The TOP-1 stabiliser sight consisted of a gyro with motor, ribbon, rotating lower prism head sight, upper and lower electromagnets, and the "contact automatic fire" and arresting device. The gyromotor which rotated at 18,000rpm, was placed in the outer ring of a gyro chamber, which provided the second and third degrees of gyro axis movement. Above and below the outer ring of the gyroscope were placed rotary electromagnets that served to correct the gyroscope in case of deviation of its axis from the position given to it (i.e. deviation of the crosshairs sight from the target). In the case of such deviation, the commander with the help of corrective control buttons applied electrical voltage to the upper or lower electromagnetic fields, which caused a change in the position of the outer ring of the gyroscope, which in turn turned the lower prism of the sight head through the ribbon. Thus, the crosshair of the sight was combined with the target. The ribbon was attached to the pulley, rigidly mounted on the axis of rotation of the prism. On the same pulley was placed a plate spring, at the end of which were installed platinum "automatic fire" contacts in the form of two hemispheres. The counterpart "contact automatic fire" was on the frame of the sight. In the zero position, when the axes of the barrel gun coincided with the crosshairs of the (gyro) sight the contacts were closed. During movement of the tank with vertical gun vibration, the contacts on the spring remained stationary and the pins on the sight moved with the gun. In that moment, when the direction of the axes of the barrel coincided with the stabilised line of sight, the contact closed, an electric voltage through the "fire" key was applied to the electro-capillary sleeve, and a shot taken. The arresting device was designed to align the axis of the gyro with the axis of the gun barrel, as well as to secure the gyro in the travel position. Disconnecting the gyro could be achieved mechanically, using a detent handle (stowed position and inoperative gyro) or electrically using the detent control buttons (in combat). With the help of a collimator device (located in the top cover of the sight head) in the sight, the visibility of a special light mark called "light re-

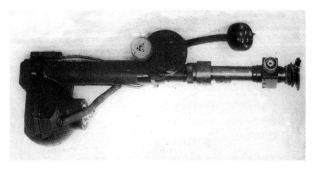

TOP-1 telescopic gun sight.

flection" was ensured, by the position of which, relative to the horizontal line of the crosshair of the sight, it was possible to judge the misalignment of the position of the gyroscope axes and the axes of the barrel bore. The coincidence of the light mark with the horizontal line of the sight crosshair identified alignment of the axis of the gyro and the axis of the gun barrel, and determined the moment of taking the shot.

To power the gyromotor stabiliser were placed in the turret a two-position main switch, transformer, circuit breaker relay and a power socket for connecting the sight to the tank on-board electrical supply. The PI-30 converter transformed 12v DC voltage into three-phase 100-100v AC voltage. The circuit breaker-relay protected the TOP-1 sight electrical supply. With the help of the TOP-1 sight, the gun and coaxial machine gun could be fired using the foot pedal using electric power from the stabiliser, with also electric firing with the stabiliser on "automatic fire". In these cases, the TOP-1 sight was used as a regular TOP sight. In the case of firing with the stabiliser mechanism operating, the commander was required to consistently perform the following actions:

1. Determine the distance to the target, side adjustment and choose armour-piercing or fragmentation projectile.
2. Use the hand-wheel on the aiming angle box to set the target distance on a scale for the selected round.
3. Move the vertical thread of the sight crosshairs to the appropriate division of the scale of lateral corrections by means of the lateral correction hand-wheel. Adjust for tank movement with the vertical thread to follow the direction of movement, and adjust for target movement in the direction opposite to target movement.
4. With the gyro retired and manual elevation utilised, to aim the gun so that the crosshairs of the aiming lines in the field of sight were aligned with the aiming point.
5. Determine the coincidence of the crosshairs of the sighting lines from the aiming point via the gyroscope.
6. Hold the crosshairs of the aiming lines at the aiming point by pressing the electromagnet control button, and pressing the "fire" button. With the coincidence in the vertical plane of the axis of the gun barrel with the aim-point, and the "auto. fire" contact closed, voltage was supplied to the electric percussion cap on the shell casing, and the shot taken.

Clearly, firing on the move with the stabiliser operating required certain skills. With proper and confident use of the TOP-1 sight, stabilised line of sight firing accuracy and operational speed was however significantly increased.

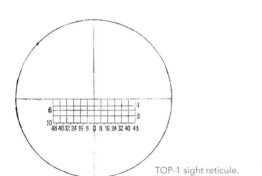
TOP-1 sight reticule.

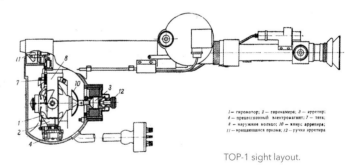
TOP-1 sight layout.

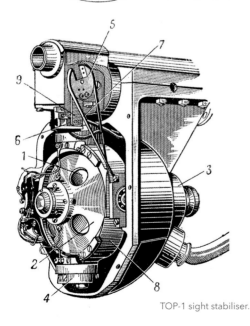
TOP-1 sight stabiliser.

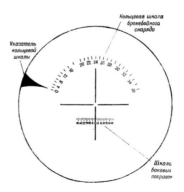
PT-1 sight reticule and field of view.

PT-1 Sight for 45mm Gun

For direct fire from the gun and co-axial machine gun, and for all-round observation from A-20 tank, the PT-1 M-1932 tank panoramic periscope sight was used, mounted in an armoured cup located on the left side of the turret roof. The sight head projected above the roof, with the eyepiece at eye level of the tank commander when seated. The sight had the following optical system characteristics: magnification-2.5x, field of view-26°, aperture-36°. The optical system of the sight used a 1:1 ratio lever and hinge parallelogram linked to the gun mantlet. The periscope sight moved vertically synchronously with the armament, with movement of the lever transmitted to the rotatable rectangular reflective prism, located in the sight head. Simultaneously, the direction of the line of sight, due to the rotation of the prism, coincided with the directions of axes of the armament bores, while the body and the ocular part of the sight were always stationary. The sight head was removable for replacement in the event of damage. In the sight field of view were: sighting crosshairs, consisting of horizontal and vertical thin line segments; distance scale with a pointer for firing armour-piercing rounds and a lateral correction scale. In the window within the sight body above the eyepiece were three scales: upper - remote for firing a shrapnel projectile; middle - remote for firing the co-axial machine gun; lower - to determine the horizontal angles between the axis of the gun barrel bore and the optical axis of the PT-1 sight. These scales in the sight window were marked with the appropriate inscriptions: ОСКОЛОЧНЫЙ (Oskolochniy - HE-Frag), ПУЛЕМЕТ (Pulemet - machine gun) and ГОРИЗ. УГЛЫ (Goriz. Ugli - horizontal angles). In addition to these three scales there were two more on the body of the sight - the lateral correction scale for when firing at night and the scale of angles of the target - to adjust when firing on uneven ground with large differences in elevation. For ease of observation and aiming in the dark, the outer scales and sighting cross-hairs in the field of sight were illuminated with low intensity electric bulbs.

All-round observation was provided by the sight head, which was rotated with the help of a hand-wheel. The sight housing and eyepiece remained stationary. To transition from "firing" mode to "circular observation" the tank commander turned off the sight lock mechanism, by rotating it clockwise. During circular observation, the value of the rotation angles of the sight head was calculated on the "Horizontal Angles" scale.

Observation Devices

For surveillance of terrain and the enemy in a combat situation in the tank A-20 was provided with three 120mmx30mm viewing slots. One placed in the driver's hatch cover, the others either side of the turret. To protect crewmembers from bullets

and shrapnel, the slots were closed internally with bulletproof glass observation devices, consisting of the base, an armoured flap that closed the viewing gap, a frame and bulletproof glass. The viewing devices were all of identical construction. The viewing slots in the turret were opened by moving the armour flap downwards, and the viewing slot of the driver mechanic by pulling the flap to the left. The glass in all devices was bul-

The PT-1 sight for the 45mm M-1934 tank gun.

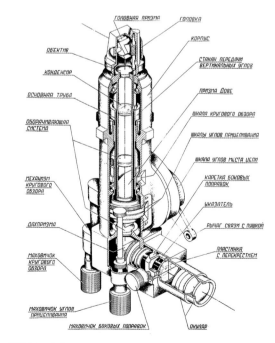

PT-1 layout diagram.

letproof multi-layer "triplex" glass, enclosed in a welded demountable steel box with a pin lock, providing quick and easy replacement of a damaged glass element. For crew protection, the viewing devices were covered with a layer of soft rubber. A 20mm armoured plate was inserted in a special groove frame during a major attack or when changing a damaged bullet-proof glass manually, so blocking the viewing slot. In this situation, the viewing angle was decreased from 50° horizontally and 20° vertically to 45° and 10° respectively. A spring-loaded latch, held the plate in its closed position. To ensure the hermetic sealing of the hull and turret when deep wading across water obstacles, the observation device design included rubber seals and plugs that covered the inspection slots, installed when preparing the machine for underwater driving.

To improve visibility, the loader's position on the A-20 tank was also equipped with a PTK M-1933 panorama sight, installed in an armoured "cup", located on the right side of the turret roof, designed for battlefield orientation, to determine the distance to a target the size of which was known, target acquisition and fire correction. The design of the PTK panorama sight was that of the PT-1, with the same optical characteristics, but without the aiming mechanisms. In the field of view there was vertical and horizontal scale crosshair, with the divisions plotted in "thousands" from 0-00 to 0-48 on both scales. Each division was 0-04 "thousandth". With these scales, the loader could determine the approximate distance to a target of known dimensions. The distance was defined as the ratio of the size of the visible target (height on vertical scale or length on horizontal scale) to the number of "thousandths" that closed the target in sight.

A-20 Engine

The A-20 tank was powered by a newly designed V configuration 12 cylinder four-stroke liquid-cooled engine, the V-2, designed and manufactured at Plant №75 in Kharkov (until February 1939 the Diesel Department - Department "400" - of Plant №183). The V-2 diesel had a double bank design, each six-cylinder block positioned at 30° to the vertical. The main technical characteristics of the V-2 engine installed in the A-20 tank are shown in the table (top right).

The main components of the V-2 diesel engine were the crankcase, two cylinder blocks, crank, distribution and transmission mechanisms. The cast aluminium alloy engine housing consisted of upper and lower halves. In the upper half of the crankcase for the installation of cylinder blocks, there were two inclined planes each located at 30° to the vertical. Additional rigidity of the upper half of the crankcase was provided by seven internal transverse partitions, to which were ttached seven suspensions of the main bearings of the crankshaft case.

For installation and mounting the engine on its frame,

Number of cylinders	12
Configuration	V-12
Angle of camber of cylinders (°)	60
Cylinder diameter (mm)	150
Piston stroke (left group/right group with trailed connecting rods) (mm)	180 / 186.75
Total working volume of cylinders (litres)	38.88
Compression ratio (x:1)	17-17.8
Crankshaft rotation direction	Clockwise
Maximum power - crankshaft rotation 1,800rpm (hp)	500
Nominal rated power - crankshaft rotation 1,750rpm (hp)	450
Operating power at crankshaft rotation of 1,700rpm (hp)	400
Maximum allowable rotational speed of crankshaft (rpm)	1.950
Minimum steady speed (idle) (rpm)	500-550
Operating rotational speed of crankshaft, rpm	1,300-1,500
Maximum torque, kgf/cm^2	230-240
Fuel consumption (max) at nominal / operating regimes l/hour	170
Number of valves per cylinder, Inlet/Outlet	2 / 2
Type of nozzle	Closed
Number of injectors per cylinder	1
Tightening the spring of the nozzle needle, kgf/cm2	200
Dry weight of diesel engine without generator (kg)	690 ± 10

in the upper half of the crankcase there were four "pads" with eight mounting bolt holes. The lower half of the crankcase covered the lower part of the crank mechanism and acted as the oil sump. The left and right cylinder blocks each consisted of a cylinder jacket, six cylinder liners, and a cylinder block closed from above by a cover. The crank mechanism, consisted of 12 piston groups, 12 connecting rods and the crankshaft. The distribution mechanism consisted of 48 valve mechanisms (24 inlet and 24 outlet valves) and four camshafts intended for opening the inlet and outlet valves in a certain sequence. Each cylinder head was mounted on one camshaft for intake and exhaust. The camshafts received rotation from the crankshaft through a set of vertical and inclined rollers with bevel gears, which also operated the fuel pumps, air distributor, generator, water and oil pumps.

The process of converting the chemical energy of fuel burned in the cylinders into mechanical operation of the diesel V-2 occurred in four working cycles - intake stroke, compression stroke, operating stroke and output stroke. Each stroke was performed in one stroke of the piston (up or down). The intake stroke was made by movement of the piston from the top dead centre point to the bottom dead centre point. As the volume of the cylinder above the piston at this time increased, the air pressure in it became less atmospheric, and the air from the engine compartment, passing through the air purifier, filled the cylinder through two open inlet valves. When the piston moved up from the lower to upper dead centre point, the inlet and outlet valves were closed and the air in the cylinder began to shrink. By the end of the compression stroke, the cylinder pressure reached 35kgf/cm²(henceforth kg/cm²)*, and its temperature rose to 550-600°C, sufficient for self-ignition of diesel fuel, which at the end of the compression stroke had been injected in spray form into the cylinder. Mixing with the air, the fuel formed a combustible (working) mixture that self-ignited. By the time the piston reached the upper dead centre point, an intensive combustion process of the working mixture began, with the cylinder pressure increasing to 85-95kg/cm², and the temperature rising to 1,700-1,900°C. Due to the gaseous expansion of the combustion the piston in the cylinder was moved under pressure to the bottom dead centre point and the compressed gas thus heated to a high temperature. At the end of its power stroke, the gas pressure in the cylinder was reduced to 3-4kg/cm² . The operating cycle was completed on the exhaust stoke as the piston moved up, exhaust gases having a temperature of 450-500°C and a pressure of 1.1-1.2kg/cm² being removed from the cylinder into the exhaust manifold and to atmosphere. When the piston reached the upper dead centre point, the operating cycle was completed, and the cylinder prepared to receive a new volume of air. The V-2 diesel engine was fitted in the A-20 engine compartment floor and lower hull sides by a riveted and welded cradle. The connection of the engine to the gearbox was semi-rigid-through a rubber coupling.

Fuel System

The fuel system included the on-board fuel reserve, and filtering and metering of fuel to the engine cylinders as required. The V-2 engine could operate with both gas-oil type "Э" (Eh) and diesel fuel "ДТ" (DT). The fuel was located in six fuel tanks; all mounted within the armoured hull in the combat and transmission compartments, with a total capacity of 530 litres.

In the fighting compartment between the housings of the 2nd and 3rd suspension units were installed in pairs the right and left front fuel tanks (upper and lower). The upper (120 litre) and lower (53 litre) fuel tanks were connected, and in the fuel system worked as one tank. In the lower tanks a drain hole was located above the discharge openings of the front hull floor plate for draining the fuel if required. The use of two tanks instead of one was dictated by maintenance requirements - if necessary the replacement of each of the four front fuel tanks could be made through the turret hatch without dismantling. The rear fuel tanks, with a total capacity of 184 litres, were installed in the transmission compartment along either side of the tank hull

and were interconnected. At the bottom of the rear tanks there were sedimentation tanks with drain holes above the drain hatches of the rear hull floor plate. The total working capacity of all the fuel tanks was 505 litres. A safety reserve capacity (25 litres) protected the tanks from fuel volume expansion due to increased ambient air temperature. Manually checking the remaining fuel in the tank was carried out with the help of a dipstick meter, dropped into the tanks through the fuel tank filling necks, which were fitted with removable filters to protect the fuel system from dirt contamination when refuelling.

The front and rear fuel tanks were connected to the fuel distribution valve connecting the tanks to the 18ПБ-1 (18PB-1) gear-type fuel pump. The fuel distribution valve was installed in the engine compartment on the bulkhead, with its four-position handle on the fighting compartment side of the bulkhead. At the lower position, fuel access from the tanks to the fuel pump was blocked. The horizontal settings allowed fuel to be fed from the corresponding front tanks, and with the lever pointed upwards, from the rear tanks. Engine operation was thereby ensured in case of damage to any one of the fuel tank groups. Before arriving via the fuel pump at one of the twelve plungers (injectors) of the NK-1 high-pressure fuel pump, the fuel was cleaned in the fine filter, located between the engine cylinder blocks above the gear mechanism. The NK-1 fuel pump was mounted between the cylinder blocks. Adjusting the amount of fuel supplied to the injector nozzles in accordance with the engine load was carried out by rotating the plungers of the fuel pump. The NK-1 fuel pump was directly connected to the driver-mechanic's fuel pedal. To maintain uniform operation of the engine (regardless of the fuel pedal) at a minimum idle speed of 500-600rpm, a centrifugal regulator was mounted in the fuel pump. The crankshaft speed was limited, ranging from 1,800-1,850rpm, to protect the engine from over-revving in the event of a sudden drop in load. In the range from 600-1,800rpm the regulator did not operate on the rail of the fuel pump, and the amount of fuel supplied through the cylinder injection nozzles changed with pressing of the fuel pedal. Engine crankshaft speed control was carried out with the help of a tachometer, the indicator of which was located on the driver mechanic's control panel. High pressure fuel lines connected the sections of the NK-1 fuel pump to the injector nozzles. As fuel from the pump was supplied to the nozzle under a pressure of 200kg/cm², the wall thickness of the high-pressure steel tube was a substantial 2.5mm.

Before starting the engine, the fuel supply to the NK-1 pump was carried out from a pressurised tank, the 0.2-0.3kg/cm² pressure being created with the help of a manual piston air pump installed in the tank control unit. The pump was connected to an air distribution valve that connected the pump to one

---

Kgs per the Russian source material refers to kg-force (kgf) often simplified to kg/cm².

of the three groups of fuel tanks. After starting the engine, the group of tanks from which the fuel was supplied by the distribution valve was transferred to communicate with the atmosphere. The fuel pressure in the system was controlled by means of a pressure gauge mounted on the driver mechanic's control panel, where a drain valve for air release from the fuel fine filter or NK-1 pump was also located.

Air Cleaning System

The main element of the air purification system was a combined type oil-air purifier mounted directly on the V-2 diesel intake manifolds consisting of a tray pan and a filter element. At the bottom of the pan was the oil bath, filled with one litre of engine oil, sufficient to provide a 10mm oil level in the bath, above which was a filter element laid between two grids in a metal casing. The operation of the air cleaner was based on a combination of inertial and filtering cleaning principles. Air containing the dust entered an annular slot formed by the upper edge of the tray and the cylindrical surface of the filter element housing. Centrifugal forces mixed the dust in the air above the oil bath heated to more than 120° C. Finer airborne dust particles lodged in the filter element, while larger dust particles settled in the pan oil bath. Purified air from the filter element entered the intake manifolds of the engine. In the presence of dust in the air measuring $0.3g/m^3$, the air cleaner design provided an average 75% cleaning efficiency during 10-hours of engine operation.

Exhaust System

Removal of engine exhaust gases was carried via the engine exhaust manifolds and exhaust pipes. The 127mm diameter exhaust pipes were affixed to the 103mm diameter engine exhaust manifolds by clamps, the connections sealed with asbestos cord. The exhaust pipes passed through the transmission compartment and exited the hull in the upper hull rear, the apertures being protected by armoured caps with flanges fastened by three studs and nuts. When preparing the tank for deep wading, the exhaust pipes were dismantled and "ПХ" (PKh) valves installed, preventing water from entering the engine in case of engine stall.

Engine Cooling System

The V-2 engine as mounted in the A-20 tank was provided with a closed type liquid circulating engine cooling system, designed to remove heat from engine parts that had been in contact with hot gases, and maintain these components within acceptable temperature limits. The cooling system, with its centrifugal pump with drain valve, two tubular radiators, centrifugal fan, and automatic steam/filling valve was filled with 90-95 litres of coolant with system circulation provided by a centrifugal

The V-2 diesel engine, which entered production in 1939.

pump mounted on the lower half of the engine crankcase on the transmission side, powered via the engine crankshaft, delivering at operating speed a flow of 450-500 l/min. The temperature of the coolant in the cylinder block was monitored by a thermometer, with the readout located on the driver-mechanic's dashboard control panel. Cooling of liquid in the system was by means of two radiators located either side of the engine compartment. The cooling system was connected to the atmosphere through an automatic valve consisting of two separate valves for steam and air. The steam valve, which opened with an increase in system pressure over $1.6kg/cm^2$, protected the radiators from boiling over. The air valve, which opened when the cooling system pressure decreased to $0.87-0.92kg/cm^2$,

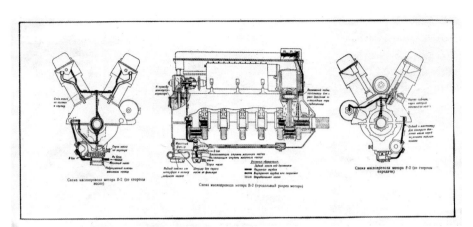

The V-2 diesel engine lubrication scheme.

protected the radiators from deformation as the coolant cooled after the engine had stopped running. The boiling point of water in the cooling system was about 110°C. The Centrifugal fan was designed to ensure forced air circulation in the engine and transmission components of the tank. The air entering the machine cooled the water and oil radiators, gearbox, and main and side friction clutches, preventing overheating of these units during operation. The fan with riveted blades was bolted to the flywheel of the main clutch and ran directly at the enginge revs. The fan design capacity running at 1,800rpm was 10m³/s.

When overcoming water obstacles by deep wading, engine cooling was achieved by drawing outboard water filtered through a cloth filter. Water supply and removal were regulated by means of a valve installed in the fighting compartment, albeit the underwater driving system was not fully developed on the A-20 tank prototype.

Engine Lubrication System

Supply of oil to the mechanical parts of the V-2 diesel and partial heat removal was in the A-20 tank provided by a circulating type pressure lubrication, the main elements being an oil pump, two oil filters, an oil sump below the engine crankcase, two oil tanks - a radiator placed in the engine compartment along the sides between the 3rd and 4th suspension units, a shut-off valve and control devices, a pressure gauge and two thermometers.

Circulation of oil brands "CO" (SO) and "CC" (SS) in the system was by means of a three stage gear type oil pump installed in the lower half of the engine crankcase and operated via a power-take-off. Oil arrived at the inlet section of the oil pump from the two oil radiator-tanks via a shut-off valve, and further through the oil filter to the high pressure outlet, lubricating the bearings and other engine components having rubbing surfaces. The circulated oil was accumulated in the engine crankcase sump, from where oil passed through another filter via two sections of the oil pump. After passing the second

filtration, the oil passed via two pipelines and the bypass valve into the cooling sections of the oil radiator-tanks, cooled by forced airflow (the total cooling surface was 7.05m²). The cooled oil was then fed into the inner cavities of the radiator-tanks and mixed with the rest of the oil. Depending on the ambient temperature, the cooling radiators placed on the internal walls of the oil radiator-tanks facing the engine could be switched on or off by means of a bypass valve. In the case of disconnection of the cooling sections, the oil, bypassing them, directly entered the tanks. The full capacity of each radiator tank was 70 litres, with replenishment being 50 litres. Controlling the oil level in the radiator-tanks was carried out through the oil filler aperture using a special meter. To protect the lubrication system from dirt when refilling with oil, removable gauze filters were installed in the radiator tank filler necks. Draining oil from the system was via the radiator tank drain holes located above the drain hatches of the rear hull floor plate, as well as from the engine crankcase - via the drain valve on the oil pump. The temperature of the oil entering and exiting the engine was monitored by means of thermometers, the indicators for which were installed on the driver-mechanic's instrument panel, together with a pressure gauge that showed the 6-9kg/cm² operating system oil pressure, with the maximum permissible oil temperature at being 110°C. During long stops, to prevent oil from flowing from the oil-radiator tanks into the engine crankcase, the tanks were isolated by means of a shut-off valve which the driver knew was open due to a glowing green light on the electrical component panel. When the light was not glowing, engine operation was prohibited.

Engine Starting Systems

Engine start-up of the V-2 diesel in the A-20 tank was by means of a 15hp ST-70 electric starter, or by compressed air in case of of electric starter failure. When starting the engine electrically, the mechanical coupling of the engine crankshaft with the starter gear was via a gear crown fixed on the flywheel of the main clutch. The air starting system consisted of two 10-litre cylinders, a reduction valve, a tee for charging cylinders from an external source, a high-pressure air duct and an air distributor mounted on the drive housing of the NK-1 fuel pump in front of the engine. The compressed air supply to the air distributor was via cylinders installed at the front of the hull via air lines and a reduction valve located in the control compartment. From the air distributor, compressed air was alternately, in accordance with the order of the engine cylinders, fed to the starting valves installed in the heads of the cylinder blocks. During the expansion stroke, compressed air through the starting valves entered the cylinders and acting on the pistons, forced the engine crankshaft into rotation. Maximum cylinder air pressure was $150kg/cm^2$. The cylinder head had a shut-off valve and a connection to the reduction valve, in the body of which was installed two pressure gauges, one showing the air pressure in the cylinders, the second showing the pressure of the air going to the air distributor (starting pressure). The minimum engine starting pressure was $45kg/cm^2$. With two fully charged cylinders, the engine could be started 12-15 times.

Transmission

Converting the transmission torque and tractive effort from the engine to the combined wheel-track drive system of the A-20 tank was carried out using a mechanical transmission, consisting of main clutch, gearbox, two friction clutches and floating band type brakes, two side and two gear drives for supplying torque to the driven road wheels when driving the tank on wheels, and drives to the control elements of the transmission. Pneumatic servos were installed in the A-20 to operate the main and side frictions, and to reduce braking forces.

Main Clutch

The multi-disk main friction clutch on the A-20 tank was intended to disconnect the engine from the transmission when changing gear, smooth the transfer of engine load when starting the tank and after gear change, and for protection of transmission components and the engine from damage due to a sudden change in engine speed or travel speed. The main clutch consisted of a flywheel, seven 3mm thick steel plates, and the pressure plate, with the driven parts consisting of a drum with nine 3mm thick steel clutch discs and a ball-type disengagement mechanism. The main clutch was rigidly connected to the engine output drive shaft via a splined coupling. Torque from the engine was transmitted to the leading parts of the main clutch, and from them to the slave parts. In turn, the hub of the driven drum was through an elastic splined coupling connected to the drive shaft of the gearbox. There were deliberately significant gaps between the coupling spines, this semi-rigid connection of the main clutch with the gearbox reducing shock loads due to misalignment between the engine and the gearbox. When the main clutch was activated, the drive and slave disks were compressed by sixteen cylindrical pressure springs with a force of $545.6kg/cm^2$ and due to the friction force they rotated as a whole. To stop the transmission of torque from the engine to the gearbox, the main clutch was disengaged, i.e. the friction discs were released from the forces of the pressure springs. The driver-mechanic via control rods operated the disengagement by a device that moved three ball bearings located in grooves on an inclined surface ("tear"). The movement was transmitted to the flywheel side of the main clutch, compacting the disk, through which the fingers released the pressure plate from the leading and slave discs. The discs were released from the force of the pressure springs, and the driving and driven parts of the

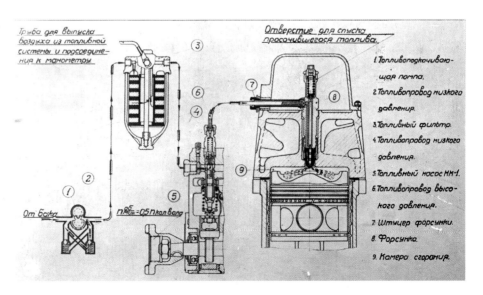

The V-2 diesel fuel and ignition system.

main clutch disconnected, and thus torque from the engine was temporarily not transmitted to the gearbox.

Gearbox

The gearbox was intended to change the traction on the drive wheels at a constant engine crankshaft speed; to change the speed in a wider range than could be achieved by purely changing the rotation speed of the engine crankshaft, to allow reverse tank movement with a constant direction of rotation of the crankshaft of the engine, and to ensure prolonged idling during stops. The 3-way, 4-speed gearbox with a transverse horizontal shaft and a mechanical actuator provided tank movement on one of the four forward gears as required, and in reverse. Gearchange was carried out by means of a gear lever shift mechanism installed to the right of the driver-mechanic's seat, via three movable slides, hence the box "three-way" nomenclature. The transmission was made without direct transmission, with the location of the shafts in one horizontal plane. The gearbox ratios for the A-20 tank, and speed in each gear is shown in the following table.

Gear	Gear Ratio	Gear ratio speed (km/h at 1,700rpm)
1	2.688	8.98
2	1.265	18.8
3	0.656	36.9
4	0.372	65.16
Reverse	2.874	8.45

The gearbox case was constructed of aluminium alloy and built in upper and lower halves with spray lubrication of gears and bearings. The gearbox was filled with 11 litres of "MK" brand aviation oil (at temperatures below -20°C - aviation "MZS"). Draining of oil from the gearbox was via a drain plug in the lower half of the crankcase, closed by a plug. The weight of the gearbox without oil was 370kg.

Side Friction Clutches and Brakes

The complex multi-disc on-board (side) dry friction clutches on the A-20 tank were designed to ensure tank movement both on tracks and on wheels. Turning the tank when moving on tracks was by means of disengaging one of the friction clutches and then braking the trailing track, and by braking the road wheels when in wheeled mode.

The on-board frictions consisted of the driving parts (the inner drum with 21 pressure plate discs) and the driven parts (the outer drum with 20 driven disks) and the ball disengagement mechanism. The internal (driving) drums were connected by a splined connection with the main transmission output shaft, the external (driven) drums being mounted on armoured flanges. The dry friction discs were compressed

together by 16 pressure springs. Disengaging the clutch, i.e. releasing the friction discs from the spring force, was carried out by a ball mechanism consisting of three ball bearings placed in inclined ball grooves ("tears") in the control mechanism box. The principle of operation of this ball mechanism was the same as that used for disengaging the main clutch. To stop and rotate the tank, floating 200mm wide steel brake bands with heat-resistant "Ferodo" composite material linings were installed on the outer drums of the on-board frictions either side of the tank. To obtain a uniform gap between the band and the drum when releasing the control lever side clutch-pedal foot control transmission brake, the band was fitted with a support spring preventing the "Ferodo" linings from arbitrarily seizing on the drums. The space between the band and the drum was ventilated by forced air, improving heat transfer.

Control of the on-board frictions and the brakes was carried out by means of two levers installed either side of the driver's seat, the intermediate, longitudinal and inclined control rods, levelling and transition rollers. Brake control was by means of pedals and a system of levers, with pulling on both brakes at the same time stopping the tank. The pedal was mounted on a common roller with the pedal of the main clutch and equipped with a ratcheted locking latch mechanism intended to hold the brakes in a tightened state while parked or when the tank stopped during rise and descent. The side frictions were attached and centred on the flanges of the side reducers through the outer drums, in the hub of which were installed ball bearing sets.

Final Drives and Road Wheel Drive System

The final drive gearboxes either side of the A-20 tank increased the torque and traction force on the drive wheels when the tank was moving on tracks. The single-stage reduction gear final drives with a 4.57 gear ratio consisted of leading and driven parts housed in steel housings welded and riveted to the hull. The side-reducer drive shaft, combined with the drive gear, was mounted in the crankcase neck supported on two

The air cleaner on the A-20 tank.

roller bearings. The driven shaft and drive gear was mounted in a removable armoured crankcase cover on two single-row tapered roller bearings. At the end of the driven shaft, located outside the cover, were splines on which the track drive wheel was mounted. In the lower part of the crankcase of the side gearbox, there was a torque transmission unit (power take-off) from the driven gear of the side gearbox to the longitudinal side drive shaft of the road wheel drive mechanism. The transmission unit consisted of a shaft mounted in the crankcase of the side gearbox on three roller bearings and ending with a bevel gear, and a movable gear that allowed engagement and disengagement with the road wheel drive shafts via the horizontal shaft drives. When activated, torque was transmitted to the road wheels via the bevel gear engaged with the longitudinal side shaft drive. Engaging and disengaging the drive to the road wheels was carried out by the driver-mechanic for each side separately by means of two levers. The drive systems were used to engage the 2nd, 3rd and 4th road wheels when the tank was moving on wheels. All the road wheel drive components were placed within the tank hull with the exception of the wheel gearboxes, which were protected by armoured covers.

The longitudinal side shaft drives consisted of three propshafts and three bevel gears on each side, connected in series (shaft-box-shaft-box-shaft-box) by means of couplings. Torque from the side gearbox was via the longitudinal side shafts, transmitted through bevel gearboxes to the telescopic universal shafts connected to the individual wheel drives. Torque was passed individually as required to the 2nd, 3rd and 4th road wheels. The drive shafts were located in a closed steel casing, protected from dirt and damage. The use of a telescopic propshaft as a drive to the individual wheel reducers was due to the position of the road wheel relative to the tank hull constantly changing in the vertical plane when the tank was moving across rough ground, with the universal joints of the telescopic gimbal allowing torque transmission to the wheel reducers over the entire range of vertical road wheel travel. The reduction gear hub was partially housed in a sealed disc cover welded to the balancer and a casing cover. Drive to the gear reducer was by means of a splined connection in constant engagement with the outer gear of the reducer. Speed synchronisation when the A-20 tank was driving on wheels and tracks was without additional gear synchronisation mechanisms, with speed equalisation by using the same gear ratios in the transmission elements of the tank, which simplified the transmission design and increased operational reliability.

Pneumatic Servo Control System

The A-20 tank was fitted with a closed type pneumatic servo control system designed to reduce the effort exerted by the driver-mechanic on the levers and pedals when controlling the main and side friction brakes, and when braking. The control system included a compressor; high-pressure receiver cylinder and three air cylinders with relief valves, aiding operation of the main clutch and the steering clutch levers. A piston-type compressor mounted on the gearbox pumped air into the high-pressure cylinder placed under the gearbox and provided a constant supply of compressed air with an average pressure of $6kg/cm^2$. The compressor was driven by a gearbox transmission shaft power take-off. When pressing the main clutch pedal or when moving the levers controlling the on-board frictions, air from the high-pressure cylinder via a differential valve mechanism entered the corresponding air cylinder. The cylinder rods were connected to the levers of the equalising roller mounted under the driver's seat. In each of the air cylinders, compressed air acted on the piston, which, via the levelling roller and the traction system operated the shut-off mechanisms of the main or side frictions and the drive levers of the brakes. As a result, the main or side clutch was decoupled, and began tightening the brake band (after side clutch disengagement). With the help of the differential valve mechanism the degree of brake tightening directly related to the application of the pedal. After the pedal of the main clutch or the lever of the side clutch returned to its original position, air from the cylinder was by means of a piston under the action of a recoil spring directed to a low-pressure cylinder mounted in the engine compartment. From the low-pressure cylinder, air entered the compressor again. Constant system pressure was maintained via working and safety valves installed on the left side of the control compartment. In case of a lack of air in the system, it was automatically taken from the atmosphere. With the pneumatic system operating, the force applied by the driver-mechanic on the pedal when disengaging the main clutch was $7-8kg/cm^2$; the force applied on the levers to disengage the on-board clutch and brake varied from $7-30kg/cm^2$ depending on ground conditions. The main and side clutches and brakes of the A-20 tank could still be operated in case of failure of pneumatic system actuators. In this case however, the force required to disengage the main clutch increased to $35-45kg/cm^2$, and the force for disengaging the side clutch and braking was $50-80kg/cm^2$.

Wheeled and Tracked Drive Systems

The combined wheel-track drive system consisted of two track drive wheels and eight road wheels. When driving in wheeled mode, the first pair of road wheels provided steering, and the 2nd, 3rd, and 4th road wheels were driven. In tracked mode the system incorporated the two idler wheels with tensioning mechanisms, track-turn skid steering and the two tracks. The design of the wheel-tracked drive system allowed the tank to move on tracks, on wheels, and simultaneously on track on one side of the tank and on wheels on the other side.

The track drive wheels were mounted on the output shaft of the side reducer. On the steel hub of the drive wheel was a flange, with twelve tie rods. Each drive wheel had six holes to release mud and snow accumulating between the wheels during tank movement, the edges of the holes being flanged for rigidity, and six holes for passage of the roller bearing shafts, the freely rotating rollers engaging with the track horns. To increase the bearing surfaces of the axles of the rollers strengthening plates (referred to in Russian as "bonki") were welded to the discs. In order to reduce the contact and wear of the track horns, the working surfaces of the rollers were made in the form of a groove. With a worn track, the drive horns on alternate track shoes entered the gaps between the rollers, and with the rotation of the driving wheel the rollers located on the horn ridge and drove the track forward. As one horned track link exited from a roller, the following horned track link was entering between other rollers. When the tank was being driven on wheels, the track drive wheels rotated freely. The hub of the track drive wheel was externally closed by an armoured cover attached to the hub with five bolts. The diameter of the track drive wheel assembly was 634mm, and its weight - 124.8kg.

The main parts of the first road wheel pair were the axle trunnion boxes, split hubs, two 7mm thick stamped armour steel discs with rubber rim (tyre) shock absorption, two ball bearing sets each, and rocker-arms with stub axles. The trunnion boxes were steel castings, forming the mounting for the road wheel and location of the stub-axle and ball bearing sets. The box had a hole for passage of the stub axle, connected with a rocker-arm, and with a mounting located in the upper part of the box, to which the steering mechanism was attached. The outer surface of the box was cylindrical in shape for mounting the inner of two ball bearings and a support collar. The inner ball bearing set rested on the inside against

the collar of the box, and the outer surface - within the thrust ring. The road wheel hub consisted of two steel discs with six holes for the coupling bolts. Each half of the hub had a cylindrical recess, housing the ball bearing races. Both halves of the hub, together with the mounted wheels of the road wheel, were tightened with six bolts, with an attached conical armour cap. On each disk was welded a steel rim, fitted with a 150mm wide rubber rim with 42 holes for cooling and better cushioning. The diameter of the first road wheel was 830mm and the width 350mm.

The rocker-arm was a box-section steel casting with an "ear" at one end to connect it with the trunnion box of the first road wheel, and a hole at the other for passage of the stub-axle. The hollow axle of the rocker arm was fixed at one end in a bracket mounted in a special niche of the tank hull, and the other in the steering control tube. Inside the hollow axle of the rocker arm was a gear rack, connected by means of screw gears with the axis of the (removable) steering wheel installed in the control compartment at the workplace of the driver-mechanic. With the tank driving on wheels, the driver steered the fron wheels via a conventional wheel and steering rack arrangement. The maximum steering angle of the first set of A-20 road wheels driving on wheels was 15° either way. The 2nd, 3rd and 4th road wheels had the same overall design as the front steering wheel set but modified for use as driven wheels. The wheels were all 830mm in diameter 350mm in width, with a road wheel with reducer and balancing arm weighing 299.4kg. To reduce rubber component wear when the A-20 tank was moving on wheels, all road wheels had a slight camber angle of 1° 30'.

The closed-hinged tracks used on the A-20 were 400mm wide, each with 72 track shoes (36 with guide horns), with the total length of a new track being 12.02m. Each track shoe

Schematics of the main friction (clutch), and gearbox.

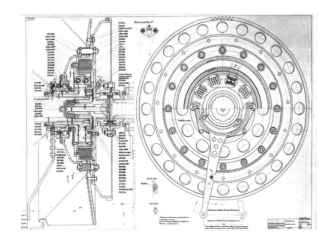

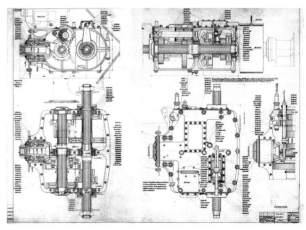

had 13 hinge fingers - 7 at the front and 6 at the rear. The tracks links were connected through floating type hinges with 18mm diameter track pins. The axial movement of the pins in the track eyelets was limited by spacer-rivets inserted into the holes in the outer eyelets of the tracks. Each track link (between eyelet centres) was 167mm, and including hinge - 172mm. Total weight of both tracks was 1,300kg. The outer surface of the tracks had stiffeners, which also acted as grousers. Additional bolt-on grousers were provided for use on soft ground or on icy roads, each fastened through holes in the track shoes by two bolts. The A-20 tank prototype was not however equipped with grousers during trials, since their design had not then been completed. The significant 400mm track width and 3.674m length of track on the ground provided the A-20 tank with good track ground floatation, with average ground pressure under 0.61kg/cm².

The idler wheel ("sloth" in Russian) guided the track return, and allowed for track tension adjustment. The idler was a cast steel wheel with two pressed rubber rims, installed in the front of the tank on the outer axis of the crank of the track tension mechanism. The crank was attached to the bracket by a nut located inside the tank body, which turned a worm drive tensioning mechanism accessed through apertures in the inclined hull glacis plate. When changing track tension, the nut was eased, and the engaged idler-crank and bracket teeth were released. The worm-drive was then rotated using the socket wrench of the track tensioning mechanism, and the distance between track drive wheel and the guide wheel centres altered, increasing or decreasing track tension depending on the crank rotation. The idler wheel could be adjusted 170mm horizontally, which in the case of severe track-hinge wear made it possible to reduce the track by as much as two links. The diameter of the guide wheel was 504mm and its weight was 104.6kg.

Suspension System

The composition of each of the eight A-20 tank suspension units a the rocker-arm (balancer), elastic spring element, helical compression spring (one spring in the suspension units of the first wheel pair and two springs in the other wheels) and a suspension travel limiter. The first road wheel pair suspension unit springs were placed horizontally; those of the 2nd, 3rd and 4th road wheels obliquely.

The main parts of the elastic elements of the suspension units of the first road wheel pair were a cylindrical screw spring, a guide rod (stock), a regulating cup with spring cushion, a spring casing and a rocker-arm travel limiter. The screw spring (OD 123mm, rod diameter 28mm) was placed in a steel cylindrical casing installed horizontally along the side within the tank hull and connected by its flange to the niche of the rocker-arm of the first road wheel. Inside the spring was an installed rod, with one end threaded into the adjusting block, and the other connected with the rocker-arm. When the road wheel moved upwards, the rod moved forward, towards the front of the hull, together with the adjusting cup and "pillow" (rubber pad), which compressed the spring with its flange. When the road wheel moved downwards, the rod moved in the opposite direction, releasing the spring. Maximum upward road wheel travel was limited by a rubber shock absorber installed in the tank hull in the rocker-arm recess; and downward travel by the spring assembly and the track.

The elastic elements of the suspension units of the 2nd, 3rd and 4th road wheels had the same design but were located at an angle of 28°30' in shafts welded within the hull. Screw springs (OD132mm, rod diameter 27mm) were located in the shaft one above the other and connected by means of a centering sleeve. Inside the springs there was a guide rod, at the top of which there was an adjusting cup, and at the bottom - a support cushion with a sleeve, which incorporated the rocker-arm (balancer) axle. The upper part of the adjusting cup was screwed into a nut, hinged in the tank body. By tightening or loosening the adjusting cup and thereby compressing or loosening the springs the weight of the tank could be rationally distributed over the road wheels. When installed correctly, the suspensions units provided the A-20 tank with a ground clearance of 400-410mm. The connecting assembly between the elastic element of the suspension unit and the road wheel was the rocker-arm balancer, which was a hollow steel unit of complex geometric shape and housed in the tank hull at the bottom of the suspension unit shaft. There was an aperture in the internal section of the balancer for passage of the telescopic drive shaft, transmitting torque to the wheel reducer of each of the six driven road wheels, internally the balancer mechanism was placed in a tube mounted across the floor of the tank hull. Axial displacement of the balancer was prevented by a removable armoured protective cover. Upward movement of the rocker-arm was limited by a rubber shock absorber attached to the steel platform welded inside the shaft of each suspension assembly. At maximum vertical travel of the road wheel, the steel platform of the balancer rested against the shock absorber and stopped further wheel movement. Downward wheel travel was limited by the suspension assembly travel, as well as by any slack in the track. The dynamic (upward) stroke of each road wheel was 150mm, the static stroke (downward) was 90mm. All suspension unit components of the 2nd, 3rd and 4th road wheels, with the exception of balancers, were interchangeable. The rocker arm/balancer units were interchangeable only within the same side.

Electric Equipment

The electrical system installed in the A-20 tank powered various equipment including engine start and operation, communications, lighting and alarm systems. The source of electric power was a generator type "ГТ-4563А" (GT-4563A) with relay-regulator "PPT-4576A" (RRT-4576A) and four batteries 6СТЭ-128 (6STEh-128). The 1kW capacity GT-4563A generator was installed on the right side of the V-2 diesel engine and was the main source of electric energy, and battery charging while the tank engine was running. The GT-4563A shunt-type generator was a DC unit driven via a power-take-off from the engine crankshaft. The RRT-4576A relay-regulator was installed to the left of the driver and combined three electromagnetic devices: voltage regulator, reverse current relay, and the current limiter. The voltage regulator was designed to maintain generator output in the range of 24-32v. With the help of a reverse current relay, the generator was automatically disconnected from the on-board electrical network at low crankshaft speed or engine stop when the generator voltage was lower than the battery voltage or connected to the network when the generator voltage exceeded the battery voltage.

Four 12-volt 6STEh-128 lead-acid starter batteries, with a nominal voltage of 12V and capacity of 128Ah each were placed in frames in the engine compartment. The battery provided power to the electric engine starter and electrical energy to the consumer units at low engine revs (when the generator was disconnected from the electrical on-board supply), or with the engine off. There was a mixed (parallel-serial) connection between the batteries, hence a nominal voltage of 24V and a total nominal capacity of 256Ah.

The consumer units on the A-20 tank requiring electric power were: starter "CT-70" (ST-70) with the starting relay PC-260 (RS-260), electric motor МБ-20 (MB-20), turret motor МВ-24 (MV-24), the fighting compartment exhaust fan, ТОП-1 (TOP-1) stabiliser sight, the 71-TK-3 radio station and ТПУ-2 (TPU-2) tank intercom, the ГФ-4702 (GF-4702) signal (horn), and internal and external lighting devices.

External tank lighting consisted of: a "КДО" (KDO) headlight with two electric lamps "large" and "small" (beam) (25w and 5w respectively), mounted on a bracket to the left of the sponson for the front machine gun (during trials, the headlight was replaced by a spotlight), as well as a "ТПП" (TPP) tank sighting spotlight with a 250w lamp, mounted directly on the armoured gun mantlet. There was also the "ЗИС" (ZIS) signal ("rear") lamp installed at the rear of the tank on the roof of the transmission compartment under a flap. To ensure blackout, the white glass lantern (top - "stop" and bottom "numbering" for showing tactical numbers) was on the inner side painted blue. Internal lamps included three ППТ-37 (PPT-37) shades and

four ОСЛТ-37 (OSLT-37) lamps, panel electrical and control panel instruments and a portable "ПЛТ-36" (PLT-36) lamp.

Control and measuring instruments monitored and provided engine oil lubrication system warning, while the Type 4 МШС (4 MShS) voltmeter and Type 4 МТС (4 MTS) ammeter indicated system voltage and amperage respectively.

The electric switching and auxiliary devices in the A-20 tank were protected by a fuse box, with electrical devices including protecting emergency (duty) lighting, shield electrical, turret electrical shield БЗС-5 (BZS-5), switch batteries (ground), the brake light switch (stop light). The emergency light, mounted on the shaft of the second right suspension assembly, illuminated the crew compartment and provided a portable lamp connection for when the batteries were disconnected. On the emergency lighting panel were located the ПТ-37 (PT-37) shaded light and its toggle switch and a plug for connecting a portable lamp.

All the tank electrical control devices were located in a single panel located to the left of the driver which mounted the voltmeter, ammeter, electric start button and electro-signal (horn), external and internal lighting switches, oil warning light and eight fuses. There was a separate control panel in the turret with fuses and switches for the turret internal lighting, the power supply of Unit №1, the TPU-2, and the bulbs in the PTK (for night firing), and TOP-1 stabiliser-sight. Supply of electric energy to the turret electrical panel was via a VKU-3A rotating contact device mounted on a special bracket on the fighting compartment floor.

The A-20 tank used a single-wire scheme, with the negative wire earthed to the tank hull. The exceptions were only the circuit (duty) lighting and warning lights for the oil-radiator valve, directly connected to the batteries via a two-wire scheme. The on-board network nominal voltage was 24V. The low-voltage copper wiring used in the electrical system varied in diameter, thickness of ПРП-1 (PRP-1) rubber wiring insulation and braiding according to use. Single wire cables and combined wiring looms were of 1.5, 2.5, 10, 35 and 95mm diameter. The wire braiding was also to reduce radio interference.

Communications

The A-20 tank was fitted with a 71-TK-3 short-wave receiving and transmitting speech and telegraph simplex radio, and TPU-2 tank intercom. The 71-TK-3 radio station, installed in the turret bustle of the A-20 tank, was an upgraded 71-TK-1 radio station that worked in the frequency range 4-5.625MHz. The radio station consisted of: transmitter and receiver in a frame with shock absorption, РУН-75 (RUN-75) and РУН-10 (RUN-10) transformers with filters and cables, 4-NKN-10 alkaline battery, main switch with cables, spare bulbs box, microphone, two double handsets (voice), telegraph keys and an

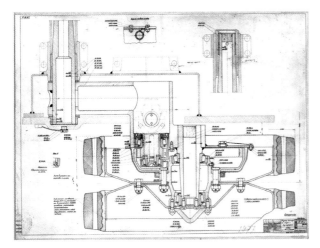

A-20 road wheel and rocker-arm balancer schematic.

antenna. The radio transmitter circuit was independent of that for the telephone and telegraph, and consisted of a master oscillator, power amplifier and modulator to obtain a 750V DC voltage in the transmitter the RUN-75 transformer was used. The receiver used three SB-112 and four УБ-110 (UB-110) lamps. DC low to DC high voltage (200V) was provided by the RUN-10 transformer. The receiver of the radio station was located on the right side of the turret bustle behind the loader's seat, and the transmitter on the left side behind the tank commander's seat. The radio station main switch could be set to "reception", "transmission" and "off". The ebonite insulator type antenna with a steel spring base through which the Аш (ASh) or АшТ (AShT) antenna was inserted, was assembled from four one-metre long jointed steel tubes. The antenna input point was located at the right side rear of the turret roof, protected by an armoured cup. The TPU-2 tank intercom was designed for two-way telephone (speech) and light signal communication between the tank commander and driver-mechanic. The TPU-2 kit consisted of: Unit №1 - tank commander, Unit №2 - driver, two pairs of ТГШ (TGSh) head phones, two

MA (MA) microphones, connecting cables and spare parts. TPU-2 unit №1 was installed in the turret at the workplace of the tank commander, and Unit №2 opposite the driver's seat mounted to the glacis plate between the driver's hatch and the front machine gun installation. On the side-wall of Unit №1 by the commander were placed two switches - single and paired. The single switch had two positions - "Talk" and "Ready to Listen". The paired switch had three positions "Internal communication" - for communication with the driver-mechanic, "Transmitter KV" and "Transmitter UKV" for receiving, and relay through a radio station. During conversation between the commander and driver-mechanic the single switches of both devices were transferred to "Talk" and the commander's switch to the "Internal Communication" position. At the end of the conversation, the single switches were returned to the "Ready to Listen" position. On the front wall of each unit there was a button to signal and a lamp with a red lens to control the call. The light alarm worked regardless of the switch position on either device.

Spare Parts, Tools and Accessories (ZIP)

The spares and tool kit (ЗИП - ZIP) consisted of general, special and entrenching tools, towing and lifting devices, spare parts, supplies and materials destined for technical maintenance and basic ongoing tank repair. The external and internal ZIP stowage for the A-20 tank was designed on paper, but not installed when the prototype was tested. The design documentation envisaged the following ZIP set on the tank:

- Two 5-tonne jacks, located on special mounting plates, attached to the front walls of the niches of the first suspension mountings, either side of the tank, secured with clamp locks;
- Two ZIP boxes for the gun, placed on the floor under the seat of the machine-gunner-radio operator;
- Two sapper shovels, mounted externally on a folding rack mounted above the transmission compartment;
- A two-handed saw placed outside the tank on the right side longitudinal plate of the engine compartment roof;
- Four spare track links (connected in pairs) attached to the upper side armour either side of the tank.

Portable tools were placed in two tool bags, the internal location of which was undetermined; nor at the time was the location of the two towing cables, axes, sledgehammers and special tools required to refill the oil and coolant.

When the tank was being driven on wheels, each track was split into three sections that were mounted on the track guards and fastened in five places by heavy-duty braid straps. A portable two-litre tetrachloride fire extinguisher was mounted within the tank.

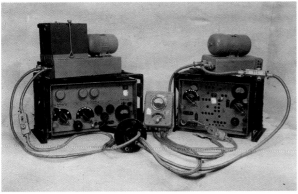

The 71-TK-3 radio transmitter-receiver station.

Chapter 8

General Arrangement of the First A-32 Prototype

The first prototype of the A-32 tank was a tracked-only version of the A-20 wheel-tracked tank, and differed from it in having more powerful armament and a modified chassis with five road wheel pairs per side, and a changed transmission design. Since the majority of the parts, assemblies and mechanisms of the A-32 tank were as for the A-20 design, the description of the A-32 given below provides information only where the A-32 differed from the A-20.

Tank Hull

The construction of the hull of the A-32 tank, with the exception of the hull front and side armour did not basically differ from the design of the A-20 hull. The hull armour thickness and inclinations were as for the A-20, with the exception that the vertical side armour plates were 30mm thick on the A-32. The hull of the A-32 tank was of uniform width along its length, i.e. without narrowing at the front of the hull as in the A-20, as the tank lacked the front steering wheels and their control mechanisms and thereby did not require the hull to be narrowed to accommodate them. The upper and lower plates of

the hull frontal armour on the A-32 tank were 132mm wider at the junction with the vertical side plates than on the A-20 tank due to the lack of narrowing of the hull as described, and the increased thickness of the side armour. The rest of the frontal part of the tank A-32 design was as for the A-20 tank.

The sides of the A-32 tank hull, as with the A-20, consisted of upper and lower sections. The design of the upper side sections (the inner fender or "wing" sections) was the same on both tanks, the only difference being the absence of welded platforms and clamps for storing the removed tracks. The lower part of the vertical hull sides of the A-32 tank, unlike on the A-20, consisted of a single armoured plate, in which was located five cut-outs for the rocker-arms of the tank suspension units. After installation of the rocker-arms and suspension springs, these cut-outs were partially closed with removable armour covers 30 mm thick, attached to the side armour with five bolts each. At the front of each vertical side sheet was welded a bracket to install the idler wheel, and at the rear there was a cut-out to install the final drive. On the inside of the A-32 sides there were welded suspension spring shafts (four on each

Frontal view of the first A-32 tank prototype.

side) with the fuel and oil tanks installed in the space between the shafts. On the insides of the hull front, pockets and brackets were welded for installation of the suspension units of the first road wheel pair.

The roof of the A-32 hull, as with the A-20, consisted of a frontal turret sub-structure and removable roof sections over the engine and transmission compartments. In front of the turret plate over the shafts for the second suspension units, and also in the rear plate over the shafts of the third suspension units there were four notches (one for each shaft) for access to the suspension components, closed by removable armour covers. The hatches for refuelling the front fuel tanks of the A-32 tank were moved forward relative to their location on the A-20 tank and placed along the frontal edge of the turret. The removable roof section above the A-32 engine compartment

was almost identical to that of the A-20, with the exception that the hatches in the longitudinal sheets of the engine roof section were modified to provide access to the 4th and 5th suspension assemblies. The longitudinal armoured roof sections above the engine also differed in detail. The design of the removable roof section over the transmission compartment, and that of the rear hull of the A-32 was identical to the A-20.

The hull floor of the A-32 consisted of two armour plates, front and rear. Due to the lack of narrowing of the hull near the front, the front plate of the A-32 hull floor, unlike the A-20, was rectangular. The dimensions of the oval shaped escape hatch in the front plate of the A-32 hull floor was, at 350×416 mm, smaller than that of the A-20. The location and number of cut-outs for the suspension components also differed, the A-32 hull floor having five rectangular cut-outs each side, one for the

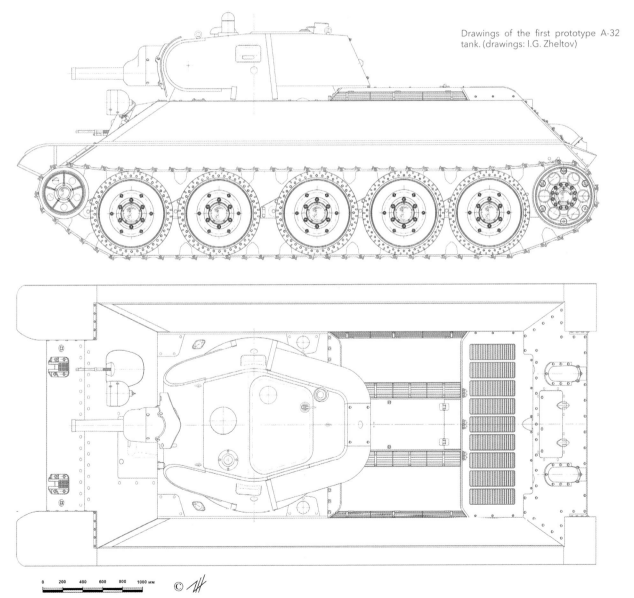

Drawings of the first prototype A-32 tank. (drawings: I.G. Zheltov)

first suspension unit, and for the shafts of the 2nd to 5th suspension units. The remaining hull floor hatches and drain holes were in design and size as for the A-20 tank, with the exception of deletion of the six lubrication access points for the multiple final drives fitted on the wheel-tracked A-20 tank.

Turret

By its design, geometric dimensions, and the thickness and inclination of its armour plates, the A-32 turret was basically no different from the A-20 turret, with two exceptions. The embrasure in the turret front was modified, and increased, due to the installation of a 76.2mm L-10 tank gun. There were also no embrasures for mounting the PTK panorama sight heads at the front of the turret roof.

The turret sides were now provided with newly designed convex-shaped observation devices for the tank commander and loader, welded into rectangular cut outs in the armour. These observation devices - a notable feature of the early series production T-34 - improved visibility relative to the A-20 and also increased the space inside the turret required for normal firing of the 76.2mm L-10 gun.

Armament

The armament of the A-32 tank consisted of a 76.2mm L-10 semi-automatic tank gun, two 7.62mm DT machine guns (one co-axial with the main gun, the other mounted in the hull glacis), with a ТОД (TOD) optical telescopic sight, and ПТ-1 (PT-1) optical periscopic panoramic sight for the 76.2mm gun.

76.2-mm L-10 Tank Gun

The 76.2-mm L-10 tank gun (GAU index-52-P-354T) was a general-purpose weapon intended for firing at tanks and other armoured vehicles, artillery located in the open, machine-gun nests and enemy infantry. The gun consisted of the following main parts: barrel, semi-automatic breech, trigger, recoil and recuperator devices, masks, elevation mechanism, shield and drive to the periscope sight. The specifications are given in the table (right).

The design of the L-10 gun-barrel belonged to the "non-bonded" barrel type and consisted of a free tube moun-

Basic data - 76.2 mm L-10 Tank Gun

Calibre	76,2mm
Number of rifling grooves	24
Steepness of the rifling (constant) (klb)	20
Barrel length (klb)	23,7
Length of threaded part of the barrel (klb)	16,5
Normal recoil length (mm)	350-450
Maximum recoil length (mm)	485
Amount of fluid in the recoil brake (l)	4,6
Initial velocity (armour-piercing projectile) (m/s)	555
Initial velocity (HE-Frag shell) (m/s)	560

ted in a conical casing with the slide mechanism welded to it, a "screw-on" breech and armour protection. The gun tube was inserted into the casing (with the breech removed) with the retention of a small diameter gap, and prevented from rotating by a special dowel key installed in the thickened collar of the breech section of the barrel. The breech was screwed on to the housing, centred on bronze bands, pressed into the housing and fixed by two wedge locks. On the muzzle section of the gun barrel were fitted three armoured rings, which protruded from the casing and protected the gun barrel from bullets and shrapnel. The armoured rings were fixed by a special nut screwed on to the gun barrel.

The bore consisted of the sealing section of the gun barrel accomodating the breech, the gate (shutter)and the rifled gun tube section with 24 clockwise cut rifling grooves to impart projectile spin. Above, there was a hole for the passage of the rod compressor recoil devices (above the chamber) and holes for the installation of the mechanism of the "semi-automatic" (breech), and the breech gate (shutter) closing and ejecting mechanisms.

Locking the barrel, firing, and ejection of the shell casing was carried out with the help of the vertical wedge breech gate with a previously described mechanical "semi-automatic". The gate consisted of locking, opening, firing and ejection mechanisms, and the mechanism of the "semi-automatic". Manual

The 76.2mm L-10 tank gun.

Rear view of the first A-32 tank prototype.

opening of the breech gate was by means of a handle placed on the right "cheek" of the breech; and production of a shot by means of the firing hammer (pin) shock, with two alternative triggering mechanisms (foot and manual). The "semi-automatic" mechanism provided for automatic closing of the breech after loading the gun, and automatic opening of the breech after firing a shell and ejection (extraction) of the spent casings, which, after being deflected from the back wall of the turret, fell into a bag. The casing catcher was located behind the fixed part of the barrel and consisted of a metal frame and said canvas bag it being attached to the brackets of the mask, and having two position - stowed (folded down) and combat (located horizon-

tally along the axis of the bore). The folding canvas bag, riveted to the gun casing, was locked by a latch, and contained up to 8 shell casings. On the left side of the breech unit there was a shield to protect the tank commander from the sliding parts of the gun during firing. Above the flap was riveted a pad for the cheek the tank commander when observing via the TOD sight. The L-10 gun was equipped with two aforementioned mechanical firing trigger mechanisms - foot and hand. The foot trigger was the main, and the hand trigger the secondary option, used in the event of failure of the foot mechanism.

When fired, absorbing the energy of the recoiling parts of the gun (with a weight of 440kg) and returning them to their

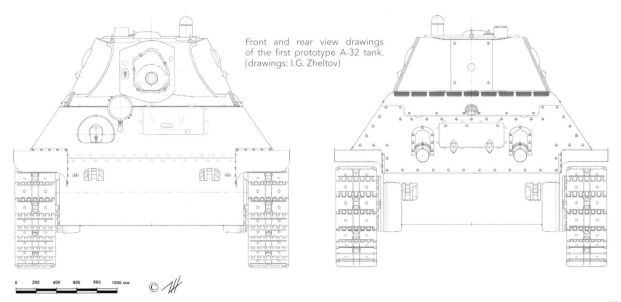

Front and rear view drawings of the first prototype A-32 tank. (drawings: I.G. Zheltov)

original position afterwards was performed using a hydro-pneumatic ПОУ (POU) recoil device. The recoil brake and recuperator were a single unit, located above the barrel and rigidly connected with the gun mask. The recoil brake cylinder was placed inside the outer "air" cylinder - which contained both liquid and air. The recoiling parts of the gun POU were fastened by a nut with a spring stopper. This design provided a recoil resistance force of up to 8,500kg/cm² and a range of recoil lengths - the standard recoil length was 400 ± 50mm, and the limit - 485mm.

76.2mm L-10 Gun and Co-Axial Machine Gun Installation

For mounting the main armament and coaxial machine gun in the A-32 tank turret there was an installation, including mask, gun, two trunnions and armour. The gun mask, intended for mounting the gun and coaxial machine gun in the tank turret was a complex quadrangular box shape. In the middle of the mask there was a hole for the gun barrel, with two slides welded to the inside of the housing which located the barrel mechanism, and on which the moving parts of the gun slid during firing and recoil. Over the embrasure for the barrel there was a threaded hole for installation of the POU cylinder. In addition, the mask had holes for the TOD telescopic sight, for the cylinder mechanism for the semi-automatic breech and the ball installation for the co-axial DT machine gun. In the side walls of the gun mask were pressed and welded trunnions on which the paired gun installation moved vertically on bronze bushings mounted in the "cheeks" of the frontal turret plate. The worm gear type manual lifting mechanism mounted in the A-32 tank provided the gun and coaxial machine gun with elevation and depression from +30° to -5°.

The outer part of the gun mask that closed the armour protection for the gun assembly consisted of an armoured shield, mask protection, front cover and screw-on shield. The gun shield was bolted to the mask using the same holes as for the passage of the gun barrel, POU cylinder, cylinder battery mechanism "poluavtomatik" (semi-automatic) breech, TOD sight and machine gun. Additional plating protected the gun shroud, and POU cylinder of the recoil mechanism against bullets and shrapnel.

In the plates were holes for the passage of securing bolts of the gun shield. A frontal armoured plate protected the POU and the recoil system of the "semi-automatic" mechanism, and another plate covered the space between the front plate of the turret and the gun mask. In the gun mask there were holes for the TOD sight (on the left side) and holes for the machine gun (on the right) paired with the gun.

Ammunition

For firing from the L-10 tank gun the following unitary artillery rounds with propellant charge as for 76.2mm M-1902 gun were used (propellant index Ж-354А (Zh-354A) - propellant charge mass 0.930kg, powder Type 7/7):

1. Unitary artillery rounds with ОФ-350 (OF-350) high-explosive "long-range steel-grenade" (HE-Frag) shells and ОФ-350А (OF-350A) "long-range steel-cast iron grenade", with KTM-1 fuses.
2. Unitary artillery shots with high explosive shells Ф-354 (F-354) and Ф-354Г (F-354G) i.e. "the old high-explosive grenade of the Russian type" equipped with KT-3, KTM-3 and ЗГТ (3GT) fuses.
3. Unitary artillery rounds with armour piercing-tracing (AP-T) shell Бр-350А (Br-350A), equipped with МД-5 (MD-5) or МД-76 (MD-76) fuses.
4. Unitary artillery rounds with "bullet shrapnel" - Ш-354 (Sh-354) and Ш-354Т (Sh-354T) equipped with 22 second and "T-6" detonating caps, respectively.

Firing unitary artillery rounds with a propelling charge for 76.2mm gun M-1902/30 (propellant index - Ж-354 (Zh-354) with propellant charge weight 1,080kg, the powder Type 7/9 of the L-10 gun was strictly forbidden.

The high-explosive shells were used to destroy enemy troops and machine-gun emplacements, to engage artillery, for the destruction of simple field shelters and obstacles, and to fight against armoured vehicles in the absence of armour-piercing tracer (AP-T) shells. There were two options available when firing high-explosive shells, depending on the installation of the fuse, with as a result two types of projectile - fragmentation

Left to right: 76.2mm OF-350 round, OF-350A round, F-354 round and Br-350A armour-piercing tracer rounds.

and high-explosive. Fragmental shells had an impact detonator on which the cap was removed before loading the round. The shell exploded immediately on impact with the target, with the explosive effect obtained via a combination of gas expansion, shock waves and, primarily, shrapnel fragments. This option was used to defeat unsheltered manpower and enemy artillery. The alternative "explosive effect" was obtained by firing with the fuse armed but with the cap still in place. In this case, the shell penetrated the target and then the explosive charge detonated, the shock wave destroyed the shelter and enemy manpower was hit by shrapnel. This firing variant was used specifically to defeat enemy troops located in field fortifications.

Armour piercing-tracer rounds were used to destroy armoured objects (tanks, armoured vehicles, armoured trains, etc.) and long-term firing points - ДОТ (DOT) in Russian. From a distance of 500m the L-10 gun could penetrate armour plate with a thickness of 40mm sloped at an angle of 30°. To enhance the overall damaging effect, the projectile body also contained 155 grams of explosive, which by means of the same gas expansion, shock wave and projectile fragments caused similar damage to that of a fragmentation shell on entering the hull or turret of an armoured vehicle target. Shrapnel projectiles were used for defeating unsheltered enemy manpower, and in self-defence (effectively firing "buckshot").

Tank Sights

The A-32 tank commander carried out observation from the tank and direct-fire aiming of the 76.2mm L-10 gun and co-axial machine gun by means of a PT-1 optical monocular sight - considered the main sight for the tank - and an additional TOD sight.

It should be noted that the PT-1 and TOD sights were not standard for the 76.2mm L-10 gun, as their distance scale were graded to the ballistics of the M-1927/32 (KT) tank gun. When firing the L-10 using the PT-1 and TOD sights, the gunner had to use special conversion tables. In April 1939, specialists at Artkom AU RKKA had developed a new ballistics scale for the PT-1 and TOD sights for use with the L-10 gun. In order to avoid confusion during production and operation, the new sight scales with the ballistics of the L-10 gun were assigned the designations PT-2 and TOD-2. The order for their production was in April-May 1939, given to Plant №69, being at that time the main manufacturer of tank sights. However, in view of the heavy workload of the plant, production of PT-2 sight was abandoned, with new production limited to the production of TOD-2 sights.

PT-1 Sight for the 76.2 mm L-10 Gun

According to the optical characteristics and design of the PT-1 M-1932 tank periscopic panoramic sight for the 76.2mm gun was no different from the sight for the PT-1 to 45mm gun,

except for the presence of different scales placed both in the field of view and in the body of the sight. Calibration of the remote scales of the PT-1 sight for the 76.2mm gun was made using the ballistics of 76.2mm tank gun M-1927/32 (KT). In the field of view of the sight were: sighting crosshairs and an annular distance scale with a pointer for firing OFS or a "bullet shrapnel" projectile (firing armour piercing-tracing projectiles was also conducted with the help of this scale) and the lateral corrections scale. In the window placed in the body of the sight over the eyepiece, there were three scales: the top - remote for firing with long-range OFS ("long-range grenade") rounds; the average - in "thousandths" (thou.) for introduction of lateral amendments; and lower-to determine the horizontal angles between the axis of the gun barrel bore and the optical axis of the PT-1 sight at target designation. In the sight window, these scales were marked with the appropriate words: "ДН.ГР" (bottom.Gr.), "ТЫСЯЧНЫЕ" (thousands) and "ГОРИЗ.УГЛЫ" (horizontal angles).

TOD Sight

The TOD M-1930 telescopic tank sight was located on the left side of the gun and was rigidly connected with the gun mask and co-axial machine gun by a fixed bracket. The sight provided for firing from point-blank range and had the following optical characteristics: magnification 2.5x, field of view 15º, aperture/luminosity-13w.

The sight was a long optical tube and consisted of the head,

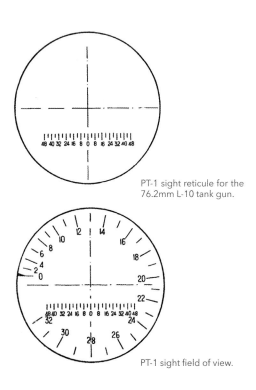

PT-1 sight reticule for the 76.2mm L-10 tank gun.

PT-1 sight field of view.

middle section, eyepiece, and the lateral correction and aiming angles mechanisms. The exit pupil diameter was 23mm. The graticule of all remote scales of the TOD sight was performed using the ballistics of the 76.2mm M-1927/32 (KT) tank gun. In the field of view of the sight were located the sighting cross-hairs, consisting of horizontal and vertical thin threads, as well as a scale to take account of lateral corrections. Lateral correction was carried out with the help of a correction mechanism handwheel, while the vertical thread of the crosshairs moved to the right or left of the centre of the field of view.

Setting the distance to the target was performed using the handwheel of the aiming angle mechanism on the scales observed in the box of the aiming angle mechanism. In the window two distance scales were visible: the left was marked ДН.ГР (Dn. Gr.) - for firing with long-range ОФС (OFS) "long-range grenade" (i.e. artillery support fire) rounds, and the right, marked "ШРАПНЕЛЬ" (shrapnel) -for firing OFS, "bullet shrapnel" or armour-piercing rounds (i.e. direct fire). Both scales were illuminated with electric lamp with a power of 3.5w.

Ammunition Complement

The A-32 tank ammunition complement consisted of 72 rounds for the L-10 gun and 26 drums for the DT machine guns. All

The TOD sight assembly.

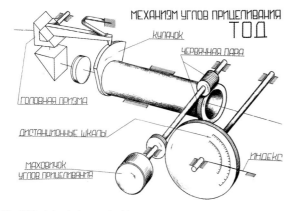

The TOD sight aiming angle drive mechanism.

ammunition stowage was located in the fighting compartment of the tank. Ammunition supply to the gun was divided into first and second stage, first stage ammunition being located in clamps mounted on the bulkhead plates covering the fuel tanks. The second stage ammunition was housed in metal "suitcases" installed on the hull floor of the tank and covered by lids, that formed the floor of the fighting compartment.

Engine

The engine of the A-32 tank was basically as for the A-20 tank. The only exception was the construction of the fuel tanks, cooling radiators and the engine lubrication system layout. In connection with the increase in the number of road wheels and suspension mounting and shafts on the A-32 tank, and the change their location in the hull, the capacity of the fuel tanks and oil radiator-tanks on the A-20 tank was reduced by 36 and 30 litres, respectively. The capacity of the four front fuel tanks located between the shafts of the second and third suspension units was 317 litres; the capacity of the two rear fuel tanks was 177 litres. Thus, the total fuel tank capacity of the A-32 tank was 494 litres, and the working capacity - 462 litres. Total capacity of the two oil-tank-radiators, located either side of the tank between the shafts of the 4th and 5th suspension units, was 110 litres.

Transmission

The main difference between the transmission of the A-32 and the A-20 tank was the lack of additional mechanisms required to drive the road wheels on the A-20 when operating in wheeled mode. The A-32 lacked the power take-offs and gearing that transferred torque to the longitudinal side and final drive shafts to the road wheels, and the mechanisms for engaging and disengaging the road wheel drives. The A-32 featured conventional final track drive wheels with no additional drive take-offs. The other elements of the A-32 powertrain - the main clutch, gearbox, steering clutches and associated brakes and actuators had the same design as the A-20 tank.

Track Drive and Running Gear

The running gear of the A-32 tank consisted of the track drive, individual road wheels and spring suspension mechanisms and return idler wheels.

The track-drive based system used on the A-32 tank consisted of two rear drive wheel-sprockets, five road wheels per side (rather than four as on the A-20), two idler wheels with tensioning mechanisms and the tracks. The drive and idler wheels with track tensioning mechanisms were taken directly from the A-20 tank.

Due to the lack of a wheeled mode drive system, the design of the A-32 road wheels was considerably simplified compared to the A-20. Each road wheel with external rubber shock absorption (i.e. rubber rims/tyres) consisted of a hub and two stamped discs made of armoured steel. The hub of the road wheel was a steel casting with a central flange. To install the discs on the hub flange, there were six annular holes for the passage of bolts that attached the discs to the hub. To increase the bearing surfaces, the bolt locations were reinforced with welded steel reinforcing discs. To increase strength of the rollers, the discs were additionally secured with six bolts with spacers (the tie bolts passed through the spacer bushings, mounted between the disks). From the outside the wheel hub were closed with a removable armoured cover, attached to the hub with five bolts. On the rim of each wheel a steel bandage rim was pressed and welded with an intermittent seam, fitted with a 150mm wide rubber rim/tyre with 42 ventilation holes. Inside the hub, on both sides, there were cylindrical recesses with recesses for the installation of two bearing sets, on which the road wheel pressed on the axis of the rocker-arm balancer. The road wheel diameter was 830mm, and the overall width 350mm. In contrast with the A-20, the A-32 road wheels were installed in the vertical plane without a camber, with all road wheels having the same construction and being interchangeable. During tank plant and polygon tests of the A-32 tank, BT-7 road wheels were as an expediency measure installed on the balancers of the 1st, 2nd and 3rd suspension units.

Due to the increase in the overall number of road wheels to ten, the track surface contact area of the A-32 tank increased by 334mm relative to the A-20 (by the length of two track shoes) to 3.998mm, which in turn, despite the increase in the combat weight of the A-32 tank, reduced the average ground pressure from 0.61 to 0.595kg/cm^2.

Suspension

The suspension system of the A-32 tank consisted of ten independent suspension assemblies located within the tank hull for the now ten rather than eight road wheels, with each assembly including: a rocker-arm (balancer), a suspension element (two helical compression springs) and balancer-stops. The suspension components of the 2nd to 5th road wheels of the A-32 tank were of identical design, and were located inside the hull within inclined steel box shafts welded to the inside of the tank hull. Coil springs with an outer diameter of 132mm and rod diameter of 27mm were located within the shaft one above the other and connected by means of a centring sleeve. Inside the springs there was a guide rod, with an adjusting cup above the assembly, and at the bottom a support cushion with a sleeve, linked to the stub axles. The rocker-arm connecting the spring element of the suspension unit and the road wheel was a hollow steel unit located at the bottom of the shaft of the suspension unit. At the ends of the balancer there were holes for the balancer stub-axle, the road wheel axle and the suspension rod connection. These assemblies were press-formed and welded. The attachment of the second to fifth suspension mountings in the A-32 hull was the same as in the A-20 tank. The suspension units of the first road wheel pair were different in design, the springs having different diameters and being located one inside the other. The outer diameter of the outer spring was 178mm (rod diameter 30mm); the outer diameter of the inner spring - 112mm (rod diameter 22mm). The dynamic travel (i.e. upward) of each A-32 roadwheel was 150mm, and static movement (i.e. downward) was 90mm. The ground clearance when adjusted correctly via the spring adjustment cups, was in the range of 385-400mm.

Electrical and Communications Equipment, Spare Parts, Tools

The electrical equipment of the A-32 tank was as for the A-20, with the exception of the mountings, provision of a stabiliser for the TOP-1 sight (not installed in the A-32 tank during trials) and a 71-TK-3 radio station. According to the requirements of the Prototype Committee, the radio in the A-32 tank was to be installed in the front of the hull rather than in the turret bustle as with the A-20 tank, which entailed a change in the electrical system layout. However, the hull-mounted 71-TK-3 radio station installation was not installed or tested in the A-32 tank prototype, which was without a radio station at this stage. Provision of on-board spare parts, tools and accessories (ZIP) for the A-32 tank, was as with the A-20 prototype, also not implemented during trials.

Chapter 9

Tank Testing - A Chronicle of Events

The A-20 and A-32 prototypes developed at Plant№183 were according to NKSM Order №21ss dated 17th March 1939 to be transferred to ABTU to conduct field trials no later than 1st June 1939. Before transfer to the army, the tanks were per Soviet norms required to pass internal factory and ABTU polygon trials that would ultimately determine which option, either the wheel-track A-20 or the tracked A-32 would be taken into Red Army service.

Factory tests actually began on 26th May 1939, when assembly of the A-20 tank was completed in mechanical workshop "530" of Department "500" of Plant №183. On this day, the A-20 tank, minus its main armament, had its first trial run, the "newborn" tank moving approximately 1km around the territory of the plant on wheels in 1st and 2nd gear. The tank underwent minor fettling over the next five days, and was the end of May 1939 transferred from machine shop "530" to prototype workshop "540", headed by engineer I. I. Kazimirov and his deputy, engineer P. N. Goryun, who would directly supervise most A-20 and A-32 plant testing.

The first endurance run of the A-20 tank, with Plant №183 test driver I. V. Kuznetsov at the controls, took place on 1st June 1939. After the 174km run, the situation report noted:

"The mechanisms worked smoothly. The temperature regime of the water and oil remained within 60-70°C. <...>
From the conversation with the driver, the machine is well controlled, has smooth running, but with significantly increased noise due to the drive mechanisms for the additional (wheeled drive) trans-

missions. From conversations with those present, the behaviour of the machine is good, and the movement sustainable."

RGVA. F.31811 L.3 C.1633. pp5

As a result of the proving run and subsequent plant technical inspection, the following defects and malfunctions were detected:
- Fuel leaks from both left and right rear fuel tanks due to poor soldering seam, incorrect fastening and lack of internal baffles
- noted to improve the structural rigidity;
- Slight coolant leak from the left radiator;
- Oil drips from the gearbox;
- Leakage of bearing grease from under the armoured caps of the 2nd, 3rd and 4th road wheels and the discs welded to the balancers (insufficient tightening);
- Destruction of the cone bearing cup, and in consequence the wheel reducer bearings, of the 3rd right road wheel (insufficient strength of the bearing cup);
- The gear spindle of the ST-70 electric starter jammed in the gear ring of the main clutch (faulty relay).

When preparing the tank for the next run, all these defects and failures were eliminated within two days.

On Sunday, 4th June 1939, the day after repair completion, employees of prototype workshop "540" with the participation of leading engineer of the 1st Department of the 8th Division of ABTU, Major I. G. Panov prepared the A-20 for a long endurance run on tracks. Informing his direct chief, military engineer 1st rank Ya. L. Skvirsky on the results of this run, Panov in the next operational summary reported:

The A-20 tank overcoming a 1.1m vertical wall.

The A-20 tank brings down a 330mm diameter oak tree.

"Distance travelled 4.6.39 on tracks 155km (corrected to 175km) on a good dirt road. The movement was steady. The mechanisms worked smoothly. The water temperature was 70°C, and the oil 85-90°C. The speed was brought to 65km/h at 1,400-1,800rpm. Noted somewhat increased heating of the gearbox and side frictions. The tank was fully outfitted (i.e. in combat order), and then driven 200km on heavy ground and rough terrain".

RGVA. F.31811 L.3 C.1633. pp6

After completion of the run, tank maintenance in workshop "530" uncovered:
- Oil leak from under the seal of the neck of the gearbox.
- On the left side clutch, the oil seal, bearing and - due to improper adjustment - the steel band brake failed.

Once again, the factory masters* did everything to quickly repair the prototype A-20 and continue the tests. By the end of the month, the A-20 had travelled a total of around 700km on tracks and wheels. During plant testing the specialists of workshop "540" checked the strength and reliability of the new tank and its individual components. The A-20 was thereafter tested for its ability to overcome natural and artificial obstacles: ascents and slopes, loose sand and dunes, forested and marshy terrain, "malozametny" (difficult to notice) obstacles and "French Grid"** anti-tank traps, as well as fording capability.

By the time the A-20 had performed more than 75% of its plant tests, assembly of the first A-32 prototype had been completed in workshop "530". Driving of the tank was entrusted to an experienced Plant №183 driver-tester, V. V. Dyukanov. By 2nd July 1939 the A-32 tank had undertaken two factory proving runs of approximately 110km. During the runs, there was a major oil leak from the right oil tank (from the mesh communicating with atmosphere) and "non-floating" (i.e. jerky) operation of the main clutch when using the servo-operated pneumatic control system. After elimination of defects, testing of the A-32 tank continued. In addition to the proving tests, by mid-July 1939 the A-32 and A-20 tanks had both passed a number of special tests, such as overcoming loose sand, dunes, slopes and the

aforementioned "French Grid" type anti-tank obstacles. In total, the A-32 tank during factory trials covered 235km, and the A-20 tank - 872km, including 217km on wheels and 655km on tracks. During these trials, the diesel engine installed in the A-32 tank worked 12h 20m, and that of the A-20 tank worked 37h and 7m. After factory testing and rework the A-20 and A-32 tanks were to pass the more challenging field testing, with the aim:

"1. To determine the tactical and technical parameters of tanks in summer conditions with a comparative assessment with the A-7 and A-8 (BT-7 and BT-7M).

2. To determine the degree of compliance with the tactical and technical requirements (TTTs).

3. To identify the durability and reliability of the tanks and individual components, and ease of maintenance and repair in field conditions".

RGVA. F.81311. L.3. C.1633. pp16

To conduct and manage the A-20 and A-32 tank field trials, the chief of ABTU, Komkor (Corps Commander) D. G. Pavlov, on 16th June 1939 by Order №207091s established a Commission under the chairmanship of the head of the 1st Department of the NIABT polygon at Kubinka, Major E. A. Kulchitsky, with senior ABTU engineer, Major I. G. Panov, appointed as his deputy. The Commission included the chief designer of Plant №183, M. I. Koshkin; engineer of the 3rd Department Glavspetsmash NKSM, N.I. Masalskaya (NKSM curator for the A-20 and A-32 tanks); senior engineer of the 4th Department of ABTU, military engineer 3rd rank N. Ya. Goryushkin; military representative of ABTU at Plant №183, military engineer 3rd rank P. P. Baikov and the representative of Plant №75, engineer-motorman I. Skorikov. According to the same order, trials were to be conducted at "Kharkov Plant №183" in the course of a month. Each tank was required to not only cover at least 2,500km (700km on cobblestone highway, 1,000km on dirt roads and 800km on virgin soil), but also to undertake a number of special tests, the types and methods of which were detailed in: "The program of range tests of tanks A-20, A-32, in summer conditions." approved on 13th June 1939.

In the event, the testing timetable specified in Pavlov's order could not be observed, with the field tests being carried out from mid-July to October 1939, with an interim long break during which the A-20 and A-32 tanks took part in a show for the government at the Kubinka polygon in the Moscow region. The tests were carried out mainly by the experimental workshop "540" within Plant №183. Participants included the deputy workshop chief engineer P. N. Goryun, the head of testing-engineer V.V. Amiragov, engineer-researchers N.S. Gutnik and G.G. Onishchenko, and driver-mechanics V. V. Dyukanov and I. V. Kuznetsov, together with the members of the Commission.

P.N. Goryun.   I.V. Kuznetsov.

---

* The term "master" in Russian engineering terms refers to a fully qualified technical specialist.

** French Grid - Russian term for mixed emplaced log and barbed wire anti-tank obstacles

The proving runs were carried out along main routes as noted in typical reports such as below:

"1. Kharkov-Belgorod-Oboyan, with departure at 53rd km of the Belgorod highway through Tsirkun-Liptsy.

2. Kharkov-Rogan-Kamannaya Yaruga.

3. Kharkov-KhTZ-Pavlinka [Pavlenky]-Rogan Station-Bezlyudovka-Vasyshchevo-Ternoyaya [Ternovoe]-Mokhnach Station-Kamennaya Yaruga-Zadorozhnoe-Sorokovka-Babki [Bolshaya Babka]-Pechenegy-Babki [Bolshaya Babki]-Saltovo Station-Nepokritoe [Nepokritaya]-Kharkov. The route Kharkov-Belgorod-Oboyan represented, is basically, a good grade-dand gravelled road allowing normal vehicular traffic. The (area of the) turn-off from the Belgorod highway represents, partially, a well-worn cobblestone highway and partially dirt country roads. The route Kharkov-Rogan-Kamannaya Yaruga is a graded dirt road. The route Kharkov-Vasyshcheve-Kamennaya Yaruga-Pechenegy- Saltovo-Kharkov has diverse surfaces including soil. Predominant are the country dirt roads. A small part of the way runs through loose sands and sandy roads".

RGVA. F.31811. L. 3 C.1607. pp69-70

During the proving runs the participants recorded, as mandated, the distance covered, route characteristics, the time spent in movement and various stops, and the working oil and water temperatures of the tank engines. After each run, the average speed of pure (uninterrupted) travel, average technical and operational speeds, and fuel and oil consumption were determined. During the runs the Commission also determined the working conditions of the individual crewmembers. Readings and test results were recorded in trip logs and test reports. All the information obtained would later be used in preparing the final A-20 and A-32 field testing report.

For the field trials, the A-20 prototype (Plant №0367-5) was transferred by the plant to military representatives on 15th July 1939; being joined on 17th July 1939 by the first A-32 tank prototype (Plant №0367-3). Neither tank was fitted with "PKh" underwater driving apparatus, or a standard set of ЗИП (ZIP) spare parts, tools and accessories. The A-32 also lacked the 71-TK-3 radio station installation and associated electrics. In addition, BT-7 road wheels were still temporary mounted on the 1st, 2nd and 3rd wheel stations of the A-32 tank, as the new wheels designed for the A-32 were not ready. The A-32 was for trials purposes also mounted on A-20 tracks rather than those specifically designed for the A-32 tank.

Before the first mobility trials, the combat weight of the A-20 and A-32 tanks was on 17th June 1939 checked by Department "500" using crane scales. When weighing the A-20 tank, its tracks were placed on the upper side armour, with a 140kg weight added in lieu of the usually stowed ZIP spare parts. Meantime, when weighing the A-32 tank, the still missing tracks, the PT-1 periscopic sight, the ZIP set, and the difference between the weight of the newly developed wheels and the temporary fitted BT-7 wheels was noted. The test-weighing established the combat weight of the A-20 tank as 18,000kg, and that of the A-32 tank as only slightly higher, at 19,000kg. The weight distribution on the roadwheels of the A-20 tank was separately determined in workshop "150" of tank division "100" at Plant №183 using eight scales. The equivalent road wheel load distribution test for the A-32 tank was held slightly later, on 14th August 1939, on the unhurried basis that if the procedure with the A-20 tank (with the same number of road wheels as the BT-7) had proven un-problematical, then for the A-32 tank the weight distribution would clearly

The A-20 wheel-track tank prototype.

V.V. Dyukanov.

The first A-32 tank prototype.

be an improvement. Due to the lack of an additional two sets of scales at Plant №183 for weighting the A-32, the following specific "procedure" had to be developed.

"Machine "A-32"

1) Place the 8 decimal scales so that the weight is only on the front and rear wheels. The 3 pairs of central wheels are located on 2 pairs of scales.

2) Scales are put on the 2nd and 4th wheels, and under the 1st, 3rd and 5th wheels. Pads of the same height as the scales are substituted.

3) The 1st, 3rd and 5th wheels are placed on the scales, and pads are placed under the second and fourth wheels, the load on the wheel, standing on the scales, thereby being fixed".

RGVA. F.31811. L.3. C.1607. pp71

The measurements indicated the load on the A-20 road wheels ranged from 1,610kg to 2,600kg, and that on the A-32 from 1,150kg to 2,330kg. On the basis of the results, the Commission concluded as reflected in Table №1* of the Appendix to the A-20 and A-32 tank polygon test report:

"1) From the table it is clear that the load on the "A-20" and "A-32" is distributed more evenly than in the "A-7" and "A-7M" (BT-7 and BT-7M).

2) The front wheels of the "A-20" machine are underloaded because the centre of gravity has been moved 157mm to the rear of the machine, and adjustment of the "candles" (suspension unit adjusters) to achieve an improvement is not achieved.

3) The load distribution on the wheels of the "A-32" is abnormal. The required unloading of the middle wheels failed due to the fact that the suspension of these wheels was fully lowered.

4) It is difficult and time consuming to adjust wheel loads:

(a) Access to horizontal candles is difficult,

(b) Loading or unloading of one wheel leads to an equivalent change of loadings on all unaligned wheels, and the need for repeated adjustment of each candle.

Representatives of the Commission and test crews resting during the A-20 and A-32 tank trials. Standing: E. A. Kulchitsky (in the tanker's helmet) and M. I. Koshkin. Sitting: in the centre N. I. Masalskaya (in the tanker's helmet), I. V. Kuznetsov (smoking). On the far right V. V. Dyukanov, and next to him N.S. Gutnik.

* The Russian term "karta" can mean table, graphic or map depending on context. The report included all of these appendixes.

In operation, the suspension can be adjusted only approximately by the (adjustment) cups, machine clearance, and deformation of the rubber on the road wheels.

5) *By the loads on the wheels and the cup status it is clear that the suspensions of the "A-20" and "A-32" tanks are unevenly loaded. Load distribution is unsatisfactory.*

It is necessary to load the front steering wheel pair of the "A-20" machine and unload the 1st and 2nd driving wheel pairs. The middle wheels of the A-32 should be unloaded".

RGVA. F.31811 L.3.C.1607. pp74

The determination of centre of gravity coordinates for the A-20 and A-32 tanks was undertaken on 14th Aug 1939 in workshop "530" of Plant №183. The results were recorded in Table №2 of the Appendix to the A-20 and A-32 field test report. The conclusion reached on the centre of gravity location on the A-20 and A-32, affecting both mobility and stability was that:

"1. The table below shows that the Cg* of the A-20 tank is moved forward, compared to the A-7, by 347mm, the Cg of the A-32 tank is moved forward 24mm compared to the A-20, and compared to the A-7, by 371mm. The vertical Cg of the A-20 tank is higher than that of A-7 by 143mm, and the A-32 by 190mm. Moving the Cg of the A-20 and A-32 tanks is due to the fact that the nose sections of these machines are heavier than the A-7 machine and the turrets are made of thicker armour than the turret of the A-7.

"Table of Cg coordinates of tanks A-20, A-32, B-7 (A-7) and BT-7M (A-7M)

Type	Weight of tank in determining Cg	Medium Clearance (mm)	Coordinates of Cg. Approx.		
			X	Z	Z¹
A-20	17,400	405 - 410	2,373	246	858
A-32	18,300	385 - 400	2,397	316	905
A-7	13,910	390	2,026	114	715
A-7M	14,520	396	1,993	167	775

RGVA F.31811. L.3. C.1607. pp75

NOTE:

X - distance from the track wheel axis to the centre of gravity horizontally. Z - distance from the track wheel axis to the vertical centre of gravity. Z¹ - distance from the ground to the centre of gravity."

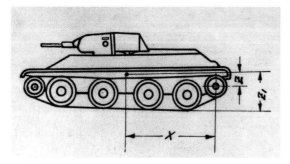

The A-20 centre of gravity diagram.

Forward offset Cg of the A-32 tank relative to the A-20 is 24mm due to the heavier (76.2mm L-10) gun system compared with the 45mm gun. Moving of the Cg of the A-20 and A-32 upward compared to the A-7 (BT-7) is due to the heavier turret and a larger engine.

2. *The location of the horizontal Cg of the A-20 and A-32 tanks is better located than on the A-7 and A-7M (BT-7 and BT-7M) tanks. This arrangement of Cg allows for more uniform load distribution on the wheels and should increase mobility over obstacles and soft ground.*

3. *Raising the Cg of the A-20 and A-32 tanks, compared to the A-7 and A-7M tanks, has practically no effect on stability, as the tracks of the A-20 and A-32 tanks are wider than for the A-7 and A-7M tanks - by 360mm. In general, the rolling of tanks is limited by the grip of the track on the ground".*

RGVA. F.31811. L.3. C.1607. pp76-77

After weighing the A-20 and A-32 tanks, and determining the road wheel load distribution for the A-20, both tanks were prepared for the first proving trials held on 18th July 1939. On this day the A-20 and A-32 tanks travelled on the route:
Plant №183-Pavlenky-Rogan Station-Bezlyudovka-Vasyshchevo-Ternovoe-Mokhnach Station-Kamennaya Yaruga-Chuguev-Zarozhnoe-Sorokovka-Bolshaya Babka-Stariy Saltov-Nepokritaya-Plant №183. During the run, the A-20 moved on its tracks. The results of the proving run were as follows:

	A-20 Tank	A-32 Tank
Total distance travelled (km)	182	184
Including on cobblestone highway (km)	5	5
Including on dirt roads (km)	161	161
Including on sand and sandy roads (km)	16	18
Including virgin lands (km)	-	-
Time of pure movement (hours-minutes)	5 - 05	5 - 47
Time spent in removing defects and failures, (hours, minutes)	0 - 03	-
Time spent on rest, meals and other stops (hours, minutes)	1 - 20	0-40
Average net speed of movement (km/h)	35.8	34.1
Average technical speed (km/h)	35.4	34.1
Average operational speed (km/h)	28.1	30.3
Average daily outside air temperature (°C)	27.5	27.5
Average water temperature entering engine (°C)	92	78
Max. water temperature entering engine (°C)	107	85
Average oil temperature entering engine (°C)	90	58
Max. oil temperature entering engine (°C)	102	70
Average oil temperature leaving engine (°C)	95	82
Max. oil temperature leaving engine (°C)	105	90

* Цт (центра тяжести) - Centre of Gravity (Cg)

Nº	Tank Type	Gear	Length of test (m)	Number of runs	Averages			Design speed (km/h)
					Time	RPM on tachometer	Test speed Achieved (km/h)	
1	A-20	I	1,000	1	6m. 53 sec.	1,700	8.72	8.98
2	A-20	II	1,000	2	3m. 19 sec. 3m. 17 sec	1,700	18.37	18.8
3	A-20	III	1,000	2	1m. 40 sec. 1m. 40 sec.	1,700	36	36.9
4	A-20	IV	1,000	2	0m. 57 sec. 0m. 57 sec	1,700	63.16	65.16

RGVA. F.31811. L.3. C.1607. pp94

The higher water and oil temperatures for the A-20 in comparison with the A-32 were due to constant leaks in the cooling and lubrication systems of the V-2 engine, which were not completely eliminated on the A-20 by the end of polygon testing. Throughout the run jerky pneumatic servo control operation of the main clutch was noted on both tanks. This defect, caused by imperfect alignment and fettling of the servo mechanism, continued on all future runs using pneumatic servo control system.

Post-run maintenance of the A-20 uncovered an oil leak from the left oil tank, due to poor soldering, and a broken speedometer cable (used to determine speed and distance travelling on wheels). The A-32 main clutch pedal would also not fully return to its original position. The following day, 19th July 1939, was taken for maintenance and repair of both the A-20 and A-32 tanks. Additional repairs on the A-20 replacement of a the pneumatic servo control system pipe connecting the compressor to the high-pressure accumulator cylinder, and replacement of a bent bracket on the turret hatch cover.

On the morning of 20th July, a convoy, consisting of A-20, A-32, BT-7 and BT-7M tanks, having travelled about 40km on the route Plant №183-Pavlenky-Rogan Station-Bezlyudovka-Vasyshchevo-Ternovoe-Mokhnach Station-Chuguev highway, arrived in the area 2km east of the village of Rogan. Here, on a long straight in the road, all four tanks were trialled for time and path of acceleration while moving on tracks. The site chosen for testing was a segment of dry, graded dirt road. The teste methods abd results were reflected in Table №3 of the Appendix to the A-20 and A-32 polygon test report. Following the tests the Commission concluded:

"a) The route and time of acceleration, i.e. pick-up for tanks A-7, A-7M, A-20 and A-32, to the speed of 30km/h is almost the same. Some of the best pick-up is with the A-20 tank in 1st and 2nd gear due to the large transmission ratio, i.e. reduced speeds, in comparison with A-7 and A-7M. The transmission benefits are not apparent on 1st and 2nd gear for the A-32 because of its slightly greater weight, obviously, lowering relative engine power.

b) The time required to accelerate to speeds above 30km/h for the

A-20 and A-32 tanks, in comparison with A-7 and A-7M, is sharply increased. This is explained by the reduced gear ratios and the greater weight of the tanks, i.e. the greater the reduction in specific power (the hp/ tonne of the weight of the tank)."

RGVA. F.31811. L.3. C.1607. pp80

Immediately after the acceleration tests on the Chuguev highway, trials were conducted to verify that the actual speeds of the A-20 on tracks were consistent with the calculated speeds. Seven runs were undertaken on a 1km section of straight road - the first run being in 1st gear, with two runs for each remaining gear. The test results were summarised in the following table (above). According to test results, the Commission concluded:

"The mismatch of the speeds obtained in the test runs with the calculated velocities is explained by inaccurate tachometer readings. Guided by the tachometer readings, calculated speed can be maintained Note: as the gearshift on the A-32 tank has the same gear ratio as the A-20, the speed will be roughly the same".

RGVA. F.31811. L.3. C.1607. pp94

In the afternoon of 20th July 1939, the column of four tanks returned to the plant along the same route as used on the outward leg. The following day, the A-20 and A-32 tanks were prepared for a new long proving run, with both tanks mounted on tracks. On the A-20 tank, the engineers at workshop "530" eliminated

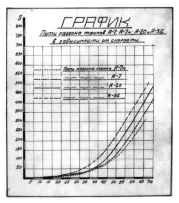

Graph of tank acceleration tests, time and distance.

oil tanks leaks; tightened the torque bolts of the V-2 diesel; replaced a broken clip on the flange of the engine intake manifolds, and replaced torn "durites" (hoses); the detached turret détente was welded back and a deformed track tension mechanism replaced. On the A-32, burrs were eliminated on the worm drive of the turret rotation mechanism, the detached turret détente also welded back in place and a manufacturing defect - an incorrectly welded locking point for the turret hatch - corrected.

Early in the morning of 22nd July 1939, a convoy consisting of the A-20, the A-32 and an escort vehicle again left the gates of Plant №183. The prototypes were to twice undertake a circular route starting and ending at Plant №183*. However, only the A-20 completed the day's trials. South east of the village of Rogan the A-32's centrifugal cooling fan disintegrated. After inspection, continued participation of the A-32 in the trial was considered impractical, and the tank returned to Plant №183 directly along the Chuguev highway. The A-20 continued on the planned trial route. The results of the run conducted on 22nd July 1939 were as follows:

	A-20	A-32
Total distance travelled (km)	440	82
Including on cobblestone highway (km)	16	5
Including on dirt roads (km)	394	70
Including on sand and sandy roads (km)	30	7
Including virgin lands (km)	-	-
Time of movement (hours, minutes)	14 - 58	2 - 42
Time spent on eliminating defects and breakdowns (hours, minutes)	4 - 25	0 - 14
Time spent on rest, meals and other stops (hours, minutes)	2 - 18	0 - 33
Average net speed of movement (km/h)	29.4	30.3
Average technical speed (km/ h)	22.7	28.0
Average operational speed (km/h)	20.7	23.5
Average ambient temperature (˚C)	14.3	14.3
Average water temperature entering engine (˚C)	85	70
Max. temperature of water entering engine (˚C)	105	75
Average oil temperature entering engine (˚C)	87	62
Max. oil temperature entering engine (˚C)	102	73
Average oil temperature leaving engine (˚C)	93	83
Max. oil temperature leaving engine (˚C)	107	90

During technical inspection of the damage incurred on the A-32 during trials and subsequent repairs carried out in workshop "530" found to be the centrifugal fan was missing its cowling, and the reinforced sections originally riveted to its blades. The self-destruction of the blades and surrounding cowling with the fan running at 1,400-1,600rpm had damaged

both the aft fuel tanks, the left and right oil radiators and two radiators of the engine cooling system. The fan destruction had also dented the engine exhaust manifolds and exhaust pipes, and bent the control rods for the main clutch control mechanism and the left brake. During technical inspection of the A-32 tank, it was also found that due to engine-transmission misalignment, the bolts on the coupling for the main clutch were losoe. Due to overheating of the external gearing of the final drives and lack of bearing lubrication, the oil seals had failed. Grease was also leaking from under the shaft seal of the right-side final drive.

As the A-20 tank had arrived at Workshop "530" from its proving run late at night, a further technical condition check was made the next day, on Sunday 23rd July. Despite the A-20 tank having covered 440km, no other serious damage was detected, except for the following:
- In the V-2 engine, the pipe connecting the fuel filter to the NK-1 fuel pump had broken due to vibration;
- On the reinforcements for 10 blades of the centrifugal fan, the riveting was weakened (poor riveting);
- Due to the bronze centering cone loosening the hub of the main clutch damper began to wobble on the engine output shaft splines;
- In the steering clutches and brake bands a number of parts had to be replaced due to overheating; the main clutch pedal was not returning fully on release.

In the period from 23rd - 25th July 1939, the A-20 and A-32 tanks were serviced, repaired and prepared for the next trial run, undertaken by both tanks in the morning of 26th July. However, the tanks managed to cover only part of the planned route. After the column had proceeded along the route: Plant №183-Pavlenky-Rogan Station-Bezlyudovka-Vasyshchevo-Mokhnach Station-Rogan-Kamennaya Yaruga, representatives of the Commission temporarily halted the tests due to side friction clutch slippage on both tanks. Defining the cause and making adjustments took slightly over an hour, after which the A-32 tank continued back to Plant №183*. On the A-20 tank, due to slippage of the drive and idler wheels, the left side clutch became excessively hot, leading to oil seal failure. During adjustments, it was found that the mounting bolts in the flange of the left side gear reducer were loose and bolt faces and lock plates damaged due to being hit by the moving track. To continue further testing of the A-20 tank was considered unwise, and the tank returned to Plant №183 directly from: Kamennaya Yaruga-Rogan to Kharkov. The results of the runs conducted on 26th July are as follows (table right).

The long trial runs conducted on tracks on 26th July 1939 were non-standard. At the end of the 1930s test runs with stops of under 10 minutes were considered non-stop. The non-stop

* The actual route was: Plant №183-Pavlenky-Rogan Station-Bezlyudovka-Vasyshchevo-Ternovoe-Mokhnach Station-Chuguev highway-Kamennaya Yaruga-Chuguev-Zarozhnoe-Sorokovka-Bolshaya Babka-Pechenegy-Bolshaya Babka -Staryi Saltov-Nepokritaya-Plant №183.

122

	A-20	A-32
Total distance travelled (km)	111	201
Including on cobblestone highway (km)	8	13
Including on dirt roads (km)	85	91
Including on sand and sandy roads (km)	18	6
Including virgin lands (km)	-	91
Time of movement (hours, minutes)	3.47	6.57
Time spent on the elimination of defects and breakdowns (hours, minutes)	1 - 07	1 - 13
Time spent on rest, meals and other stops (hours, minutes)	0 - 05	0 - 30
Average net speed of movement (km/h)	29.2	29.0
Average technical speed (km/ h)	22.6	24.7
Average operational speed (km/h)	22.3	23.2
Average ambient temperature (°C)	28.1	28.1
Average water temperature entering engine (°C)	95	78
Max. temperature of water entering engine (°C)	105	90
Average oil temperature entering engine (°C)	99	75
Max. oil temperature entering engine (°C)	110	88
Average oil temperature leaving engine (°C)	105	86
Max. oil temperature leaving engine (°C)	115	98

run of the A-20 tank was 60km on that day, and the A-32 tank some 6km longer. Due to the abnormal operation of the side friction clutches the tests were completed on this day.

After the return of the A-20 and A-32 tanks to workshop "530" at Plant №183 they were thoroughly inspected and repair crews then began to restore both tanks. The A-32 continued the proving run tests the following day, while the A-20 tank remained in workshop "530" undergoing repair. On Thursday 27th July, the A-32 went on another overnight run by the same route. After travelling 76km, near Kamennaya Yaruga, during a technical check of the tank, a significant failure was detected with the main clutch - all 16 bolts connecting the damper of the main clutch with its outer drum and the attached centrifugal fan were sheared. As the damage could not be repaired on site, the tank was towed back to workshop "530". According to the results of the interrupted run, the average rate of net movement of the A-32 tank on the day was found to be 32.3km/h, the average technical speed being 32.3km/h and the average operational speed of 28.2km/h.

During inspection of the engine and transmission compartments of the A-32 tank, it was also found that due to misalignment between the V-2 diesel output shaft and the gearbox, in the outer drum of the main clutch damper there were cracks at the connection with the central fan to a depth 1.7mm and the bolt holes connecting the outer drum with the damper had eliptical wear of up to 2mm. In addition, the drive and slave discs of the

main clutch were warped from 0.15 to 0.35mm, and the thrust ball bearing had axial backlash of 0.84mm and radial backlash of 0.12mm. External inspection revealed that as a result of towing the ribs of the front rims were dented. For the next three days, the A-32 remained under repair in workshop "530". By the evening of 27th July, when the broken-down A-32 was delivered under tow to workshop "530", the workers there had just completed repairs on the A-20 tank after its own proving run.

In the morning of 28th July 1939, the repaired A-20 wheel- tracked tank continued its proving runs. According to the trip journal, the tank on that day travelled 253km on tracks, of which 157km was on dirt roads, 75km over virgin soil, 18km on sand and 3km on cobblestone road, with the average speed for the entire run being 28.2km/h. In the afternoon the A-20 was returned to the plant and minor damages repaired. Because of an unreliable cotter pin, the linkages for the 1st and 2nd gears had become disconnected. On Saturday, 29th July the A-20 was again inspected for defects in workshop "530", during which the Plant №183 specialists identified the following defects:
- difficulty changing gears (due to sand and mud build-up, and overly rigid retainer springs in the gearbox);
- large burrs on driven shafts, caps and "O" rings of both final drive gearboxes due to destruction of the tapered roller bearings. (bearing lubrication difficulty due to unfinished design);
- leaking lubrication in the final drive gearboxes past the seals on the gears for the transmission of torque from the driven gear final drives to the longitudinal side shafts for the road wheel drive shafts in wheeled mode;
- failure of the copper pipe connecting the compressor to the low-pressure cylinder;
- Loosening roadwheel conical armour cap bolts.;
- one-sided wear of the rollers of the track drive wheel due to misaligned axes of the drive wheel and road wheels;
- no bracket on the turret détente (due to bad welds);
- inability to open the engine and transmission compartment hatches due to unfinished lock construction;
- inability to control opening and closing of the transmission compartment louvres from the driver's seat;
- failure of the manual gun elevation mechanism due to jamming of the lifting mechanisms.

It was also found that the rods of the 2nd and 4th suspension units developed "teardrop" wear in their mountings due to rod misalignment from excess suspension movement. On 29th and 30th July the A-20 and A-32 tanks remained in workshop "530" in preparation for the continuation of field trials.

On Monday, 31st July the A-20 wheeled tank (on tracks) and the A-32 undertook the next test run. The tanks were expected to pass twice along a circular route starting and finishing at Plant №183*.

---

* The return route was: Kamennaya Yaruga-Zarozhnoe-Rogan-Mokhnach Station-Vasyshchevo-Bezlyudovka-St. Rogan-Pavlenky-Plant №183

Damages - ventilator fan, fuel tank, right side radiator and exhaust pipe.

The A-20 made it through the day's trial, covering 438km. The A-32 by contrast had a successful morning followed by a problematical afternoon. The tanks covered the morning's run after which the test participants had lunch and rested. On the afternoon run, however, the A-32 stopped after only 18km due to failure of the main clutch. Technical inspection revealed that all the bolts securing the centrifugal fan to the external drum (flywheel) of the main clutch were sheared off. To continue on was impossible, and the tank was towed back to the factory and to workshop "530". Thus, the results of the run were as follows:

	A-20	A-32
Total distance travelled (km)	438	235
Including on cobblestone highway (km)	10	6
Including on dirt roads (km)	400	120
Including on sand and sandy roads (km)	28	18
Including virgin lands (km)	-	91
Time of pure movement (hours-minutes)	13 - 06	6 - 06
Time spent on the elimination of defects and breakdowns (hours, minutes)	5 - 06	1 - 32
Time spent on rest, meals and other stops (hours, minutes)	1 - 11	1 - 51
Average net speed of movement (km/h)	33.5	38.5
Average technical speed (km/ h)	24.1	30.8
Average operational speed (km/h)	22.6	24.8
Average ambient temperature (°C)	22	22
Average water temperature entering engine (°C)	93	72
Max. temperature of water entering engine (°C)	110	90
Average oil temperature entering engine (°C)	88	68
Max. oil temperature entering engine (°C)	102	95
Average oil temperature leaving engine (°C)	94	85
Max. oil temperature leaving engine (°C)	108	100

Non-Stop Run Trials

The Commission also conducted a test to determine the duration of a non-stop run and the reasons limiting such a run. The non-stop run of the A-20 tank reached 116km, with a duration of 3h 15m, and with an average speed of 35.9km/h, before being interrupted due to a copper pipe fracturing in the pneumatic control servo system.

While the A-20 tank completed its run, the broken-down A-32 was being checked in workshop "530" of Plant №183. It transpired that in addition to the sheared bolts, the main clutch had other damages. The steel master and slave disks of the main clutch were warped from 0.15-0.20mm. There was scoring and cracks to a depth of 1.5mm on the surface of the fan cowling, and the holes for the bolts connecting the cowling had scoring ellipses to 0.8mm. Scoring was also found on the teeth of the main flywheel ring. In addition, technical inspection revealed other malfunctions in the A-32 tank:
- Due to overheating the right steering clutch was out of commission, the outer drum, steel master and slave drives and bearings were discoloured due to heat;
- The brake bands of both side friction clutches lost effectiveness due to uneven circumference of the outer drums.
- The right-side gear reducer required repair;
- The relay drive of the ST-70 electric-starter malfunctioned, such that on engine start the starter gear drive starter jammed in the crown of the main clutch;
- Broken turret détente handle.

The A-20, which had returned from its test run late at night on 31st July, was during a technical inspection the following day also found to have a number of serious malfunctions:
- Exhaust gases were escaping between the cylinder heads and cylinder sleeves of the V-2 diesel due to warped aluminium cylinder block head gaskets;
- The torque nuts, connecting the V-2 cylinder block to the crankcase were loose;
- Coolant was escaping from a crack on the outside of the left engine cylinder block;
- Breakage of the copper pipe connecting the fine fuel filter with the NK-1 high-pressure fuel pump;
- Loose mounting of the compressor pneumatic servo-control to the gearbox (damaged lock pins);
- ST-70 electric starter failure (jamming of the electric starter gear with the flywheel on engine start).

The A-20 Takes The Lead

By the evening of 3rd August 1939, the A-20 and A-32 tanks were both repaired and being prepared for continued testing.

---

* The route followed was: Plant №183-Pavlenky-Rogan Station-Bezlyudovka-Vasyshchevo-Ternovoe- Mokhnach Station-Chuguev highway-Kamennaya Yaruga-Chuguev-Zarozhnoe-Sorokovka-Bolshaya Babka, Pechenegy-Bolshaya Babka-Stariy Saltov-Nepokritaya-Plant №183.

The next morning both tanks left the territory of Plant №183 for a long route on tracks, mainly on dirt roads.

The route was Plant №183-Pavlenky-Rogan Station-Bezlyudovka-Vasyshchevo-Ternovoe and back. Again, only the A-20 completed the route. The A-32 suffered another breakdown near Rogan, on this occasion failure of the main clutch control linkage. Repairing this seemingly minor malfunction took four hours, which adversely affected the overall test results. The distance travelled by the A-32 tank had been only 53km, including 4km on a cobblestone highway, 39km on dirt roads and 10km on sand and sandy roads, with a net driving time of only 2h 27m. The performed calculations showed that at this average rate of net movement of the A-32 amounted to only 21.6km/h, and the average technical and average operational speed was 8.3km/h. These statistics were important, in that at this stage in the testing of what prototype would become the next Red Army medium tank, the average technical and operational speeds of the A-20 were far better - by a factor of four - than the A-32.

During the 110km run (8km on cobblestone highway, 87km on unpaved roads, 15km on sand and sand roads) the A-20 crew spent 2h 56m and another 6 minutes for checks, with no defects found. The A-20 during this run achieved the best performance over the entire period of field tests, with an average technical speed on unpaved roads of 38.8km/h. The Average operational speed was, at 36.4km/h, not significantly lower. On the same day, the A-20 had achieved a record average rate of movement on tracks on a cobblestone road. The A-20, rather than the A-32, was looking to be the more successful design variant for the future Soviet medium tank.

In connection with the troubleshooting of the A-32 tank, the A-20 tank left for the cobblestone road test run on its own. The routing this time was more direct, namely several trips from Plant №183-Rogan-Chuguev and back. The morning's travel was without incident. After checking the technical condition of the tank, having lunch and then a short rest, the test participants continued their journey towards Chuguev. Approximately 3km

Damaged cylinder head gaskets on the V-2 diesel engine installed in the A-20 tank.

from the village of Rogan the right brake band broke due to a stripped thread on its mountings. The crew repaired the damage in 45 minutes and the run continued, but directly back to Kharkov. At the end of 4th August, the A-20 tank was now on a cobblestone highway having covered altogether 112km, but at the same time, the net movement was 2h 3m. The testers had spent 45 minutes troubleshooting, and 1h 11m on breaks and other operational stops. In accordance with the calculations, the average speed of the A-20 tank on tracks along the cobblestone road was 44.4km/h, which was the best average speed for either tank during all of the polygon tests. The average technical and average operational speed was meanwhile significantly lower - 34.4km/h and 25.2km/h respectively.

After return from this run, the workshop "530" in the afternoon of 4th August 1939 during technical inspection of the A-20 tank were found a number of defects and malfunctions in the transmission and running gear:

- leakage of lubricant in the wheel housing of the gear drive welded to the rocker-arm, and also from under armour caps of the first (driven) road wheels and hubs of the driving wheels of the tracks (due to incomplete seal design);
- weakening of the tapered bearing retainer and, as a consequence, an increase in the axial backlash of roller bearings in the wheel gearboxes of the 2nd and 4th left road wheels;
- partial or complete destruction of the track drive wheel rims;
- increased wear of the roller bearings of the track drive wheels;
- f ormation of cracks in welding seams on the track drive wheels;
- unreliable couplings on the longitudinal side shafts of the drive units transmitting torque to the road wheels.

Within two days the staff of workshop "530" had repaired the A-20 tank and prepared it for further tests. Renovating the A-32 tank meantime took three days, with the main friction (clutch) replaced and a range of other repairs, including the tracks which had suffered from excessive track hinge wear. In addition, the fastenings on the upper inclined rear armour plate to the tank body were restored.

Ascents and Descents

In the morning of Monday, 7th August 1939, the A-20 tank left the territory of Plant №183 for the completion of special tests. On this day, the Commission had to determine the ability of the A-20 wheel-track tank to overcome natural obstacles, gradients and slopes when driving on tracks, on wheels and on one track only and to affirm the minimum turning radius on tracks, wheels and on one track.

Testing to determine the capability of the A-20 tank on slopes when driving on tracks was conducted in a ravine located 1.5km southwest of the village of Pavlenky. During these tests, the tank had to traverse a section of road along the slopes of the

№	Gear	Turning Point	Direction of Rotation	Angle of Rotation (°)	Crankshaft rotation speed (rpm)		Time of Rotation (sec)	Diameter of outer trail (m)	Turning Radius (m)
					Start	Finish			
1	I	In Place	Right	360	1,800	1,700	18	7.49	3.745
2	I	In Place	Left	360	2,200	2,200	13	9.00	4.5
3	II	In Place	Right	360	1,400	1,200	12	6.30	3.15
4	II	In Place	Left	360	1,800	1,700	8	7.30	3.65

RGVA. F.31811. L.3. C.1607. pp100

ravine, which effectively provided a 500-550m long test circuit with slopes ranging from 0° to 34°. The soil in this area was dry and solid black earth covered with short grass. Before the tests, two links were removed from each track due to significant stretching as a result of excessive hinge wear. During the first attempt, the A-20 in 1st gear overcame the circuit in 4m 30s. Traversing the slope in the opposite direction took 5m 30s, while in situ on a steep slope the tank made a turn of 90°. The second run was on a slope of 34° which it traversed without changing the direction of movement. The testers recorded that the tank slipped sideways on the slope by 400-500mm, before the slipping was arrested by firmer ground. The test results were recorded in Table №12 of the Appendix to the report on the A-20 and A-32 field tests. In the test conclusions drawn by the Commission, the mobility and stability of the A-20 tank on slopes was found to be good.

The Commission then conducted special tests in the same ravine to determine the maximum angle of ascent to be overcome by the A-20 tank when moving on tracks. During the test, the A-20 tank in 1st gear quite easily and without need for over-revving overcame slopes of 35° and 37° with a travelled distance of 28m and 24m respectively. The tank failed however to overcome a slope of 40° even on the 4th attempt - every time the tank had climbed about 18m up the slope, the engine stalled. When driving in 2nd gear, the A-20 tank without over-revving could not climb the slope at 19°, but with revving the tank managed to climb 6m up a 20° slope and 29 metres up a 16° slope. After overcoming each rise the tank descented in the opposite direction, which was easily overcome, both in forward and reverse motion. The results of the tests were illustrated in Table №10 of the Appendix to the A-20 and A-32 tank field test report. Regarding the potential of the A-20 tank to overcome gradients when driving on tracks, the Commission concluded:

"a) The Maximum slope overcome by the A-20 machine, with the engine working 101 hours, 10 minutes in 1st gear was a slope of 38°- 39° (limited by engine output).
b) In 2nd gear the machine overcame (limited by engine output), - 14° - 16° slopes.
<...> >
Slopes of 20-22°, length less than 45 metres, were overcome with over-revving in 2nd gear".

RGVA. F.31811. L.3. C.1607. pp104

Wheels and Tracks

The following tests required the A-20 tank to travel on wheels, and on one track, for which purpose the tank crew removed the left track and the drive mechanisms transferring torque to the 2nd, 3rd and 4th left side roadwheels was engaged. The test was then performed on dry solid clay, covered with sparse grass to determine the minimum turning radius of the tank A-20 when driving with one track missing in 1st and 2nd gear. The results obtained during the tests are shown in the table above. The following conclusions were drawn in the Annex to the report on the A-20 and A-32 tank range tests in Table №9:

"1. The turn radius in wheeled mode requires more than with tracks, due to slipping of the wheels on the ground.
2. The time required to turn in the direction of travel is less than with tracks, due to wheel slippage on the ground when turning in the direction of the tracks.
3. The turning circle of a single-track machine on dry hard ground in all gears is the same as for a machine with both tracks fitted.
4. Movement and turns in the direction of the track on very moist ground is impossible, due to wheel slip."

RGVA. F.31811. L.3. C.1607 pp101

Lastly, the 4th special test for the A-20 tank, held on 7th August 1939, was to determine the maximum slope that could be surmounted when driving on wheels, and on one track. The first heat was with the tank mounted on track on the right side and on road wheels on the left side; the tank without much difficulty on the first pass overcoming a 19° slope with a length of 25m. In the next two heats the A-20 in 2nd gear overcame a 25m long, 29° slope, but both times with a slip to the right. The following attempt to overcome a slope of 33° was unsuccessful.

In order to determine the maximum slope that could be overcome by the A-20 tank while driving simultaneously on wheels and one track on wet ground, the test participants moved to the territory of a nearby range. At the final test stage the weather deteriorated and by the time of arrival at the new testing location the depth of the wet layer of black soil covered with sparse grass, was 40mm. Unsurprising in such circumstances the tank failed to drive up a 30m long slope at 10° in 2nd gear. The tank moved forward 5-10m, and then slipped to the left due to slippage of the road wheels in the wet earth. The

The A-20 tank overcoming a 35° slope.

The A-20 tank on a 37° descent.

results of the tests were shown in Table №11 of the Appendix to the A-20 and A-32 field test report. In the same table, the following conclusions were drawn by the Commission on the identified capabilities of the A-20 tank to overcome the ascents while driving simultaneously on wheels and one track:

"a) On dry, hard ground covered with black earth to a length of 30m, the tank can overcome on a single track in 1st gear a climb of up to 30° with slippage to the track side of the tank.
b) On solid wet ground (after rain), the tank may in 2nd gear overcome on a single track, slopes up to 5°.
b) On solid dry ground the tank in 2nd gear can climb 15-16°, i.e. the same as on two tracks. As in the first, and in the second case - the limit is the engine (power output)".

RGVA. F.31811. L.3. C.1607. pp111-112

In the afternoon, all participants returned to Plant №183, where the technical condition of the A-20 tank was checked in workshop "530". Despite the fact that on 7th August 1939, the distance travelled was minimal - only 19km - faults were discovered in the engine and transmission that prevented the tank from continuing trials the next day, the same being the case for the A-32 tank.

On Tuesday 8th August, the A-32 tank left the territory of Plant №183 for the next run, travelling 180km for the day (120km on virgin land, 42km on dirt roads and 18km on cobblestone roads). The overall elapsed time for the trial was 6h 17m, with 35 minutes spent on rest, eating and operational stops.

The performed calculations showed that the average technical speed was 28.8km/h, and the average operational speed slightly lower at 26.3km/h. The V-2 diesel engine mounted in the A-32 performed per norms during the trial, with the water temperature, oil cooling and lubrication all within acceptable limits. The following morning the A-32 was prepared for the next run at workshop "530".

On Wednesday, 9th August a further testing run of the A-20 and A-32 tanks was held in various road conditions. The A-20 tank in the day moved on tracks predominantly on unpaved roads and gravelly highway, and the tank A-32 tank moved over open ground. For the day test results of the run were as follows:

	A-20	A-32
Total distance travelled (km)	304	225
Including on cobblestone highway (km)	12	18
Including gravelled roads (km)	164	-
Including on dirt roads (km)	108	42
Including on sand and sandy roads (km)	20	-
Including virgin lands (km)	-	165
Time of pure movement (hours, minutes)	7 - 57	8 - 31
Time spent on the elimination of defects and breakdowns (hours, minutes)	7 - 20	1 - 37
Time spent on rest, meals and other stops (hours, minutes)	0 - 0.6	-
Average net speed of movement (km/h)	37.9 / 35.6*	26.4
Average technical speed (km/ h)	37.9 / 13.7*	22.2
Average operational speed (km/h)	36.8 / 13.7*	22.2
Thermal mode of the engine		
Average ambient temperature (°C)	21.4	21.4
Average water temperature entering engine (°C)	94.5	70.5
Max. temperature of water entering engine (°C)	110	85
Average oil temperature entering engine (°C)	94.6	69.6
Max. oil temperature entering engine (°C)	105	80
Average oil temperature leaving engine (°C)	102	88
Max. oil temperature leaving engine (°C)	112	100

Note: * - average speed when driving on dirt roads / on gravel highway.

During the afternoon when driving on the route Belgorod-Kharkov, the actuator control for the right-side clutch in the A-20 tank failed. The fault was found to be that due to a stripped bolt thread, there was a gap between the stub-shaft and the disengagement mechanism of the right-side clutch. Delivery of replacement components from Plant №183 and repair under field conditions required more than 7 hours, and only in the morning did the test participants return to plant. Due to such a long downtime, the average technical and operational speed of the A-20 tank while driving along crushed stone gravelled highway was obviously significantly lower than in previous runs.

On 9th August during trial runs the Commission also defined the duration of non-stop movement of the A-20 and A-32 tanks. On this occasion, the non-stop run of the A-20 lasted for 3h and 8m at an average speed of 41.8km/h, travelling 131km, of which 75km was on gravelled highway and 56km on dirt roads. Non-stop travel was interrupted due to failure of the control mechanism for the right-side clutch, as noted.

The A-32 travelled a total of 107km on virgin ground during tests at the aviation training ground, taking 2h 35m with an average speed of 41.2km/h. The A-32 tank proving run was interrupted due to required to make adjustments to the brake band clearances and slave drums of the steering clutches.

The following day, in workshop "530", factory teams were engaged in troubleshooting problems with the A-20 and A-32 tanks, as identified during the technical inspection. By the end of the working shift, the A-32 had been prepared for new tests, but repairs on the A-20 had not been completed.

Less than 10 hours later, there was another proving run of the A-32 tank held on 11th August*. The total distance travelled by the A-32 tank on this day was 226km on dirt roads, 203km on sand and sandy roads, 18km and 5km on cobblestone highways. The time of clean movement of the tank was 6h 36m, with 3h and 14m spent on troubleshooting and adjustment of the onboard friction clutches. The average speed of clean movement of the A-32 tank during this run was 34.2km/h, with an average technical and operational speed of 23.0km/h. The temperature of water and oil in the engine cooling and lubrication systems remained within standard operating limits throughout the trial. Since during the run serious breakdowns in the A-32 did not occur, by the following morning the tank, along with the repaired A-20, was ready to continue trials, now to show their capabilities to cope with local marshes and wetlands.

Early on the morning of Saturday 12th August, the column, which included prototypes of the A-20, A-32 and A-7M (BT-7M) tanks, a series production BT-7 tank and a prototype "Voroshilovets" heavy artillery tractor left Plant №183, to the village of Khotomlya on the route: Plant №183-Nepokritaya-Stariy Saltov-Torfyanoe marsh (1.5km north of the village of Khotomlya). There, at a straight-line distance of 43km from Plant №183, the tanks underwent special tests in "mud baths". The area selected for this testing was an area of marsh

The A-20 tank overcomes a 29° slope in 1st gear with the left track removed.

The A-20 tank on a 10° descent in 2nd gear with the left track removed.

with water and liquid sludge, the land surface of which was a layer of peat with a thickness of 0.3-0.6m. The dry upper layer of peat, covered with tall sedge grass, was densely covered with tussocks with a height of 0.3-0.5m. At one side, the bottom of the marsh was flat and shallow, and the other was sloped. The depth of water and silt on the "gentle" side was 10cm, gradually increasing to 40cm towards the opposite side.

The tanks overcame the selected area of marsh from the gently sloping side in 1st and 2nd gear with an engine crankshaft rotational speed of 1,800-1,900rpm, with the tanks moving through the marsh in a straight line. The first tank to tackle the marsh site was the A-20, which began to move in 1st gear and was able to advance only 20m in total, as at the 17 metre mark the tank tracks began tearing the peat layer, which gradually built up in front and under the tank, such that after 20m the tracks began to slip without finding traction. The tank sank 0.8m into the marsh at the rear, and was able to reverse out only with the help of two BT tanks and a Voroshilovets tractor. Because of the earlier engine breakdowns, the A-20 tank did not participate in further tests so as to avoid likely further transmission complications. The other tanks failed altogether to overcome the wetland trials. On its first attempt, the A-32 overcame 18 metres of marsh before slipping into the track ruts left earlier by the BT-7M tank, on which it bottomed out, and

---

stalled. During the second and third trials, the A-32 tank overcame 9 metres and 11 metres respectively, then the tracks tore up a two-metre length layer of peat and which built up under the tank which again bottomed out and stuck in the marsh. The immersion depth of the tank near the rear was 0.65m during the first trial, 0.8m on the second, and 0.7m on the third attempt. Each time the A-32 tank was towed out of the marsh.

Only the A-32 and BT-7M prototypes overcame the 25-metre long marsh area, in 2nd gear, with the maximum submerged depth of each tank being 0.6m. In the afternoon of 12th August, all trial participants returned to Plant №183 in Kharkov. To determine mobility on other soil types, identical tests were carried out on 23rd August near the Ehskhar farm, which will be described below.

Elimination of the defects found in the A-20 and A-32 tanks during technical inspection was carried out by workshop "530" at Plant №183 on Sunday, 13th August. On the A-20, leaks due to poor soldering were sealed on the left and right oil tanks. The following parts were replaced: brake band springs; bolts and thrust washers on the left side gear reducer and a broken suspension rod on the first left side road wheel. The A-32 received a new left-side friction clutch and, together with the A-20, a new set of tracks - also due to excessive track elongation caused by heavy wear of the track hinges. It was not possible to reduce the track length by removing links from each track (as done on the A-20 tank) due to insufficient travel of the track tensioner, hence the A-32 tracks had to be replaced.

On Monday, 14th August 1939, in Acceptance Workshop "150" of Tank Department "100" of Plant №183 the Commission measured the load on the A-32 roadwheels with the eight aforementioned decimal weights; and then in Workshop "530" determined the centre of gravity coordinates for the A-20 and A-32 tanks, as detailed earlier. After carrying out these procedures the tank prototypes were prepared for another long run, held the next day, after which all the A-20 endurance trials were carried out exclusively with the tank running on wheels.

A New Location for New Trials

Due to the prototype tanks now being planned to undergo different testing procedures, the A-20 was dispatched to the north of Kharkov, in the direction of Oboyan, and the A-32 tank sent south-east in the direction of Chuguev. The route travelled by the A-20 tank on 15th August 1939 was Plant №183-Tsyrkuny-Lipsy-53rd kilometre of the Belgorod highway-Belgorod-Oboyan and back, a total of 326km. A large part of the distance travelled, some 218km, was on the unpaved roads, 16km on cobblestone roads, 10km on sand and sandy road and 82km on dirt roads. The total time of tank travel was 8h 45m, with 42m spent on rest, meals and other operational stops, with another 10m spent on the elimination of minor malfunctions detected during the run. The performed calculations showed that the average rate of net movement of the A-20 tank on wheels on the day was 36.8km/h, the average technical speed 36.5km/h, and the average operational speed 34.3km/h. During the route, the testers also determined the duration of the non-stop run of the A-20 tank on wheels and the reasons limiting that. This time the distance travelled during the nonstop run was 121km, the time of non-stop movement was 3h 8m, and the average speed 38.7km/h. The reason for the stop was again to eliminate leaks from the oil tanks.

Unlike the A-20 tank, which moved mainly on gravel-asphalted highway, the A-32 tank moved mainly over ground and dirt roads on the same route as undertaken on 11th August. A total of 209km was covered by the tank during this run, almost half of this distance on virgin ground, 73km on dirt roads, 16km on sand and sandy roads and only 15km on cobblestone highway. The travelling time was 7h 16m. The testing team spent 2h 37m on the elimination of two faults (failure of a turret retainer bracket and sheared bolt heads attaching the drive wheel to the drive shaft of the right-side final drive). The average net speed of movement of the A-32 tank was 28.7km/h, and the technical and operational speed - 21.2km/h.

On the same day, the A-32 was subjected to another test, to

The A-32 tank unsuccessfully attempting to overcome a peat marsh in 1st gear.

determine the duration of movement on virgin ground in 3rd gear at the lowest possible speed, until reaching the maximum permissible water and oil temperatures in the engine cooling and lubrication systems. During the tests conducted 3km south of Plant №183, the A-32 tank travelled 25km before reaching the maximum oil temperature of 105°C. Driving time was 1h 30m; the minimum speed in 3rd gear was 10-12km/h; the engine crankshaft rotational speed was 900-1,100rpm; and the maximum water temperature in the engine cooling system reached 95°C.

After the return of the A-20 and A-32 tanks to Plant №183, the technical condition of both tanks was checked in Workshop "530", and the machines readied for the next test. On Wednesday, 16th August, the first tank to leave the territory of Plant №183 was the A-20. For the day's proving run the tank was to travel on wheels to Oboyan and return along the same route. However, the A-20 failed to perform a number of tests scheduled for the day, as after it had travelled 24km along the road from Belgorod in the direction of Oboyan, the left steering clutch began to malfunction. The tank was forced to stop in the area of the Krapivinskie Dvori farm, located 7km south of the village of Yakovlevo. During the inspection it was found that the drive control for the left side friction clutch was bent. It took less than 4 hours to detect and repair this defect, but continued travel in the direction of Oboyan as required for the trial was considered unfeasible, and the repaired A-20 tank headed back in the direction of Kharkov (today Kharkiv). No other serious breakdowns occurred during the return run.

In total for the day the A-20 tank travelled 214km, of which 133km was on gravelled highway, 68km on dirt roads, 8km on cobblestone highway and 5km on sand. The time of actual travel was 5h 37m, the time spent on troubleshooting was 3h 47m, with rest, meal and other operational stops being 27m. As a result, the average speed of pure (i.e. uninterrupted) movement of the A-20 tank was 38.1km/h, the average technical speed was 22.7km/h and the average operational speed was 21.8km/h.

The number of tests scheduled for the A-32 tank for 16th August 1939 was substantially more than for the A-20. On this day, the A-32 had to undergo tests to overcome ascents and descents, and then make a run through an area with varying road conditions. To determine the capabilities of the A-32 tank to overcome ascents, the trial participants on the morning of 16th August, assembled in Yar, located only 1km southeast of Plant №183 in Kharkov. At the initial stage of the test, the A-32 tank consistently overcame in 1st gear two steep climbs of 35.5° and 37° with an ascent length of 28m and 24m respectively. The tank failed however to overcome a steeper rise of 40° with a solid surface without grass cover even on the seventh attempt. Every time the machine moved in 1st gear up the slope 18-20m, then due to insufficient traction the tracks began to spin. During the plant tests, the A-32 had easily overcome an identical slope, but with grass cover. After overcoming the slope on every occasion, the tank then effortlessly carried out the descent, with the slopes overcome easily in forward and reverse gears. The results of the tests were recorded in Table №10 of the Appendix to the A-20 and A-32 tank field test report. On the capabilities of the A-32 tank on gradients, the Commission concluded:

"The maximum possible ascent for the A-32 tank on dry hard ground, without grass cover, is 38-39° for grip of tracks to the ground."

RGVA. F.31811. L.3. C.1607. pp104

After the "ascent and descent" trials, the A-32 was tested to determine cross-country capability. For this purpose, the test participants moved from Yar to a ravine located 1.5km southwest of the village of Pavlenky. At the new location the soil rather than being dry solid clay was dry "chernozyom" (black loam soil) covered with short grass. The A-32 was tested on its ability to overcome slopes on the same plot of land on which similar tests had been carried out on the A-20 on 7th August 1939. The route on which the tanks were tested passed along the slopes of the ravine and represented an overall circuit of 500-550m with slopes ranging from 0° to 34°.

Ahead of the A-32 testing the tracks were tightened as much as possible. During tests the machine in 1st gear comple-

The A-32 tank successfully overcomes a 37° slope.

The A-32 tank attempting unsuccessfully to overcome a 40° slope.

The A-32 tank about to descend a 35° slope.

The A-32 tank about to descend a 37° slope.

ted the circuit on the ravine slopes in 6m 20s, about-turned, and moving in the opposite direction overcame the same route in 6m 10s, with no sliding or locking of tracks. However, when driving on a slope of 34°, the Commission noted lateral slipping of the machine down the soil slope. The results of the tests were reflected in the Appendix to the A-20 and A-32 field test report in Table №12. Mobility of both tanks on the test slopes was recognised by the Commission as good and sufficient.

According to the testing route records the A-32 tank on 16th August in addition to ascent and descent tests also completed 192km of mobility proving trials, including 93km on dirt roads, 9km on cobblestone highway and 90km on virgin soil. As the movement was carried out mainly in 3rd and 4th gears, the average net speed of the tank was higher on this day, at 39.4km/h. Despite the relatively high (24.8°C) ambient temperature that day the oil and water in the lubrication and cooling systems remained within their permissible values. The A-20 and A-32 tanks were again duly returned to workshop "530" at Plant №183, where minor repairs were conducted, the tanks refuelled, and prepared for the next day of trials.

On the morning of 17th August, the A-20 and A-32 prototypes, and a series production BT-7 moved from the territory of Plant №183 to the area of Pavlenky village for undertaking the trials, to determine the minimum turning radii of the machines when driving on tracks on lower gears. Tests were carried out in two stages, at first on a dirt road in the ravine, and then in a nearby field. In total, on dry and hard ground, the A-20 tank made 14 360° skid turns in different directions, and the A-32 made an equivalent 6 turns. The results obtained during these tests were reflected in Table №8 of the Appendix to the A-20 and A-32 tank polygon test report. Following tests the Commission concluded:

"a) A-20 tank turning radius on a dirt road: in 1st gear - 4m, in 2nd gear - 3.8m. On stubble: in 1st gear - 4.3m, in 2nd gear - 7.5 m.
b) A-32 tank turning radius on a dirt road: in 1st gear - 3.35m, in 2nd gear - 3.6m. On stubble: in 1st gear - 5.2m, in 2nd gear - 9.5 m.
c) A-7 tank turning radius in 1st gear - 3.2m, in 2nd gear - 3.2m.

Some of the worst turning of tanks A-20 and A-32 in 2nd gear on stubble was due to reduced available power due to significant lateral track resistance, and also a lack of braking power. The slewing capacity of the A-20 and A-32 tanks is satisfactory, but to increase slewing capacity it is necessary to increase the engine power and install more powerful brakes."

RGVA. F.31811. L.3. C.1607. pp104

After completing the turning radius tests near Pavlenky, the A-20, A-32 and BT-7 tanks returned in the morning to Plant №183, where at Workshop "530" a comprehensive inspection of the technical condition of the A-20 tank was undertaken. Meantime, the A-32 tank and its participating test crew after a short rest moved directly to the next proving run. During this run, which lasted 7h 43m, the A-32 travelled 171km, including 115km on virgin soil, 35km on dirt roads, 5km on cobblestone highway and 16km on sand and sandy roads, with the time of pure (uninterrupted) motion being 5h 15m. A total of 2h 28m was spent eliminating faults revealed during the run, which had a negative impact on the average operational and technical speed - that day they did not exceed 22.1km/h. Conversely, the average speed of net movement on virgin lands on this day was higher than in three previous runs, at 32.6km/h.

Top Gear and Closed-Down Tests

During the run, the Commission conducted two additional tests. The first was to determine the duration of the tank on the cobblestone highway and dirt road in 3rd and 4th gears at the lowest possible speed, until reaching the maximum permissible water and oil temperatures in the engine cooling and lubrication systems. The results were recorded in Table №7 of the Appendix to the polygon test report. The Commission conclusion noted:

"On the highway and a dirt road, to determine the duration of movement at a minimum steady speed to raise the temperature of the water and oil up to 100°C - failed. The average temperatures did not rise above 86°C. Hence in 3rd and 4th gear at 500-600rpm with

The A-32 tank negotiating a descent.

A-20 and A-32 minimum turning radius track skid marks.

a speed of 10-18km/h a tank can move on a dirt road and on the highway for a long time."

RGVA. F.31811. L.3. C.1607. pp96

The second test was to determine the temperature of the engine and the reliability of the mechanisms of the A-32 tank with long-term movement in combat order (with closed hatches and engine compartment louvres). This test was carried out twice - at the beginning and at the end of a long run. The first test was conducted when the ambient air temperature was 29.6°C. The A-32 tank with closed hatches and blinds moved over ground in 3rd gear for 4 minutes, until the water temperature in the engine cooling system exceeded the permissible limit of 105°C. In combat order the A-32 tank had traversed 1.43km of virgin ground at an average speed of 21.4km/h. The second test of the A-32 tank in combat order was held at 17:00, when the outdoor temperature had dropped to 26.8°C, the tank moving with closed hatches and louvres in 3rd gear on a dirt road. After 7 minutes, with the temperature of the water in the engine cooling system having still not reached its permissible limit the tank had traversed 2.73km with an average speed of 23.4km/h. The results of these tests was reflected in Table №23 of the Appendix to the test report. The Commission concluded:

"The "A-32" tank in combat order in 3rd gear can move over virgin

ground for 4 minutes; on a dirt road - 7 minutes. Under the same conditions, on a dirt road at an ambient temperature of 30°C, the A-7M (BT-7M) tank can move for 28 minutes, while the M-17 engine on the A-7 tank (BT-7) overheats after 2 minutes. Despite the best results obtained on the A-32 compared to the A-7, the service endurance of the tank in combat is still insufficient. It is necessary to change the design of the louvres in the transmission compartment, to increase the working time under these conditions to at least that of the A-7M".

RGVA. F.31811. L.3. C.1607. pp157

As the A-32 arrived at the plant late in the evening, technical checks were undertaken the following morning, 18th August 1939, with the malfunctions noted as:
- Breakthrough of exhaust gases in between the cylinder heads and the V-2 diesel cylinder linings; battery terminal broken off; wire breakage in the generator winding.

Thanks to the skills and efforts of the workers at Department "500" the tank was restored to full operational condition by the same evening and prepared for a new run the following day. The number of detected defects and malfunctions in the A-20 tank was significantly higher, so their elimination in Workshop "530" continued the next day. Within two days, the completed repairs included elimination of coolant leaks from the left radiator and the water pump, with leaks from both oil tanks now sealed. Three bearings, an oil seal and the universal joints in the drive shaft for the gear reducer of the 4th right road wheel were replaced. In addition, the bolts for the tapered bearing cups were tightened on the final gear reducers for all road wheels, and all fastenings in the longitudinal side drive shafts for the driven road wheels tightened.

In the evening of 19th August 1939, as repair of the A-20 tank was being completed, the A-32 tank returned to workshop "530" from its next run. On this day, the A-32 tank made its final (and at 346km the longest) test run: Plant №183-Tsirkuny-Liptsy- 53rd km of the Belgorod highway-Belgorod-Oboyan and return. The main part of the run, some 226km, was on gravelled roads, with 103km travelled on dirt roads, 12km on cobblestone highway, and 5km on sand and sandy roads. The net travel time was 9h 38m, with rest, meal and other operational stops taking 35m, and with 42m spent on fixing minor malfunctions. The calculations showed that the average speed of pure movement was 35.9km/h, the average technical speed - 33.5km/h and average operational speed - 31.7 km/h.

During the same trial the Commission performed a test to determine the duration of a continuous run, and the reasons for limiting that when travelling on a gravelled highway. Thiscontinuous run of the A-32 tank amounted to 226km, the run duration being 5h 35m, with the average speed being 40.5km/h. The stop was due only to making a small field camp at the 53rd km of the Belgorod highway after the A-32 had returned to the gravelled main highway.

Returning from the run in the afternoon of 19th August, the A-32 tank was left in workshop "530" for regular maintenance. In a form of "relay race" the testing runs were then transferred from the A-32 back to the A-20 tank.

On Sunday, 20th August, the field test participants, despite it being a day off, could not rest. In the early morning they went with the A-20 tank to the next test run, with the A-20 covering the same route driving on wheels as the tracked A-32 had completed the previous day. The A-20 failed however to complete the day's tasks. About 20km from Oboyan, the test participants made a short stop, during which was discovered a leak from the oil tank. The test crew decided to continue the trial, but returning in the opposite direction directly back to Plant №183 at Kharkov rather than onward towards Oboyan. During another regular inspection of the tank, carried out 6km southwest of Belgorod, the crew spent 57 minutes eliminating the oil tank leak, which had become worse. After returning to the plant, the results of the run were summarised. For the day, the A-20 tank had on wheels covered exactly 300km, of which 188km was on gravelled highway, 81km on dirt roads, 26km on cobblestone highway and 5km on sand and sand roads. The time of pure movement was 7h 18m, with 57m for troubleshooting and 43 minutes for rest, meals and other operational stops. The average speed of pure movement was 41.2km/h, the average technical speed 36.3 km/h, and the average operational speed 33.4km/h.

On 20th August, the A-20 tank also underwent a non-stop proving run on a gravelled-asphalt highway, as with the A-32 tank. The length of this run was 152km, with a non-stop travel time of 3h 58m, and an average speed of 41.9km/h. The reason for the stop was the aforementioned oil tank leak. All of next day, 21st August, two crews in workshop "530" fettled and prepared the A-20 and A-32 tanks for the next tests.

In the morning of 22nd August, the A-20 tank undertook the final long-range test provided for by the trial program. This time the run was done mostly on dirt roads*. On this day, the A-20 tank drove on wheels for a total of 7h 19m, traversing 173km, of which 141km was on dirt roads, 18km on cobblestone highway and 14km on sand and sandy roads. According to the test log, the net travel time was 4h 26m, the time spent on the elimination of breakdowns and defects was 2h 25m, and the time spent on rest, meals and other operational stops was 28m. The average net speed was 39.1km/h, the average technical speed 25.3km/h and the average operational speed 23.6km/h.

The mobility runs on the prototype A-20 and A-32 tanks in a variety of road conditions had been successfully completed. To complete the field-testing program for the tank prototypes there now remained only a series of special tests.

In the morning of 23rd August, A-32 and A-7M (BT-7M) prototype tanks, together with a prototype "Voroshilovets" heavy artillery tractor moved in a column on the Chuguev highway towards the settlement of Kamennaya Yaruga. In an area 2km east of the village of Rogan on a straight section of the highway tests to determine the time and path of acceleration of the A-32 tank were repeated (the first time this test was undertaken on the A-32 tank had been on 20th July). Repeated tests of the A-32 tank on the same section of road were carried out in order to obtain objective data on the time and path of acceleration of the tank with significant wear of components and assemblies during intensive operation. During the first such test, the distance travelled by the A-32 tank had been 420km, and its engine had run for 17h 5m. For the second test, the distance travelled was 2,912km and the engine running time was 100h 59m, a vast increase in stress loadings and wear.

The tests showed, unsurprisingly, that the performance of the A-32 tank was worse than for the same tank the month before. The acceleration time with a gradual transition from the 1st to the 4th gear in earlier testing had been 47 seconds, but at the end of testing was now increased slightly to 50 seconds, with the distance to reach 4th gear increased from 470m to 640m. The deterioration in the performance of the A-32

The A-32 tank fording at depths of 0.7m (left) and 1.4m (right).

* *The route followed on 22nd August was: Plant №183-Pavlenky-Rogan Station- Bezlyudovka-Vasyshchevo-Ternovoe-Mokhnach Station-Kamennaya-Yaruga-Chuguev-Zarozhnoe-Sorokovka-Bolshaya Babka-Stariy Saltov-Nepokritaya-Plant №183.*

The A-32 tank attempting to overcome a 12m wide, 0.7m deep marshy ditch.

tank was mainly due to a substantial (100hp) power loss in the engine, caused by significant wear and tear during testing. The summary results of this special test and its conclusions were reflected in Table №3 of the Appendix to the A-20 and A-32 tank testing report. The following graph in the report appendixes, Table №4, presented the results of another special test conducted on the same day on the same section of the Chuguev highway. The purpose of this test was to determine:

- Time to stop the A-32 tank; time spent and the path covered by the tank when switching from the lower to higher gear; the time and path of movement of the tank by inertia.

The test showed that from a speed of 57.5km/h, from the moment of simultaneous tightening of both brake belts, via operation of both clutch control levers, that to bring the tank to a full stop took 6 seconds, with the distance travelled to a complete stop being 28m. When braking under similar conditions with the foot controls, the braking time and the path were reduced to 5 seconds and 27m, respectively. Moving from 1st to 2nd gear took 4 seconds, with the tank travelling 5.5m in that time. Moving from 2nd to 3rd gear took 4.5 seconds with the tank accordingly travelling 13.3m. Finally, the shift time from 3rd to 4th gear was 3 seconds, with the according distance travelled being 23.6m. In determining the time and deceleration distance of the tank by inertia, it was found that for the 1st gear at a speed of 8.98 km/h, it was 4 seconds and 9m respectively. When driving the tank in 2nd gear at a speed of 18.8 km/h the parameters increased to 11 seconds and 27m respectively. In 3rd and 4th gears, at speeds of 36.9km/h and 51km/h respectively, the deceleration times for the A-32 tank were 16 and 25 seconds, and the distance travelled 93m and 160m respectively. According to the results of tests, the Commission concluded:

a) *the time and braking distance of the A-32 tank on tracks is substantially the same in both braking methods and is sufficient to permit movement in a convoy.*

b) *The time required to change gear is 3-4 seconds. The distance travelled while shifting from a lower to higher gear is 5-25m.*

c) *Moving-off from a static position can be made from 2nd gear in all soils, with the exception of loose sand".*

RGVA. F.31811. L.3. C.1607. pp86

Fording and Marshland Mobility

After determining the overall mobility performance of the A-32 tank, all the test participants moved to an area near the village of Ehskhar, 8km southwest of Chuguev, where the A-32 tank was to be tested first crossing water obstacles and "mud baths".

To determine the maximum depth the A-32 tank could ford without special preparation, a section of the Donets river with a solid sandy river bed was chosen. The A-32 entered the river from the sloping shore under its own power, and was deliberately stopped at a depth of approximately 0.5m for a period of 15 minutes. During inspection, water entry into the hull was found. The second stop, with a duration of 45 seconds was made when the tank was at a depth of 1m, which showed a small leak from the transmission hatch in the hull floor. A third stop of 57 seconds duration was undertaken when the front of the tank was at a depth of 1.47m. Water entered the hull through the driver's hatch seal, his viewing device, the gaps in the machine gun ball mount shield, and via the bolt holes for the hull side armour plates. The significant flow of water into the A-32 tank was due to the driver's hatch cover rubber seal being damaged. In addition, the joins and fastenings where the upper side armour plate joined the hull allowed water ingress.

After the A-32 had been in the water with the engine running for 10 minutes, it was pulled ashore by a "Voroshilovets" tractor. With the tank back on the riverbank, about 250 litres of water was drained from the hull, including 12 litres drained from the right side final drive and 1 litre from the left. The test results were recorded in Table №14 of the Appendix to the field test report. Regarding the capability of the A-32 to ford water obstacles without special preparation, the Commission concluded that:

"The A-32 tank can overcome a maximum fording depth of 1,400mm. It is necessary to make the hull impervious and eliminate leaks in the connections of the on-board gears (reducers - final drives)".

RGVA. F.31811. F.3. C.1607.pp120

After the "water procedures" the testing moved on to a shallow marsh area overgrown with sedge grass. Here the tanks continued the tests on marshland mobility begun on 12th August. On the first attempt, the A-32 tank moved in the marsh for 38 metres in 1st gear, after which the tank came to a halt due to spinning tracks while immersed to a depth of 0.35 metres. The tank was towed out of the marsh. On the second attempt the tank, again in 1st gear, managed to move 50m with immersion to a depth of 0.15m, and then moved to the opposite shore of the marsh. The 70m long marshland obstacle was also successfully overcome by the BT-7M tank and the "Voroshilovets" heavy artillery tractor, with the depth that both machines sank into the ground not exceeding 0.26m. The following test selected for the tanks was a wetland area water-filled ditch 7-12m in width with a viscous bed and steep banks. The A-32 tank easily crossed the 7m wide ditch but failed to overcome the 12m section of the same obstacle, being forced to a halt at an immersion depth of 0.7m. The tank was towed out of the ditch. The test results for the (A-7M) BT-7M tank were similar.

The last obstacle the prototype tanks faced on the day was an earth pit 6-8m wide, filled with water to a depth of over 1 metre, with steep banks, and a viscous bed, which neither the A-32 nor the BT-7M tanks could overcome.

The results of the special marsh and wetland tests, as conducted from 12th to 23rd August 1939, were reflected in Table №15 of the Appendix to the A-20 and A-32 tank test report. The Commission concluded:

"a) Peat bogs with a solid sandy base 25m wide, depth 0.6m, the A-20, A-32 and A-7M (BT-7M) machines moving in 1st gear did not overcome. In 2nd gear, the A-32 and A-7M machines overcame the marshes.

b) Marsh, consisting of thick sticky mud, to a depth of 0.35m and overgrown with tall grass, the A-32 tank overcame 38m in 1st gear, while the A-7M (BT-7M) tank overcame 25m. The depth of immersion of the tank tracks was for the A-32 - 0.35m, and for the A-7M - 0.38m.

c) The marshy ditch 7-8m wide and 0.7m deep with a viscous base and steep banks was for the machines tested in 1st gear impassable.

d) A marshy pit with a width of 7-8m, a depth of 1.1m with a viscous base and steep banks, was for both the A-32 tank and A-7M tanks impassable in 1st gear.

Summarising the above, we come to the following general conclusion:

1. In wetlands the tractability of the A-20 and A-32 tanks is slightly higher than A-7 (BT-7) and A-7M (BT-7M) tanks, which should be explained by the lower ground pressure and better track characteristic of the A-20 and A-32. The increased all-terrain capability of the A-20 and A-32 tanks is insignificant.

2. Mobility in marshes, for the A-7 and A-7M tanks, and A-20 and A-32 tanks is insufficient".

RGVA. F.31811. L.3. C.1607. pp127

After completion of the marshland trials in the afternoon of 23rd August, the participants returned to Plant №183. The next morning the Chairman of the Committee on field testing of the A-20 and A-32 tanks, Major E. A. Kulchitsky was informed by the Director of Plant №183, Ya. E. Maksarev that the day before, the plant had also received an order from the People's Commissar of Medium Machine Building (NKSM),

I. A. Likhachev, to suspend tank testing. According to the order, prototypes of A-20, A-32, BT-5M and BT-7M tanks were to be prepared and sent to Kubinka near Moscow to participate in a demonstration to the military and political leadership of the country, scheduled for the second half of September 1939, only three weeks hence. With regard to the suspension of field-testing of A-20 and A-32 tanks, Major Kulchitsky on the same day reported to his superiors in Moscow. At 15:00, he sent from the Central Telegraph office in Kharkov a telegram directed to the assistant chief of ABTU, military engineer 1st rank B. M. Korobkov and to the chief of the 8th Department of ABTU, military engineer 1st rank Ya. L. Skvirsky:

"TWENTY-FOURTH (day) STOPPED WORK. DIRECTOR RECEIVED ORDER TO SEND TO KUBINKA "TWENTY" (the A-20) (No) 4137 - ENGINE 143 (and) "THIRTY-TWO" (the A-32) (No) 3000 ENGINE 103 - BOTH RUNNING. UNCOMPLETED MOVEMENT WITHOUT WHEELS. QUESTIONS INVITE EXPERTS. REQUEST PERMISSION TO COME MOSCOW FOR TWO DAYS. - KULCHITSKY".

RGVA. F.31811. L.3. C.1633. pp178

Over the next 12 days the A-20 and A-32 tank prototypes were prepared in Department "500" at Plant №183 for the forthcoming demonstration. Both tanks were provided with newly installed V-2 diesel engines, with warranted service life (i.e. fully tested engines). As of 23rd August, the A-20 tank had during plant and field tests travelled some 4,139km, of which 1,239km was while mounted on tracks, 2,831km on a single track and 69km driving on wheels. The total distance travelled by the A-32 tank was slightly less, at 3,121km. The tanks prepared for the demonstration at Kubinka were on 5th September sent by rail to the NIABT test polygon at Kubinka. The show to the military and political leadership of the country of new and modernised armoured weapons, held on 22nd September, including the A-20 and A-32 tanks will be described in detail in the next Chapter.

Two Tank Designs To Adopt for Service

At the end of September 1939, the senior military leadership of the Soviet Union was of the opinion that it was necessary to adopt into the Red Army and put into serial production two medium tank types: the wheeled-tracked A-20; and the tracked A-32, with it being planned to series produce a version of the A-32 tank with enhanced armour. For the manufacture of two prototypes of the latter machine, which received the index A-34, and also for conducting military trials of these new prototypes, Contract № 8/678 was signed between ABTU and Plant №183 on 28th September. In connection with the foregoing, it was decided to involve only the wheel-track tank A-20 in what was the originally planned final stages of field testing of the A-20 and A-32 tanks. While the A-20 and A-32 tanks were located at Kubinka, specialists at the NIABT test polygon carried out additional testing of the A-20 tank, mostly regarding its armament:

- Firing trials to determine the reliability of the gun and coaxial machine gun installation in the turret;
- Tests to determine the sectors of fire and maximum elevation and depression angles of guns and machine guns;
- Tests to determine the usability of elevation and traverse mechanisms and any rework required;
- Tests to determine visibility from the tank and ease of use of observation devices and optical sights;
- Tests to determine the degree of carbon dioxide (CO_2) and carbon monoxide (CO) and its removal from the inhabited compartments of the machine when firing the machine guns.

The tests were carried out according to the program, signed on 28th September 1939 by the assistant chief of ABTU, military engineer 1st rank B. M. Korobkov and the chief of the 8th Department of ABTU, military engineer 1st rank S. A. Afonin. The latter had been appointed to this position at the end of August 1939, replacing Ya. L. Skvirsky, who had for health reasons been transferred to the post of senior lecturer of the Department of Tanks and Tractors at the VAMM technical university of the Red Army. The results of the NIABT polygon tests were reflected in Tables №37, №38 and №39 of the Appendix to the report on A-20 and A-32 tank field tests.

The strength of the A-20 armament installation mountings was tested with ten rounds fired from the 45mm gun at angles of from +30° to -4°. Regarding gun laying in the vertical and horizontal planes, as well as the ammunition complement, in the section "conclusions" Table №38, was stated:

"1. Eliminate the possibility (during recoil) of the breech handle striking the hinge of the turret hatch at maximum angle of depression. 2. Install a gun depression stop limiter to prevent possible damage to the turret.

3. Resolve the ammunition stowage, the construction of which should be: a) Convenient and easy to use. b) Protect from penetration of dust and dirt.

4. Increase the horizontal field of fire of the machine gun to the left of the radio operator.

5. Gun elevation and turret rotation mechanisms to be constructively modified.

6. Strengthen and improve the turret accent fastening.

7. To link the location of all devices, traverse and lifting mechanisms, as well as the electric motor, so that there is complete security and convenience in the management of weapons and surveillance."

RGVA. F.31811. L.3. C.1607. pp265

Determination of concentrations of carbon monoxide (CO) and carbon dioxide (CO_2) in the habitable compartments of the A-20 tank was carried out during tank movement with closed hatches when firing simultaneously from two 7.62mm DT machine guns located in the combat compartment and in the control compartment. Firing from each machine gun was conducted with a rate of 63 rounds (1 disk magazine) within two minutes with a break for three minutes for air sampling. In total, 6 disk magazines were used up during the test. Air samples were taken three times from the breathing zone of the radio operator and the loader, with the ventilation switched on and off. The results obtained during this test were recorded in Table №39 of the Appendix to the report on the A-20 and A-32 tank polygon tests, with the A-20 tank ventilation system evaluated as follows:

"The concentration of CO when ventilation is switched on and off is slightly higher than the hygienic norm, but not at poisonous levels. The concentration of CO with the fan off exceeds the hygienic norm (standard conditions) by 20 times, reaching 0.424mg/litre in the turret. Activation of the fan reduces the concentration of CO, but is not effective enough, especially in the control (driver's) compartment. Maximum found was 0,371mg/litre in the control compartment and 0.331mg/litre in the turret, i.e. 15 times above health standard norms. Prolonged firing at this concentration can cause initial signs of poisoning (headache, nausea). In order to create acceptable conditions, the crew in the "A-20" and "A-32" tanks need improved ventilation, reducing the concentration to at least the level of the "A-7" (BT-7) tank (without ventilation 0.286mg/litre, with ventilation 0.05-0.17mg/litre)."

RGVA. F.31811. L.3. C.1607.pp264-267

After the A-20 and A-32 tank prototypes had returned from Kubinka to Kharkov in the first days of October 1939, new trials were conducted on the A-20 tank at Plant №183 and in and near Kharkov between 14th and 17th October. The purpose of these tests was to determine the size of trees that the tank could fell, the maximum height of vertical obstacle the tank could overcome, and the probability of burning liquid entering the tank.

Trials against Trees

Tests on determination of the size of trees that the A-20 tank could topple were carried out on 14th October 1939 in a mixed wood area near the village of Guty, 64km northwest of Kharkov. The first test felled an oak tree with a trunk diameter of 337mm. On the first attempt, the tank drove 10m from a standing start and dislodged but did not fell the tree, which was felled on the second attempt. Two oak trunks with diameters of 180mm and 330mm subsequently were knocked over from the first hit when accelerating 12m in 1st gear from a standing

The A-20 tank felling a pine tree with a diameter of 630mm from the first impact.

The A-20 tank overcomes a 1.1 m high vertical wall.

start. For the felling of larger trees, the run of the tank and its speed correspondingly increased. A 630mm diameter pine tree was felled from the first impact in 2nd gear with an acceleration run of 50m. In the final part of the test, the A-20 tank from a 55m acceleration run in 2nd gear felled a 675mm trunk diameter pine tree on the third impact.

The findings from the test near the village of Guty were recorded in Chart №16 of the Appendix to the test of the A-20 and A-32 tanks. Following the results of tests the Commission made the following conclusions:

"Tanks "A-20" and "A-32" can:
1. With a 50-55 metre acceleration run in 2nd gear with the first impact down a pine (tree) Ø 630mm and with three impacts to Ø 670 mm. 2. With a 10-12 metre acceleration run in 1st gear at the first strike down an oak (tree) Ø 330mm".

RGVA. F.31811. L.3. C.1607. pp130

Vertical Obstacles

The next additional test of the A-20 tank, to determine the ability to overcome artificial obstacles, was carried out on 16th October 1939 in the settlement of Yar, not far from Plant №183. For testing, the plant built a vertical reinforced concrete wall 1.1m high and 1.16m wide, the top of which was a truncated cone with a width of 0.28 m. The rear of the wall was an incline, being 1.08m at the base and merging with the upper part of the wall. The outside the wall was lined with bricks. The A-20 overcame the obstacle on the first attempt. The conclusions drawn from the test results and reflected in Chart №17 of the Appendix to the A-20 and A-32 tank field test report noted:

"The A-20 tank can overcome a vertical wall up to 1.1 metres in height; BT tanks can overcome a vertical wall of 0.7-0.8 metres".

RGVA. F.31811. L.3. C.1607. pp133

Trial By Fire

The final test conducted was to determine the degree of protection that the hull and turret provided from penetration of burning liquid (i.e. "Molotov cocktails") into the tank. This test was carried out on 17th October 1939 in the same location where the day before the A-20 tank had overcome the concrete wall. 25 sisal rope torches impregnated with aviation fuel and gasoline were attached with wire to the A-20 tank prototype. Before beginning the test, the participants closed all the hatch covers on the tank and then lit the torches. The driver-mechanic (sitting in his seat during the test) started the engine. With the engine idling, 0.6 litre capacity "Molotov cocktail" bottles filled with fuel were thrown at the tank; the first two bottles thrown on the upper hull rear, the third on the rear turret plate, and eight others on the engine compartment roof. The duration of intensive burning of the ignited fuel was 15-20 seconds. The results obtained during this test were recorded in detail in Table №18 of the Appendix to the A-20 and A-32 tank test report. In particular, it was noted that:

"During inspection of the tank after the test, the following was found:
1. Transmission compartment - detected scorching in places of flame penetration under the water drain around the seal perimeter. Rubber seal without traces of burning. Traces of flame destruction of mechanisms and assemblies detected in the compartment. The electric distribution system has no traces of flame damage.
2. Hatch over the engine - intense scorching around the hatch perimeter is detected, indicating flame penetration under the covers. The sealing of the rear of the hatch cover has a 30mm lesion in the rubber caused by flame penetration.
Traces of destruction by fire of units and mechanisms in the engine compartment via the hatch over the engine is not detected. The Durite* hoses, pipelines and air purifier are covered with light soot. The inner surface of the engine hatch cover over the engine is badly scorched.

---

* The hoses were specifically named by make.

Testing the A-20 for the probability of burning liquid penetrating the tank.

3. *Covers above the radiators - after removing the right cover over the radiator the following was discovered: the rear of the radiator was badly scorched, the upper soldering melted, but no water leaks were detected. The (heat transfer) fins at the top of the oil tank are melted, the tank itself at the top had a melted seam 35-45mm in length in two places, but with no oil leak detected. The oil tank and radiator have scorching on all top surfaces. The left water radiator and oil radiator tank have burn marks similar to the right side, but with melted soldering not detected. The rubber seals of the covers over the radiators have fire damage to the rear of the machine with a length of 50-60mm.*

4. *The turret hatch had no rubber seal and the inner surface of the hatch had traces of intense flame penetration. Traces of flame penetration near the turret (race) shoulders were not found. The driver, who was inside the machine when the bottle hit the back wall of the turret bustle, observed a large flame that penetrated under the hatch cover. The driver was unharmed. After the test, the A-20 machine was driven 14km and was able to continue driving.*

Summary:

1. *Gradual burning of petrol - 11 bottles - in different places of the roof did not cause a general fire.*

2. *Flames penetrated into the pockets between the radiators through the inlet louvres and caused damage to the soldering joints in the oil and water radiators, which with longer burning can cause a radiator leak.*

3. *The sealing of the engine and turret hatches does not provide protection from the penetration of burning fluid.*

4. *It is required to make the roof more sloped or design an addition. Modify the sealing of the hatches."*

RGVA. F.31811. L.3. C.1607. pp138-40

Test Conclusions

At this point, the testing of the A-20 and A-32 tank prototypes was complete. The Commission had however to execute one more, final point in the field test program, namely to issue the report, preparation and registration of which took a week. The report on range testing of the A-20 and A-32 tanks, printed on 24th October 1939 in six copies and duly signed by all members of the Commission, consisted of the introduction, ten sections, and a 35-page conclusion. An integral part of the final report was drawn up at the end of November 1939 by specialists of the Prototype Workshop "540", which had conducted factory and polygon tests on both tanks, a 276 page document entitled *"Appendix to the report on polygon tests of the tanks A-20 and A-32".* The Appendix contained the text of the test program, a brief description and detailed tactical and technical characteristics (TTKh's) of the A-20 and A-32 tanks, and 41 tables and charts each containing the methodology, objectives and results of individual tests. The results obtained during the factory tests of the A-20 and A-32 tanks conducted before 18th July 1939 were also included in the final report and its appendixes. In the introductory part of the report regarding compliance of the prototype A-20 and A-32 tanks to their design requirements, the Commission noted that:

"Tanks meet tactical and technical requirements, except for the following main points:

1. *Flamethrower installation, specified in the tactical-technical requirements (TTTs) for the tank, is not provided.*

2. *The weight of the tanks was more than specified in TTTs - the A-20 by 1.5 tonnes and the A-32 by 2.5 tonnes.*

3. *Obtained ground pressure for the A-20 tank was $0.61kg/cm^2$ and the A-32 - $0.595kg/cm^2$; against TTTs for the A-20 of $0.58 kg/cm^2$ and the A-32 - $0.53kg/cm^2$.*

4. *TTTs were provided for equipment for underwater movement, but designing tanks for PKh operation the plant has not finalised. On the outstanding points of TTT requirements, the Commission considers necessary:*

1. *To provide for the installation in the tank of a flamethrower and submit drawings for approval to the ABTU.*

2. *The tank weights and ground pressures (i.e. their TTTs) should stand without change, because deviations from the requirements have not had any significant impact on the tactical-technical characteristics of the tanks.*

3. *Urgently to finish the equipment of tanks for underwater movement and to carry out tests on a prototype.*

The samples are made of (standard) materials used in tank and tractor manufacture. Alloyed materials are used in samples on critical mechanisms: gears, side transmission shafts and gearboxes. The same materials are used for production of responsible mechanisms in serial production machines - tanks and tractors. All bearings installed on tanks are selected according to the standard range ma-

nufactured by the 1st and 2nd GPZ (manufacturing plants). The Exception being two bearings installed in the main clutch. For one bearing, Plant №183 manufactured a separator (bearing retainer cage), and for the second cage the ball bearings are standard, and the rollers are manufactured by Plant №183)."

RGVA. F.31811. L.3. C.1606. pp7-9

In the first section of the report, the Commission identified shortcomings in the design of the armoured "korpus" (referring to both hull and turret) of the A-20 and A-32 tanks, as well as recommendations for their elimination, and the strengthening of armour protection. Overall, the Commission positively evaluated the design of the armour layout of both tanks:

"The tank hull, for the most part, is made of inclined plates, which increases its resistance to damage and protects against 12.7 mm (DK) rounds.

Armour plate connections (welds, riveting, etc.) during trials proved reliable, but require testing by (artillery) fire.

To increase the reliability of the protective properties of the tank, to increase the frontal armour plates from 20mm to 25mm, while maintaining the same angles.

The hull floor armour when overcoming the "French Grid" (embedded log anti-tank defences) is deformed, but the deformation during tests did not cause damage to vital components. When overcoming (emerging from) trenches and ditches, the underside of the bow does not protect against bullets (note the armour thickness of 10mm). The (hull floor) armour from the bow to the engine compartment should be increased to 13mm.

The hull roof has an insufficiently sloping form, such that tests showed the possibility of grenades thrown on it being retained. Burning liquid on the roof of the tank is trapped until it is completely combusted in the formed pockets near the inlet louvres. Flames from the burning fluid in these pockets are drawn by air flow into the engine compartment. During the test, the gradual burning of petrol in the amount of 11 bottles in different places of the roof, did not cause a fire, but the ingested flame damaged soldering on the water and oil tank-radiators, which can lead to putting the tank out of commission.

If the roof is hit with bullets, or grenades in the area of the inlet louvres, there is the possibility of penetration of shrapnel and (bullet) splashes inside these apertures, which can cause punching of the radiators. It is required, to execute a more sloping hull roof, or to establish additional shielding. On the inner side of the covers over the apertures to place a flap, to provide protection from shrapnel and splashes hitting the radiators. The recess on the roof under the turret bustle forms a pocket which captures grenades thrown into this place. It is necessary to provide protection against grenades dropping in this place.

The driver's hatch must be mounted on internal hinges, and

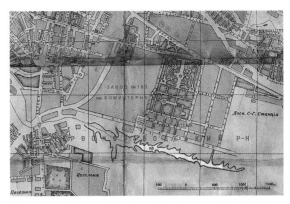

The area used for special testing at Yar, adjacent to Plant №183.

for greater reliability and better tightness of the hatch be fitted with hermetically tight seals.

The manhole (escape hatch) at the front of the tank hull floor is geometrically too small for the crew to exit; is hermetically sealed, and will require a long time to open. The hatch requires to be modified so that it will be possible to quickly to open to an angle of 90° and to close the crew access with a secret lock".

RGVA. F.31811. L.3. C.1606. pp9-10

In the section devoted to the turret construction, the armament installation and the sighting and observation devices the Commission listed the shortcomings identified during the trials, together with recommendations for their elimination:

"In terms of the turret's geometric dimensions, the crew can be comfortably accommodated. The single turret hatch does not allow two people to be in place at once, and in the marching position tires the crew. It has sharp edges that can cause injury to the crew. The mounting in the stowed position is unstable and loose. In a combat situation the hatch does not have a snug fit around the perimeter ensuring against penetration of burning liquid.

It is necessary to improve the fastening of the hatch in the marching position, eliminate the sharp edges and ensure hermetic tightness in the fighting position.

The strength of the turret and armament mountings was checked by firing from the 45mm gun at angles of +30° and -4° and overcoming trenches, and shown as quite sufficient, but requires validation when dynamically overcoming earth obstacles in higher gears.

Observation from the turret with the help of observation devices and panoramas is weak, and the visibility dead zone is large (12-12.5 metres). It is necessary to improve visibility from the turret by placing additional viewing devices on the turret roof or providing a special cap [commander's cupola]. For the pistol-port to provide protection from being knocked out, and to add a ring for more convenient closing of the port.

The PT-1 and PTK vision devices are protected by an armoured cup. The removable head remains however unprotected from bullets and shrapnel. The position of the instruments relative to the seats ensures normal monitoring.

The location of the PT-1 relative to the TOP-1 does not ensure mutual operation of weapons, since the devices touch at an elevation angle of +1° and it is not possible to obtain the lowest gun depression. It is necessary to install the devices in a position that provides for maintenance of weapons.

The paired 45mm gun and DT machine gun allows an elevation angle of 42.5°, but firing and or adjustment at that elevation angle is impossible, as the PT-1 and PTK allow fire only at the elevation angle of 30°.

Before production of a (modified) PT-1 providing firing at an elevation angle of 45°, install an additional mechanical sight that allows firing up to 43°.

To ensure gun recoil does not potentially damage the hull, a recoil stop limit is required.

Air pollution in the tank during firing is high and can cause crew poisoning. The analysis showed that after firing 6 magazines from two machine guns located in the bow of the tank and the turret at a rate of 2 minutes of burst fire and a break between these bursts of 3 minutes, the concentration of CO with the ventilation turned off was 0.424 mg/l., with the included 0.371mg/l, which is 15-20 times higher than the hygienic norm. In the A-7 tank the concentration of CO under the same conditions is equal to 0.286mg\l without the inclusion of ventilation and 0.17mg/l. with ventilation included.

It is necessary to improve the ventilation in the tank, providing acceptable conditions for the crew when conducting intense fire. The ammunition layout is of the BT type.

The ammunition complement can be increased through the use of vacant areas. It is required to protect the main armamant rounds and machine-gun magazines from contamination. To hermetically seal the rounds "suitcases" (containers), with convenient latches should be used. To develop stowage for 20pcs. grenades, and to increase the ammunition through the use of free space".

RGVA. F.31811. L.3. C.1606. pp11-12

In the third section of the report "Mobility of Tanks", the Commission assessed the identified capabilities of the A-20 and A-32 tanks to overcome natural and artificial obstacles. Concerning overcoming of natural obstacles in the report it was noted:

"1. Ascents.

The mobility of tanks A-20 and A-32 on dry slopes is better than BT tanks, due to better weight distribution on the road wheels and better track characteristics.

Tanks A-20 and A-32 overcame maximum rises of almost equal magnitude, in the range of 39-40°, for dry solid soil, overgrown with grass, while wet soil slopes of 16 -17° can be overcome. The limiting factor of climb on dry slopes, during tests was for the A-20 insufficient engine power, and for the A-32 lost track grip with the ground.

The mobility of prototypes on dry ascents is quite sufficient, limited only by the track grip with the ground. For this purpose, it is desirable to increase the power of the V-2 engine by 50-100hp at 1,700rpm, so having enough power to overcome earthen obstacles with the tank on a slope of about 40°. The track grip with the ground will be significantly higher than at the maximum slope with dry soil. This power reserve is necessary to overcome the maximum slope at the end of the engine warranty period, when the power loss (through wear in service) reaches 100hp. The mobility of tanks on wet ground is insufficient and similar to that of BT tanks without grousers. It is necessary to develop a device that improves the performance on wet, icy ascents and descents.

2. Slopes.

The mobility of prototypes on slopes is higher than that of BT tanks. The movement of A-20 and A-32 tanks on slopes of up to 32° allows directional change. Without turns in movement, slopes of 34° are possible.

The mobility of the prototypes is quite sufficient for movement on rough terrain.

3. Marshes and Wetlands.

The mobility of A-20 and A-32 tanks in marsh is the same and little different from that of BT tanks. As with these other tanks, it is insufficient to overcome marshes. On marshland areas the mobility of the prototypes, despite their greater weight, is slightly better than for the BT tanks, but insufficient for reliable movement. BT tanks, and the A-20 and A-32 prototypes, can only with difficulty overcome marshes and wetlands. It is necessary to increase the mobility of tanks on marshes and wetlands through the use of special devices (i.e. grousers), sharply reducing the ground pressure and increasing the engagement of tracks with the ground.

4. Fording.

Tanks A-20 and A-32 can ford to a depth of 1.4m. Fording depth is insufficient. The use of "PKh" (deep wading) equipment is required to provide the crossing of (short, 20-25m) fords to a depth of 1.7m and 1.9m".

RGVA. F.31811. L.3. C.1606. pp13-15

The report did not mention the mobility of A-20 and A-32 tanks in sandy areas, although the respective tests were conducted on 28th June in the area between Vasyshchevo village and the village of Shubino, some 15km southeast of Kharkov. On that day, the tanks alternately travelled in a 1km long circuit in 1st gear and on the sand dunes; while en-route the machines overcame three slopes varying in steepness from 18° to 24°; a 26° descent; and a slope of the same steepness. According to the test results the participants made the following conclusions recorded in Table №13 of the Appendix to the field test report:

*"1. The mobility of tanks A-20 and A-32 in deep sand is satisfactory.
2. In 1st gear the tanks overcame long slopes of 24°, short banks of 26°".*

RGVA F.31811 L.3. C.1607. pp117

Regarding the capabilities of the A-20 and A-32 tanks to overcome artificial obstacles, the Commission noted:

"1. Triangular and trapezoid earth ditches.
For prototypes and BT tanks when driving in lower gears the maximum surmountable obstacles are:
- triangular ditch, width 3.5m, depth, breastwork 1.2m.
- trapezoid ditch, width 4m, depth 1m. breastwork 1.2m.

When overcoming obstacles in higher gears, the mobility of the tanks is increased, but this requires the crews of the BT, A-20 and A-32 prototypes to be provided with protection from (impact) injuries. For overcoming such obstacles (at speed) it is necessary to increase the strength of the A-20 and A-32 tank idler wheel and turret mountings.
2. French Grid.
The test samples of the A-20, A-32 and BT tanks cannot overcome French Grid (emplaced logs and wire) obstacles in low gears. The most advantageous gear with which to overcome these obstacles was the 3rd gear for all the tanks BT, A-20 and A-32. The maximum surmountable obstacle for tanks of this type should be considered a grid with logs Ø 240-300mm and 8mm wire in 6 rows. In overcoming the French grid and other obstacles all tanks have deformed hull floors. Denting of the hull floor of the A-20 and A-32 does not cause (internal) damage, but with the BT-5M tank damaged the water pump. Tank hull floors need to be made more rigid to prevent damage.
3. Felling trees.
The (A-20 and A-32) prototypes can fell larger individual trees than BT tanks, which is explained by the use of greater horsepower. Pines Ø 0.25-0.4m. The A-20 and A-32 tanks can fell in 1st gear with the first blow and without bypassing the fallen trunk. Trees of the maximum dimension that the A-20 and A-32 can fell are downed in 2nd gear with maximum engine revs. The maximum tree size that can be felled by the prototypes, should be considered a pine tree of Ø 670mm. A tree of this size takes 1-3 impacts, but the tank without manoeuvring around the tree cannot continue driving, being stopped by the twisted roots. For felling of trees, as well as to overcome other obstacles, the tanks must be equipped with adequate protection for the crew at their work places.
4. Vertical wall.
The (A-20 and A-32) tanks overcome a higher vertical wall than the BT, due to the higher height of the tow hooks and better track characteristics. The maximum height of a brick wall that can be overcome is 1.1-1.2m".

RGVA. F.31811. L.3. C.1606. pp15-16

The mobility of the A-20 tank when driving with one track removed, as well as when driving on wheels on dry ground was recognised by the Commission as satisfactory; on wet ground, the machine performed less well, as was noted in the report:

"On one track the BT and A-32 cannot reliably move, even on roads and on dry soil. The A-20 driving on one track has quite satisfactory cross-country ability on obstacles, good capability on dirt roads and on up to 30° slopes, in dry weather. On wet ground, with a large immersion of the wheels, mobility is unsatisfactory, because the machine strongly leads towards the wheeled mode side of the tank. BT tanks can move on wheels on the road and hard ground in dry weather. The A-20 tank, on wheels, has higher mobility than the BT, because of the large number of driven wheels. In dry weather the A-20 tank driving on wheels overcomes roadside ditches, reliably traverses terrain with ascents of 20-25°, but not loose sand and wetland areas, or on dirt roads. Movement on wheels, on wet dirt roads is poor due to insufficient wheel engagement with the ground. For movement on wheels, and on one track, on wet dirt roads and ground, it is necessary to improve the required engagement of wheels with the ground".

RGVA. F.31811 L.3. C.1606. pp16-17

The fourth section of the field test report reviewed the agility and controllability of the A-20 and A-32 tanks. The Commission noted:

"The minimum turning radius of BT tanks on tracks is 3.2m., tanks A-20 and A-32 - 3.5-4m. The turning radius, and turning of tanks A-20 and A-32 in all road conditions is good. During the tests, the cornering of the A-20 and A-32 tanks was often unsatisfactory due to the lack of reliable operation of the brake bands and the on-board frictions (i.e. side clutches). Handling of the A-20 and A-32 tanks with (pneumatic assisted) power steering is much better than the handling of BT tanks, because it requires less effort. With failure (of the pneumatic assistance) or abnormal steering, to drive a tank for a long time is almost impossible, as the required leverage effort reaches 60-80kg. It is necessary to reduce the effort required on the levers of the steering clutches when the servo is off, to reduce and bring them to the level required on the BT. Tanks A-20 and A-32 on tracks are stable when driving at all speeds and under any road conditions. The A-20 in wheeled mode has poor road holding when driving on a broken highway or country road with potholes. This is due to insufficient load on the driven wheels. The load on the driven wheels must be increased."

RGVA. F.31811. L.3. C.1606. pp17-18

The, fifth section of the report noted the parameters and characterising relating to the operational range of the A-20 and A-32 tanks, and comparison with the BT-7 and BT-7M tanks:

"Fuel reserve (range), depending on road conditions, varies: BT-7 on tracks: 300-350km; BT-7 on wheels: 480-510km; BT-7M on tracks: 520-630km; BT-7M on wheels: 1,070-1,250km; A-20 on tracks: 350-400km; A-20 on wheels: 900-1,000km; A-32 on tracks: 300-440km.

Fuel consumption for 1km,

On tracks (l/km): BT-7: 2.2-2.56, BT-7M: 0.82-0.90, A-20: 1.18-1.28, A-32: 1.08-1.10.

On wheels (l/km): BT-7: 1.25-1.35, BT-7M: 0.45-0.52: A-20-0.54. Compared with the range of BT-7 tanks, the range of tanks A-20 and A-32 is much greater, due to the efficiency of the V-2 engine. The range of the BT-7M is however more than that of the A-20 and A-32 tanks, which should be explained by the larger quantity of carried fuel and lesser weight of the BT-7M tank, with identical engines. The range of the A-20 and A-32 tanks is sufficient to ensure the necessary manoeuvrability of tanks of this type. The service range of tanks A-20 and A-32 is 150-200km, close to that of BT-7 tanks, which is 100-150km. At the range limit of the BT it is required to lubricate the main and side frictions (main and side clutches), and on the prototypes - adjust the track tension.

Preferably, the range of the A-20 and A-32 tanks, before maintenance (tensioning the tracks simultaneously with lubrication to the main and side clutches) should be increased to 250-300km. The driver's endurance on the A-20 and A-32 tanks is signifi cantly hig-

Artificial tank testing obstacles as used for the A-20 and A-32 tank tests.

her than on BT tanks, and does not limit both non-stop movement and daily transition. Reduction of driver fatigue on the A-20 and A-32 is explained by the installation of servo controls. After lengthy transitions the driver has however a tired back from poor design of the seat and incorrect seat mountings."

RGVA. F.31811. L.3. C.1606. pp18-20

The sixth section of the report provided test result statistics on the maximum and average operational and tactical speeds of the A-20 and A-32 tanks when driving in different road conditions. This section also gave the reasons that retarded, in the opinion of the Commission members, the average tank speeds, and recommendations thereon:

"The maximum speeds of tanks A-20 and A-32 was 74.7km/h on tracks. On wheels the A-20 tank developed the same speeds, as gear ratios on track and wheel-track drives are the same. Average speeds (km/h) during the tests were obtained:

		Operational	Technical	Pure Motion
A-20 on tracks	On road	25.2	34.3	44.4
	On ground	22.3	24.6	31.7
A-20 on wheels	On road	25.5	31.6	38.6
	On ground	23.3	25.3	39.1
A-32 on tracks	On road	22.7	24.9	35.9
	On ground	22.6	24.7	32.5
	On soil	22.7	23.1	28.7
БТ-7M on tracks	On road	32.6	32.6	32.6
	On ground	20.6	26.5	31.7
	On soil	22.8	28.4	33.6
БТ-7 on tracks	On ground	25.6	20.6	34.6
	On soil	25.6	27.8	31.2

The average test speeds were somewhat understated. The decrease in average speeds on the tests should be explained by the fact that the tanks A-20 and A-32 are new tanks, prototypes and first checked to determine the maximum possible speed. In addition, average speed has decreased greatly due to the unreliable operation of steering clutches and brake bands. With the current dynamics of the A-20 and A-32 tanks, characteristics of their engines and improved suspension, the average speed can be increased. There is insufficient engine power output when driving on 4th gear on dirt roads. When determining the pick-up (acceleration) a discontinuity in the acceleration of the tank in various gears was found. In 4th gear the engine is slow picking up momentum, and at the end of the engine warranty period it proved almost impossible to raise the engine revs. above 1,500rpm. The gear ratio of the 4th gear needs to be increased and thereby to reduce the speed to better utilise the 4th gear. This will allow, in addition to im-

proving acceleration and average speeds, improvement of the thermal regime of the engine in 4th gear. The medium operational and tactical speeds obtained over 3,000-4,000km (of travel) are high and show the good quality of the prototype tanks".

RGVA. F.31811. L.3. C.1606. pp21-22

The main indicators characterising operational mobility of the A-20 and A-32 tanks were stated by the Commission in the seventh section ("Non-Stop and Daily Transitions") of the test report:

"During the tests, non-stop movements of the A-20 tank were in the range of 60-150km and 60-200km for the A-32. The limit to nonstop movement of both tanks was the need to make control inspections and lubrication, before reaching the deadlines. Very often, movement was stopped due to violations of regulations and unreliable operation of brake bands and the on-board frictions (side clutches). The maximum trial distances made by the A-20 tank on tracks were 290-440km and on wheels 250-320km. And on the A-32 - up to 346km. The daily distance travelled by the A-20 on wheels was limited by the unreliabile fastening of the drive-shaft couplings and insufficient strength of the wheel bearings. On tracks, the daily transition was reduced for the same reasons as non-stop movement, and due to crew fatigue from troubleshooting. The reasons limiting the results of both the non-stop and the daily transition are typical of prototypes and will be eliminated in the subsequent manufacture of tanks. The length of the daily transitions and non-stop movement is for prototype tanks quite satisfactory. After elimination of the shortcomings revealed by tests, non-stop transitions will increase and have to be limited by terms of service. Daily endurance will also increase, and will have to be limited to the total time for the movement, maintenance and resting of the crew."

RGVA. F. 31811. L. 3. C. 1606. pp. 22-23

The quoted thermal regime of the V-2 diesel engine installed on the prototype A-20 and A-32 tanks was significantly different from the thermal regime of the M-17T petrol engine installed on serial production BT-7 tanks. The Commission thereby paid special attention to the operation of the cooling and lubrication systems of the V-2 diesel engine installed in the A-20 and A-32 tanks. The data obtained during the field tests on the operation of these systems were reflected in the eighth section of the report: "Temperature regime":

"The temperature regime of the V-2 diesel engine is sharply different from that of petrol engines, which is explained by the feature of the diesel to emit less heat into the cooling water. In addition, the A-20 and A-32 tanks have improved engine cooling conditions due to increased fan performance, increased cooling surfaces, and improved

radiator design. During the test, the maximum water temperature in the A-20 was 110°C, and in the A-32 - 90°C. The maximum oil temperature of the A-20 was 108°C and the A-32 - 90°C.

The highest recorded temperature of the A-20 tank engine was the result of a malfunction of the cooling system, which was accopanied by leakage of water and oil. In addition, the engine of the A-20 during trials suffered a breakthrough of gases into the cooling water. With a correct cooling system, the thermal mode of the engines on the A-20 and A-32 ensures normal operation of the tanks in summer conditions with an ambient temperature of up to 30-32°C. Under these conditions, the A-32 tank can move in 3rd gear in combat order with closed (engine) louvres from 4 to 7 minutes, while the BT-7 overheats after 2 minutes, the (diesel-engined) BT-7M in 28 minutes. The cooling performance of the A-20 and A-32 tanks in a combat situation should be increased at least up to the level of the BT-7M tank.

At a higher ambient temperature, the tanks can still be operationally exploited, but in order to create better engine cooling conditions, it will be necessary to maintain certain engine revolutions and frequently change gears to do so.

Considering the temperature regime of the V-2 engine on the A-20 and A-32 tanks is quite satisfactory for exploitation in summer conditions, the need to install a special heating device against freezing in winter conditions should be considered."

RGVA. F.81311. L.3. C.1606. pp23-24

In the ninth section of the report, the Commission listed the shortcomings of the crew members' working arrangements identified during the polygon trials of the A-20 and A-32 tanks. Characterising the overall working positions of the A-20 and A-32 tank crew members, the Commission stated:

"The (crew) working positions in the tanks and all equipment connected with them (internal lighting, shields, handles, locks, etc.) are not yet completed, and in the prototypes are unfinished. The plant, having done a lot of work on the creation of new prototypes, equipped the tanks with servo-control and allocated a large working area for the crew, left the equipment of the working areas unchanged and in poor condition. The driver's seat is high, causing a driver of abve-average height to rest his head on the hull roof. The seat does not protect from sliding sideways when moving on slopes, and when changing gears. The driver's position causes muscle fatigue. The driver's head is in proximity to outstanding and sharp handles, bolts, sharp edges and angles. There are no retention belts for the crew seats. There is no windshield, despite the fact that the plant itself has been using a good shield for several years that works well against dust, dirt and rain. Working positions in the turret do not give the opportunity to move efficiently with a full crew. Seats are rigid, turn on brackets and do not protect from sliding. There are no footholds

and handholds. In the fighting compartment there are many sharp corners, brackets, and there are no protective shields, and no thermos for water. Monitoring of instruments is inconvenient, because the main instruments are not concentrated in one place. Devices are lit unevenly and can be blinding when being viewed. Lighting of the road ahead when driving at night is insufficient. The manufacturing plant needs to modify workplace equipment components in new model machines, drastically different from all existing tanks."

RGVA. F.31811. L.3. C.1606. pp24-25

The tenth and final section of the report on range testing was the section devoted to service and repair of the A-20 and A-32 tanks, and a review of the reliability of the main mechanisms and components of these machines. Regarding the convenience of maintenance and repair, the Committee noted:

"The prototypes from the point of view of maintenance and repair performed satisfactorily, but there remains the testing of individual issues. Servicing of fuel and lubricants takes too much time. It is necessary to reduce the time required to access the tanks. Oil tank access requires too much time and access to some of the lubrication points is inconvenient. MTK oils are unsuitable. The factory recommends 4 separate varieties of lubricants which complicates the logistics supply to the army, this not being caused by necessity. Grades of grease should be reduced to two types. The transition from track to wheeled mode and back requires too much time, and for the crew is impossible without breaking the tracks into six links (sections). It is necessary to mechanise the mounting of tracks. The service life of the brake bands and side frictions is insufficient. The time taken to replace the brake bands is very long and requires the removal of the gearbox with the side friction - it is necessary to ensure the change of the brake bands without removing the gearbox. The side wheel reducers require verification of the fastenings (bolts) during operation, and it is required to ensure secure fastening to provide for the entire warranty period. It is necessary to develop a maintenance and machine repair system for these new samples. Development of these issues should facilitate the conditions of maintenance and repair, reduce the working time for repairs, increase the time between maintenance and repair, and distribute the work volume, completing the main operations in 30-50 hours."

RGVA. F.31811. L.3. C.1606. pp25-26

The tenth section of the report also contained information about the reliability of the engine, transmission and chassis of the A-20 and A-32 tanks. The Commission identified defects and design deficiencies found in testing, together with recommendations for their elimination. As the V-2 diesel design had at the time of the A-20 field tests not yet been finalised by Plant №75, particular attention was paid to this new type of tank eng-

ine. The advantages and disadvantages of the V-2 diesel engines installed in the A-20 and A-32 tanks were noted in the report:

"Engines V-2 mounted on tanks A-20, A-32 and A-7M [BT-7M] showed a number of positive qualities during parallel testing of the A-7 series tank with the M-17T engine. The main ones are the following:

1. *The tractive qualities of the V-2 engine provide machine movement on all types of road and in all gears, and the engine delivers the necessary power and revolutions. It should be noted that for tanks A-20 and A-32, it is desirable to increase the power by 50-100hp at 1,700rpm, so that after 80-90 hours of engine operation the overcoming maximum slopes and obstacles by the machines can be assured.*
2. *The temperature regime of the V-2 engine is steady at any rpm limits. The temperature regime of the V-2 engines in the A-20 and A-32 when moving in combat position showed an unsatisfactory time result (4-7 minutes) due to the absence of additional (hot) air outlets.*
3. *In the summer, the V-2 engine does not limit the choice of speed and does not require frequent switching of speeds to a lower gear for cooling, as occurs in the M-17T (petrol) engine.*
4. *Fuel consumption of the V-2 engine is economical.*
5. *The V-2 engine is less of a fire hazard than with the M-17T engine.*
6. *When driving at night there are no flames from the exhaust pipes that unmask the tank.*
7. *The flexibility of the V-2 engine in road conditions is better than the M-17T engine. This is due to the ability of a diesel engine to accept greater overload due to separate fuel supply, regardless of the amount of ingested air. When working with overload the V-2 engine does not suffer a sharp rise in water temperature.*
8. *The diesel (engine) allows long-term operation at low speeds. In the summer, the engine is easily started from the electric starter and a reliable air start is also provided.*
9. *In terms of operational use, the maintenance of the V-2 engine is easier than the carburettor engine M-17T, because the engine V-2 has no ignition devices.*

Engine faults:

1. *Insufficient engine operation warranty period to rebuild (100h).*
2. *Unreliable sealing of the cylinder head - the unit allows the penetration of gases into the cooling water. Note: this defect can be corrected without removing the engine from the tank. This requires about a day of working time for 3 - 4 people (at first experience).*
3. *The change of advance angle of the fuel injection has reduced the power and lowered the engine temperature regime. This was the result of the installation on the engine of the NK-1 fuel pump with "Bosch" metering.*
4. *Water leaks through the seal of the water pump.*
5. *Smoke exhaust from the V-2 engine is significantly more than the*

M-17T engine. This defect may be corrected by the appropriate fine-tuning of the fuel system."

RGVA. F.81311. L.3. C.1606. pp26-28

With regard to the fuel and control systems, that in turn ensured the operation of the V-2 diesel, the Commission noted that during tests, the fuel system and the engine lubrication system showed "not reliable operation" because of the insufficient strength of the (internal) fuel tanks. The Commission recommended to Plant №183 that "tanks be made of more durable material" by installing "communicating partitions" (i.e. baffles) within the fuel tanks as well as improvement of the fuel tank mountings within the tank hulls.

Regarding the reliability of the transmission mechanisms on both tanks, including the main clutch, main gearbox, onboard frictions, brakes and onboard gear reducers, and the noted design shortcomings, the report stated:

"Main clutch: On the A-32 machine the main clutch two times failed because of misalignment between the engine and the gearbox. On the A-20 machine the main clutch worked 4,200km, with no serious defects. The flexible coupling (damper) of the main clutch did not give positive results due to a defect (sticking of the drum hub to the damper hub).

Coupling: for warranty purposes a 100 working hour engine guarantee is not advisable. With an increase in warranty up to 200 hours, a modified flexible coupling must be installed in some of the installation batch (pilot production/establishment lot) machines for verification. To reduce dust on the friction surfaces of the main clutch, to install seals.

Fan: in terms of performance provides a normal thermal regime of engine operation and its durability is reliable, but the fan blades are made of special steel 30-XMA (30-KhMA - chromium molybdenum steel).

It is required to increase the gaps: a) between the bulkhead of the transmission compartment and the fan cowling, b) between the control rods of the main clutch and the fan (due to lack of clearance there was scoring damage).

Gearshift and connecting coupler: 3-way 4-speed gearshift during testing worked on the A-32 tank - 3,000km on the A-20 tank - 4,200km. The mechanism worked reliably and stably. Disassembly after testing showed the gears and bearings to be in good condition and with the change of two gears the box is suitable for further work.

Requires: a) Eliminate the flow of oil from the neck of the P.P. gearbox. b) Increase the strength of the vertical roller (bearing) of the P.P. gearbox and its fixing. c) Eliminate the separation of the rods of the 1st and 2nd gear.

Coupling between the main clutch and gearbox is working reliably and is fully acceptable. It is desirable to increase the absorption of misalignment (slack take-up) capability.

Steering clutches and brakes: During tests the onboard frictions were for adjustment and parts replacement twice removed on the A-20, and on the A-32 - three times.

The brake bands had to be replaced - on the A-20 tank - 3 bands, and on the A-32 tank - 4 bands.

The operation of the onboard frictions and brakes is unreliable, with high heating temperature (120-180°C) and there were cases of failure when turning of the tank.

Required:

a) To improve the quality of regulation of on-board frictions.

b) To increase brake torque.

c) Reduce the required pressure on the brake bands (6-6.5kg/cm² - too great).

d) Achieve full and uniform circumference of the drum brake band.

e) Ensure that the transmission compartment is cooled.

Final drive: For the time of tests worked normally and reliably. During the period of being driven 4,200km on the A-20 and 3,000km on the A-32, the outer bearings and shafts were replaced on both machines (after 1,500-1,700km). The bearing wear was due to insufficient lubrication. When viewed at the end of the test, the onboard (final drive) transmission gears were in good condition and suitable for further exploitation.

Required:

a) To Improve lubricant access to the tapered bearings.

b) To Increase the rigidity of the tie strings and improve alignment.

c) Strengthen the outer bearings."

RGVA. F.81311. L.3. C.1606. pp28-30

Regarding the reliability of the pneumatic driving control system servos, as well as the feasibility of installing this system on tanks in the future, the Commission noted:

"The power steering makes it easier to operate a tank and increases the efficiency of the driver. During tests mechanisms worked reliably, but the piping was unreliable. Needs:

a) Instead of copper pipelines to use steel.

b) The drive on the pedal of the main friction (clutch) to exclude for these types of machine as use of it is rare, and efforts are small (35kg)".

RGVA. F.81311. L.3. C.1606. pp31

The tenth section of the test report was completed with a description of issues related to the reliability of the main components and assemblies of the A-20 and A-32 tanks. About the individual spring suspension, in particular, it was noted:

"Before the change of (suspension) rods during the tests, the A-20 ran 420km, the A-32 - 3,000km.

Suspension design and characteristics of the springs, provide in comparison with the BT, a softer stroke and attenuation of os-

cillations occurs faster. The suspension of the A-20 compared with the A-32 is more elastic. As a firing platform - has not been checked. During the tests, the suspension worked reliably, but with a large one-way wear of the stem nut and stem. Required to reduce wear".

RGVA. F.81311. L.3. C.1606. pp30

Regarding the reliability of the A-20 wheel-tracked drive-tank and the tracked A-32 the Commission noted:

"The steerable wheels have worked 4,200km and can be used for further operation. Required to fix a grease lubricant leak.
Supporting (i.e. road) wheels of the wheeled drive are unreliable due to insufficient strength of the roller bearings of the wheel reducers. Required to replace with stronger bearings.
The track drive wheel on the A-20 worked 4,200km, on the A-32 worked 3,000km, and is suitable for further exploitation, but with a large one-sided wear of the road wheels. It is necessary to improve the durability of the (drive) wheels. The idler during tests showed unreliable work.
Required: a) structural modification of the idler mount, b) to strengthen the idler mounting bracket.
The (track) tensioner device does not provide fast and convenient tensioning of tracks.
The track has a better performance than the A-7 tank and its strength (as regards partition and shedding of tracks) during the tests provided the warranty requirements on both A-20 and A-32. The road wheels of the A-32 tank worked 3,000km and are suitable for further exploitation.
The rubber on the wheels at an ambient temperature of 25-30°C, with an average net speed of movement of 40km/hour in a continuous run of between 25km and 100km, worked until destruction at 700km on a gravelled highway and to 400km on a dirt road, while the A-7 [BT-7] under the same conditions achieved 50-100km. In tracked mode the rubber lasted 3,000km.
Increasing the resistance of road wheel rubber in the A-20 tank has been achieved through more uniform load on the wheels, 1.5° camber and widening of the tyre rubber. The dependence on increasing the resistance of rubber between the camber and the widening of the tyre (rim) could not be established due to the lack of rubber. The camber justified its purpose and its use on wheel-track prototypes is mandatory."

RGVA. F.81311. L.3. C.1606. pp26-28

The final part of the report on the prototype A-20 and A-32 tank trials was the conclusion. The Commission conclusion was a comparative evaluation of the A-20 wheel-tracked and tracked A-32 tanks, and also listed the advantages of these rototypes ahead of the series-produced BT-7 wheel-track tank:

"I. Performance of prototypes.

The A-20 and A-32 tank prototypes made by Plant №183 proved themselves well for durability and reliability - being ahead of all previously produced prototypes.

II. Comparative evaluation of A-20 and A-32.

The wheeled-tracked A-20 tank compared to the tracked A-32 has the following advantages:
1. Has ammunition complement of up to 80 rounds, and 17 more machine-gun discs than the A-32.
2. Has the ability to move on one track on dry dirt roads, terrain and overcome obstacles.
3. After the failure of 1-2 wheels on one side, the tank can still move on highways and hard ground.
4. In the emergency state and when the engine is destroyed, it can be towed in wheeled mode.
5. Can move on wheels on the highway in any season and on dry dirt roads in a convoy.
6. The A-20 tank is 1 tonne lighter than the A-32.

Along with these advantages, it has the following disadvantages compared to the A-32:

1. Armed with a less powerful gun.
2. Side armour is 5mm thinner.
3. The engine is more loaded, because it has two less supporting wheels (greater ground pressure).
With the exception of the final drives and wheels all the components are the same and interchangeable. The A-20, as a wheeled-tracked tank, in comparison with the presented sample A-32 has more advantages.

III. Advantages of prototypes in comparison with the BT-7 serial tank.

The prototypes are more modern (than the BT-7) and have the following main advantages:
I. Hull and Turret.
a) Installed more powerful armour.
b) Most of the korpus (hull and turret) consists of inclined sheets.
c) The korpus is much better protected from grenades, combustible liquids and OV (chemical attack).
d) The useful area inside the korpus is greater.
e) The crew consists of 4 persons.
2. Armament.
a) A more powerful gun is installed on the A-32.
b) On both samples a second machine gun is installed.
c) The prototype tanks, as fire platforms, are more stable.

3. Mobility.

a) The range of the A-20 tank is significantly higher on wheels and provides for convoy travel on country roads in dry weather.

b) The cross-country ability on tracks of both samples is better on ascents, slopes, fords and when felling trees.

c) A-20 has the ability to move on ground and obstacles on one track.

4. On non-stop movement and daily transitions.

Tanks A-20 and A-32 by design and equipment allow for major modifications.

5. Working Positions

a) For both tanks A-20 and A-32, a large working area is reserved for the crew.

b) Servo control is installed.

6. Engines.

Engine V-2 is better than the M-17 and gives an improvement on the tank with the following key benefits:

a) At high ambient temperatures and heavy loads the engine has the optimal temperature regime.

b) In difficult periods may move in combat order (i.e. closed down).

c) When overcoming water obstacles, the engine is not concerned with water splashes.

d) More Economical in all respects.

e) Less dangerous with regard to fire.

f) Easier to maintain.

7. On reliability and durability.

a) The A-20 and A-32 are more reliable in design than the BT-7 and may have a longer warranty period.

b) Test samples, with the exception of the idler, side clutch and brakes, are stronger than BT-7 tanks".

RGVA. F.31811. L.3. C.1606. pp32-34

In contrast to the findings, which took three pages in the report, the polygon test conclusion was rather concise:

"CONCLUSION.

The test samples of tanks A-20 and A-32 fully comply with the TT requirements (i.e. the TTTs) presented. The A-20 and A-32 are suitable for use in the Red Army.

The A-32 tank, having a margin to increase weight, it is advisable to protect with more powerful armour, respectively increasing the strength of individual components, and changing the transmission gear ratios. In this case, the strengthened parts should be used to the maximum, and also used on the A-20. All shortcomings noted in the report need to be urgently eliminated to provide to ABTU for approval the list of works with an indication of timing".

RGVA F.31811 L.3. C.1606 pp35

Finally, the 35-page report on field testing of the A-20 and A-32 tanks was signed; by the Chairman of the Commission, the head of the 1st Department of the NIABT polygon, Major E. A. Kulchitsky; the Deputy Chairman of the Commission - senior ABTU engineer, Major I. G. Panov and all members of the Commission; the chief designer of Plant №183, M. I. Koshkin; the engineer of the 3rd Department Glavspetsmash NKSM N.I. Masalsky; senior engineer of the 4th Department of ABTU, military engineer 3rd rank N. Ya. Goryushkin; military representative of ABTU at Plant №183, military engineer 3rd rank P. P. Baikov and the representative of Plant №75, the engineer-motorman I. I. Skorikov. The first copy of the report remained at Plant №183, with the remaining five sent out in the third week of October 1939. Three went to ABTU Red Army and one to Glavspetsmash NKSM, with one copy to the NIABT range at Kubinka. The Appendix to the report on testing the A-20 and A-32 tanks was by volume almost eight times greater than that of the report itself, and therefore much more time was spent on its drawing up and registration. Only on 7th December 1939 was the Appendix sent from Plant №183 to the same addresses as the main report; and in the same quantities. This document was signed by the deputy head of workshop "540" at Plant №183, P. N. Goryun, workshop engineer V.V. Amiragov and engineer-researchers of workshop "540" N.S. Gutnik and G. G. Onishchenko. Three copies of the Appendix to the report arrived in a secret unit of ABTU on 11th December 1939 and the following week, on 19th December 1939, at a meeting of the Defence Committee of the SNK USSR, the question of acceptance into the Red Army of one of the participant tanks was finally resolved.

The cover of the A-20 and A-32 tank testing report dating from July-October 1939.

Chapter 10

Adoption into Red Army Service

After the suspension of field trials in late August, the A-20 and A-32 tanks were repaired in Department "500" of Plant №183 and on 5th September 1939 sent to the NIABT ABTU polygon at Kubinka near Moscow for participation in a show of new and modernised armoured vehicles for the military and political leadership of the country. Three days before the scheduled show, on 19th September 1939, the head of ABTU, D. G. Pavlov and the Military Commissar of ABTU, P. N. Kulikov sent the People's Commissar of Defence K.E. Voroshilov Letter №210089ss, which reported on the implementation of the decisions of the Defence Committee of the USSR on the production of new models of tanks and armoured vehicles. In this document, Pavlov and Kulikov for the first time in official correspondence proposed adoption of the A-20 and A-32 tanks into the Red Army. In the section "tanks medium type" the letter stated:

A-20 Tank:

"The A-20 tank is a wheel-tracked (design), with three pairs of driving wheels. The tank has completed factory and field tests totalling 4,200km. In the process of testing the following deficiencies were identified:

a) The on-board friction (clutch) and brakes require strengthening.
b) To change the design of fastening the idler wheel.
c) Weak reducer wheel bearings.
d) There is insufficient visibility from the tank.

The plant has eliminated these shortcomings.
The A-20 tank has great advantages over existing BT tanks - armour, engine, operational and combat qualities. The tank is adopted into the Red Army. To manufacture an installation batch (establishment lot) in the amount of 15pcs. by 1st January 1940, preparing for serial production in 1940.

A-32 Tank:

The tank completed factory and field tests totalling 3,000km. During the tests were revealed the same shortcomings as on the A-20 tank. The A-32 tank meets the specified tactical and technical requirements, but since the tests revealed available reserves for strengthening the armour of the korpus (hull and turret), it is advisable to strengthen the armour to 45mm throughout. Tank is adopted into the Red Army. Prior to 1st January 1940 to make an installation batch of A-32 tanks with 45mm armour in the quantity of 5pcs.

RGVA. F.4 L.14. C.2222 pp25-26

Side view of the A-32 tank prototype, loaded to a combat weight of 24 metric tonnes.

The leadership of ABTU proposed to adopt both the wheel-track A-20 and tracked A-32 tank types, significantly increasing the amour protection of the latter. Even before the start of A-20 and A-32 polygon tests in late June 1939, D.G. Pavlov instructed the leading engineer of the 1st Division of the 8th Department of ABTU, Major I. G. Panov, who was at the time at Plant №183, to consider strengthening the armour protection of the A-20 and A-32 tanks without making fundamental changes in their design. This decision was due primarily to the known quantitative and qualitative development of anti-tank guns in several foreign armies in the late 1930s, while the experience of war in Spain had also confirmed the need for new tank designs with shellproof armour. The armoured hull and turret of the A-20 and A-32 tanks protected the tank only from 12.7mm equivalent calibre armour-piercing rounds. This requirement to increase the armour was immediately implemented by Pavlov. In the summary *"About progress at the Plant №183 as of 6.7.39."*, compiled by Panov, it was reported in particular, that:

"On the instructions of the Komkor the estimation with regard to increasing the armour for the A-20 is that it can be increased by 5mm throughout without a rework, for a weight gain of 700-750kg; the A-32 by 10mm all around, which will require rework of the transmission and involve a weight gain of 1,600-1,650kg, hence the weight of this machine will be 19,500-19,600kg".

RGVA. F.31811 L.3 C.1633 pp112

That Pavlov's wish to strengthen the armour protection of new tanks could be implemented became obvious during field tests of the prototype tanks, particularly the A-32, which, as test results showed, had the essential reserve power allowing an increase in combat weight. Accordingly, in mid-August 1939, before the field tests, the KB-520 design Bureau at Plant №183 were tasked to carry out preliminary calculations on the possibility of installation on the A-32 tank armour plate with an overall thickness in vulnerable areas of 45mm that guaranteed the protection of the crew and internal tank equipment from 37mm anti-tank gun fire at all ranges.

According to the calculations, increasing the armour thickness to 45mm would increase the tank combat weight to 24-25 tonnes. To analyse the effect of increasing the combat weight of the A-32 tank on its dynamics, as well as on the reliability of its components and mechanisms, it was decided to utilise a second prototype of the A-32 tank, the assembly of which was nearly complete within workshop "530" of Plant №183. The tank was to be loaded-up to the noted design weight and subjected to comprehensive tests. In the second half of August 1939, Major Panov, who was at that time the Deputy Chairman of the Commission on polygon tests of the A-20 and A-32

Petr Stepanovich Glukhov.

tanks, in the report *"on the progress of experimental work on the Plant №183 as at 18.8.39"* stated:

"Machine A-32 (second) is in the assembly stage and should be complete by 25-26.8. It will be loaded to 21.5-22 tonnes and subjected to mobility tests up to 1,000-1,200km and to other special tests. Runs are expected to start from 27.8 and finish on 5.9.
The plant Director is instructed to assign calculating and estimates for production of the A-32 machine with 45mm armour on the front and sides and 35mm below the track guards, rear, etc. respectively, and indicate weight gain, complete and outline alterations".

RGVA. F.31811 L.3 C.1633 pp376.

Major Panov's forecasts on the readiness of the second A-32 tank prototype were destined not to materialise. In mid August 1939 the Director of Plant №183 Ya. E. Maksarev received from the People's Commissar of Medium Machine Building (NKSM), I. A. Likhachev, guidance on preparations to send to the NIABT polygon at Kubinka near Moscow prototypes of the A-20, A-32, BT-7 and BT-5M tanks (the latter being a BT-5 fitted with a V-2 diesel engine) to participate in the review of new and modernised tank types. Prototype preparations fully occupied almost all of the specialists in Department "500" and in consequence work on the second prototype A-32 tank was temporarily suspended.

Simultaneously with preparations at Plant number №183, the teams of several other plants of the Commissariats of Medium and Heavy Machine Building (NKSM and NKTM) also prepared existing and modernised samples of armoured vehicles for display on the NIABT polygon at Kubinka. The acting chief of the polygon, military engineer 1st rank P. S. Glukhov on 8th September 1939 sent to the assistant chief of ABTU, military engineer 1st rank B. M. Korobkov with transmittal Letter №0922s prepared by E. A. Kulchitsky a scheme and an explanatory note regarding the show of military machines. The next day, 9th September 1939, Glukhov with transmittal Letter

№0923s sent Korobkov in ABTU a list of the personnel participating in the prototype demonstration. From Plant №183 were specified: the plant chief designer - Mikhail I. Koshkin; the Deputy head of the KB-520 design bureau - N. Kucherenko; the tank driver-mechanics (A-20 - I. V. Kuznetsov, A-32 - V. V. Dumanov, BT-7M - N.F. Nosik and BT-5M - I.G. Bitensky); the assistant driver-mechanics (A-20 - S. A. Dushin, A-32 - A. Pashin, BT-7M - M. A. Olkhovatov, BT-5M - Parfenov), and a group within the group of L. P. Evtushenko, namely engineers, P. S. Gupalov and V. G. Matyukhin, engineer-motorman I. I. Skorikov, master electrician M. E. Kalugin, master N.K. Maksimikhin, and mechanical fitters V. Ya. Danilchenko, Ya. N. Yurovski, F. M. Masenko and P. A. Tertishno.

The list of participants was edited on 11th September 1939 with transmittal Letter №209792s signed by D. G. Pavlov and P. N. Kulikov addressed to the chief of the NKO administration, Komkor M. G. Snegov. In the part relating to representatives of Plant №183, to the revised list had been added the Plant Manager, Maksarev and the assistant chief of ABTU, Korobkov, with a redesigned demonstration programme for the NIABT polygon, signed by the acting head of the polygon P. S. Glukhov, and military Commissioner of the polygon A. S. Davydenko, on 14th September 1939. By 20th September, everything was ready for the reception of distinguished guests.

On Friday 22nd September 1939 the planned demonstration of new and modernised tanks and armoured vehicles was held for the military-political leadership of the country at the NIABT polygon at Kubinka. The demonstration was attended by the People's Commissar of Defence K. E. Voroshilov, Deputy Chairmen of the SNK of the USSR, N.A. Voznesensky and I.A. Mikoyan, Member of the Economic Council of People's Commissars of the USSR A. A. Zhdanov, and the People's Commis-

sars of Medium and Heavy Machine Building, I. A. Likhachev and V. A. Malyshev. The show was also attended by industry representatives, including directors and chief designers of the plants that had developed and manufactured the new prototypes. The show was managed by the acting chief of the polygon, military engineer 1st rank P. S. Glukhov, the polygon commander, battalion Commissar A. S. Davydenko and the head of the polygon test department, Major E. A. Kulchitsky.

Placed in a row together with upgraded T-26 light tanks, the BT-5M and the BT-7M, were presented prototypes of the T-100, SMK and KV heavy tanks, the A-20 and A-32 medium tanks, the T-40 amphibious tank and the BA-11 armoured car, the combined result of two years of collaborative work by the People's Commissariat of Defence (NKO) and defence industry organisations to create new combat vehicles. The show was conducted per schedule, without incident or breakdown of any prototype. The memoirs of the representative of Military Department of SNK of the USSR A. A. Vetrov - a veteran "tankist" who had participated in the civil war in Spain, and who was present at this show, recalled in part that:

"Marshal of The Soviet Union K. E. Voroshilov arrived. It was clear that the People's Commissar of Defence was not in the mood. Absent-mindedly after hearing the report of Komkor D. G. Pavlov, he, dryly greeted the approaching military leaders and representatives of the industry, and without stopping went directly with A.A. Zhdanov, A.I. Mikoyan and N. A. Voznesensky to the tank observation tower. The Marshal and his entourage headed to the tower, and we, to a small grassy hill nearby. Here, looking around, I saw at the edge of the forest sprinkled with sand an area on which were lined up six brown painted tanks. On the right flank standing out by its impressive size was the twin gunned SMK land dread-

Front view of the A-32 tank prototype loaded to 24 metric tonnes. The weights added to the glacis, hull upper sides and turret roof are evident in this view.

Rear view of the same A-32 tank prototype with weights added to test capability with an increased combat weight of 24 metric tonnes.

nought. Standing next to it was a single-turret KV heavy tank, the model of which we saw at the end of last year at the plant of Zh. Ya. Kotin (the Leningrad Kirov Plant), which (alongside the SMK) looked almost like a small child. The A-20 wheel-tracked light tank and very similar tracked T-32 (A-32) differed (from the other tanks) with an unusually compact and beautiful shape. They stood side by side with the modernised T-26 and BT-7M still the main tank park (fleet) of Red Army. <...> We heard the voice of K. E. Voroshilov: "Why don't you start?" On the command tower there began a fuss, with lots of coloured signal flags. The tank crews, standing slightly in front of the machines, quickly took their places. And now, the dull roar of the engines rose and bluish-brown cloud of exhaust smoke signalled the readiness of the tanks. <...> But a not typically recognized tank subdued the lively talk caused by the test successes of the KV, as on an even more complex path, designed for light tanks, rushed the tracked T-32 tank. <...> Here, at a good pace and with some even grace the tank crossed the moat, escarpment, contra-escarpment and the track bridge. I, as a former driving instructor, was well aware of what skills the driver must possess, but that being said, to without a hitch overcome such challenging obstacles, a powerful and agile machine is required to withstand such high loads. At this time M. I. Koshkin, was seemingly smiling, talking nearby with N.V. Barykov, and only his feverishly gleaming eyes and pale lips betrayed his state of mind. And now, the T-32 has left behind the last obstacle. It would seem that the tests had been successfully completed. But what is this? The tank suddenly turned again to the right and approached a very steep slope up which it crawled to the summit. "Stop him!" shouted one of the observers. "There's a rise of more than 30°, it may tip over!" Alarmed, we looked towards the tower. There, surprisingly, all is quiet. Corps commander D. G. Pavlov, smiling, saying something to the People's Commissar. Accordingly he shakes his head. It is understood that the rise of the experimental tank to the "mountain" is not by an amateur driver but is stipulated in the testing plan. Meanwhile, the T-32 has already climbed to the maximum height. "Here is the machine!" - already admiration escaped from my neighbour. "Yes, and, indeed a superb tank! What we need!" - confirmed the other. There was friendly applause. The tank abruptly turned and moved now down the hill. Along the way, the driver-mechanic drove the tank into a fairly thick pine tree and knocked it over, thus showing the ability of the tank to overcome wooded areas. Then the T-32 slid into the river, with surging waves almost entering the driver's hatch. But the tank, as if nothing had happened, is already approaching the opposite shore. On the second crossing of the river, the tank easily climbs the sandy shore and only after that under the general roar of approval races to its place at the finish site. The mood of Marshal K. E. Voroshilov, was clearly corrected. He already laughs, says something lively to A.A. Zhdanov, A.I. Mikoyan and N. A. Voznesensky around him.

Then, calling the tank designers M. I. Koshkin, N. L. Dukhov and Zh. Ya. Kotin to the tower, he heartily thanks them."

A.A. Vetrov. Military Memoirs. Voenizdat, Moscow, 1982. pp31-34

The following day after the successful demonstration of the machines, A. A. Goreglyad on 23rd September 1939 held a meeting in the Moscow office of the Deputy People's Commissar of Medium Machine Building (NKSM) at which the directors of factories and chief designers discussed the current state of affairs and directions for future work taking into account comments and suggestions made by the military during the show. As can be seen from the surviving transcript of this meeting, Mikhail I. Koshkin in his speech stressed that the completion of the A-20 and its serial production should be carried out at Plant №183, which had extensive experience in the production of wheel-tracked tanks. According to Koshkin, Plant №183 was to master serial production of A-20 tanks in the second half of 1940. The meeting noted that the A-32 tank had significant advantages over T-26 and T-28 tanks, while being relatively simple to manufacture and produce "in any plant". In his final speech, summing up the results of the meeting, Goreglyad noted that:

"the teams at the tank plants have done a lot of work, and we had the opportunity to fulfil the decision of the party and the government - samples of machines were presented, which were approved. Designers need to make every effort to finalise them as soon as possible and put the tank into service. It is also necessary to think that the tanks are not only better, but also cheaper and possibly reduce the use of scarce materials - this is a huge job for the designers. As for the production workers, they have to prepare for production in order to inform the government once again that we are already producing these machines, that these machines have been used by the army and that these machines are beginning to displace the old tank park. These tasks must be completed as soon as possible. The work of the teams and workers involved in the development of these samples should be noted. The Directors of plants, chief engineers are to consult with party organisations and to submit lists of employees to be awarded, starting from drivers, workers and designers. The teams should show even more energy and finalise the machines as soon as possible and put them into production."

RGAEh F.8115 L.8. C.14 pp216

From 25th September 1939, the chief of ABTU, Pavlov and the Military Commissar of ABTU, Kulikov endorsed the prepared draft decision of the Defence Committee about the new models of tanks and armoured vehicles based on testing. The same day, two copies of the draft resolution were sent to the office of NKOs for consideration by the People's Commissar of Defence, Voroshilov. According to the prepared draft resolution the Red Army proposed to take into service the KV heavy tank, developed at the Kirov plant in Leningrad, and remove the T-28 from serial production. The fate of the T-100 and SMK heavy breakthrough tanks was to be finally determined after carrying out comparative tests. With regard to the A-20 and A-32 medium tanks, sections IV and V of the draft resulotion proposed the following:

"IV.

Tank A-32 (tracked, with a diesel engine), made by Plant №183 NKSM to adopt in the Red Army. To increase the armour thickness up to 45mm, providing full visibility of the tank and ensuring uniformity of the greatest number of components and assemblies with the A-20 tank.

1. Samples of A-32 tanks manufactured by Plant №183 to transfer to STZ with all materials for testing, drawings and separate developments.

2. STZ to by 1.6.40 build a pilot batch of A-32 tanks in the amount of 10pcs. with an armour thickness of 45mm and fully prepare the production technology for the series production of tanks A-32 by 1.6.1940. Annual program for STZ for the production of tanks A-32 - establish (production of) 2,500 units a year, starting by 1.6.1940, leaving STZ a year in the production of T-26 tanks.

3. Armament of the A-32 tank in serial production should consist of the 76mm F-32 gun with co-axial 7.62mm machine gun, a separate 7.62mm machine gun for the radio operator and one anti-aircraft machine gun.

4. Mariupol "Ilyich" plant NKSP to manufacture parts for STZ armoured hull and turret sets for the A-32 tank in the amount of 10 sets, with armour thickness of 45mm, providing them on schedule to STZ by 1.5.1940. To oblige the STZ in cooperation with selected designers of Plant №183 to provide the Mariupol plant complete sets of drawings for all A-32 hull and turret parts by 15.11.39.

5. Factory "Red October" NKChM to prepare for the production of

45mm armour by 1.6.1940. Serial production of A-32 armoured hull and turret parts to start by 1.6.1940, providing an annual programme at STZ of 2,500 sets.

6. Krasnoarmeyskaya Shipyard NKSP [Plant №264] to conduct preparation for production of A-32 armoured hull and turret sets to launch serial production by 1.6.1940, with the annual program of 2,500 hull and turret sets. At the same time, capability for T-26 hull and turret set production in wartime remains at the shipyard.

V.

Tank A-20 (wheel-tracked with diesel engine and 3 pairs of driven wheels), made by Plant №183 NKSM, to adopt in the Red Army, providing full visibility from the the tank.

1. Plant №183 to produce an installation (pilot) batch of tanks A-20 in quantity 10 pcs by 1.1.1940. To prepare for the series production of A-20 tanks by 1.3.1940 with an annual program of 2,500 pcs. By 1.3.1940 to have in production a BT tank fitted with a diesel engine.

2. The Mariupol "Ilyich" plant NKSP to manufacture for Plant №183 NKSM hull and turrets sets for the A-20 tank in a quantity of 10 sets on schedule: 4 pcs. by 25.10.39, 6 pcs. by 1.12.39, preparing to secure production by 1.2.1940 of armoured parts for the A-20 hull for Plant №183 NKSM- 2,500 sets per year".

RGVA. F.4 L.14. C.2222. pp38-40

It was proposed that work on the STZ-25 and STZ-35 light tanks developed at STZ to replace the T-26 tank be discontinued, as they did not meet modern requirements. T-26 production was to be continued at Plant №174 in Leningrad, while the T-26 was to be equipped with an upgraded chassis design by the Experimental* Plant №185. In addition, the Red Army was to adopt into service the T-40 amphibious tank with torsion bar suspension developed at Plant №37 to replace the T-37 and T-38 tanks.

Two days later, on 27th September 1939, the draft resolution on new models of tanks and armoured vehicles, without

T-100 heavy tank prototype.

SMK heavy tank prototype .

The original Russian term "Opitny Zavod" can be translated as trial, experimental, pilot, or prototype plant.

any changes, was together with the report of Voroshilov from the NKO command in Letter №81088ss sent to the Chairman of the Defence Committee of the USSR SNK, V. M. Molotov. Thus, after the demonstration of new models of armoured weapons, the highest military leadership of the country had concluded with a decision on the need to adopt two new medium tanks for the Red Army - the wheel-tracked A-20 and the tracked and more heavily armoured tracked A-32. Series production of A-20 tanks was proposed to be undertaken at Plant №183, with A-32 series production at the Stalingrad Tractor Plant (STZ).

For the urgent conduct of military tests of the A-32 tank with enhanced (to 45mm) armour protection, ABTU leadership decided to make prototypes of this combat vehicle in the shortest possible time. For this purpose, on 28th September 1939 Contract №8/678 was signed between ABTU and Plant №183 for the manufacture of two such up-armoured machines, to receive the index A-34. The new prototypes were given the tank index "A-34" rather than the consecutive and more logical index "A-33" because the index "A-33" was already assigned to another KB-520 engineering development - a tracked assembly for the ZiS-5 truck resulting in the ZiS-33 half-track conversion, on which Plant №183 had started work earlier than on the A-34 tank. Under the terms of the agreement, Plant №183 was to produce and prepare two A-34 tanks for army trials no later than 15th January 1940.

At the end of September 1939 the Director of Plant №183 Maksarev addressed the chief of ABTU, Pavlov with a proposal to organise in the assigned plants serial production of two tank types - the A-20 and A-34. According to Maksarev, Plant №183, if released from other production such as the "Voroshilovets" artillery tractor, could produce A-20 and A-34 tanks in the required quantity. The chief of ABTU agreed with the proposal of the Director of the Plant №183 and on 30th September 1939, the Military Commissar of ABTU, Kulikov prepared a draft letter addressed to the People's Commissar of Defence of the USSR, Marshal of the Soviet Union, K.E. Voroshilov as follows:

"Report to the Director of Plant №183 comrade Maksarev said that in terms of production capacity, he has the opportunity, from the 1st quarter of 1940, to produce the T-32 (A-32) tank in the layout in which it was presented to you, and from the 2nd half of 1940 the same machine with 45mm armour. The plant director asks you to produce this T-32 (A-32) machine into production in his plant as it is easy to manufacture and can be produced with 45mm armour. Production of the machine T-20 (A-20) with its all driven wheels at Plant №183 will delay production because of its complexity.

Considering that the installation of new production in STZ or

another plant of a new class of machine will require 6-8 months, the Plant Director offers to arrange for the production of both machines at their plant in quantities T-32 - 2,500pcs. and T-20 - 2,500pcs. (in wartime), but with the removal of non-tank production, including the Voroshilovets tractor, with the transfer of the latter to production at ChTZ in the amount of 800pcs. a year, starting with 1940. Reporting on the substance of the above, I believe it is possible to agree with the proposal of the Director of Plant №183 for 1940 production, while developing production of the T-32 at STZ. Given that with the development and production of the T-32 with 45mm armour, the army receives a good quality, fast, economical tank weighing no more than 23-24 tonnes that will be impervious to 37mm calibre anti-tank gun rounds, I think it is possible to stop production of the T-26 class of machines in 1941, i.e. since the mass serial production of the T-32 will be at the STZ plant, stopping the further development of the production of the T-26, replacing completely the existing tank types with new machines: T-20 replacing the BT, T-32 replaces the T-26 and T-28, and heavy machines of the "KV" type with a diesel engine, and if they are adopted in the Red Army, the "SMK" and "100"(T-100) (the Red Army) will be armed as a new class of machines".

RGVA. F.31811. L.2. C.928 pp124-125

After reviewing the text of the draft letter, Pavlov made the following hand-written note on the document:

"Comrade Kulikov. It is only necessary to agree with the document. If the People's Commissar disagrees with the draft resolution, then report that the draft is written in accordance with the decision at the Review. But for the system of production of weapons for the next 10 years it is urgent to implement this".

RGVA. F.31811. L2. C.928. pp124-125

However, the *"urgent to implement"* proposed *"system of production of weapons"* failed. Looking ahead, we will detail that coordination at the level of the Government of questions of acceptance by the Red Army of new types of tanks and armoured cars, including the A-20 and A-34 tanks, and about the choice of plants for their serial production began in October and ended on 19th December 1939 with the adoption of KO Resolution №443ss. We will review in detail about how there was an approval of the draft resolution between interested ministries and what options were considered in the Defence Committee (KO pri SNK SSSR).

With a relatively small number of enterprises capable of carrying out large-scale tank production, the country's leadership reviewed the best options to make the most effective use of the existing plant production capacities. It should be noted that only three tank plants could undertake the mass production of A-20 and A-34 tanks, Plant №183 - the "Kom-

The KV M-1939 (U-0) heavy tank prototype.

intern" plant in Kharkov, Leningrad Plant №174 in the name of Voroshilov and the Stalingrad Tractor Plant in the name of F. E. Dzerzhinsky (STZ). All these enterprises were under the authority of the People's Commissariat of Medium Machine Building (NKSM). The Leningrad Kirov plant, which belonged to the people's Commissariat of Heavy Machine Building (NKTM) was not considered for the production of new medium tanks, since its capacities were to be used for the production of new KV heavy tanks.

It was not a simple task to ensure the production of new medium and heavy tanks. According to calculations, for the manufacture of armour for one hull and turret set for the KV heavy tank, metallurgical plants needed to smelt 100 tonnes of

steel; for the A-34 tank - 37.5 tonnes and for the A-20 tank - 25 tonnes. The following metallurgical plants were considered as manufacturers of steel for the A-20 and A-34 tank hull and turret sets; the Mariupol plant in the name of Lenin, the Izhorsky plant and the Kulebakskiy plant in Kirov, which were under the authority of the People's Commissariat of the Shipbuilding Industry (NKSP), and also the Taganrog plant in the name of Andreev, the "Krasniy Oktyabr" (Red October) plant in Stalingrad, and the Enakievsky and Kramatorsky metallurgical plants - both subordinate to the People's Commissariat of the Iron and Steel industry (NChM). Forging and the rolling of ingots into steel plate was planned to be undertaken at these same plants. Production of armoured hull and turrets sets for the A-20 and A-34, and their mechanical and thermal treatment was to be provided by the Mariupol plant in the name of Lenin, the Izhorsky plant, and in part by the Krasnoarmeiskaya shipyard (Plant №264). The following production capacities of the main armoured and metallurgical enterprises of the USSR were specified in the reference prepared by Military Engineer 2nd rank I. A. Burtsev at ABTU regarding the question of tank armour production as of the 4th quarter of 1939:

As noted, in October 1939, the Defence Committee (KO) began approval of the agreement drawn up in ABTU on the draft resolution on new models of tanks and armoured vehicles with all the interested people's commissariats - NKO, NKTM, NKSM, NKSP, NKNP and NKChM. The leadership of the People's Commissariat of Medium Machine Building (NKSM),

№	Name of Plant	Open-hearth furnaces		Rolling mill		Forging press		Number of thermal furnaces	Number of presses and rollers	Mechanical workshops	Assembly of hull & turret sets
		Quantity	Production Capacity per year of cast metal (000 tonnes)	Can roll thickness (mm)	Production capacity per year in thousand tons	Quantity					
1	Izhorsk Plant	8	220 – 240	From 10 and higher	50-60	1	20-30	17	3	2 workshops	Fully provided
2	Mariupol Plant	16	680 – 750	10-300	60 – 70	1	35-40	16	2	1 workshops	Fully provided
3	Taganrog Plant	7	360 – 400	10-45	45 – 50		No	3 for annealing	No	NO	No
4	Kulebaksky Plant	5	130 – 150	6-35	50-60		No	3 for annealing	No	No	No
5	Krasny Oktyabr Plant	13	700 – 750	3-35	70 – 100 with the launch of a new mill*		No	8 for annealing 3 for hardening	3	No	No
6	Vyksa Plant	7	120 – 147	4-13			No	2 for annealing 1 for hardening	No	1 repair workshop	No
7	Ordzhonikidze Plant (Yenakievsky)	5	250 – 300	6-35	94		No	No	No	No	No
8	Zaporiozhstal	8	480 – 520	To 200	225 – 250		No	No		No	No
9	Red Army Shipyard		No		No		No	5	5 straightening machines & 2 presses	1 repair workshop	Fully provided

* - Before the start of the new mill, the rolling mill can produce 30 - 40 tons of armour plate.
Deputy. HEAD OF THE 8th DEPARTMENT OF THE ABTU of the Red Army (signed) Burtsev (Rogachev).

RGVA F.31811. L.2. C.1010. pp12

before making its proposals in the draft resolution, decided to ascertain the views of the factory teams about the production of these or of other tanks in their enterprises. With this goal, on 10th October 1939 the chief of the Glavspetsmash NKSM, G. S. Surenyan sent several variants of the special production program for 1940 to the plant directors subordinate to him, including the Director of Plant №183, with transmittal Letter №4214s. In response to this document, the Director of Plant №183, Maksarev, chief engineer of the plant S. N. Makhonin and plant chief designer Mikhail I. Koshkin on 30th October 1939 sent to the chief of Glavspetsmash - Surenyan, the Deputy People's Commissar of NKSM - A. A. Goreglyad and the chief of ABTU - D. G. Pavlov, Letter №S06415, which confirmed the readiness of Plant №183 to put the A-34 tank into mass production in 1940:

"On the Question: Programs 1940, specialisation and production preparation.
In regard to Letter №4214s from 10/10, this is to inform you that our factory in 1940 finds acceptable the 2nd option as the most appropriate for the following reasons:
a) Machines "A-34" in their tactical and technical data should be machines of large-scale production and only produced by a large powerful plant - our equipment can certainly produce a tank of this tonnage. Other tank factories should be used for the manufacture of the lighter "A-20" tank, where you should make the installation batch of "A-20" machines.
b) In addition, the "A-20" machine in our view, as a less heavy machine, can be given to secondary plants.
c) Our plant cannot produce the "A-34" and "A-20" simultaneously in the large quantities demanded with existing facilities.
d) Currently we are working on a tractor to replace the "Voroshilov" on the basis of the same "A-34" tank. In these two machines, "A-34" and the tractor on the basis of "A-34" most mechanisms and parts are common. This makes it possible to increase productivity and mass production in departments 100, 200, 500, 700. The latter further emphasises the expediency of manufacturing the machine "A-34" in our plant. The plant has already started to prepare the production of the "A-34" machine guided by the planned program, which was sent to you. From the above it can be seen that our plant can and does take in 1940 the second option:
(I) Under this variant, the 1940 programme would be expressed in
- 1,000 machines "A-7D" [BT-7M]
- 150 machines "A-34".
(see Order №SO6134 to factory from 16/10., sent to you, as well as Annex №1 approximate release plan for special machines in 1940).
II) Comparing the program of 1940 on commodity output by Spetsmash. in the above 1939 costs - it is clear that production costs in 1940 will be 23% above 1939 costs (see Annex №2).

III) Considering the release in 1940 of 150 "A-34" machines and prototype tractors on the basis of "A-34", we have constructed the schedule of preparation and development of these machines (see Schedule №1-2). The specified schedules of preparation for serial production we ask you to approve.
IV) To allow pre-production of Spetsmash. (special machines) in 1940, for calculation, we adopted an increased cost coefficient for the "A-34" machine of 1.75x that of the "A-7" (BT-7.

RGVA. F.31811. L. 2 C.1101. pp139-140

Later in the letter was a request that the management of Plant №183 should prepare for series production of the A-34 and an artillery tractor on its basis, which later received the index "A-42". It was clear the plant did not have the capacity to produce both the A-20 and A-34 while also producing steam locomotives and artillery tractors. It should be noted that steam locomotive and tracked tractor production was the major output of KhPZ as the name would suggest. In 1939, for instance, the plant assembled 288 "SO" steam locomotives, 117 tenders, 467 "Komintern" medium artillery tractors, and 67 "Voroshilovets" heavy artillery tractors.

However the view of the NKSM Kommissar, I.A. Likhachev was not in alignment with that of the management of Plant №183. At the time it was planned to put both the A-20 and A-34 into series production as the T-20 and T-34, and as Plant №183 had significant experience of building the BT series of wheel-track tanks, then logically preparation for and series production of the more complex A-20 should be undertaken at Plant №183, with series production of the tracked-only A-34 undertaken at Plant №174 in Leningrad. In connection with this, on 2nd November 1939 NKSM prepared its own draft variant with a resolution about tank and armoured car types in the fourth section of which it was stated:

"2. Organise production of the A-34 tank at Plant №174 NKSM in cooperation with the Kirov Plant NKTM, Plant №232

STZ-25 wheel-track tank prototype.

155

NKV, Plant №213 NKAP, Plant №203 NKAP and other with the following production schedule:

A. Two (standard) prototypes to be completed at Plant №183 by 15.1.40 in collaboration with Plant №174.

B. Installation batch (10 tanks) to be built by 25.9.1940 at Plant №174.

C. Preparations for series production to be complete by 31.12.1940 with series production of the A-34 tank beginning from 15.11.1941. Production output at Plant №174 to be 2,000pcs. per annum.

3. People's Commissar of Ship Building (NKSP) comrade Tevosyan to organise at the Izhorsky plant production of the hull, turret and armoured parts for the A-34 tank.

4. Oblige NKSP to provide armour sets for the A-34 in accordance with the following schedule:

A. For the prototypes by 20.11.1939 deliver to Plant №183 three sets (of armour) from the Mariupol plant.

B. For the Installation Batch by 15.8.1940 deliver 10 hull and turret sets to Plant №174 from the Izhorsky plant.

C. For series production, 200 hull and turret sets for the A-34 tank to be delivered from the Izhorsky plant by 1.8.1940 in accordance with the production schedule.

RGVA F.31811 L.2 C.928. pp116-117

As regards plans for A-20 production, the resolution contemplated:

"1. Organise the production base for preparation of the A-20 tank and associated hull and turret sets at Plant №183 NKSM with the following schedule:

A. 10 examples of standard series tank by 1.5.1940.

B. Prepare (for) series production of the A-20 tank by 1.8 with production of 300 series tanks in 1940. Production output of A-20 tanks at Plant №183 in the quantity of 1,500pcs. in 1941 and 2,500pcs. in 1942.

The "Voroshilovets" heavy artillery tractor.

2. NKSP comrade Tevosyan to organise armour (hull, turret, armoured parts) at the Mariupol plant for the A-20 machine.

3. Oblige NKSP to produce armour (sets) for the A-20 for Plant №183 HKSM in the following quantities:

By 1.1.1940 - 3 sets

By 1.3.1940 - 7 sets

NKSP Commissar, comrade Tevosyan, to prepare the production of armour for the A-20 from 1.8.1940 with delivery of 350 sets in 1940, 1,600 hull and turret sets in 1941 and 2,750 hull and turret sets.

RGVA. F.31811. L.2. C.928. pp117-118

The Stalingrad Tractor Plant, according to this version of the draft resolution, was during 1940 to prepare for production of a T-26 light tank with a modified chassis, with an expected production of 5,000 tanks in 1941 increasing to 8,000 in 1942. Production of the T-26 light tank replacement and spare parts from Plant №174 was planned to start on 1st January 1941.

To review the T-34 production drawings, and to clarify issues related to the potential organization of its serial production at Plant №174 in Leningrad, the deputy chief designer of Plant №174, K. P. Gavrut and the head of the Assembly shop, Fratkin were sent to Plant №183 in Kharkov. During their visit, they were to prepare proposals on the timing and procedure for the receipt and transmission of design documentation for the A-34 tank, and in addition to provide preliminary considerations on the equipment and organisation required for production of the A-34 tank at Plant №174. About the trip to Kharkov, Gavrut reported to the chief of GlavSpetsmash NKSM, G. S. Surenyan, and also the plant management, on 13th November 1939 in Letter №3456. According to Gavrut, even under the most favourable conditions Plant №174 in Leningrad could begin serial production of A-34 tanks not earlier than the second half of 1941. In this proposed scheme of cooperation, the production of hull and turret sets, as well as the main components and assemblies of the T-34 tank was planned for other plants, including: Izhorsky (hull and turret sets), Plant №75 (V-2 diesel engine), Plant №234 (transmissions, and vision devices) and other factories in Leningrad. Plant №174 was considered, first of all, as an assembly plant. On the same day - 13th November 1939 -that deputy chief designer Gavrut reported on his visit to Kharkov, another letter was sent from Plant №174 concerning the organisation of A-34 tank production in Leningrad. The chief designer of Plant №174, military engineer 2nd rank S. A. Ginzburg in Letter №3453 sent to I. V. Stalin, K. E. Voroshilov and I. A. Likhachev addressed the following:

"Before Plant №174 in the name of Voroshilov, People's Commissar, comrade Likhachev has set the task of developing a new type of tank

"34". My experience as a designer and tanker, and analysis of the prospects of development of armoured weapons and real possibilities of our tank industry leads me to conclusions somewhat different from the task assigned by the People's Commissar comrade Likhachev. Knowing that this issue is in the near future to be resolved by the government of the USSR, I considered it my duty to write you this report on the necessary development of tank weapons to take part in the discussion of this particularly important issue for the defence of our homeland. I have stated my point of view in the attached article."

RGVA. F.4. L.14. C.2222. pp60-61

In an attachment to the letter was an article entitled *"Modern tasks in the domestic tank building industry"* by S. A. Ginzburg that set forth his views on the further development of armoured vehicles for the Red Army. According to Ginzburg, in connection with the trend of qualitative and quantitative strengthening of anti-tank defence in the armies of the most probable enemies, the Red Army required the adoption of the following new types of tanks:

"We need the additional presence on a medium tank of heavy armour, protecting at least against 37mm projectiles. It will be a tank for supporting small tanks [small tanks in the article referred to the T-26] in direct support of the infantry. This tank will have to suppress anti-tank gun defence to its full depth and thus free the battlefield for small tanks, in turn clearing the battlefield from firing points that impede the advance of infantry. This new medium tank should be a powerful tank, at least with double the current engine power output (20-25hp/tonne) and be armed with a calibre of 75mm (76mm). Taking into consideration possible future gun developments, with divisional anti-tank defence having a calibre of up to 60mm it is necessary in special cases to break through heavily fortified areas in tanks with even more powerful tanks - they must have a heavy tank with the armour, at least against the action of 60mm armour-piercing shells and armed with one 75mm or more 45-47mm guns.

Finally, given the future possibility of the strengthening of the infantry battalions re-equipped with company machine guns of 12.5mm it is necessary to prepare a new type of small tank, protected by armour 20-25mm against the action of the new enemy large-calibre automatic weapons, because to suppress the latter with a medium tank certainly will not succeed. The dynamic qualities for this tank may remain the same as those of its predecessor.

Thus, in conclusion, now is the time to adjust the quality of the tank weapons in the first place by creating a powerful new medium tank, in the second phase by creating a new heavy tank, and in the third - a new small tank.

Technically, these tasks are solvable and will give the necessary combat and economic effect, provided the creation of these new machines is as purely tracked tanks, without complicating the addi-

tional requirements for wheeled travel. (Example: a requirement to withdraw tanks from the battlefield at the loss of a track - can save a few tanks, but will greatly overload the entire tank park and make all the machines considerably heavier and less economical). This will make it possible to use the weight of the machine more efficiently and will make the completion of the task more real."

RGVA. F.4. L.14. C.2222. pp65-66

In S. A. Ginzburg's opinion, the tracked A-34 perfectly suited the role of the new "heavily armoured" medium tank, and it was proposed to abandon adoption of the high-speed wheel-tracked A-20 as excess to requirements. In the final part of the letter, Ginzburg proposed to use plant capacity for the production of tanks as follows:

"- Production of T-26 light tanks to be left at Plant №174 and STZ (as back-up plant);
- To organise production of the A-34 medium tank at Plant №183;
- To organise production of the heavy breakthrough tank at the Kirov plant (replacing the T-28 tank) and to use the Chelyabinsk tractor plant (ChTZ) as back-up plant".

Acceptance of the A-20 wheel-track design into Red Army service and the establishment of series production was, in accordance with the recommendation of Ginzburg, to be rejected on the basis of the following:

"Provided that the program for the main types of T-26 and T-34 tanks is carried out, the main tank Plants №174 and №183 will be fully loaded. This "20" type of machine is the most laborious and complex. To transfer it for development to other plants - almost guarantees it will not be produced. To release it for production either at Plant №174 or Plant №183 represents a threat of disruption of (prodcution of) either small or medium tanks. The right solution is to abandon this intermediate tank type. For dynamic qualities the tank can be replaced by the "34" type tank which costs about the same but with much superior armour and weapons. As a small tank with intermediate armour this (A-20) machine will not be economical due to being almost twice the cost of the T-26".

RGVA. F.4. L.14. C. 2222. pp68

S. A. Ginzburg, being the main designer of Plant №174, was undoubtedly personally interested in trying to keep the long obsolete T-26 tank in production rather than the "foreign" tank imposed by the People's Commissariat. Whether a significant role in the ultimate fate of the A-20 tank was played by Ginzburg's correspondence is not presently possible to document, but in mid-November 1939 at State level, the decision on the need to adopt only one type of medium tank, the A-34 tracked tank, for the

Red Army, and the organisation of serial production, was most critical. Contributing to the adoption of this decision was the fact that plant trials of a test-loaded A-32 tank in mid November 1939 had confirmed the ability to enhance the armour protection of the A-34 tank to 45mm, thereby confirming its advantages over the A-20 wheel-tracked tank type. Ultimately, after numerous discussions, on 20th November 1939 in NKSM was prepared the next version of the draft resolution of the Defence Committee on *"Adoption into the Red Army, of tanks, armoured vehicles and artillery tractors, and producing them in 1940"*. In this version of the draft resolution, specifically on medium tanks, was stated:

"Tank A-32 tracked, diesel engine V-2, produced by Plant №183 NKSM to adopt by the Red Army, with the following changes:
a) Increase the thickness of individual armour plates to 45mm;
b) Improve visibility from the tank;
Install the following weapons on the A-32 tank:
a) A 76.2mm F-32 gun paired with a 7.62mm machine gun;
b) Separate machine gun of 7.62mm calibre for the radio operator;
c) Separate machine gun of 7.62mm calibre;
d) Anti-aircraft machine gun of 7.62mm calibre.
To assign a name to the specified tank - "A-34". <...>
To oblige the Commissar of Medium Machine Building (comrade Likhachev):
A. Organise the production of A-34 tanks at the Kharkov Plant №183 named after the Komintern (Communist International):

a) Manufacture 2 prototypes by 15.1.40;
b) Make an installation batch in number of 10pcs by 15.9-4.;
c) Produce in 1940 not less than 200 A-34 tanks;
d) Increase the capacity of Plant №183 for the production of A-34 tanks by 1.1-1941, up to 1,600pcs."

RGVA. F.31811. L.2. C.928. pp90,92

It's notable that no word in the text of this document mentioned the A-20 tank. Thus, the decision process had reverted to the originally envisaged decision of the Defence Committee (KO) №198ss/s *"On the system of tank weapons"*, of from two proposed variants of a medium tank for the Red Army to take only one tank (now the A-34) as: *"most fully satisfying tank requirements."* A similar decision had been arrived at by the high command of the Red Army. At the meeting of the Main Military Council (GVS) of the Red Army held on 21st November 1939, devoted to the organisation, number and deployment of the Red Army, the following decision was made regarding the reorganization of tank troops, reflected in the resulting Protocol №6:

"To have within the Red Army, instead of the existing tank corps and separate tank brigades a similar structure of separate BT and T-26 tank brigades, consisting of four tank battalions armed with T-26 and BT tanks, with future rearmament with T-34 tanks. The T-28 and T-35 tank brigades, with further re-equipment of tanks KV, will have a three battalion composition".

RGVA. F.4. L.18. C.49. pp6-7

The proposed "A-42" (AT-42) armoured artillery tractor.

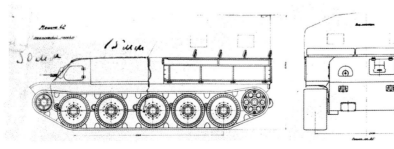

Blueprint of the "A-42" artillery tractor.

As can be seen from the of the Protocol text, equipping tank brigades with A-20 wheel-tracked tanks was not planned. On the same day, 21st November 1939, endorsed the People's Commissars of Medium Machine Building (NKSM) I. A. Likhachev and Heavy Machine Building (NKTM), V. A. Malyshev was a draft resolution of the Defence Committee *"On adopting into the Red Army tanks, armoured vehicles and artillery tractors, and producing them in 1940"* which was sent with transmittal Letter №3434 to ABTU for approval. This procedure did not require a lot of time, and on 24th November 1939 the approved draft Resolution was sent by D. G. Pavlov to the People's Commissar of Defence, Voroshilov with Letter №211981ss stating:

"Please endorse the attached draft Resolution. Adding:
1. In the resolution not included - new running gear for the T-26.
2. Consider that the resolution needs to include: "Since 1940 to start preparing STZ plant for T-34 tank production, preparing for production by 1.1.1941".
3. The order for tanks "KV" - 50 tanks for 1940 is too small. The minimum order ABTU RKKA deems necessary is to make 100 "KV" tanks. Tank "KV" although having not finished all tests (covered more than 700km), has given good performance in tests, and components and assemblies are identical to the SMK tank, which are tested on that machine. We consider it necessary to put the "KV" tank in production and in the course of production of the installation batch to eliminate insignificant defects which can be found out in the course of further tests".

RGVA. F.31811. L.2. C.928. pp88

Ultimately, on 26th November 1939, the draft Resolution *"On adopting into the Red Army tanks, armoured vehicles, artillery tractors and their production in 1940"* was amended within the NKO, according with serial production of the T-34 tank being in addition to Plant. №183 now also assigned to STZ. Moreover, the "A" development designation used for the A-34 medium tank was now replaced by the letter "T" with the tank henceforth becoming known as the "T-34". The following day, 27th November 1939, the the draft resolution, endorsed by Likhachev, Malyshev and Pavlov sent with transmittal Letter №81354ss was sent by the NKO to the TsK VKP(b) in the name of I.V. Stalin and to the SNK in the name of V. M. Molotov. In the covering letter, signed by the People's Commissar of Defence, K. E. Voroshilov, it was requested to approve the attached draft resolution of the Defence Committee *"On adopting the Red Army tanks, armoured vehicles, artillery tractors and their production in 1940".*

Looking ahead, it can be said that this version of the draft Resolution, with minor amendments made by Stalin not rela-

ting to the T-34 tank, was adopted at the meeting of the Defence Committee of the USSR on 19th December 1939 with the number 443ss.

In addition to the draft decree, in an attached Letter №81355ss, People's Commissars Voroshilov, Likhachev and Malyshev reported to I. V. Stalin and V. M. Molotov on the implementation by industry of Defence Committee Resolution №198ss/s. In the introductory part of the report it was noted:

"As a result of exceptionally hard work, tremendous effort, and most importantly the enormous enthusiasm of all the factory workers who conducted these works, and NKO engineers who controlled and governed them, the most important Resolution of the Government on further strengthening the striking power of the Red Army - Fulfilled. For today the following machines are created:...".

RGVA. F.4. L.14. C. 2222. pp82

There followed an impressive list of armoured vehicles created by government order, including the KV, SMK and T-100 heavy tanks, A-20 and A-32 medium tanks, the T-40 small amphibious tank, BA-11 armoured car, the GAZ-61 and a GAZ-AA variant with all wheel drive; the ST-2 and Voroshilovets artillery tractors, and the V-2 diesel engine. The development work by defence plant teams on creating the new prototypes was praised, and the report ending with a request for government awards for a cast of people. However, not all tasks on creation of new samples of armoured weapons specified in the Resolution KO №198ss/s, had been completed by industry. As of the end of September 1939, the following works remained outstanding:

"- Increase engine power for the T-26;
- Manufacture of chemical and chemical dispensing (equipped with flamethrower and smoke-generator) tanks on the basis of modernised T-26 and BT-7M tanks and the A-32;
- Installation of a 76.2 mm gun in the T-26 and BT-7M tanks;
- Production of T-26, BT-7M and T-28 tanks, suitable for "underwater travel" (PKh). "

In early October 1939, the Deputy People's Commissar of NKSM, A. A. Goreglyad sent to the Defence Committee a letter with the motion to dismiss these works. At the request of the Deputy Chairman of the Defence Committee N. A. Voznesensky, the People's Commissariat of Defence (NKO) requested ABTU experts to prepare a conclusion on the matter, in which NKO agreed with the termination of some of the developments specified by A. Goreglyad due to their overall inexpediency. The conclusion on the issue raised by Goreglyad, signed K. E. Voroshilov, was sent to the Defence Committee in the name of N.A. Voznesensky on 23rd October 1939 by Letter

№81232ss. Meanwhile, while the question of adopting by the Red Army of new tank types and selection of plants for their serial production was debated in the higher echelons of power, work continued at Plant №183 in Kharkov in October 1939 on field testing of the A-20 prototype now returned from Moscow. From the report: *"On the progress of experimental work on Plant №183 as at 10 October 1939"* compiled by Major Panov and the chief of the 8ᵗʰ Division of ABTU, military engineer 1ˢᵗ rank S. A. Afonin was stated:

"Machine A-20:
The machine arrived from Kubinka and we began testing. Works on modification of the prototype plant did not start. By the decision of comrade Koshkin, before 1.11 there will be no work on the machine as all forces are thrown at completing the A-32. The general opinion of the plant is not to start such work, because there is a rumour (project Glavspetsmash NKSM) that A-20 will be manufactured at KhTZ (the Kharkov Tractor Plant), and therefore rework will be done by KhTZ. A pilot production batch we have no reason to do, and without a contract we cannot even open an order account. Please take all measures to manufacture the A-20 at Plant №183, as otherwise the machine will be built in inexperienced hands, and the proceedings cannot be brought to the desired result, and there will be legitimate criticism from (Red Army) units. The desire of Plant №183 in the transfer of A-20 is, apparently, to get rid of the manufacture of a more difficult machine, and leave easier work for themselves. KhTZ is under the control of a different Commissariat, and in virtue of this division and GlavK came under the influence of the plant, and pushes the project from above, although Koshin completely agrees with me that the A-20 needs be to produced at Plant №183 as having extensive experience in high-speed machines and an established production base. Consider it necessary to achieve the most urgent decision on this matter in the Council of People's Commissars and to end this uncertainty. The Plant should be given the letter with appropriate signatures on the manufacture of a pilot production lot of A-20 tanks. Not starting revisions at Plant №183 may delay the roll-out of works for the production of hull and turret sets in the Mariupol plant. These questions cannot be delayed, especially the preparations for manufacture. Reinforced parts-running gear bearings, side frictions, brakes the plant has not manufactured, motivation - no money. The plant on prototypes overspent about one million Roubles, and I am afraid that it will not be possible to secure funds to complete the work".

RGVA. F.31811. L.3. C.1633. pp433-434

As indicated in the document, in the first half of October 1939 KB-520, according to Panov, had paid little attention to the A-20 prototype; design efforts being focused on the creation of the A-34 tank. Fearing that the A-20 tank would not be brought "to mind", the military Commissar of ABTU, Brigade

Semeon Aleksandrovich Ginzburg.   Vyacheslav Aleksandrovich Malyshev.

Kommissar P. N. Kulikov, on 21ˢᵗ October 1939, sent to the Director of Plant №183, Maksarev Letter №211174s stating:

"ABTU Red Army has information that work on the elimination of defects noted on the A-20 tank during testing is not conducted because it is assumed that production will be transferred to another plant. I think this phenomenon is clearly abnormal even with such a solution. Regardless of the decision on the production base for the A-20 tank, which will be decided by the Government, ABTU RKKA categorically insists that Plant №183 brings the tank to completion, makes all the corrections not only in drawings but also in metal, so that even if transferred to another plant, the machine must already be completely finished.

In addition, ABTU RKKA considers that on the A-7 tanks fitted with a diesel engine, starting with series production, must be installed servo-controls on steering clutches. The plant has all the possibilities in this respect. On the measures taken and the timing you are asked to immediately report".

RGVA. F.31811. L.3. C.1633. pp448

In November 1939, KB-520 had begun to address the deficiencies identified in the A-20 tank design during plant and field tests, as well as preparairing drawing and design documents for establishing series production. These works were undertaken by designers KB-520 in parallel with the development of drawings of the prototype A-34 (T-34) tank. As is clear from Letter №SO7204, signed by Maksarev and Koshkin and sent 9ᵗʰ Dec 1939 to ABTU, completion of the A-20 drawing revisions was planned for not earlier than second half of January 1940:

"To Your letter №211174s, it is reported that at the present time, the main work of the Design Bureau of the plant is the process of reviewing all drawings and all documentation of machine A-20 for the preparation for serial production. The revision of the latest

drawing revisions shall be based on all the comments of the Commission as set out in the test report of the prototypes. At the same time, drawings of parts and assemblies as a whole are checked from the point of view of serial production technology. The deadline for the above work we have made the second half of January 1940".

RGVA. F.31811. L.3. C.1632. pp140

However, to complete the preparation of drawing and design documentation for the A-20 tank for serial production was not required. According to Resolution №443ss adopted on 19th December 1939 at the meeting of the Defence Committee of the USSR, serial production of the A-20 wheel-tracked tank was not to be. Regarding the T-34 tank, KO Resolution №443ss indicated the following:

I"I. T-32 - tracked, diesel engine V-2, produced by Plant №183 NKSM, with the following changes:

a) Increase the thickness of the main armour plates to 45mm;

b) Improve visibility from the tank;

c) Establish on the T-32 tank the following weapons:

1) 76mm F-32 gun with co-axial 7.62mm machine gun; 2) separate 7.62mm machine gun for the radio operator; 3) separate 7.62mm machine gun; 4) 7.62mm anti-aircraft machine gun. To assign a name to the specified tank "T-34". <...>

2. To ensure the production of tanks, tractors and armoured vehicles in 1940 and the development of necessary capacities: <...>

2) To Oblige the People's Commissar of Medium Machine Building (NKSM) (comrade Likhachev):

At Plant №183.

a) To organise production of T-34 tanks at the Kharkov Plant №183. (the Komintern plant); b) to produce 2 prototype T-34 tanks by 15 January 1940 and a pilot batch of 10 pcs. by 15 Sep 1940; c) produce in 1940 not less than 200 T-34 tanks; d) to increase the capacity of Plant №183 for the production of T-34 tanks by January 1, 1941, up to 1,600 pcs; e) from now until full development of serial production of T-34 tanks to produce from 1 December, 1939 the BT tank with V-2 diesel engine installation; f) manufacture at Plant №183 in 1940, not less than 1,000 tanks BT with diesel engine V-2; g) in 1942 to stop production of the BT tank with V-2 diesel engine, replacing it fully with T-34 production;ww <...>

At the STZ plant.

a) To organise at STZ during 1940, the capacity for production of 2,000 tanks per year;

b) to produce in 1940 20 T-34 tanks;

c) prepare production on STZ for release in 1941 - 1,000 T-34 tanks. To stop production of T-26 tanks at STZ.

Narkomsredmash (NKSM) (comrade Likhachev I. A.). The exis-

ting stock, stamps, fixtures and tools are to be used at Plant №174 for the production of the T-26. To submit to the Defence Committee of the SNK SSSR a reasonable calculation of unused costs for the organisation of T-26 production at STZ to cover the costs at the expense of the Reserve Fund of the SNK USSR. <...>

3) to Oblige Narkomsudprom (NKSP) (comrade Tevosyan):

<...>

3. To ensure the armour production for new models of tanks, to oblige comrade Saburov (Gosplan SSSR), comrade Tevosyan (NKSP), comrade Merkulov (NKChM), comrade Likhachev (NKSM) are by 10 January 1940 to submit to the Defence Committee (KO) proposals for the organisation of production of armour with a thickness of 90mm and less for tanks: KV, T-34, T-40 and armoured cars. The proposals are to provide for the full production of tanks and armoured vehicles, both under the plan of peace and wartime, based on the use of existing armoured and metallurgical plants.

4. According to this resolution since 1 January 1941 to establish and leave on production the following types of tanks:

1) Heavy tank "KV"; 2) T-34 tank; 3) Tank "T-40""

GARF. F.8418. L. 28. C.92. pp121-129

It should be noted that the KO pri SNK SSSR Resolution №443ss *"On adopting the Red Army tanks, armoured vehicles, artillery tractors and about their production in 1940"* was of great importance not only in the fate of the T-34, but also in equipping the Red Army with new weapons and military equipment in general. In addition to the T-34, the Red Army by this resolution adopted the KV heavy, BT-7M fast and T-40 amphibious tanks; the "Voroshilovets", ST-2 and STZ-5 tracked artillery tractors; the BA-11 armoured car, GAZ-61 wheeled artillery tractor and the ZiS-32 truck, and also the V-2 diesel engine. The management of Plant №183 learned about the adopted Resolution №443ss and its content (the parts relating to the plant) only at the very end of the year from Order №188ss, signed on 28th December 1939 by the People's Commissar NKSM, I.A. Likhachev.

T-40 light amphibious tank.

Chapter 11

The A-20 Prototype in Service & Combat

After enactment of the KO pri Defence Comittee SNK SSSR Resolution №443ss of 19th December 1939, the main efforts of design team "500" at Plant №183 were aimed at urgently creating two A-34 prototypes for the future T-34 medium tank. The prototype A-20 and A-32 tanks now at Plant № 183 were after polygon testing now in Department "500" awaiting major repairs. However, despite the fact that in December 1939 priority was now given to the creation of the A-34 tank, KB-520 worked on revising the design documentation of the A-20 tank, taking into account the comments of the Commission set out in the polygon testing concludions, while mechanical shop "530" manufactured parts for rebuilding the tank with reinforced transmission and chassis elements. Summarising the experimental work undertaken in December 1939, the senior ABTU military representative at Plant №183, military engineer 2nd rank D. M. Kozyrev noted:

"I. Design office:

a) Rework of A-34 drawings.

b) Completion of A-20 working drawings, which will be completed in January 1940.<...>

II. Mechanical Shop and Assembly.

<...> 2.Manufacture of a number of parts for the A-20 which needs to be rebuilt with enhanced transmission (for the) wheeled drive in January 1940".

RGVA. F.31811. L.2. C.1181. pp1

Workshop "530" was for various reasons unable to repair the A-20 and A-32 prototypes in January, February or March 1940. At the beginning of 1940, the staff of the machine shop and Department "500" were preoccupied with the production of the two A-34 tank prototypes and their subsequent testing. Moreover, in order to accelerate assembly of the first A-34 prototype, the original A-32 tanks had been cannibalised for parts. At the end of January 1940, when installing the 76.2 mm L-11 gun in the A-34 tank, a temporary elevation mechanism was installed, removed from the L-10 gun of the A-32 prototype tank. Only after two A-34 tanks had been assembled, tested, undergone plant production and almost half their military trials were the staff of Department "500" in mid-March 1940 able to return to the issue of rebuilding the original A-20 and A-32 tanks.

Secondly, there was no contract between ABTU and Plant №183 for the overhaul of the A-20 and A-32 tanks, and accordingly, no allocated funds. Plant №183 could have repaired the

The A-20 tank at the NI Polygon at Kubinka (summer 1941).

tanks without a contract at its own expense, but the A-20 and A-32 were the property of ABTU and not the plant. To settle the legal side of this issue, on 18th March 1940, the Director of Plant №183 Ya. E. Maksarev sent to the chief of ABTU, Kom-Kor (Corps Commander) D. G. Pavlov Letter № SO1913:

"According to our intended plan of experimental work on 1940 the plant was to undertake capital rebuild of the prototypes of tanks A-20 - 1pc. and A-32 - 1pc. In order to avoid losses in time waiting for approval we began to repair the A-20 tank. At the moment the work comes to an end, and by 1.4. of this year machine A-20 m. b. [can be] fully renovated. To repair the "A-32" tank we assume to start work on 1. 4. of this year. We ask to confirm your consent and to give the corresponding instruction to sign the contract for repair of all 3 tanks. After completing the repair, we consider it expedient to leave the A-20 tank with us at the plant for further tests, and the A-32 tank - send by your orders to another factory or a military unit for training purposes. We look forward to your decision."

RGVA. F.31811. L.2. C.1141. pp219

Following from this letter, the assistant chief of ABTU, Co-lonel A. P. Panfilov and acting military Commissioner of ABTU military engineer 2nd rank N. N. Makarov agreed to the specified works and prepared Contract №142 for restoration of three pro-totypes of the A-20 and A-32 tanks. Two copies of this agreement signed by the Deputy Director of Plant №183, I. M., Shulman, were on 23rd April 1940 under transmittal Letter №2170 sent from Kharkov to Moscow for signature in ABTU. Contract №142 between Plant №183, and the client - ABTU stated in part that:

"1) The Supplier shall undertake restoration of the first three proto-types of A-20 and A-32 tanks manufactured in 1939, one A-20 tank and two A-32 tanks.

2) Restoration of the specified machines is made according to supp-lier drawings with tolerances as determined by the supplier.

3) Rebuild period:

a) For machine A-20 - April

b) For machine A-32 - July-August

4) Acceptance of tanks is made by the Representative of the client at the plant (subject to) the supplier undertaking a proving run of 50km. Note: the proving run certificate is drawn up as acceptan-ce of the machines serving as a document for payment.

5) Supplier for the A-32 tank warrants the run (mileage) of 1,000km, but for a period not above one year, from the date of dispatch of the machine from the plant. Note: non-ferrous metal parts are not included in the warranty.

6) The Client undertakes the requirement to replace parts that have not passed the warranty, to confirm acts indicating the cause of failure of the parts.

7) The Client is obliged to leave the A-20 machine at the factory of the Supplier for the production of further tests, and for the machine A-32 to give the address to which it is to be sent.

8) The Cost of repairing the three machines is roughly determined at 150.000 Roubles per machine.

9) The contract sum is determined at roughly 450.000 (four hund-red fifty thousand) Roubles.

10) Final payment is due by the accounting-recovery cost calcula-tion estimates of 5.3 % of the profits.

11) All other conditions are in accordance with the main contract dated 19/1-40 №4-074".

RGVA. F.31811. L.2. C. 1141. pp220

It should be noted that in April 1940 in Moscow the draft resolution of the Defence Committee (KO): *"About the deve-lopment of prototypes of armoured weapons"* was agreed between several Commissariats (ministries). The draft resolution in part reviewed the further fate of the A-20 tank. Ultimately, at a meeting of the KO on 4th May 1940, a Resolution No191ss was adopted. The fifth point of this document specified that the prototypes of tanks A-20, T-100, "SMK" and the LB-23 armoured car "with all drawings and specifications" were to be stored at plants №183, №185, and the Kirovsky and DRO (Vyksa) plants. This decision radically differed from the pro-posals made by the leadership of the ABTU in preparation of this resolution. Hence, the chief of ABTU, D. G. Pavlov, and Commissioner P. N. Kulikov on 20th May 1940, sent to the Pe-ople's Commissar of Defence (NKO) S. K. Timoshenko Letter №73084ss stating:

"The decision of the Committee of Defence SNK SSSR №191ss dated 4 May decided, that the prototypes of tanks "A-20", "100", "SMK" and the armoured "LB-23" with all drawings and technical condi-tions are to be kept by Plants №183, №185, Kirovsky and DRO. During its consideration of the draft resolution the KO was presented another version of paragraph 5 - that these tank and armoured car prototypes, with all drawings and specifications be conveyed to the NI Polygon ABTU RKKA (i.e. to the Kubinka polygon).

All prototypes are paid for by ABTU K.A., reflected in the amount 12,375,000 Roubles. These prototypes do not represent any value for the manufacturing plants since they are not accepted for production, as a result of which they can be dismantled for scrap be-cause they now need to be repaired. Storing them on the NI Polygon will enable the designers of tank factories, studying real samples of the history of tank production of the USSR, to improve and to move tank designs forward. I present a draft letter to the Chairman of the KO, Marshal of the Soviet Union comrade Voroshilov. - Please sign".

RGVA. F.4. L.14. C.2831 pp24

Also attached to the letter was another document - the draft resolution of the KO on the amendment of certain Paragraphs of the resolution of the KO Resolution №191ss:

"1. Paragraph 5 of Resolution №191ss of the Defence Committee dated 4 May - to cancel.

2. Manufactured by industry, but not meeting all the latest tactical and technical requirements: A-20 wheel-track tank with diesel V-2 and three pairs of driving wheels; T-100 and SMK breakthrough tanks; and armoured car LB-23, are not accepted for production.

3. In order to study and summarise experience of tank designers of the factories and improvement of armoured vehicles, prototypes with all drawings and specifications are to be conveyed to the NI Polygon ABTU Red Army."

RGVA. F.4 L.14C.2831 pp.26

Letter №16495ss, signed by Timoshenko and addressed to Voroshilov, requesting transfer of the A-20, T-100 and SMK tanks and the LB-23 armoured car to the NI Polygon at Kubinka, with the NKO draft Resolution sent to the KO on 25th May 1940. However, the issue of amending KO Resolution №191ss had not been resolved. The signing of the Customer agreement №142 on the repair of the A-20 and A-32 tanks was delayed until the beginning of June 1940. And ABTU was ready to pay only for the repair of the two A-32 tanks. To pay for the repair of the A-20 tank, which according to Resolution KO №191ss to be stored at Plant №183, and that the company's management planned to use for experimental work, was according to ABTU, to be at the plant's own expense. Concerned about the protracted process of signing several agreements, including an agreement for the repair of the A-20 and A-32 tanks, Plant №183 on 6th June 1940 sent to ABTU in the name of A. P. Panfilov Letter №SO2924, which, in part, stated:

"Despite our reminders to the 4th Department of ABTU KA, we have not received the mentioned agreements so far and have not received a response on this issue from the 4th Department of ABTU KA. We ask for your guidance in instructing the 4th Department ABTU KA to immediate sign and send to us, the above mentioned agreements".

TsAMO. F. 38 L. 11355. C.32. pp.10

A. P. Panfilov received the letter no earlier than 10th June 1940, and on 11th June, he instructed the head of the 4th Department of ABTU, military engineer 1st rank N. N. Alimov to draw up a contract to repair only the two A-32 prototypes. The order of Panfilov was executed on 17th June 1940 as contract №213 on the repair of the two A-32 tanks, sent to Plant №183 in Kharkov with the forwarding Letter №73726s. ABTU at the time still refused to pay for the capital rebuild of the A-20 at

Plant №183. However, repairs of the two A-32 tanks specified in Contract №213 could nevertheless not begin, as from the beginning of July 1940 the A-32 tanks were being used in the Operational Department "70" of the plant for training T-34 tank crews. In addition, the A-32 tanks were also being used for classroom study of the new medium tank design by the tank command and commanders of military units of the Kharkov Military District, the Kharkov and Kiev tank engineering and Orel armoured schools; Kazan school refresher courses and the command structure of the Military Academy of Mechanisation and Motorization of the Red Army (VAMM KA) in the name of Iosef Stalin. In addition to the two A-32 prototype tanks, in the operational Department "70" of Plant № 183 were located; two T-34 and two BT-7M tank types, for the training of crews that arrived at the plant to take delivery of new production from the plant. For the period from 1st July 1940 to 25th January 1941, the training of over 60 mid-ranking officers, 229 tank commanders and 239 driver-mechanics was undertaken with the participation of the A-32 tank prototypes.

Throughout the second half of 1940, the prototype A-32 tanks were involved in driver training. Plant №183 in Letter №SO6070 dated 12th November 1940 and Letter №SO6945 dated 22nd December 1940, addressed GABTU requesting the postponement of essential repairs from 1940 until 1941. Correspondence on this matter between Plant №183 and GABTU KA (before 26th June 1940 - ABTU RKKA) lasted as long as both prototypes of the A-32 tank while training military personnel in the Operational Department "70" had not completed their warranty period. In the end, negotiations between Plant №183 and GABTU ended with the signing in April 1941 of an additional Agreement №100-2/B1-314 to Contract № B1-221 dated 8th March 1941, printed at Plant №183 in five copies; the document stating:

*"**Customer:** Main Auto-Armoured Command of the Red Army (GABTU KA) in the person of the head of the Armoured Directorate of the Red Army, military engineer 1st rank comrade Korobkov, Boris Mikhailovich.*

***Supplier:** Plant №183 (the Komintern plant) in the person of the Deputy Director of Plant №183, comrade Makhonin, Sergei Nestorovich, have concluded the present agreement as follows:*

1. The supplier undertakes to overhaul two prototypes of the tank A-32, manufactured in 1939.

2. The restoration of these tanks is made according to the drawings of the supplier agreed with the GABTU KA military representative. Maximum use of A-34 tank parts is allowed.

3. Rebuild time September - October 1941.

4. Acceptance of the machines is made by the representative of the customer at the supplier plant with a (proving) run of 50km.

5. The cost of repair of one tank is 150,000 Roubles - negotiable.

The parties reserve the right to make a final calculation on the basis of defect Acts of replaced parts and mechanisms.

6. The total amount of the contract is 300,000 Roubles.

7. All other conditions according to the basic contract is as for contract № B1-221 dated 8 March, 1941".

TsAMO. F. 38 L. 11355. C. 99. pp. 97

And so, the further "destiny" of the A-32 tanks was determined by a capital rebuild six months in the future and a new "life" in the Red Army. However, the outbreak of the Great Patriotic War on 22nd June 1941 did not allow the prototypes to return to the ranks of the Red Army. In the summer and autumn of 1941, all efforts at Plant №183 were focused on maximising the series production of T-34 tanks, and there was simply no time available to rebuild the A-32 tank prototypes.

Whether the A-32 tanks were used as stationary firing points in the defence of Kharkov in October 1941 is not definitively known. In all probability they were not, as the A-32 prototypes do not appear in any notification about sending tanks from Plant №183 for the period from 22nd June to 19th October 1941. Unlike the A-32 prototypes, the A-20 wheel-tracked tank was however able to perform the task for which it had been created - to come to the defence of the Motherland. The A-20 tank moreover began its combat activity after having become an exhibit at the GABTU NI Polygon museum at Kubinka near Moscow, of which more will be said later.

Meanwhile, back in pre-war Kharkov, on 19th February 1941, the district engineer of GABTU at Plant №183, military engineer 2nd rank D. M. Kozyrev in Letter №123s addressed to the chief of the 3rd Department of BTU, GABTU military engineer 1st rank and S. A. Afonin, with a request to give instruction on the A-20 tank at Plant №183. According to the letter by Kozyrev, the tank A-20 was *"on the move and was not needed the plant."* Around the same time, another similar document

was sent from Kharkov to Moscow. In Letter №SO1055 dated 21st February 1941 addressed to the chief of BTU GABTU, military engineer 1st rank B. M. Korobkov, the Deputy Director of Plant №183, S.N. Mahonin also asked to resolve the issue regarding the A-20 tank:

"According to your instructions, the prototype of the A-20 tank restored by us in 1940 should be stored at our plant until further notice. Due to the absence of the necessary storage space, please allow the transfer of this tank to any educational or research organisation. The tank has been in storage since the second half of 1940".

TsAMO. F.38. L. 11355. C.6. pp.46

The leadership of GABTU responded quickly to the Kharkov request. On 26th February 1941 the Deputy chief of BTU GABTU, military engineer 1st rank N. N. Alimov and the chief of the 3rd Department of GABTU, military engineer 1st rank S. A. Afonin sent to the district engineer of Plant №183, military engineer 2nd rank D. M. Kozyrev Disposition №145025s, in which, inter alia, it stated: "Ship the A-20 tank located at the plant to the NI Polygon (rail) station Kubinka". S. A. Afonin informed S. N. Makhonin about the instructions given on the A-20 tank in Letter №145039s dated 10th March 1941. In pursuance of the decision made by GABTU, the A-20 wheel-track tank prototype was on 1st April 1941 sent from Plant №183 by rail to Kubinka near Moscow.

On 14th April 1941, the Commission at the NI Polygon of GABTU, consisting of the acting head of the junior ammunition technician Kulapin, head of tank park Lieutenant Mescheryakov and warehouse manager Sergeant Shkelev made the inspection and acceptance of the weapons from the A-20 tank delivered from Plant №183. Acceptance Act № 58-14 / 4, drawn up in triplicate, noted, inter alia:

"At the actual acceptance has appeared:

№	Description	Quantity	Factual per quantity:	1	2	3	Total
1	45mm M-1934 gun. №Э4896	Pc		–	1	–	1
2	ZIP - 45mm gun, in special box	Set		–	1	–	1
3	7.62mm DT machine guns. №Ж6176 и ЖГ352	Pc		–	2	–	2
4	ZIP - machine guns, in special box	Set		–	2	–	2
5	DT magazines	Pc		–	44	–	44
6	PTK sight, №3964 in special box	Pc		–	1	–	1
7	PT-1 sight, №9700 in special box	Pc		–	1	–	1
8	TOS sight, №4524 in special box	Pc		–	1	–	1

TECHNICAL CONDITION.

1. Machine gun DT Ж6176 with spare barrel № 1 - carbon deposits and scratches, with muzzle rash in the rifling.

2. Machine gun DT ЖГ352 with spare barrel № 1. In the breech

there is muzzle rash in the rifling. There is no cover on the box.

3. The boxes for the optics and spare parts-are fading in colour.

4. The gun, the sight PTK has no documents".

TsAMO. F.38. L.11355. C.18. pp122

All of the equipment specified in the acceptance certificate, except for the 45mm tank gun, was dismantled from the tank and stored. The A-20 was initially kept in the open tank storage area at the NI polygon of GABTU KA at Kubinka but not used for any purpose. The small collection of combat and secondary machines was in April - May 1941 with incomplete configuration, as noted in the *"Act on inspection report on operation, maintenance and storage of combat and support vehicles - NI Polygon GABTU KA"* dated 5th April 1941, drawn up by the Commission under the chairmanship of the head of the 1st Department of BTU GABTU KA military engineer 1st rank I. D. Pavlov. Only two months later, on 20th June 1941, the assistant chief of the NI Polygon GABTU KA for scientific and technical work, military engineer 1st rank P. S. Glukhov sent to the head of the 3rd Department of BTU GABTU KA Letter №0575s follows:

"The polygon has received from Plant №183, an A-20 prototype, I ask for your guidance on its assignment".

TsAMO. F. 38 L. 11355. C. 12 pp.324

On the same day the head of the 3rd Department of BTU GABTU KA, military engineer 1st rank S. A. Afonin instructed his immediate subordinate - the head of the 1st Branch of the 3rd Department of BTU KA, Lieutenant Colonel I. G. Panov to write the NI Polygon that the wheel-tracked tank should be kept in the open-air museum of prototype and trophy vehicles. This assignment was executed on 21st June 1941, the A-20 tank prototype thereby officially becoming a museum exhibit the day before the beginning of the Great Patriotic War. It was not however destined to remain in this status for long. On 8th August 1941 the tank, along with four museum exhibits and eight serving Red Army tanks became part of a separate tank company under the command of Captain Karpenko. Before returning the A-20 tank and other museum exhibits to service, the previously removed machine guns, sights and observation devices were re-installed, and the ammunition loaded for operational use of the tank.

On the basis of a GABTU order, a separate tank company was formed from the fighting vehicles of the tank company and the park of museum and trophy vehicles at the NI Polygon GABTU, as part of the Mozhaisk fortified region (№36), deployed as a mobile reserve. Until the beginning of October 1941 the staff of the company were engaged in combat training while in their place of permanent deployment on the polygon site at Kubinka. At this time Semyonov began to command the company, three BT-7 tanks and BT-7M tank were transferred from the company to other units.

On 6th Oct 1941 Semenov, as with all other commanders within the Mozhaisk defence line, was ordered by the commander of the Moscow Military District (MVO) Lieutenant-General P. A. Artemyev to bring the company into full combat readiness. Because during combat preparation the T-100, T-111, BT-7 and BT-IS tanks remained out of order and under repair, there were only five serviceable tanks concentrated on 7th October 1941 in the area Novosumino (4km southwest of Mozhaisk): an amphibious T-40, two T-26 light tanks, and the A-20 and T-29 prototypes. From a separate tank company in the area there was also an AT-1 self-propelled gun, a BA-20 light and BA-10 medium armoured car, seven trucks and two mobile "repair flyers" (TRM tank repair workshops).

The rapid deployment of the Moscow and other garrisons to strengthen the Mozhaisk defence line was due to the fact that from 30th September 1941 in the Bryansk area, and from 2nd October in the Vyazma area, German forces began their offensive on Moscow, with large enemy forces surrounding the Red Army in the areas of Vyazma and Bryansk on the approaches to Moscow creating an extremely dangerous situation for the country. Moscow quite unexpectedly came under direct and major enemy attack. By the time the German tank formations broke through the Vyazma line, there were no intermediate defensive lines or troops capable of delaying the offensive of the enemy tank groups in the whole area before the next defence line at Mozhaisk. On the Mozhaisk line there was at the beginning of October only a very small number of Soviet troops that could delay the onset of enemy tank forces on Moscow. They could withstand the advanced units of the German Army Group "Centre" but not its main strength. Combat-ready units, which were transferred to Moscow from the Far East and Central Asia, as well as reserve units formed in the European part of the Soviet Union, hastily moved to the Front, but were still at the time at a considerable distance from it. In the evening of 7th October 1941, the Mozhaisk defence line was alerted for immediate engagement and troops took their defensive positions. On the Moscow - Minsk road near Novosurino the A-20 tank and its crew within the separate tank company commanded by Semenov acting as a mobile reserve, stood ready for combat.

On 12th October 1941, the chief of the Mozhaisk combat area sent a separate tank company of the district of Mozhaisk in the direction of Verei, from which the enemy was already only 12km away, and the Company became part of a combined detachment under the command of the chief of staff of the 36th fortified region, Colonel I. V. Klyaro. On 13th Oct 1941 at the line of Pafnutovka - Volchenki (4km southeast of the village) the A-20 entered combat. In the second half of October, the crew of the A-20 tank within the composition of the separate tank company was involved in the fighting in the area east of Mozhaisk, where on 26-27th October 1941 the unit had finally stopped the enemy offensive on a line west and southwest of Kubinka.

After a two-week respite, on 15th November 1941, now reinforced German Wehrmacht troops launched a new offensive on Moscow. The A-20 prototype was again involved in the fighting on the approaches to Moscow, but now located in the 22nd Tank Regiment (TR) of the 22nd Tank Brigade (TBr), into which the Semenov's tank company was transferred in the afternoon of 28th November, 1941, after the brigade was put in reserve of the commander of the 5th Army for replenishment and resupply.

At 21:00 on 28th November 1941 the A-20 tank, together with four more T-34 tanks, two T-30 tanks and a T-50 tank was located in a wood 1km to the south of Pavlovskaya Sloboda (30km west of Moscow).

All day on 29th November 1941 the crew of the A-20 tank was, as with all the 22nd TBr, engaged in tank technical maintenance and the cleaning of personal weapons. To stall the enemy in the area of Pavlovskaya Sloboda, on 29th November 1941 on the basis of the 22 TBr was created a the mobile group under the command of Colonel I. P. Ermakov, commander of the 22nd TBr. The group also included remnants of the 36th Motorcycle Regiment (MTsP), the 18th TBr and 2nd Infantry Battalion of the 601st Motorized Infantry Regiment (MSP). At 09:00 on 30th November 1941 the chief of staff of the 22nd Tank Brigade, Major N. P. Konstantinov, in Combat Report №13, reported to the head of the armoured division of the 5th Army, Colonel D. I. Zaev, that:

The A-20 tank during reconnaissance training. NIP (NI Polygon) GABTU KA, autumn 1941.

"1. Parts of the mobile group: 22 TR with attached tanks of the 18 TR, 18 MSPB, 36 MTsP, 2/601 MSP, 22 Recce Co., 18 Recce Co., 22 Anti-Aircraft Div. - are formed and concentrated in the district of Pokrovskoye, Yurievo, Pavlovskaya Sloboda. <...>

9. Units are kept in readiness to act in directions:

1) Rozhdestveno - Snegiri,

2) Rozhdestveno - Kryukovo,

3) Pokrovskoye - Borki.

4) Pokrovskoye - Kozmino <...>

10. Conducted exploration in the probable directions of actions of the brigade".

TsAMO. F. 326 L. 5068 C. 4 pp.262

At 16:00 on 30th November 1941, the 22nd Tank Regiment was replenished with two T-34 tanks, four T-60 tanks, two T-26 tanks and armoured cars. All tanks of the regiment, including the A-20, were to the end of the day refuelled and replenished with ammunition. In the morning of 1st December 1941 the Germans on the flanks of the defence line of the 108th Infantry Division of the 5th Army launched an offensive and broke through the Red Army defences, and by the evening had taken Boriskovo, Borki, Slavkovo, Piskovo, Voronino Abushkovo. The mobile group, including the A-20, was ordered to restore the position. A successful night attack was carried out by parts of the mobile group in the regions of Pokrovskoye, Voronino and Obushkovo.

At 12:00 on 2nd December 1941, a German force with two regiments of infantry with tank support attacked in the regions of Pokrovskoye, Abushkovo, Yurevo and Kozenki. There was fierce fighting through the night, with the German forces occupying these towns, albeit with heavy losses. For a day of fighting, the 22nd TBr lost two T-60 tanks and a T-50 (all burned out) and also and undefined number of T-26 and T-34 tanks.

Mobile repair personnel of the 25th PRB. In the lower right corner - A. V. Lunev.

On 3rd Dec 1941 the A-20 tank within the 22nd TBr, attached to the 108th Rifle (Infantry) Division, participated in an offensive in the area west of Pavlovskaya Sloboda. During the day of fighting three Soviet tanks were knocked out, including the A-20. In a Memorandum dated 3rd December 1941 to his immediate superior Captain M. Krivolapov, senior assistant to the chief of the 1st Separate tank armoured division of the 5th Army, Captain V. E. Galchin stated that in the mobile group of Lieutenant Colonel I. P. Yermakov had in operation: T-34 (7), KV-1 (1), T-26 (2), T-30 (2), T-60 (5), BT-4, BA-10 (1), FAI (1), T-50 (under repair?), and the A-20 - under repair".

The A-20 tank, being damaged in combat beyond the field capability of the repair company of the 22nd TBr, was evacuated and transferred to 25th mobile repair base (PRB) of the Western Front. In December 1941, the 25th PRB was stationed on the territory of the "Krasnaya Truba" (Red Pipe) plant in the Moscow suburb of Fili. Due to the lack of V-2 diesel eng-

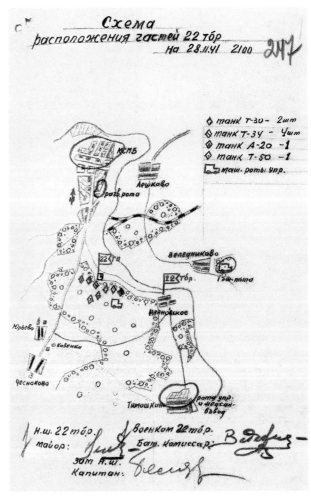

The arrangement of the 22nd Tank Brigade at 21:00 on 28th November 1941

ines, A-20 repairs were completed only in the spring of 1942. The commander of the Department of Installation Works of the 25th PRB, Sergeant A. V. Lunev wrote of the A-20:

"In the first days of war at Plant №183 plant where I worked, from among volunteers - workers and technical workers - some mobile tank-repair bases (PRB) were assembled. They were assigned the task to repair damaged vehicles in the field and to assist soldiers in mastering the new T-34 tank. In a pretty broken truck, covered with a sun-bleached tarpaulin, we seven workers rushed along front line roads, hurrying where our assistance was so needed. Together with the troops we made a difficult retreat from Smolensk to Moscow. When our soldiers were on the outskirts of the capital, we settled in the village of Fili near Moscow. Dozens of repaired vehicles were re-

turned to duty there to participate in the historic battle for Moscow.

Once within a number of damaged tanks came into our hands a prototype A-20. Meeting it was like meeting an old friend. I remembered hot days working on the creation of this tank, together with the designers standing vigil over her assembly and completion. The A-20 was restored (at Fili). With pain in my soul, I escorted the tank to the edge of the village, mentally wishing it success in battles with the fascists. We never met again."*

The last known location of the A-20 was while undergoing repairs in the region of Fili in the western outskirts of Moscow. Unfortunately in surviving archives there is no information as to the subsequent fate of the A-20 prototype.

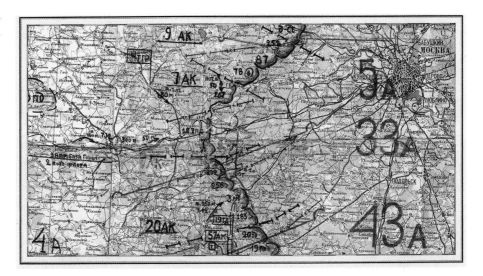

Map of the combat deployment of the A-20 within in a separate tank company in October 1941

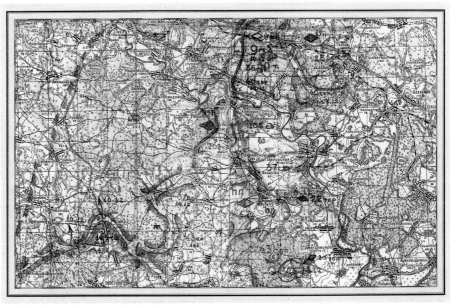

Map of the combat manoeuvres of the 22nd Tank Brigade 1st - 3rd December 1941

* *T-34: Path to Victory: The Memoirs of Tank Builders and Tank Crews.* Ed.: K. M. Slobodin, V. D. Listrovoy, *Publishing House of Political Literature of Ukraine, 1989, pp194-195*

Chapter 12

The T-34 enters Production
- Assigned Plants, Secrecy, Allies and Enemies

According to the Decision of the Defence Committee of the SNK №443ss dated 19th December 1939, serial production of the T-34 tank was to in 1940 be organised at Plant №183 (the "Komintern" plant) in Kharkov and at the Stalingrad Tractor Plant (STZ) named after F. E. Dzerzhinsky. The choice of these plants for the production of a new medium tank was not incidental.

Plant №183 was established on the basis of Order №6 of The People's Commissariat of the Defence Industry (NKOP) dated 30th December 1936 as a reorganisation of the Kharkov Steam Locomotive Plant (KhPZ), which had begun the production of tanks in addition to locomotives in the autumn of 1928. A contract was concluded between KhPZ and the Artillery Department of the Red Army (at the time responsible for tank building) on 18th September 1928 for the production of a T-12 prototype tank constructed of boilerplate steel. The T-12 prototype was completed a year later, on 15th October 1929, and was modified on an ongoing basis at KhPZ until 25th February 1930 when factory testing of the new prototype began. As a result of these trials the Main Design Bureau of the Gun-Arsenal Trust in Moscow in collaboration with the KhPZ design bureau in Kharkov under the leadership of I. N. Aleksenko designed a modernised version, the T-24 - the first "mass production" Soviet medium tank - albeit with a total of only 25 T-24 tanks being

assembled at KhPZ in 1931. The Kharkov KhPZ plant had nevertheless gathered invaluable experience in the design and development of the prototype T-12 and "series" production T-24, which would form the basis for an exponential expansion in tank production at the plant in the years ahead.

After production of a pilot batch of T-24 tanks for service evaluation purposes, T-24 assembly was discontinued at KhPZ in order to prioritise on the series production of another new tank type, based on a technology principle imported from the United States. The new tank, the BT-2 (Bystrokhodny Tank - Fast Tank-2) was a wheel-track design capable of fast travel on roads in wheeled mode. The BT-2 was assembled at KhPZ in Kharkov in 1932-33, being thereafter replaced in production with the modernised BT-5, which featured a new turret unified with the current T-26 tank series, and armed with a 45mm 20K tank gun. The BT-5 was produced at KhPZ for the Red Army in 1933-1934, before being in turn replaced in production by the BT-7, which was assembled at KhPZ (renamed Plant №183 in 1936) from 1935-1939. The last series production BT series wheel-track design developed and produced at KhPZ in Kharkov was the BT-7M tank, powered by a V-2 diesel engine. In total, KhPZ (Plant №183) produced more than 8,100 BT series wheel-track "fast tanks" of all modifications. The main design elements of the future T-34 medium tank were latent in the BT

The A-32 had by 1940 been developed into the series production T-34 in the form it would become world famous. (T-34 of the installation batch).

The T-24, the first Soviet "series" production medium tank. Combat weight: 18.5 tonnes; crew - 5; Armament: 45mm gun, four 7.62mm machine guns; bulletproof armour; petrol engine - 250hp; maximum speed - 25.4 km/h.

The BT-7M wheel-track fast tank. Combat weight: 14.65 tonnes; crew-3; Armament: 45mm 20K gun, three 7.62mm machine guns; armour protection - bulletproof; Diesel engine - 500hp; maximum speed on tracks - 62km/h, on wheels - 86km/h.

series of tanks, and continually refined based on the results of service in the Red Army, and also as a result of operational service abroad in Spain.

Concurrently with the production of the BT series of "fast tanks", KhPZ (Plant №183) also assembled a limited production series of 61 T-35 multi-turreted heavy tanks in the years 1933 to 1939. In 1939, as T-35 production was being curtailed, Plant №183 constructed and tested prototypes of the new A-20 wheel-tracked and A-32 tracked medium tank prototypes, followed in February 1940 by the A-34 - the prototype for the T-34. As part of their military service acceptance trials, the prototype A-34 tanks made their now famous 1,500km round-trip proving run from Kharkov to Moscow and back over the period 12th March - 10th April 1940, accompanied by the T-34 lead designer,

Mikhail Koshkin. These tank prototypes were on 30th March 1940 demonstrated to Iosef Stalin and the Soviet leadership, including Kalinin and Voroshilov, within the walls of the Kremlin.

On 31st March 1940, the day following the successful demonstration at the Kremlin, a further meeting was held, attended by the People's Commissar of Defence of the USSR, Marshal of the Soviet Union K. E. Voroshilov, his deputy - Commander 1st rank G. I. Kulik, the chief of ABTU, Commander 2nd rank D. G. Pavlov, the People's Commissar of Medium Machine Building I. A. Likhachev and his deputy - A. A. Goreglyad, together with the chief designer of Plant №183 and of the T-34 tank, Mikhail I. Koshkin. Taking into account the preliminary results of the military tests of the A-34 tanks, the meeting concluded that:

An A-34 prototype for the series-production T-34 medium tank. Combat weight - 25.6 tonnes; crew - 4; Armament: 76.2mm L-11 gun, two 7.62-mm DT machine guns; armour protection - shell proof; Diesel engine - 500hp; maximum speed-54km/h.

The first four tanks of the T-34 "installation batch" were handed over to the Red Army by the military representative of GABTU KA at Plant №183 in June 1940. In addition to the ten tanks of the pilot batch, the plant had by the end of 1940 delivered another 105 T-34 tanks.

"1. Tank-T-34, made in full compliance with the Resolution of the Defence Committee of the SNK of the USSR №443/ss of 19.12-39, (has) passed State tests and the journey from Kharkov-Moscow without any breakdowns or significant defects, and is recommend for immediate series production at Plants №183 and STZ.

2. It is considered necessary to provide for an increase in working space within the turret, for more convenient command and operation of the armament. Increase the turret internal space without changes in the turret armour inclination, the tank hull or the diameter of the turret race. Place the radio elsewhere than in the turret.

3. Instruct the State tank testing Commission to within five days approve the T-34 tank drawings for production in 1940."

RGVA. F.4. L.14. C.2831. pp17-18

While the fate of the "thirty-four" was being decided in Moscow, Plant №183 in Kharkov was already preparing for production of an initial batch* of ten T-34 tanks, in the time-honoured Soviet norm of tank designers and plants working in advance of the bureaucratic paper trails that latterly formalised permission for them to do so.

Even at this early stage of production, changes were incorporated to maximise future production output. The original welded turret design was complex and labour intensive to manufacture. As the T-34 was being prepared for series production, designers at Plant №183 thereby worked with the Mariupol "Ilyich" plant, which had for years supplied hull and turret castings to KhPZ (Plant №183) in Kharkov to design a new, cast turret for the forthcoming T-34 medium tank in order to simplify tur-

ret production, and hence reduce overall tank assembly time. The Mariupol plant developed the alternative cast T-34 turret in the summer of 1940, with the first batch of final modification cast turrets for the T-34 being sent from Mariupol to Plant №183 on 15th August 1940. T-34 tanks would initially be assembled at Plant №183 in Kharkov with both welded and cast turrets according to available supply. From March 1941, the plant also began to produce tanks armed with the more powerful 76.2mm F-34 tank gun, replacing the earlier L-11, with a new fabricated gun mantlet replacing the distinctive "pig snout" type of the earlier T-34 production model. In total, over 1,500 T-34 tanks were assembled at Plant №183 in Kharkov and delivered to the Red Army in 1941 before the plant was evacuated by rail to the safety of Nizhny Tagil in Siberia beyond the Ural mountains.

By comparison with Plant №183 in Kharkov, the development of tank production at the other plant designated for T-34 medium tank assembly - the Stalingrad Tractor Plant named after F. E. Dzerzhinsky (better known as STZ) located on the banks of the River Volga was before the outbreak of war much slower and more modest in scale. As the name suggested, STZ was originally built to produce wheeled and tracked tractors for use in industry and agriculture; and subsequently for the Red Army. The first STZ-1 "International" wheeled tractor came off the STZ production line on 17th June 1930. Three years later, in August 1933, the construction of (assembly) Workshop №2 was completed, intended for the assembly of T-26 light tanks in addition to their main production location in Leningrad. The first five T-26 tanks produced at STZ were delivered to the Red Army by the end of 1933. The plant delivered only a fur-

---

* Referred to in Russian as an "Installation Batch" and some countries as an "Establishment Lot".

A T-34 medium tank as produced in August-September 1940.

T-34 medium tank with cast turret and early 76.2mm L-11 gun. Combat weight-26.8 tonnes; crew-4; Armament: 76.2mm L-11 gun, two 7.62mm DT machine guns; armour protection-shellproof; Diesel engine developing 500hp; maximum speed - 54km/h.

ther 23 T-26 tanks to the Red Army in 1934, rising to 115 tanks delivered in 1935. These numbers were particularly modest by Soviet standards, but pre-war, STZ was as indicated primarily a tractor rather than a tank production plant.

In the mid 1930s, a special design and experimental department КЭО (KEhO) was organized within STZ, headed by the engineer N. D. Verner. Under his leadership, STZ designers modified technical documentation to adapt the T-26 tank for production at STZ, and from 1940 the same was done for the T-34 medium tank. STZ used the technical documentation provided by Plant №183 in Kharkov to develop T-34 production in Stalingrad, with the STZ design modifications being undertaken to allow for local production requirements and al-

ternative sub-component contractors. T-34 series production was slow to start at STZ, with 226 STZ built T-34 tanks being delivered to the Red Army before the outbreak of the Great Patriotic War on 22nd June 1941. The plant continued to assemble new T-34 tanks during the war, and also undertook the capital repair of damaged T-34 tanks and the repair of V-2 diesel and M-17 petrol engines; remaining one of the main suppliers of new tanks to the Red Army until the summer of 1942. T-34 tank production was finally stopped at STZ only on 13th September 1942, when the front line fighting was literally on the territory of the plant. STZ produced a total of 3,405 T-34 tanks during the war before being overrun as the Battle of Stalingrad engulfed the factory.

T-34 medium tank with cast turret and 76.2mm F-34 gun.

T-34 medium tank with cast turret and 76.2mm F-34 gun, during factory testing near the plant STZ, May 1942.

Newly produced T-34 medium tanks being prepared for delivery at STZ. Note the cast and welded turrets.

The T-34 and Soviet Secrecy

The creation, production and first operational use of the T-34 medium tank occurred in the late 1930s and early 1940s of the 20th Century, the exact time that war in Europe expanded into World War Two. At the time the T-34 was designed, much of Europe was already at war, and the tank entered series production in Kharkov and Stalingrad only months before "Operation Barbarossa", the German invasion of the Soviet Union. In the context of the impending threat, which was far better understood than the Soviet leadership - particularly that of the Red Army - is often given credit for, the Soviet leadership took a number of even more specific than usual measures to protect information that constituted a State Secret. This additional security requirement concerned in particular issues related to the creation of new weapons, including tanks. At the stage of initial development of the A-20 and A-32 tank prototypes, all the materials on these tanks were already marked "Secretno" (Secret - s) or "Sovershenno Sekretno - (Top Secret - ss) and the same was true of the later T-34. This might be considered a standard with regard to tank design and development, however as the new immediate pre-war tank designs began to enter service with the Red Army, the leadership of GABTU undertook additional measures to preserve the secrecy related to the T-34 medium and KV heavy tanks.

On 16th April 1941 the chief of GABTU, Lieutenant-General of Tank Forces, Ya. F. Fedorenko sent to the commanders of armoured forces districts, armoured corps and tank divisions, Directive №140385ss, which stated:

"Take the following measures to keep the KV and T-34 machines secret:
1. Prohibit driving machines of the specified types in cities and settlements in the daytime. Driving to the polygon (testing ground) and back is to be undertaken only at night. Tanks not sent for firing trials or remaining on the polygon after firing trials are to be securely guarded.
2. Only personnel attached to the unit composition, or involved in training and maintenance of the machines are allowed access.
3. Machines at the end of their work must be sealed and protected.
4. When transported by rail, the machines are to be carefully covered with tarpaulins, as well as to be guarded in transit and when at a halt. Unloading from railway cars should be done where possible at night.
5. Material part (tank inventory) is to be stored in sheds, or in their absence to be stored under tarpaulins.
6. All correspondence on these machines is to be marked "Secret".
7. Pay special attention to the preservation of the secrecy of information on the "Tactical and Technical Properties" of these tanks, which should be known only to the command staff and crews directly working on these machines.
8. Vetting of all personnel and demand for data confidentiality about these machines is required".

Soviet tradition during the 1930s had been to show new Soviet tank technology at the annual May and November Red Square parades. These displays, ostensibly for the Soviet leadership and the Soviet "narod" or public, were also a showcase for the foreign military attachés present, such that they could report back to their respective governments as to the undoubted progress of Soviet military technology developments. Soviet tanks such as the successive production models of the T-26 light, BT fast and T-28 and T-35 multi-turreted "crowd pleasers" had been shown on Red Square immediately after series production had commenced, and in some cases before. But as war approached, there was a subtle change in what the Soviet Union chose to demonstrate in public to foreign audiences.

In order to keep secret the presence in the Red Army of fundamentally new T-34 medium and KV heavy tanks from probable future opponents, these tanks did not participate in the last pre-war parade in May 1941, nor had any inkling been provided in earlier parades. This was in stark contrast with the parades of earlier years, when the latest Soviet armoured might was always on proud public display. The parade debut of both these tank types was on Red Square only on 7th November 1941, long after the invading Wehrmacht had met both the T-34 medium and the KV heavy tank in combat. The well-known Soviet poster "Не болтай!" (Ne baltai! - "do not gossip!") by the artists Nina N. Vatolina and Nikolai V. Denisov accurately summarises the general atmosphere of secrecy in the Soviet Union in 1941.

As subsequent events would indicate, measures taken to preserve the secrecy of the T-34 tank had a significant effect, and the use of albeit limited numbers of poorly coordinated

T-34 and KV tanks caused consternation well beyond the surprise impact of unknown tank types appearing on the battlefield in the summer of 1941. On 25th June 1941, only four days into "Operation Barbarossa", the Chief of the General Staff of the land forces of Nazi Germany, Colonel-General Franz Halder, made the following entry in his military diary: *"We have received information about the appearance of another new tank, armed with a 75mm gun and three machine guns."* Halder was of course referring to the new Soviet T-34 medium tank, but note the ominous use of the word *"another"* before *"new tank"*. The Chief of the General Staff had inaccurately noted the gun calibre, and the number of machine guns, but the notation was prophetic. Four days into the war on the Eastern Front, and the Wehrmacht was already encountering unwelcome surprises from the Russians, when their own former military attaché in Moscow, Colonel Hans Krebs, had attended the 1st May Red Square parade only the previous month, and with no sign of any new technology on display had advised Adolf Hitler that that the Red Army and its equipment were well behind Wehrmacht levels of preparedness. The surprises continued, and the coming Russian winter, the coldest in years, would at the gates of Moscow be yet another.

T-34 Samples for the British and American Allies

The Soviet Union in late 1942 and mid 1943 magnanimously delivered sample T-34 medium and KV heavy tanks to two of

The famous Soviet poster - "Не болтай!" (Do not Gossip!).

their wartime Allies, the United States and Great Britain, for them to evaluate at their leisure. The subsequent evaluations generally endorsed the Soviet tank for its overall good design and effectiveness, something the Wehrmacht had by late 1942 known for quite some time.

The T-34 and KV tanks delivered to the United States were loaded on the steamship "Диролдж" as noted in Soviet loading documents, in the northern port of Arkhangelsk, on 28th

T-34 tanks during their public debut on Red Square, 7th November 1941.

August 1942. The ship departed in early September 1942, arriving at the port of New York on 10th November 1942 and being delivered to Aberdeen Proving Ground (APG) in the State of Maryland on 26th November. Three days later, on 29th November 1942, concurrent testing and analysis of the T-34 medium tank and KV heavy tank began at APG, lasting until September 1943. Great Britain received its T-34 and KV evaluation tanks a few months later, during the following summer months.

American Evaluation

The American test report conclusion noted in part that:

"The Russian medium tank T-34, is in general, a good tank, convenient for mass production by a medium-skilled labor force. <...> Distinctive features of the tank are: low silhouette with a pleasant appearance; simplicity of design. The choice of angles of inclination of the armor plates of the hull and turret indicates excellent projectile resistance <...> Placing the ammunition complement at the bottom of the hull is convenient <...> The sights are excellent; the observation devices are roughly made, but satisfactory. General visibility is good. The diesel start-up system with compressed air is an effective additional method."

The study of design and technical documentation sent together with the tanks and the test results served as a model for the creation of new American and British tanks.

The following are transcribed remarks pertinent to analysis of the T-34 medium tank at Aberdeen Proving Ground in 1942. The report details the T-34 and KV simultaneously. The text has been abridged to reflect the parts of the report specific to the T-34 medium tank.

The Second Partial and First Consolidated Aberdeen Proving Ground report including the 10th Report of Ordnance Program No.5887.

APG report: Foreign Material Section APG Report FMCV 13 Dec 1942

Report No.7 on O.P. No 5887
The following is the Proving Centre's impression of the Russian (T-34 and KV) Tanks based on the brief tests conducted:

The engines should be extremely light for their displacement since a greater portion of the material is aluminum. The (engine) design appears to be very compact. The connecting rods are of a master and articulated type, thus producing a 6.7mm shorter stroke on left bank than on the right. The engine can be started by either electric starter or compressed air, the two compressed air bottles being located just to the right of the driver. Complete results of dynamometer tests are not available but from observations however, the engines appear to be efficient, economical and the driver has a

The T-34 delivered by the Soviet Union during initial inspection at Aberdeen Proving Ground in the United States. (Steven J. Zaloga)

feeling of ample power when operating these tanks.

T-34 stows 77 rounds of 76.2mm and 46 drums of 7.62mm (2,898 cartridges).

The medium tank has four forward speeds and one reverse. The transmissions are located to the rear of both as is to be found in the Christie type tanks, having one main clutch and two brake-clutches for steering. It might be interesting to note that compared to our transmission in the M4 Tank, which uses approximately 32 gallons of oil, the Medium Russian Tank contains 3 gallons of oil in the transmission. The transmission housings are also made of aluminum. The transmissions are difficult to shift making this operation a particularly fatiguing one for the driver, and despite the little operation to date, the clutch and clutch brakes have required almost constant adjustments.

Suspension, Tracks and Bogie Wheels:

The Medium Tank has a Christie suspension, having five rubber tired individually sprung dual wheels on each side, with rear sprocket drive and front idler. It also has an integrally linked center guide, a single pin steel track approximately 20" wide, giving a ground pressure of 10 lbs. per sq.in. Floatation is good; the suspension stays clean This tank, however, does not have the ride ability afforded by the torsion bar suspension, (of the KV). The vehicle pitches and rolls quite readily. While the ride afforded to the crew is quite comfortable, this vehicle does not compare to our M4 tank in going over washboard courses or maintaining stability as a firing platform.

Fighting compartment:

The turrets on both tanks are equipped with hand and power traversing, the power being used only for slewing and is fully electric

without hydraulic control. The traversing gearbox is a combination of two irreversible mesh worms, one for hand and the other for power, coupled through a differential so that the turret be traverses by hand or with power without one affecting the other. This seems to be a very desirable feature

The turret is mounted on an all-ball race, which takes the downward and radial load. The hold down of the turret is accomplished by several forged plates that hook under the fixed- portion of the race. This arrangement simplifies the turret ring construction over what we use and would seem to be quite satisfactory. Both (the T-34 and KV) have a comparatively low silhouette over our vehicles. There is no integrated fighting compartment and the seats are hung from the turret. The guns are fired manually by hand or foot. The foot control is accomplished through Bouden cable both for the 76 mm. and the co-axial gun. The tanks are very well lighted and all the lighting is shock-mounted on rubber.

The vehicle lends itself to mass production very well, since many of the parts that we machine very carefully where it is unnecessary, are left rough on the Russian vehicles. For example, all the plates are flame - cut and welded. Many parts on the gun are also left unfinished and they show mill machine marks, and the forged flange is barely ground off. These practices would seem to result in labor saving and should be considered for adoption on our tanks.

Sighting and Observation Equipment

The sighting equipment was separately analyzed at Frankford Arsenal.

Position of the Crews

The Medium Tank has a crew of four; the driver sits slightly to the left in the front of the tank, the radio operator immediately to his

The Soviet delivered T-34 and a captured Pz. Kpfw IV during trials at APG in 1945. (Steven J. Zaloga)

T-34 tank with 76.2mm F-34 gun at Aberdeen Proving Ground in the USA, 1943.

right. The radio operator also operates the bow machine gun in this tank. The tank commander is the gunner, sitting directly to the left of the gun and the loader sits on the right of the gun.

All crew positions appear very cramped when viewed in comparison with our M4 tank. The driver's position is extremely uncomfortable, causing even a middle-sized man to be in a very cramped position. This was pointed out to representatives of the Russian Government who viewed the tanks in a demonstration and evoked the comment that it was not uncomfortable for the Russians since they fought in their tanks and did not live in them. However, both the proof officer and civilian personnel operating the Russian vehicles believe that these tanks are such more fatiguing than ours. The crew positions appear to be well located.

Both tanks handle very much as would be expected with clutch brake and brake steering, and the operation appears to be brutal to personnel used to driving our vehicles with controlled differential steering.

While the vehicles have commemoratively little mileage on them and no clutch brake trouble has developed to date, constant adjustment has been required. Since the Russians included spare parts for both main clutches and clutch brake systems, this is evidently one of the weak points of this tank.

While tests are not nearly completed, operation to date and flotation afforded by the tracks on both vehicles indicate that good cross-country operation in all kinds of going can be obtained from these vehicles.

The tests on these Russian Tanks that have been conducted to date are listed below with the results as found:

A critical mechanical inspection of the vehicles was made on their arrival at the Proving Centre. The vehicles were opened in the presence of two Russian officers and both vehicles appeared to be in good condition. A preliminary analysis of the engine and transmission oils and diesel fuel in these tanks has been made. The diesel fuel used in these tanks corresponds roughly to current specification diesel fuel used at the proving center. The engines are now using diesel fuel used at the Proving Centre. The ground pressure on both tanks has been determined and found to be 10 lbs/sq. inch. on the Medium and Heavy Russian tanks. The limits of vision on both vehicles have been determined and found to be good.

The Medium Tank was operated through snow, mud and ice and no difficulty was experienced going anywhere on the Perryman cross-country course. The vehicle handled very nicely with the exception of shifting into third and fourth gears, which might be attributed to the operators not being familiar with the vehicle. Steering at high speed is accomplished by declutching and accelerating. In first and second gear sharp turns are best accomplished by locking the track in the direction of travel desired. While the snow was not of sufficient depth to offer serious difficulty, no clogging or icing up of the track was noticed and the suspension was clean when the vehicle was returned to the shop even after having gone through several deep mud holes.

The T-34 delivered to the US was after its evaluation at APG kept in the open-air museum collection for several decades and has survived to the present day.

British Evaluation

The T-34 (№420-690) sent to Great Britain for testing was handed over to the British Army in June 1943 by the acting Commissioner of the People's Commissar of Foreign Trade of the USSR, V. N. Povalishin, in the Soviet Arctic city of Arkhangelsk. The tank was formally handed over to the acting Military Commandant of the 126th British (shore) Base at Arkhangelsk, referred to in Russian sources as Major A.J. "Райс" (which may be Reese or Rice). The tank was delivered in full combat order, right down to the provision of a penknife in the tool kit. With the tank were despatched 17 boxes of spares and tools (ZIP) including wrenches, spanners, a spare drive sprocket wheel, roadwheel, idler and a full spare track set. The ammunition provided consisted of 53 HE-Frag, 19 armour-piercing and 5 shrapnel rounds. The T-34, together with a KV delivered from Chelyabinsk was loaded onto the vessel named in Russian as "Эмпайэр-Поршна". (Empire-Porschna) at the port of Bakaritsa (Arkhangelsk). The tank was evaluated at the Military College of Science School of Tank Technology in Chertsey, Surrey, west of London. The tank was as with the earlier American test report noted as being remarkable in respect of the armour configuration, and the use of an aluminium V-12 diesel engine. The report also highlighted the practice of ensuring fine tolerances on wear surfaces but leaving surfaces rough where cleaning up served only an aesthetic purpose, noting that the practice was something British tank manufacturing might consider in wartime conditions. The tank was during evaluation dismantled for individual component testing, with only the 76.2mm F-34 armament and transmission surviving today at the Tank Museum, Bovington, in Dorset.

The following is the Foreword from the preliminary report:

An example of the T.34 cruiser tank reached the School on 22nd November, 1943. The vehicle was new and complete in all respects, being fully stowed with ammunition, wireless and other fighting equipment. It was accompanied by an impressive selection of spare parts, including some major assemblies, and a supply of fuel and lubricants.

Copies of the Russian handbooks were received and translated in the School prior to the arrival of the tank and these have been used in the preparation of this report. As the vehicle is to be submitted for gunnery and field trials at an early date no major components, except the engine, have been desmantled.

As in the case of our own cruiser tanks, the T.34 owes its origin to the Christie design. Subsequent developments in Russia and Britain, however, have not been on parallel lines, the Russians having aimed at mechanical simplicity, a large general purpose gun, stout armour and above all a design facilitating quantity production with limited resources in specialised machine tools and skilled labour. As a result of the latter factor, certain features have received less attention than they would have had in this country, but a realistic outlook and a practical approach to the requirements of a fighting vehicle are strongly manifest.

The welded hull and cast turret appear excellent from the ballistic point of view, except that there is but limited splash protection. With a few exceptions, only three different thicknesses of rolled plate are employed. Exceptional accessibility of the transmission has been secured by a hinged tail plate, but it is not easy to get at the engine.

The 76.2mm gun is mounted in a two-man turret. The crew space appears to be restricted to an extent impairing the efficient service of the gun, but final estimate of the fighting qualities must await the completion of gunnery trials. The internal stowage arrangements are simple and the aim has been to carry the maximum quantity of ammunition irrespective of its accessibility.

The 39 litre 12 cylinder direct injection compression-ignition engine has been developed from an aircraft power unit and, in contrast to other components, it is relatively costly to manufacture. The weight of all components is low - the main castings are in light alloy - and considerable courage has been shown by the designers in the adoption of certain features uncommon in modern British C. I. practice. It is a matter for surprise that although the Germans have developed apparatus for delivering hot water from another tank or other external source, the Russians include no special provision for starting in extreme cold, although a compressed air starter is provided as well as an orthodox electric starter. A translation of a report published in the German paper "V.D.I", which gives a fairly detailed description of the engine, appeared in "The Oil Engine" for December, 1943.

The suspension is arranged so that the springs are protected by main armour without recourse to double skin construction. The spaces between the spring cases are occupied by fuel tanks.

The suspension follows the original Christie design very closely and roller sprockets are employed. The tracks are in cast manganese steel with detachable grousers.

The simplicity of clutch brake steering has been retained and is in striking contrast with British and German practice. There is no power assisted control gear.

Materials have not yet been fully investigated, but there is no reason to suspect that they are not good. The machined surfaces of castings show no flaws. Aluminium is freeley used for engine castings and gear cases. Where necessary for efficient functioning, e.g in the periscopic dial sight, the fuel pump, and certain engine components, excellent finish is attained, but where not essential, it is often rough. No military or mechanical advantage appears to be sacrifi-

The cover of the British preliminary test report on the Soviet delivered T-34 tank undertaken in February 1944.

ced thereby, but a more fully developed industry might be expected to show more refinement without necessarily expanding more man-hours. Many components bear an unusual number of inspections stamps which may indicate a high degree of control in production.

The design shows a clear-headed appreciation of the essentials of an effective tank and the requirements of war, duly adjusted to the particular characteristics of the Russian soldier, the terrain and the manufacturing facilities available. When it is considered how recently Russia has become industrialised and how a great proportion of the industrialised regions have been over-run by the enemy, with the consequent loss or hurried evacuation of pland and workers, the design and production of such useful tanks in such great numbers stands out as an engineering achievment of the first magnitude.

Initial German Analysis

Several T-34 tanks captured in the early weeks of "Operation Barbarossa" were shipped to the Wehrmacht testing grounds at Kummersdorf near Berlin for evaluation. T-34 tanks had been met in combat in the first hours of the war; being together with the appearance of the KV heavy tank a shock to Wehrmacht forces, and as such the capability of the T-34 tank was known

long before examples and their component parts were tested by German military engineers at Kummersdorf. The "discovery" of the T-34 led to an immediate German drive to replicate the best features of the tank, with the angular armour configuration being integral to the design of the German Pz.Kpfw V "Panther". The T-34 had made its mark on history as a Soviet weapon even before the production output began to bite its enemies as much as the tank design itself.

The distinctive "pig snout" cast gun mantlet for the L-11 gun.

A captured T-34 M-1940 with cast turret and 76.2mm L-11 gun during German evaluation.

A side view of the same tank during Wehrmacht evaluation trials.

A rear view of the T-34 M-1940 with welded turret. Note the rectangular transmission access hatch used on early production T-34 tanks.

Chapter 13

The Hot Summer of 1941

The T-34 medium tank began to enter service with the Red Army in the autumn of 1940. The first units to receive the "thirty-four" tank for urgent familiarisation were the Academy of Armoured and Mechanised Forces of the Red Army, and the Kharkov, Orel, Kazan, Kiev and Leningrad tank schools. By the summer of 1941, there were 49 T-34 tanks located in educational institutions for training purposes.

The first military units to receive the T-34 tank - each receiving 30 T-34 tanks in November 1940 - were the 8th Tank Division of the 4th Mechanised Corps* and the 12th Tank Division of the 8th MK, which were part of the Kiev Special Military District (KOVO). An additional 50 T-34 tanks joined these units and also the 32nd Tank Division in December 1940.

From January to April 1941, T-34 tanks entered service with the 5th Tank Division of the 3rd MK of the PriBaltic (Baltic) Special Military District (PribOVO) - 50 tanks; the 4th Tank Division of the 6th MK, Western Special Military District (ZOVO) - 60 tanks; the 29th Tank Division of the 11th MK ZOVO - 26 tanks; the 8th Tank Division of the 4th MK (KOVO) - 90 tanks; The 32nd Tank Division of the 4th MK (KOVO) - 124 tanks; the 12th Tank Division of the 8th MK (KOVO) - 70 tanks; the 10th Tank Division of the 15th MK (KOVO) - 20

tanks; and the 11th Tank Division of the 2nd MK of the Odessa Military District - 50 tanks.

The formation of large combined units such as mechanised corps began in the Red Army in the second half of 1940, influenced by the success of the "Blitzkrieg" tactics of massed German army tank forces in Poland. Mechanised corps were considered by the Soviet command as the main strike means for ground forces. In the autumn of 1940, the formation of nine mechanised corps was almost complete; each consisting of two tank and one motorised divisions, together with support units. In turn, a tank division consisted of two tank regiments and motorised rifle and howitzer artillery regiments, with divisional anti-aircraft, pontoon bridge and reconnaissance battalions, and other specialised units.

According to the wartime statutes or establishment norms, a Red Army tank division was to have 375 tanks (63 KV heavy, 210 T-34 medium and 102 BT or T-26 light types), 95 armoured cars, 28 field guns, 12 37mm anti-aircraft guns and 45 mortars. A total of 6,354 T-34 medium and KV heavy tanks would be required to complete these units in accordance with Red Army norms. Given the production capabilities of the tank plants at the time, this task could be completed only by the

T-34 medium tank on the territory of the Academy of Armoured and Mechanised Forces of the Red Army in the spring of 1941.

Mechanised Corps will be abbrevated to MK in this chapter

spring of 1942. In March 1941, the Soviet government adopted new measures for the deployment of armoured troops. Besides the nine already formed mechanised corps, an additional twenty corps were to be formed during 1941. These new units would require 16,600 T-34 and KV tanks. In the immediate pre-war years of 1940-41, tank industry production capacity was such that to equip the new formations with the quantity of tanks required would take at least 4-5 years to fulfil.

By the time of the outbreak of the Soviet "Great Patriotic War" in June 1941, the total tank park of serviceable tanks available in the five Western border districts had reached a significant number - 10,540 tanks, but the T-34 represented only 904 of these tanks. For the 20 newly created mechanised corps, this number of tanks was clearly insufficient - the actual fulfilment of T-34 delivery requirements averaged 11.5% of the planned norms. The situation in the KOVO and ZOVO districts was slightly better, but the overall shortage of new tanks was very high. For example, in KOVO, of the 16 tank divisions equipped with T-34 tanks, T-34 strength versus actual requirements per norms was as follows - 8th Tank Division (88%), 32nd Tank Division (71%), 12th Tank Division (60%) and 10th Tank Division (57%). In ZOVO, T-34 medium tanks were in service only in the tank divisions of the 6th MK (238 tanks) and the 11th MK (28 tanks), the strength against actual requirements being 56.7% and 0.7 % respectively.

Combat training of mechanised corps was organised and conducted in accordance with the requirements of the People's Commissar of Defence of the USSR: "to teach troops only what is needed in the war, and only as it is done in the war". Red Army mechanised corps, regiments and divisions received a large number of new conscripts in the spring of 1941, with the combat training of armoured troops in the Red Army given a special instruction in May regar reduction in the overall time required to pass training.

The training schedule for young recruits determined that training was to be completed by 1st October 1941; with the preparation of individual soldiers and crew to be complete by 1st July, at platoon level by 1st August, at company level by 1st September; and at battalion level by 1st October 1941. Clearly, those drafted in the spring would under favourable conditions be trained and capable of conducting combat actions within armoured and motorised divisions only by the end of 1941.

Due to a lack of available tanks for training purposes, the personnel of most mechanised corps had by the summer of 1941 mastered neither the new T-34 medium nor the KV heavy tank. Driver-mechanics, due to lack of time and a very limited availability of tanks allocated for combat training, never learned to drive these tanks in difficult terrain conditions with closed hatches, or how to overcome anti-tank obstacles. Dri-

The Cover of a short temporary instruction on the design and operation of the T-34 tank. These books were used as training manuals for tankers until the publication in the spring of 1941 of the official manual: "T-34 Tank. Service Manual".

ving tanks in a column was not practiced. Many driver-mechanics by the summer of 1941 had only received 1.5-2 hours tank driving practice. At the beginning of the Great Patriotic War the combat capability of the newly created mechanised corps of the Western border districts was, due to the weak allocation of military equipment, tanks and support vehicles, trained command and line unit personnel, as well as a lack of ammunition (especially armour-piercing rounds) in consequence very limited. This was as a direct result of the major miscalculation involved in attempting the simultaneous formation of such a large number of mechanised corps. In addition, there were shortcomings in the planning with regard to the combat use of mechanised corps. Most of these corps were assigned to combined arms armies in the Western border military districts, covering the State border. Thus, of the 20 mechanised corps in the districts, 11 were subordinate to the armies of cover (i.e. front level organisations). In accordance with the general plan of covering the State border, mechanised corps, which were part of the armies of cover, had with the beginning of hostilities to concentrate in the planned areas in readiness for counter-attacks on enemy forces that had broken through the defences. Mechanised corps, which were subordinate to the fronts, were not set specific tasks; rather they were supposed to be used depending on the situation during the outbreak of combat actions. Such was the situation in the armoured and mechanised forces of the Western border districts on the eve of the war.

At dawn on 22nd June 1941, Hitler's Germany together with its Axis allies attacked the Soviet Union in violation of the 1939 Soviet-German Non-Aggression Pact (the Molotov-Ribbentrop Pact). Fierce fighting erupted along the entire Soviet border from the Baltic region in the north to the Carpathian Mountains in the south. At the time of the attack on the Soviet Union - "Operation Barbarossa" - Adolf Hitler's command had concentrated and deployed 120 fully manned, technically equipped and well-trained divisions and 2 brigades against the Soviet Union. In addition, on the southern flank were 13 divisions and 9 Romanian brigades. In total, Germany and its Axis satellites deployed 5.5 million soldiers on what became known as the Eastern Front. The 17 German panzer divisions that invaded the Soviet Union were equipped with 3,266 tanks, of which more than 1,400 were medium types. Moreover, in the armed forces of Germany's allies - Finland, Hungary and Romania - were located another 227 tanks.

By the summer of 1941, German troops already had two years of experience in modern warfare, and had been pre-concentrated on the borders of the Soviet Union, deployed in strategic offensive groups. Germany and its Axis allies had a carefully drawn up and thoroughly thought-out plan of attack, developed in the process of long-term preparation for the invasion of the USSR. In a perfidious and sudden attack on the Soviet Union, the German armed forces seized the initiative and were able to launch a powerful offensive in three main directions, towards Leningrad, Moscow and Kiev. Caught by surprise, unprepared to repel a sudden enemy attack, units and formations located in the border districts of the Red Army were unable to deploy in a timely manner along the lines provided for by the State border defence plan. They often entered combat in a disorganised manner, and, despite feats of heroism, were unable to contain the enemy offensive; and gradually retreated with heavy rear-guard fighting. Together with all the armed forces engaged in the initial defensive operations, Red Army armoured troops heroically fought against enemy forces as best they could with the resources at hand.

There were 20 Red Army mechanised corps in the border military districts, of which 9 were armed with T-34 tanks. As indicated, mechanised corps were, at the beginning of the war

unready to conduct large-scale hostilities, and were scattered over a large area along the western border of the Soviet Union. Tank divisions within Corps structure were located at a distance of 50-100km or more from each other. Such a dispersion of tank units could not adequately counter the massive and concentrated enemy tank attacks as had occurred. From the first days of the war, mechanised corps entered into heavy battles with superior German forces. As the most mobile combat means available to Army and Front level commanders, they were used primarily for counterattacks on advancing enemy forces.

The greatest and most persistent battles in the first weeks of war with the deployment of large combined-arms forces of infantry, tanks and aircraft developed in the Northwest (Leningrad), Western (Moscow) and South-West (Kiev) directions. In simultaneous actions, troops of the North-Western Front engaged the attacks by all forces of the German Army Group "North" and also the 3rd Panzer Group and part of the forces of the left flank corps of the 9th Field Army of Army Group "Centre", with a total of more than 40 divisions. The German command focused its main efforts in the Shaulyisk and Kaunas-Vilnius directions. Halfway between the state border and Vilnius was the town of Alytus, where the 5th Tank Division of the 3rd Mechanised Corps, which was under the operational command of the commander of the 11th Army, was stationed. The 5th Tank Division, commanded by Colonel F. F. Fedorov, had 50 T-34 medium tanks, 30 T-28 medium tanks, 165 BT-7 wheel-track "fast" tanks, 18 T-26 light tanks and 27 T-27 tankettes. Moreover, 46 T-34 tanks were in the 9th Tank Regiment, commanded by Colonel I. P. Verkov. Another four T-34s were part of the 5th Separate Battalion intended for communications and command of the division. The division had received its new T-34 medium tanks in February and March 1941.

Filming of the T-34 training film "Crew actions in battle" 1941.

T-34 Tanks abandoned in the equipment park due to lack of spare parts and evacuation means.

A few days before the start of the war, the 5th Tank Division was withdrawn from its permanent deployment to its pre-assigned concentration area. The 9th Tank Regiment was stationed in a forest on the eastern outskirts of Alytus; however due to breakdowns and tanks awaiting repair, there were only two T-34 tanks, six T-28 tanks and eight BT-7 tanks in the tank park at the point of permanent deployment of the regiment. In the concentration area, regimental engineering units constructed berms and hides, and carefully camouflaged the tanks and other military equipment. Attacked by large-scale armoured and infantry forces, rifle formations of the 11th Army were unable to repel the sudden blow and were forced to retreat, suffering heavy losses in personnel, weapons and military equipment.

The force of the initial strike allowed Axis forces to rapidly advance in the direction of Alytus, where two bridges crossed the River Neman. Each bridge was guarded by 21 NKVD regiment soldiers. In the 7th and 20th Panzer divisions of the 39th Motorised Corps the Germans had about 200 light tanks and 60 Pz.Kpfw. IV medium tanks.

By 14:00 the mobile group of the German 7th Panzer Division approached Alytus in order to seize and hold the bridges across the River Neman. On the orders of the command of the 11th Army, the Russian 5th Tank Division advanced to meet the enemy group that had broken through. In the first minutes of the engagement, the 5th Anti-Aircraft Division opened fire against the advancing tanks at a distance of 200-300m, knocking out 14 tanks. Another 16 enemy tanks were knocked out by gunners of the 5th Motorised Rifle Regiment, which had limited quantities of armour-piercing ammunition available. Axis tanks crossed the northern and southern bridges to the left Bank of the river Neman. The German advance slowed, but with the Nazis inflicting several artillery barrages on the positions occupied by Soviet tankers on the west Bank of the Neman in order to force the situation. Within 30-40 minutes, the Germans managed to suppress the Soviet artillery acting in an anti-tank capacity and knock out the Soviet tanks located on the left bank of the river. This allowed the enemy tanks to break through via the south bridge on the River Neman, with the north bridge being captured soon after.

The German units that had broken through were immediately counterattacked by units of the 5th Tank Division. Tanks of the 9th Tank Regiment burst into Alytus on the northern bridge, and tanks of the 10th Tank Regiment on the southern one. In the area of bridges, on the streets of the city, in its squares and its parks, there was fierce fighting until late at night. The 5th Tank Division suffered heavy losses. Fuel and ammunition were running out, and communication between units had been disrupted. Closer to midnight, the remaining defenders of the western part of Alytus began to retreat to the east towards Vilnius. Losses in the 9th Tank Regiment were significant - 27 of 44 T-34 tanks, 16 of 24 T-28 tanks, and 30 of 45 BT-7 tanks were lost in combat.

The battle of Alytus on 22nd June 1941 was one of the first battles of the Great Patriotic War involving the use of T-34 tanks. The action held up the German offensive for ten hours, the 5th Tank Division making a significant contribution to slowing the "blitzkrieg" attack on the Soviet Union; which began to meet strong opposition and falter on the very first day of the war. The headquarters of the 3rd Panzer Group, commanded by German General G. Goth, in a brief report on the results of the first day of the offensive on the fighting in the area of Alytus reported to the leadership of Army Group "Centre" as follows:

"in the Evening of 22 June, East of Olita [Alytus], the 7th Panzer Division fought against the (Red Army) 5th Tank Division - the largest tank battle during this war. We destroyed 70 tanks and 20 aircraft (at airfields) of the enemy. We lost 11 tanks"

TsAMO. F.500 L.12462. C.118. pp21

After suffering heavy losses in the fighting in the area of Alytus, the scattered units of the 5th Tank Division slowly retreated to the east, trying to delay the Axis advance on the Lithuanian capital - Vilnius. The hastily organised defence on the southern and western outskirts of the city did not last long, the city being taken by the Germans on 24th June 1941.

By order of the division commander Colonel F. F. Fedorov, divisions and units of the 5th Tank Division departed to the north-west suburbs of the city and for several days continued to slow the enemy approach. On 26th June the division commander, firing from his own T-34 tank, personally destroyed 6 enemy tanks.

A German crewman in a 38(t) light tank of the German 20th Panzer Division, Otto Karius, was lucky during the battles of Alytus and Vilnius, his tank being hit slightly later, on 8th July 1941. However, his impressions of the Russian "34" during the first days of the war, remained with him for life:

"Another event," he wrote after the war, *"hit us like a ton of bricks: the first Russian T-34 tanks appeared! The amazement was complete. How could it be that up there (i.e. in the high command), they did not know about the existence of this excellent tank? The "T-34", with its good armour, ideal form and a magnificent 76.2mm long-barrelled gun was held in awe by all, and it was feared by all German tanks until the end of the war. What were we to do with these monsters thrown against us in great numbers? At that time, the 37mm gun was still our strongest anti-tank weapon. If we were lucky, we could hit the turret race of the T-34 turret and jam it. If even more lucky, the tank will then not be able to act effectively in combat. Of course, this was not a very encouraging situation! The only way out left remained the 88mm anti-aircraft gun. With its help, it was possible to act effectively even against this new Russian tank."*

Otto Karius. Tigers in the Mud. ZAO Tsentrpoligraf, Moscow 2002 pp16

In contrast to the troops of the North-Western Front, which at the beginning of the war had only 50 T-34 tanks, in the mechanised corps of the Western Front there were 266 brand new medium tanks. 238 T-34 tanks were located within the 6th Mechanised Corps, and 28 in the 11th Mechanised Corps.

The forces of the North-Western front, as with the forces of the Western Front, not having time to tactically manoeuvre, took the brunt of the Wehrmacht onslaught and suffered heavy losses on the first day of the war. The situation was particularly difficult in the Grodno and Brest-Baranovich directions, where the Germans concentrated the forces of the 2nd Panzer Group, and the 9th and 4th Field Armies. In the first half of the first

A Czech built 38 (t) light tank. Over 280 tanks of this type were available in the 7th and 20th Panzer Divisions at the time of the attack on the USSR.

T-34 Tanks abandoned by their crews due to lack of fuel, June 1941

day of the Great Patriotic War fierce battles began approximately 15-20km to the West of Grodno, units of the Soviet 11th MK and the Axis 20th Army Corps began major combat engagements. The 29th Tank Division, deployed on an 8km front northwest of Grodno, attacked the enemy, but having advanced 6-7km was forced to suspend the offensive.

A few days before the start of the war, this division had 24 T-34 tanks built at Plant №183 and armed with the 76.2mm F-34 gun. In addition, the division had two "34" tanks received earlier for the training of tankers. In the division, in addition to the 26 T-34 medium tanks, there were two "KV" heavy tanks, 22 T-26 light tanks and 16 flamethrower tanks. Instead of the wartime fulfilment requirement of 375 tanks, the division at the start of the war had a total of only 66 tanks available.

Regarding the action of the 29th Tank Division in the early days of the Great Patriotic War, the commander of the 11th Mechanised Corps, Major General of tank troops D. K. Mostovenko in the report of Deputy People's Commissar of Defence of the USSR, Lieutenant General Ya. N. Fedorenko on 1st August 1941 reported the following:

"The command of the 3rd Army, 11th Mechanised Corps, was on 22.6.41 tasked to destroy the advancing enemy and cover the retreat of the infantry. <...> Part of the 4th Rifle Corps, covering the border and border areas could not hold the advancing enemy and quickly retreated. The 29th and 33rd Tank Divisions, as previously concentrated and engaged, took the brunt of the fighting. <...>. The enemy, attacked by tank divisions, suspended the offensive and moved to the defence, using settlements and rivers for cover. Tank units met with organised strong anti-tank (gun) defence, artillery

and air attack aircraft and suffered heavy losses. <...> Enemy tanks that tried to attack our tanks were destroyed, and the rest held by defending infantry. <...>. For all the time of the mechanised corps combat action there was not one of our planes in the air and enemy aircraft acted with impunity, shooting and burning literally separate machines. <...>. During the day on 24.6, parts of the Corps continued to engage the advancing enemy. By the end of the day on 24.6. the enemy, having occupied Grodno, began to move to the south and I was ordered to withdraw the 29th Tank Division (there remained in the division about 60 tanks, of which 10 were T-34 tanks, and the rest were T-26 tanks). <...>

The 29th Tank Division and 204th Mechanised Division on the morning of 25.6 held back the enemy offensive from the area of Grodno, Korobchitsy and Strupka. Axis forces attempts to cross the River Neman in the area of Migovo, Komatovo were repulsed. There was especially intensified bombardment on this day by aircraft and artillery and survivors from previous days were destroyed. No machine could show itself in the open without being destroyed. The location of the units was also subjected to continuous bombing and shelling by aircraft. <...>. During the night of 26-27.6, part of the Corps departed and on the following day 27.6 occupied defence positions on the River Neman. <...> By the time of departure of the Corps was the following state: 29th Tank Division-no more than 350-400 people, 25 tanks and 15 armoured vehicles; 33rd Tank Division - 153 people without combat materiel. <...>. On the night of 28-29.06 the order to withdraw was given <...> The forcing of the River Shara by the village of Vel was successful. The difficulty was in bridging the river, which was up to 60 metres wide in parts, to allow transfer of the remaining materiel. There were no crossing regular means, no saws, axes and other tools, no pontoon or sapper specia-

T-34 Tank with welded turret and L-11 gun, abandoned by the crew due to lack of recovery means.

T-34 Tank with F-34 gun, also abandoned by the crew due to lack of recovery capability, Summer 1941.

lists. The work was done by soldiers and officers, despite air attack and artillery shelling. <...> By 23:00 on 29.6. a bridge was completed to allow the passage of infantry and wheeled vehicles. The bridge could not take the weight of combat vehicles, and an attempt to ferry the tanks led to sinking of the tanks and armoured vehicles. Two T-34 tanks managed to ford the river but at Novogrudok had to be destroyed due to lack of fuel. The remaining combat vehicles were destroyed, some by enemy aircraft, which bombed day and night. <...>. By the end of the day on 30.6. the unit went into the woods to the south of Venzovets. The condition of the soldiers and commanders after continuous fighting and transitions during the 9 days, without regular nourishment, partly unarmed or without ammunition, was grave. At stops on the march all collapsed and immediately fell asleep. <...>. Combat material in the period 22.6. - 1.7.41 was worked to the limit. During the day units waged battle, and tanks regrouped during the night. Tanks, as a rule, covered the withdrawal of infantry to the next defence line. <...>. In the first attack of our tanks, the enemy suffered heavy losses in tanks and in subsequent battles with the appearance of our tanks left for (the safety of) defending infantry. <...> Typical losses for the T-34 included being taken out of commission due to track, drive wheel and idler wheel damage, with 20 of 24 tanks lost being for these reasons. During our tank attacks, the enemy concentrated the fire of several anti-tank guns on one tank, followed by the transfer of fire to the next tank. Two T-34 tanks hit but with incomplete penetration of the frontal armour subsequently went on the attack. Two of the KV tanks were destroyed the first day in combat south of Sapotskin. One tank overturned and sank in the swamp, the second was hit in the running gear; the third could not be repaired due to a lack of parts. <...>

The Commander of the 5th Tank Division Colonel F. F. Fedorov.

Commander of the 11th Mechanised Corps, Major General of tank troops D. K. Mostovenko.

German tanks break through the guns of our tanks and also burn. After 23.6.41 the Germans mainly used anti-tank guns and bombing aircraft against our tanks, which burned about 6 tanks. German tanks, after the clash on 22.06 with the 29th Tank Division, having suffered losses of around 30 tanks, withdrew and were used as anti-tank guns from dugouts and shelters. <...>

Conclusion. T-34 tanks require improvement of the quality of the metal tracks, drive and guide wheels. The quality of the material should be equal to the resistance of the frontal armour of tanks, for running gear damage in battle denies the possibility of further use of the tank, especially in the absence of a sufficient number of suspension spare parts and an insufficient number of tractors, able to evacuate directly from the battlefield. <...>

In the current situation at the Front of the 3rd Army, the 11th Mechanised Corps, and in the composition in which it found its for-

T-34 tank with welded turret and 76.2mm F-34 gun.

mation, fulfilled its task. It delayed the enemy advance for five days, inflicting heavy losses and prevented the forcing of the River Neman and covered the departure of units of the 3rd and 10th armies, and the consequent retention of the front line allowed our military units to escape and redeploy".

TsAMO. F. 38. L. 11360. C. 2. pp. 375 - 385

In contrast to the 29th Tank Division, in which T-34 crews almost from the first hours of the war had to participate in combat, the 7th Tank Division of the 6th MK of the same Western Special Military District (ZOVO) entered combat on the third day of the war. This division had almost six times as many T-34 tanks as the 29th Tank Division. The 7th Tank Division had received new T-34 medium tanks, all armed with the 76.2mm F-34 gun, in May-June 1941. 92 tanks were received from Plant №183 and 58 from the Stalingrad Tractor Plant (STZ). In addition to the "34", the division at the beginning of the war had 51 KV heavy tanks, about 125 BT-7 light wheel-tracked tanks, and 42 BT-5 and 42 T-26 light tanks. In terms of the number of T-34 tanks, this division was the best equipped with new medium tanks in the district, which at the beginning of the war was reorganised into the Western Front.

It should be noted that for the T-34 tanks that arrived on the eve of the war, the 7th Tank Division had only "Oskolochno-Fugasnimi" (i.e. "ОФ" (OF) or high-explosive HE-Frag) shells - and no armour piercing ammunition for the 76.2mm F-34 gun available at all. In addition, as of 22nd June 1941, the division had run out of ДТ (DT) - diesel fuel. All this, especially the lack of fuel, had an inevitable negative impact on the combat use of the "34."

On 22nd June 1941, at 02:00 a communications runner delivered to the headquarters of the 7th Tank Division the password on allowing the opening of the "red package" on combat alert. After 10 minutes, units of the division were in combat order and at 04:30 they focused on the collection points in the area northwest of Bialystok. At 04:00 enemy aircraft bombed divisional units in Bialystok, in the towns of Khorosh and Novoselki. From the entire division, in the 13th Tank Regiment alone during the bombardment four people were killed and 26 wounded. The material part of the division was unaffected. Until late in the evening the staff of the division were located in the concentration areas and carried out measures to bring the units to full combat readiness. At 22:00 on 22nd June the division received the order to move into a new area of concentration (40km East of Bialystok) to engage enemy tank divisions. The division, carrying out the order, wedged into the columns of traffic on the roads of the randomly retreating rear of the 10th Combined Arms Army and civilians leaving Bialystok. The division while on the march and in the area of concentration was repeatedly subjected to enemy air strikes. For the period from

04:00 to 14:00 hours on 23rd June the division lost 63 tanks destroyed or lost in an unknown direction while dispersing during enemy air raids. The rear regiments were all in disarray.

As no enemy tank divisions were located in the deployment area, the division was at 14:00 on 23rd June ordered to undertake a 50km march to an area 35km north-east of Bialystok, where the division was in place by the end of the morning of 24th June redeployed to engage advancing German tank divisions. Reconnaissance operations had found no tank division strength enemy forces in the area, only small groups of tanks interacting with infantry and cavalry. On 24-25th June the division, acting on the orders of the commander of the 6th Mechanised Corps, Major-General M. G. Khatskilevich advanced in the area of 25km southwest of Grodno, where it destroyed and dispersed up to two battalions of infantry and two batteries of artillery. After the task of the division was concentrated in the area of operations. During this operation, the division lost 18 tanks burned out and bogged down in the swamps.

On 25-26th June, the 7th Tank Division fought a defensive battle in the area 25km southwest of Grodno. By the end of the day on 26th June, Axis forces deployed reserves to increase the force of impact. The weakened Red Army motorised infantry units began to withdraw randomly to the south-east.

Part of the 7th Tank Division covering the retreat of parts of the 10th Army consistently engaged enemy units during this time. On 29th June at 11:00 with the remnants of the unit (three T-34 tanks) and a detachment of infantry and cavalry, the commander of the 7th Tank Division, Major-General of tank troops S. V. Borzilov organized the defence in the area of forest east of Slonim. On 29-30th June the division commander's unit was the one platoon of T-34 tanks that engaged directly with the enemy.

In his report on the status and actions of the 7th Tank Division, S. V. Borzilov after leaving the combat environment at the end of July 1941, indicated with regard to material losses: *"The materiel part is all left in the territory occupied by the enemy, from Bialystok to Slonim. The abandoned materiel was put into disrepair. The majority was abandoned because of lack of fuel or repair. The crews joined the retreating infantry."*

TsAMO. F. 38. L. 11353. C. 5. pp. 54

Regarding the combat qualities of the T-34 tank, the commander of the 7th Tank Division wrote: "I personally encountered four "KV" and "T-34" machines hit by anti-tank guns. In one tank was a damaged roof hatch, in another machine, the "yabloko" (literally apple - meaning ball mount) for the "TPD" (Degtyarev DT tank machine gun ball installation); otherwise it should be noted that the main reason for the tanks being out of service was damage to the gun and machine guns; the rest of the "T-34" tank has very good resistance to the impact of 37mm guns".

TsAMO. F. 38. L. 11360. C. 2. pp. 294

In analysing the actions of the 6th MK in General, S. V. Borzilov the report noted that *"for combined arms units such as with the 6th MK, there were no such tasks, as to provide the possibility of using an entire mechanised corps. The use of the 6th MK was mainly at divisional or regimental level, where it fulfilled its tasks."*

TsAMO. F. 38. L. 11360. C. 2. pp. 293

Thus, the use of 238 T-34 tanks, which was the basis of the 6th MK at the beginning of the war, failed as regards providing a united steel defence barrier. Unlike the tank divisions of the 6th MK, the tank divisions of the 4th MK operated jointly in the early days of the war. However, the nature of these actions was different.

An abandoned T-34 Tank with cast turret and 76.2 mm F-34 gun.

With regards to T-34 tank composition at the beginning of the Great Patriotic War, the 4th MK was the best equipped in the Red Army - on 22nd June 1941 it had 313 "thirty-fours". The 8th Tank Corps had 140 T-34 tanks. It was the first tank corps in the Red Army to receive 23 T-34 tanks, armed with 76.2mm with L-11 guns, which entered service in November 1940. Through until April 1941, the divisional tank parks were being monthly replenished with new medium tanks delivered from Plant №183. All T-34 tanks of this division were armed with the 76.2mm L-11 gun. Another tank division of the 4th MK - the 32nd Tank Division at the beginning of the war had 173 T-34 tanks in its composition. All T-34 tanks in this division were armed with 76.2mm F-34 guns, all of which had arrived from Plant №183 in March-June 1941. The 4th MK was stationed in Lvov (today Lviv) and was part of the 6th Army. At the beginning of the war all tank regiments of the tank divisions were located in their places of permanent station (i.e. "in barracks"). A few days before the outbreak of hostilities, the command of the corps received the order to disperse the tanks in the forests surrounding the city. The 8th Tank division on the nights of 17-18th and 18-19th June 1941 reached the forests, located 20km northwest of the city. The 32nd Tank division was to leave its permanent station on the night of 22-23rd June, and therefore the outbreak of hostilities caught it in Lvov.

Starting from the first day of the war, the higher command of the 4th MK was given orders to undertake marches to va-rious areas where the enemy was assumed to be developing an offensive. Armoured divisions moved a considerable distance and, having failing to service the materiel part (i.e. suffered from problems with breakdowns, repairs and fuel shortages) were ordered to new areas of concentration.

The former head of the operational Department of the 4th Mechanised Corps, Colonel D. Kh. Cherniyenko, in October 1941 described the use of the corps in the initial period of the Great Patriotic War:

"Use of the Corps on the side of the 6th Army, especially in the first period combat action, was clearly wrong. The case was set the task as a squadron of cavalry, giving absolutely no time for technical examination of tanks. <...> Of the total number of tanks, only 25% (approximately) were destroyed in combat, the remaining tanks failed due to their technical condition. <...> Emergency evacuation of tanks was badly handled. There was no recovery means. It was (and remains) necessary to tow the faulty tank using a serviceable tank until that tank also breaks down".

TsAMO. F.38. L.11351. C.21. pp205

A report by the commander of the 32nd Tank Division also noted that:

"In the early days of the fighting, divisions were set the task of continuous forced marches with an offensive intent and the subsequ-

T-34 Tank with damaged running gear, abandoned after an attempted recovery, summer 1941.

An abandoned T-34 tank of late spring 1941 production.

ent destruction of the tanks and infantry of the enemy. For the first three days 23-25.6, the division travelled a total of 350km on the march without adequate rest for crews and repair of the material parts. <...> During this period, the division was in constant contact with the enemy in these areas with the exception of the 3 battalions of the tank regiments of the 32nd Tank Division, which were scattered fighting in the area of Radzekhuv [70km north-east of Lvov]".

TsAMO F.38. L.11360. C.2 pp163

The tank regiments of the 8th Tank Division did not engage the enemy for the first time until the third day of the war. On 24th June 1941, when making the next march, the 15th Tank Regiment of the 8th Tank Division finally engaged with enemy units in the area of Nemirov. An attempt to break through enemy occupied Nemirov was unsuccessful. In this battle, up to a battalion of enemy infantry, up to 12 anti-tank guns, an artillery battery and 10 heavy machine guns were destroyed, with the 15th Tank Regiment loosing 19 T-34 tanks in the battle.

TsAMO. F. 38. L. 11360. C. 2. pp. 148

During the period of hostilities in the so-called Lvov protrusion, over the period 22nd June to 17th July 1941, losses of T-34 tanks in the 8th Tank Division and 4th MK amounted to 137 tanks. Of these losses, 54 T-34 tanks - less than half - were destroyed in combat; 32 tanks were evacuated and sent back to the tank plants

One of the numerous T-34 tanks abandoned by its crew due to the lack of evacuation capability.

T-34 Tank with welded turret and 76.2 mm L-11 gun, abandoned by the crew due to lack of evacuation means.

for repairs; 31 tanks had to be abandoned and destroyed by their crews; eight were missing; two were stuck in a swamp, and the reasons for the loss of ten other tanks were not established.

TsAMO. F. 38 L. 11360 C.2 pp. 156

The 32nd Tank Division of the 4th MK suffered even greater losses of T-34 tanks in the first weeks of the war. From 22nd June to 31st July 1941, the 63rd and the 64th Tank Regiments, armed with 173 "thirty-fours" at the beginning of hostilities lost 146 tanks of this type in a single week.

Compared with the 4th Mechanised Corps, the outfitting of the remaining mechanised corps of the Kiev Special Military District (KOVO - at the beginning of hostilities reorganised into the South-Western Front) with new T-34 medium tanks was significantly less. In the 8th MK on the morning of 22nd June 1941, there were 100 T-34 tanks; in the 15th - 72; in the 19th - 43; while in the 9th and 22nd there were no "thirty four" tanks present at all. T-34 tanks in these mechanised corps from 26th to 29th June participated in the Front counterattack, in three counter tank battles in the areas of Lutsk, Brody and Dubno.

On the South-Western Front of the combined arms units involved in the counter-attack on the flanks of the enemy 1st Panzer Group in the area of Dubno, the 8th MK operated the most successfully. The 12th Tank Division of this corps, having in its composition 98 T-34 tanks, despite the very difficult conditions of the situation, boldly and decisively engaged in battle with superior enemy forces with considerable success, though incurring heavy losses in the process. And yet the deep wedge of the 8th MK in the rear of the 1st Panzer Group forced the enemy to temporarily suspend the offensive and instead repel counter-attacks and regroup.

"On the right flank of the 1st Panzer Group, the 8th Russian Tank Corps" - as recorded on 29 June, 1941 in his military diary, the former chief of the General staff of the land forces of Nazi Germany, Colonel-General F. Halder - *"deeply wedged into our location and went to the rear of the 11th Panzer Division. This interposition of the enemy caused a great disorder in our rear in the area between Brody and Dubno."*

Halder F. War Diary. Vo. 1 (22.6 1941-30.9 1941). Moscow, Voenizdat, 1971. pp58

Thus, units of the 8th Mechanised Corps, largely due to the

A T-34 tank of autumn 1940 production, from the 15th Tank Regiment of the 8th Tank Division, knocked out during the battle at Nemirov.

high maneuverability and firepower of its T-34 tanks, proved the ability to inflict painful blows on the flanks and the rear of German forces. Despite the counter-attacks of the mechanised corps not leading to a decisive defeat of the German and Axis shock groups, they still played a role: the enemy suffered losses in manpower and equipment, and the pace of progress was slowed. The main reasons for the low efficiency of counter-rattacks and large losses of materiel were stated by the chief of the South-Western Front armoured command, Major-General of tank troops R. N. Morgunov in a report to the chief of the Red Army armoured command (ABTU) Lieutenant-General Fedorenko on 3rd July 1941:

"The lack of evacuation means, spare parts for KV and T-34 (tanks), the presence of manufacturing defects, not mastered exploitation, insufficient training of personnel, poor reconnaissance of enemy armoured capability, systematic exposure to bombardment on the march, in assembly areas and attack with great movement over 800-900km without cover by our aircraft and no interference by artillery in almost all areas (forests and marshes), the stubborn resistance on the part of the enemy, the lack of armour-piercing rounds for KV and T-34 (tanks) led to huge losses and consequent unfit for action, M.K. (mechanised corps) with the remaining available materiel parts."

TsAMO. F. South-Western Front. L. 151. C. 8. pp. 28

As of 17th July 1941, the 8th MK had a total of 57 tanks, 14 of which were T-34s. The same number of "thirty-fours" was to be found in the 4th Mechanised Corp. In the 15th Mechanised

Corps; of the 10 remaining tanks, only one was a T-34. The largest quantity of "thirty-fours" was available in the 19th MK - which had only 31 tanks.

TsAMO. South-Western Front. L.151.C.8.pp45

Summarising the combat use of T-34 tanks in the first fierce battles of the Great Patriotic War, it can be argued that the crews of T-34 tanks performed their military duty with honour, opposing the enemy onslaught with great courage and bravery. Only the courage and fortitude of the tankers, coupled with the high combat qualities of the T-34 tank where deployed, allowed the Red Army at that time to partially compensate for the lack of forces and serviceable defence capability at the Fronts. Meetings with the T-34 in the sultry summer of 1941 more and more undermined the formerly invincible spirit of the German panzer crews, accustomed to easy victories on the battlefields of now enslaved Europe. One of the reports of the commander of the 1st Battalion of the 36th Panzer Regiment of the 14th Panzer Division, stated the difficulties faced by German Panzer crews:

"On shelling an enemy tank with ordinary armour-piercing shells at close range (50 metres) it is necessary to strive to get around the rear of the tank, or hit under the turret from the front, or hit the armour for the gun recoil mechanism. When firing from a distance of 100-150 metres, the tank can be disabled by a fortuitous hit to the running gear."

TsAMO.F.228. L.738. C.8. pp29

And yet the high individual fighting qualities of the T-34 could not affect the overall combat situation in the initial period of the war, as the so-equipped mechanised corps in the summer of 1941 operated in extremely unfavourable and difficult combat conditions as noted. Bearing heavy losses, the Red Army was forced to move to strategic defence while thousands of enterprises and organisations were evacuated to the interior of the country; and industry was reconfigu-

red for almost exclusively military production. Gradually the production of weapons and equipment in the Soviet Union increased. T-34 tank output also over time increased, due to organisation of its serial production at several assembly plants. T-34 tanks first outfitted individual tank battalions and brigades, then tank and mechanised corps, and from 1942 also tank armies. Gradually, the "thirty-four" became the main tank of the Red Army, for the duration of the "Great Patriotic War".

T-34 and BT-7 tanks during the first weeks of "Operation Barbarossa", summer 1941.

T-34 Tank with L-11 gun, destroyed in combat, summer 1941. Note the burned off road wheel rims.

Chapter 14

Conclusion

In conclusion, the final word on the development of the T-34 is an extract translated directly from an article by one of the lead designers of the legendary "Thirty-Four" - Alexander A. Morozov. The original work was published in 1985 in the departmental scientific and technical collection article *"Questions of Defence Technology"* under the title: "T-34 - The Main Tank of the Great Patriotic War". *

T-34 - The Main Tank of the Great Patriotic War
(Alexander A. Morozov - Article Extract)

In mid 1940 (assembly of) the pre-production pilot batch of T-34 tanks began, with teething problems resolved and series production underway by the beginning of 1941. The technology inherent in the development of the A-20 and A-32 tanks formed the pre-history of the famous Soviet "Thirty Four". The T-34 tank, unlike some tanks, was not created from scratch from the first line of a drawing, but was rather the ultimate result of a series of other tank developments. The start of T-34 development was initiated with the A-20, and particularly the later A-32. The T-34 tank was the ultimate result of further development of the A-32 "initiative" tank, by further strengthening its armour protection, its armament, and carrying out a number of other changes. The T-34 would become the most mass-produced Red Army tank of the Great Patriotic War.

The first prototypes of the T-34 tank were completed in early 1940, with their high technical and combat qualities confirmed during tests. For the first time in the history of tank construction, the armour of the T-34 tank was "stronger" than anti-tank shells of the period: The T-34 tank was invulnerable when fired on from a 45mm calibre anti-tank gun. The increase in combat weight of approximately five metric tonnes, compared with the tanks' direct predecessor, the A-32, reduced the mobility of the tank slightly in lieu of firepower and armour protection. On tests in the presence of the high command of the Red Army the T-34 showed an excellent ability to overcome standard anti-tank structures and obstacles, which had caused difficulty for other Soviet designs.

In the spring of 1940, two prototype T-34 (the A-34) tanks made a run of approximately 1,500km from Kharkov to Moscow and back, demonstrating sufficient reliability of all

A.A. Morozov.

components, with high performance speed, power reserve and fuel efficiency. At the end of the outward leg of the proving run, the tanks were driven directly to the Kremlin, for inspection by members of the Soviet government including Iosef V. Stalin himself. With undisguised satisfaction at the result of the tests and obviously successful proving run, Stalin thanked the designers, testers and crew for their efforts, briefly saying in conclusion about the T-34 that: *"It will be a harbinger in our tank forces"*. This Kremlin demonstration, which became a key moment in the history of "Thirty Four", finally determined its fate. The initial batch of T-34s was assembled in the summer of 1940, and in early 1941 the plant completed all the necessary training and started serial production.

After completion of the design according to the results of tests and screenings to determine the performance characteristics of the tank, comparing that with the performance characteristics of foreign tanks of the period, one can see the significant superiority of the serial production T-34 over all foreign medium tanks.

At a time when the calibre of mass production domestic medium tanks usually did not exceed 45mm, with their armour providing reliable protection from small-arms fire and small shell

---

* Editor's note: the original text has been left as far as possible in the original Russian word format to preserve the original context.
Due to the length of the extract, the Italics have been omitted for ease of reading.

Main performance characteristics of the T-34 medium tanks and foreign, produced in the late 1930s.

Characteristics	T-34 (USSR)	Pz.Kpfw-IIIE (Germany)	Pz.Kpfw-IVF1 (Germany)	S-35 (France)	Mk-IIA (Great Britain)
Weight (metric tonnes)	25,6	19,5	22,3	19,5	25
Crew	4	5	5	4	4
Engine output (hp)	500	300	300	220	190
Power to Weight ratio (hp/tonne)	19,5	15,4	13,5	11,3	7,6
Maximum speed (km/h)	54	50	40	45	25
Road range (km)	300	175	200	240	130
Ground Pressure (kg/cm²)	0,61	0,9	0,9	0,9	1,0
Gun calibre (mm)	76	37	75	47	40
Armour thickness / slope (mm/°)	45/60	30/0	50/0	45/45	78/0
Hull front glacis plate / slope (mm/°)	40/40	30/0	30/0	45/21	40-70/0

fragments, and only partially protecting from 37-50mm anti-tank gun fire, the "thirty four" had a 76mm gun, and its armour protected against tank and anti-tank artillery of this calibre. Indicators of mobility: specific power, range, speed, potency of the T-34 were much higher than other medium tanks of the time. This was achieved primarily by equipping the T-34 tank with the V-2 diesel engine, developing up to 500hp peak output. This engine met the requirements for power, fuel efficiency, fire safety, weight, cost, manufacturability, range, etc. Note that the goal of fitting diesel engines to foreign tanks was solved

only in the 1960s. During the war, only the Soviet Union possessed such tanks. Foreign tanks were equipped with uneconomical petrol engines which also presented a serious fire hazard.

The V-2 diesel became the default engine for Soviet future heavy armoured vehicles; for all modifications of medium and heavy tanks, and other military tracked vehicles. This testifies to the high technical level of the engine, the talent and labour feat of its creators.

In solving the task of creating a tank, machines can be developed with high technical characteristics, embodied even in

T-34 tank of the installation (pilot) batch, armed with the 76.2mm L-11 gun.

the metal prototype. But whether such a tank will be suitable for production and for operation depends on the fate of the development. Tanks, especially in wartime conditions, must be produced quickly, with minimal material costs, with an acute shortage of qualified personnel and often a lack of some materials. The pursuit of the "most perfect" model of a tank embodying the latest technology, often interferes with rapid mass production of inexpensive tanks, quickly recoverable in time of war, and complicates training of personnel in the effective use of "tricky" techniques in combat.

There are well-known examples of these "advanced" models of tanks that after the huge cost of labour remained at the prototype stage. In this regard, the T-34 tank is good not only for its combat qualities, but its utmost simplicity in production, operation and repair, reliability, low cost and the possibility of mass production at any machine-building plant. These valuable qualities were achieved as a result of the persistent struggle of designers and technologists for the minimum weight and labour input of each component of the tank, in aspiration everywhere and in everything it is reasonable to save, achieving utmost simplicity, cheapness and reliability.

The Soviet Union managed to create such a tank, and it became not only the tankers' favourite formidable weapon, but also the image of a simple and reliable combat vehicle. At the beginning of World War Two on the Eastern Front, the Soviet Union managed to create and put into serial production a new medium tank, superior in fighting qualities and in adaptability to the mass production medium tanks of Nazi Germany.

The success of the T-34 entering series production was marred by the premature death of Mikhail Ilyich Koshkin on 26th September 1940; a wonderful specialist and organiser, who managed to rally and by personal example to inspire a young engineering team in solving large and complex problems; with bold technical confidence in their implementation of the T-34. From 1937 until the last days of his life, Mikhail Koshkin was associated with the work on the creation of the T-34, for which he was posthumously awarded the title of Laureate of the State Prize.

Each test, be it a separate component or a tank as a whole, took place under the direction of, and with the direct participation of, Koshkin. Energetic, restless, temperamental, he much valued his time, spent only at work, showing us an example of a high level of labour organisation. Also to Koshkin's credit was that he laid down the principles of organisation of development work at the plant, which stood the test of time and was particularly effective during the war.

So, in 1940 mass production of the T-34 tank began. Oddly enough, the Germans knew nothing about the existence of this tank, and in direct combat the T-34 tank proved a formidable opponent from the beginning of the war; enemy anti-tank

Assembly of T-34 tanks armed with the 76.2mm F-34 gun, Plant Nº183, Nizhny Tagil, May 1942.

weapons found great difficulty in destroying them. However, due to the small number of T-34s built and deployed by June 1941 their use did not have the significant impact it might have had if it been in production longer when hostilities broke out. The difficult situation at the front and the temporary loss of suppliers of materials, components and accessories, and the evacuation of a number of enterprises created many difficulties for the production of T-34 tanks.

Many production issues were resolved with exceptional efficiency and technical ingenuity, so as not to stop the release of tanks for the Front. A lack of V-2 diesel engines, rubber, ferrous and especially non-ferrous metals, electrical equipment, armour plate, and various small parts were constant concerns. Substitutes had to be procured or manufactured to produce the missing components and parts.

The difficulties were compounded by the evacuation of the Kharkov plant (Plant №183) to Nizhny Tagil to continue the production of tanks at the rail wagon-building plant, which had at the time no prior experience in tank manufacture. The relocation of the plant in September 1941 was extremely fast and organised, despite the fact that thousands of different enterprises and organisations with a large number of employees and their families were evacuated simultaneously in difficult conditions and with a lack of railway transport. The main personnel, equipment, materials and unfinished tanks from Khar-

kov were preserved, which allowed for a short lead time in organizing the production of T-34 tanks at their new location.

In the most difficult industrial and domestic conditions, aggravated by the harsh Ural winter of 1941, it was necessary to quickly organise the mass production of T-34 tanks, not only to meet the current demands of the Front, but also to gradually surpass the enemy in the number of produced tanks.

The relatively simple yet efficient design of the "thirty-four" and its adaptability to mass production at the plant with only an average level of equipment and insufficiently qualified personnel was paramount to its overall success. Now such an approach to the design of the tank seems elementary, but at that time it was not generally recognised as such and was a matter of survival. It also allowed for the relatively rapid production of T-34 tanks at plants in Stalingrad, Gorky, Sverdlovsk, Omsk and Chelyabinsk. The production output of these tanks was constantly increasing, and the cost decreasing, despite the introduction of various design improvements.

The T-34 tank was well adapted for its operation by the crew, being easy to operate, maintain and repair, and in its reliability and unpretentiousness corresponded to the harsh conditions of the war. Our Western allies, although criticising the tank for a lack of refinement in the design of a number of areas, were in general nevertheless forced to recognize that: *"Soviet tanks, mostly of good design, are suitable for mass production even*

T-34 tanks with commander's cupola, delivery inspection workshop, ChKZ, Chelyabinsk, 1943.

*with semi-skilled labor".** In British newspapers can be read the following lines: *"the Russians surpassed the Germans, not only in the production of tanks, but also on the quality of weapons. The Russian T-34 tank is the only tank that Germans are afraid of. They believe the tank is the most effective and best Russian tank, which they have had to meet. High maneuverability, gun operation and armour quality of the T-34 tank are excellent, which makes it a favourite of Russian tank crews."*

The same conclusion was emphasized by the Americans: *"the New Russian tanks, representing the standard of decent construction, were released in a strikingly short time. The most formidable tank of the Red Army is the T-34 tank. The effectiveness of the weapons, the design is very good slope armour, and mobility make this tank very dangerous to the enemy."* *

In the future, American and British designers when creating their new tanks borrowed from the construction solutions of the T-34, and their new tanks became more and more similar to our "thirty-four". Already I have already stated that we were on the right track, setting the tone and direction for foreign designers. Interesting is the opinion of the enemy about our "thirty-four", having themselves experienced its power. Already after the first engagements with participation of T-34 tanks their superiority over the German T-II, T-III, T-IV tanks** was obvious. Despite the noisy advertising specially created around its own tanks, and the cry to the whole world about their invincibility, the German command was forced to declare: *"currently, the T-34 tank is the best tank of the Red Army. It is very fast, has good armour, armed with 76mm gun and equipped with a modern optical sight. The greater angle of slope of the armour increases its protection".*

Numerous captured documents indicate that all the command authorities of Hitler's Wehrmacht were engaged in the

T-34 hull production at Plant №112 (Krasnoye Sormovo), Gorky.

T-34 with forged turret and 76.2mm F-34 gun, UZTM, Sverdlovsk.

* *T-34 study and test conclusions, Aberdeen Proving Ground.* ** *Soviet term for German Pz.Kpfw II, III, IV tanks*

fight against Soviet tanks up to the level of the Supreme Command. The need to combat the T-34 and KV tanks forced the German command during the war to seriously engage in the creation of more powerful anti-tank weapons and new tanks.

Having its industrial base in occupied Europe, Germany quickly provided troops with more effective means of combatting tanks, namely anti-tank guns and self-propelled guns mounted on light and medium tank chassis. By the summer of 1943, German armoured units began receiving the new "Panther" and "Tiger" tanks and "Ferdinand" self-propelled guns. The German command had high hopes for these new models of armoured vehicles with powerful weapons and thick armour, and therefore did not skimp on their advertising to raise the morale of the army. Indeed, in firepower and armour protection, the T-34 was inferior to the new German models. But in practice, the new German tanks did not meet expectations because of insufficient mobility, which did not allow them to realize their high firepower and protection. Another reason for the failure of the new German weapons was the relatively small number of new tanks in the army, which was a consequence of the erroneous decision to rearm the tank troops with new equipment directly during the war. Despite the use of enterprises and the resources of the occupied countries of Europe, the industry of Nazi Germany was not under force to implement the decision in practice.

In response to the creation of new German armoured vehicles, the Soviet Union meantime developed projects for the substantial modernisation of the T-34 tank. Stalin, as usual, personally considered these projects. All that was proposed by the designers to improve the T-34 tank was very attractive and consistent with the situation and development of firepower, that belligerent armies had already reached in the course of the war. However, the proposed modernisation, associated with a significant alteration of the T-34, as a result of which an essentially new tank could appear, naturally raised concerns about the possibility of reducing its mass production and even limiting for some period the receipt of new tanks in the army. The firm position of I. V. Stalin on this issue was reduced to the requirement not to waste energy and money on the development of new tanks for the simple reason that *"...during a fire,* (as he vividly expressed his thoughts) *design pumps and carry water around that you can use"*. At this stage he forbade further development of new tanks, as the T-34 tank was in all respects, in his personal opinion, already *"a good tank."*

It is inappropriate to even think about any "best" tanks without the associated restructuring of industry that might be required for their production, Stalin gave instruction to expand T-34 tank production in every possible way and to limit their modernisation to strengthening the armament and improving visibility. In accordance with this instruction, a more powerful 85mm gun was mounted on the T-34, which practically equalized the firepower of the T-34 tank with new German tanks; and a commander's cupola was introduced to improve all-round vision.

Today, after much time has passed and the results of the decisions taken at that time have been evaluated, it is clear that the

A T-34 tank with 76.2mm F-34 gun moving past a destroyed Pz.Kpfw III.

firm line enforced by Stalin on this matter - improving existing tanks rather than introducing entirely new designs - was entirely appropriate for the time. The course of events in the second half of the war fully confirmed the correctness of the Soviet government in the development of tank weapons. By this time, the production capacity of the tank industry had reached its peak, and the stability and simplicity of the T-34 design allowed production to increase exponentially, which advantage during wartime largely determined Soviet superiority over enemy tanks that might have had individual qualitative advantages.

In conclusion, it should be again emphasized that the T-34 tank has never been claimed by the Soviet Union to have been some inimitable and all-conquering "miracle tank". It was simply designed as a fit for purpose tank, which corresponded to specific Soviet requirements with regard to production and operating conditions, and the requirements of a Soviet tank at a time of total war, to the great credit of its creators.

The T-34 tank, which became the default Red Army medium tank, and the most used tank of the Second World War, was also the only tank of the combatant armies that featured no significant design changes throughout the war.

No weapon by itself wins a war however - wars are won by the people that have such weapons at their disposal. The history of the Great Patriotic War showed the world an extraordinary example of mass heroism of the Soviet people, who by their courage, bravery, and frequently by laying down their lives raised the glory of Russian weapons to unprecedented heights. This high honour was awarded to the T-34 tank, with which the tank heroes performed countless feats in the name of freedom and independence of our Soviet Motherland*.

Prototype of the first variant of the T-43 medium tank, 1942.

T-34-85 tank armed with the ZiS-S-53 gun, Plant №183, Nizhny Tagil, 1944.

*Morozov. Alexander A. Questions of Defence Technology. Series 6. Armoured Vehicles. TsNII (Central Research Institute of Information) Moscow 2nd Edition (20) 1985 pp17-21

A-20

The A-20 prototype during evaluation trials. The A-20 was used in combat in the autumn and early winter of 1941 but its only known paint finish was the standard 4BO paint used during field trials.

T-34-76 L-11

T-34 armed with L-11 gun, Plant №183, January 1941 production. Tank was sent to Military High School in Oryol and later received 3-tone camouflage which was officially adopted in early May 1941. After the outbreak of war, a battalion was formed on base of the High School (3 BT-7, 6 KV-1, 27 T-34 tanks), which was subordinated to 115th tank regiment of 57th Tank Division. This tank was lost in combat near Tolochin (Belorussia) on 6th July 1941.

T-34-76 8TH TANK BR 1941

T-34 armed with F-34 gun, Plant №183 spring 1941 production, 8th Tank Regiment of the 8th Tank Brigade under the command of Col. Pavel Rotmistrov. This tank was lost in combat during the last days of September 1941 near Luzhno village (Demyansk area). The white number "8" painted on the turret sides and transmission hatch on a hull rear plate was a brigade designation, and common practice for 1941.

T-34-76 101TH TANK DIV. DIV. ZAP. (WESTERN) FRONT JULY 1941

T-34 armed with F-34 gun, Plant Nº183 spring 1941 production, 101ˢᵗ Tank Division during combat against German 7ᵗʰ Panzer Division near Yart-sevo, July 1941.

T-34-76 KARELIA, AUTUMN 1941

T-34 armed with F-34 gun, Plant Nº183 spring 1941 production, belonging to a tank group supporting the 946ᵗʰ Rifle Regiment of the 265ᵗʰ Rifle Division. The tank was damaged by Finnish anti-tank gun fire near Kaukola village and captured on 14ᵗʰ August 1941.

T-34-76_MOSCOW, 1941

T-34 armed with F-34 gun, Plant Nº183 spring 1941 production; an unknown tank unit of the Soviet Western front, winter 1941-42. This winter camouflage scheme was adopted in 1940 and used only during the winter months of 1941-42.

T-34-76 UNKNOWN UNIT, 1942

T-34 armed with F-34 gun, Plant Nº183 summer 1941 production, from an unknown unit. The tank underwent at least one overhaul and survived until late spring 1942. The red tactical markings on the turret sides were added to by red stars on both front mud guards.

Author Biographies

Igor Gennadyvich Zheltov

For 15 years Igor Zheltov worked as Deputy Director for research at the museum and memorial complex "History of the T-34" near Moscow. Since 1997, he has worked in the Russian state archives on issues related to the history of the development of Russian armoured combat vehicles. He is the co-author of more than 20 books on the history of tank building and types of armoured weapons and equipment. Twice winner of the literary prize "Prokhorov readings", Igor Zheltov is one of the creators of the website "T-34inform", dedicated to the history and design features of the T-34 tank and its modifications.

Alexey Yurevich Makarov

For several years Alexey Makarov was a researcher at the Museum and memorial complex "History of the T-34" near Moscow. Since 2006, he has worked intensively within the Russian state archives on issues related to the history of Russian tank building in the pre-war and war years, and mainly on the topic "Development and Production of the T-34 tank".

The author has published numerous articles in Russian naval historical and scientific-technical journals, and is co-author of a series of books in Russia on the history of the legendary T-34 tank. He is also one of the creators of the site "T-34inform", dedicated to the history and design of the T-34 tank and its modifications.

Note on Translation and Abbreviation

This book, the result of years of combined research by the named authors, has been translated from the original Russian text, which has required some modification for ease of reading in English. Many Russian terms used in the book are long and regularly quoted, and so have been shortened to their well-known Russian acronyms, for example ABTU RKKA (the Auto-Tank Directorate of the Workers and Peasants Red Army) which has shortened to ABTU, without the full suffix in order to save repetition. The definition RKKA is also sometimes abbreviated as Red Army (KA) in the original Russian text. Defence Committee of the SNK of the USSR (KO pri SNK SSSR) is also shortened to KO for brevity. The full list of abbreviated terms and their acronyms is located in the glossary.

For ease of reading in English, the original Russian alphabet when describing original Russian lists has also been changed to the Latin alphabet, hence the first five letters of the Russian alphabet А, Б, В, Г, Д have been changed to the Latin A, B, C, D, E. etc.

Weights and dimensions are in metric per the original Russian documentation. The use of "tonnes" as translated from the original Russian text is metric tonnes (1,000kg).

With regard to place names, Soviet era names and spellings are used; hence Kharkov is the correct contemporary name of the Ukrainian city where the T-34 was developed. After the fall of the Soviet Union the city reverted to the Ukrainian spelling Kharkiv.

The book uses extensive quoted references, which have also been shortened for brevity, e.g. the original Russian reference РГВА. Ф. 31811. Оп. 2. Д. 842. Л. 172 (RGVA archives, File 31811, List 2, Case 842, page 172) is shown as RVGA F.31811 L.2 C.842 pp.172, etc.

Some explanatory words have been added in brackets by the authors or editor for clarification where the source material wording might not be obvious outside the original context, for-instance in contemporary technical reports.

Glossary

ABTU	Avtobronetankovoe Upravlenie (Auto-Tank Command)
ANIOP	Artilleriskiy Nauchno-Issledovatelskiy Polygon - Artillery Scientific Experimental Test Range
ArtKom	
GAU KA	Artillery Committee Main Artillery Command of the Red Army
BTU	Bronetankovoe Upravlenie - Tank Command
DOT	Dolgovremennaya Ognevaya Tochka (hardened fire-point)(bunker)
GABTU KA	Glavnoye AvtoBronetankovoyea Upravlenye KA - Main Auto-Tank Command of the Red Army
GARF	Gosudarstvenniy Arkhiv Rossiiskoi Federatsiy - State Archive of the Russian Federation
GAU	Glavnoye Artilleriiskoye Upravleniye - State Artillery Directorate
GKO	Gosudarstnenny Komitet Oboroni - State Defence Committee of the USSR
KA	Krasnaya Armiya - Red Army (also known as RKKA)
KB	Konstruktorskoye Bureau - Design Bureau
NKAP	Narkomat Aviatsionnoi Promishlennosti.
NKO	Narodny Kommisariat Oboroni - State Defence Committee
NKV	Narodny Kommissariat Vooruzheniya - People's Commissariat of Armaments

NKSM	Ministry of Medium Machine Building (Narkomsredmash) - responsible for tank production
NKTM	People's Commissariat of Heavy Engineering
NKTP	People's Commissariat of Tank Production
OF	Oskolochno-Fugasny - High-Explosive Fragmentation
RGAEh	Rossiskiy Gosudarstvenniyi Arkhiv Ekonomiki - Российский Государственной Архив - Russian State Economic Archives
RGASPI	Rossiskiy Gosudarstvenniy Arkhiv Sotsialno-Politichesko Istorii - Russian State Archive of Social-Political History
RGVA	Rossiskiy Gosudarstvenniy Voenniy Arkhiv - Russian State Military Archive
SNK	Sovet Narodnikh Kommissarov - Council of People's Commissars
TsaMO RF	Tsentralniy Arkhiv Ministerstva Oboroni Rossiskoi Federatsii - Central Archives of the Ministry of Defence of the Russian Federation
TsVKP(b)	Central Committee of the CPSU(b) - Communist Party (Bolshevik) of the USSR
TTT	Taktiko-Tekhnicheskiye Trebovaniya - Tactical Technical Tasks
USA	Upravlenie Samohodnoy Artillerii - Self-Propelled Artillery Department